SWAZILAND

INVESTMENT AND BUSINESS GUIDE

VOLUME 1

STRATEGIC AND PRACTICAL INFORMATION

International Business Publications, USA
Washington DC, USA - Swaziland

SWAZILAND

INVESTMENT AND BUSINESS GUIDE

VOLUME 1 STRATEGIC AND PRACTICAL INFORMATION

UPDATED ANNUALLY

Cover Design: International Business Publications, USA

We express our sincere appreciation to all government agencies and international organizations which provided information and other materials for this guide

2015 Edition Updated Reprint International Business Publications, USA
ISBN 0-7397-9385-3

This guide provides basic information for starting or/and conducting business in the country. The extraordinary volume of materials covering the topic, prevents us from placing all these materials in this guide. For more detailed information on issues related to any specific investment and business activity in the country, please contact Global Investment Center, USA
Please acquire the list of our business intelligence and marketing reports and other business publications. We constantly update and expand our business intelligence and marketing materials. Please contact the center for the updated list of reports on over 200 countries.

in the USA: **Global Investment Center, USA.**
P.O.Box 15343, Washington, DC 20003
Phone: (202) 546-2103, Fax: (202) 546-3275, E-mail: rusric@erols.com

For additional analytical, marketing and other information please contact Global Investment Center, USA

Printed in the USA

SWAZILAND

INVESTMENT AND BUSINESS GUIDE

VOLUME 1
STRATEGIC AND PRACTICAL INFORMATION

TABLE OF CONTENTS

STRATEGIC AND DEVELOPMENT PROFILES

STRATEGIC PROFILE

Capital	Lobamba (royal / legislative) Mbabane (administrative) 26°19′S 31°8′E26.317°S 31.133°E
Largest city	Mbabane
Official languages	Swazi English
Demonym	Swazi
Government	Unitary parliamentary absolute monarchy
- King	Mswati III
- Ndlovukati	Ntfombi Tfwala
- Prime Minister	Sibusiso Dlamini
Legislature	Parliament of Swaziland
- Upper house	Senate
- Lower house	House of Assembly
	Independence
- from the United Kingdom	6 September 1968
	Area
- Total	17,364 km^2 (157th) 6,704 sq mi
- Water (%)	0.9
	Population
- 2015 estimate	1,119,000 (154th)
- 2007 census	1,018,449
- Density	68.2/km^2 (135th) 176.8/sq mi
GDP (PPP)	2015 estimate
- Total	$8.859 billion
- Per capita	$7,917
GDP (nominal)	2015 estimate
- Total	$3.634 billion
- Per capita	$3,248
Gini (2015)	▼49.5 high
HDI	▬0.530 low · 148th
Currency	South African rand Swazi lilangeni (SZL)
Time zone	SAST (UTC+2)
Drives on the	left
Calling code	+268
ISO 3166 code	SZ
Internet TLD	.sz

Swaziland, officially the **Kingdom of Swaziland** is a sovereign state in Southern Africa. It is neighbored by Mozambique to its east and by South Africa to its north, west and south. The country and its people take their names from Mswati II, the 19th-century king under whose rule Swazi territory was expanded and unified.

At no more than 200 kilometres (120 mi) north to south and 130 kilometres (81 mi) east to west, Swaziland is one of the smallest countries in Africa. Despite its size, however, its climate and topography is diverse, ranging from a cool and mountainous highveld to a hot and dry lowveld. The population is primarily ethnic Swazis whose language is siSwati. They established their kingdom in the mid-18th century under the leadership of Ngwane III; the present boundaries were drawn up in 1881. After the Anglo-Boer War, Swaziland was a British protectorate from 1903 until 1967. It regained its independence on 6 September 1968.

The country is an absolute monarchy, currently ruled by *Ngwenyama* ("King") Mswati III. He is head of state and appoints the country's prime ministers and a number of representatives of both chambers (Senate and House of Assembly) in the country's parliament. Elections are held every five years to determine the House of Assembly majority. The current constitution was adopted in 2005.

Swaziland is a developing country with a small economy. Its GDP per capita of $7,917 means it is classified as a country with a lower-middle income. As a member of the Southern African Customs Union (SACU) and Common Market for Eastern and Southern Africa (COMESA), its main local trading partner is South Africa. Swaziland's currency, the lilangeni, is pegged to the South African rand. Swaziland's major overseas trading partners are the United States and the European Union. The majority of the country's employment is provided by its agricultural and manufacturing sectors. Swaziland is a member of the Southern African Development Community, the African Union and the Commonwealth of Nations.

The Swazi population faces major health issues: HIV/AIDS and, to a lesser extent, tuberculosis are serious challenges. As of 2013, Swaziland has an estimated life expectancy of 50 years. The population of Swaziland is fairly young with a median age of 20.5 years and people aged 14 years or younger constituting 37.4% of the country's total population. The present population growth rate is 1.195%.

Swaziland is well known for its culture. *Umhlanga*, held in August/September and *incwala*, the kingship dance held in December/January, are the nation's most important events

Background: Autonomy for the Swazis of southern Africa was guaranteed by the British in the late 19th century; independence was granted 1968. Student and labor unrest during the 1990s have pressured the monarchy (one of the oldest on the continent) to grudgingly allow political reform and greater democracy.

GEOGRAPHY

Location: Southern Africa, between Mozambique and South Africa
Geographic coordinates: 26 30 S, 31 30 E
Map references: Africa
Area:
total: 17,363 sq km *land:* 17,203 sq km *water:* 160 sq km
Area - comparative: slightly smaller than New Jersey
Land boundaries:
total: 535 km *border countries:* Mozambique 105 km, South Africa 430 km
Coastline: 0 km (landlocked)

Maritime claims: none (landlocked)
Climate: varies from tropical to near temperate
Terrain: mostly mountains and hills; some moderately sloping plains

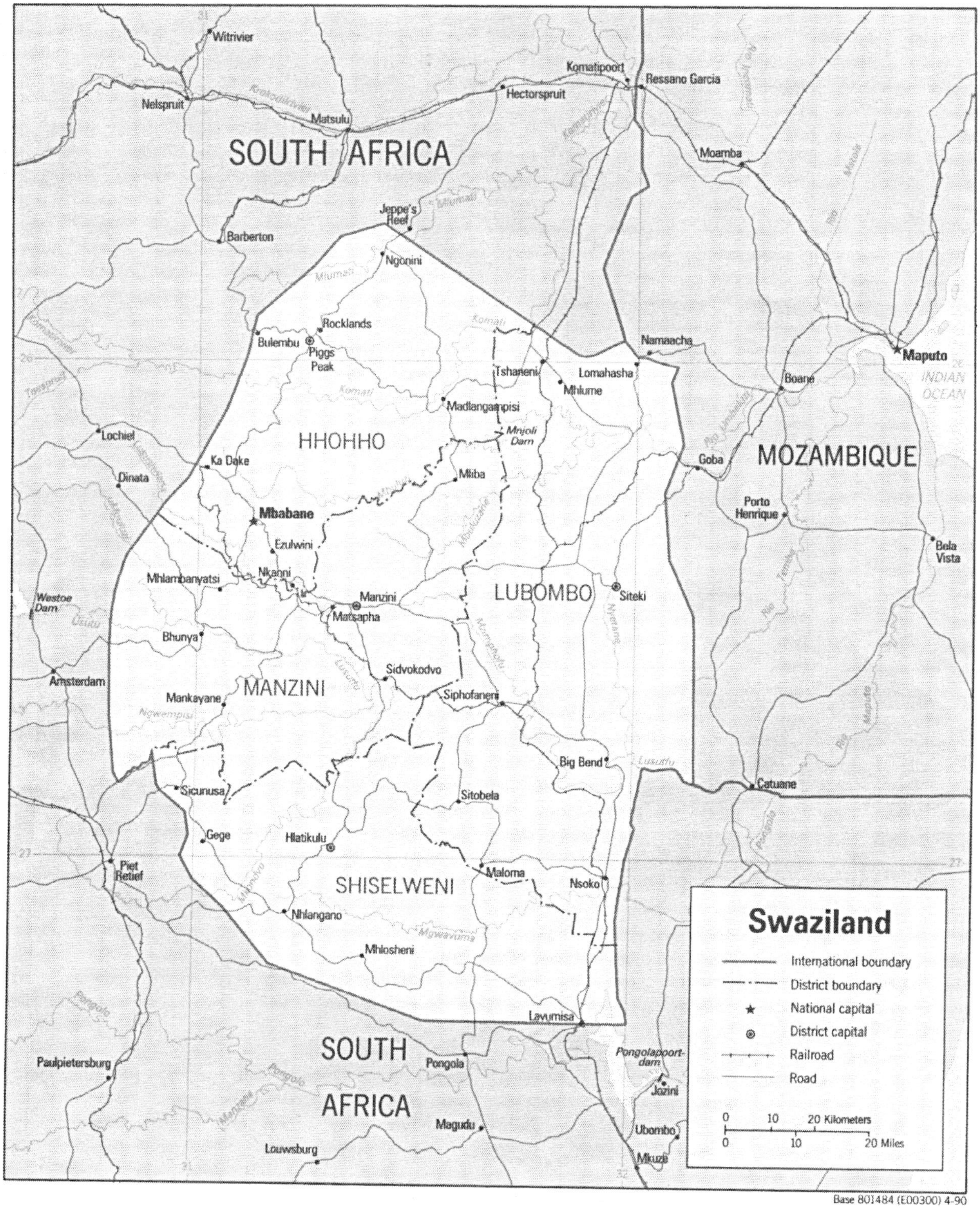
Swaziland
International boundary
District boundary
National capital
District capital
Railroad
Road
0 10 20 Kilometers
0 10 20 Miles
SOUTH AFRICA
MOZAMBIQUE
HHOHHO
LUBOMBO
MANZINI
SHISELWENI
INDIAN OCEAN
Mbabane
Maputo
Manzini
Siteki
Piggs Peak
Hlatikulu
Witrivier
Nelspruit
Matsulu
Komatipoort
Hectorspruit
Ressano Garcia
Moamba
Barberton
Jeppe's Reef
Ngonini
Rocklands
Bulembu
Namaacha
Lomahasha
Tshaneni
Mhlume
Madlangampisi
Mnjoli Dam
Boane
Lochiel
Dinata
Ka Dake
Mliba
Goba
Porto Henrique
Bela Vista
Ezulwini
Nkanni
Mhlambanyatsi
Matsapha
Westoe Dam
Bhunya
Amsterdam
Sidvokodvo
Mankayane
Siphofaneni
Big Bend
Catuane
Sicunusa
Sitobela
Gege
Piet Retief
Maloma
Nsoko
Nhlangano
Mhlosheni
Lavumisa
Paulpietersburg
Pongola
Pongolapoort-dam
Jozini
Magudu
Ubombo
Louwsburg
Mkuze
Base 801484 (E00300) 4-90

Elevation extremes:
lowest point: Great Usutu River 21 m
highest point: Emlembe 1,862 m

Natural resources: asbestos, coal, clay, cassiterite, hydropower, forests, small gold and diamond deposits, quarry stone, and talc

Land use:
arable land: 11%
permanent crops: 0%
permanent pastures: 62%
forests and woodland: 7%
other: 20%

Irrigated land: 670 sq km
Natural hazards: NA
Environment - current issues: limited supplies of potable water; wildlife populations being depleted because of excessive hunting; overgrazing; soil degradation; soil erosion
Environment - international agreements:
party to: Biodiversity, Climate Change, Endangered Species, Nuclear Test Ban, Ozone Layer Protection
signed, but not ratified: Desertification, Law of the Sea
Geography - note: landlocked; almost completely surrounded by South Africa

PEOPLE

Population: 1,083,289
note: estimates for this country explicitly take into account the effects of excess mortality due to AIDS; this can result in lower life expectancy, higher infant mortality and death rates, lower population and growth rates, and changes in the distribution of population by age and sex than would otherwise be expected

Age structure:
0-14 years: 46% (male 245,626; female 247,825)
15-64 years: 52% (male 270,308; female 291,884)
65 years and over: 2% (male 11,357; female 16,289)

Population growth rate: 2.02%
Birth rate: 40.64 births/1,000 population
Death rate: 20.4 deaths/1,000 population
Net migration rate: 0 migrant(s)/1,000 population

Sex ratio:
at birth: 1.03 male(s)/female
under 15 years: 0.99 male(s)/female
15-64 years: 0.93 male(s)/female
65 years and over: 0.7 male(s)/female
total population: 0.95 male(s)/female

Infant mortality rate: 108.95 deaths/1,000 live births

Life expectancy at birth:
total population: 40.44 years
male: 39.54 years
female: 41.37 years

Total fertility rate: 5.87 children born/woman

Nationality:
noun: Swazi(s)
adjective: Swazi

Ethnic groups: African 97%, European 3%
Religions: Christian 60%, indigenous beliefs 40%
Languages: English (official, government business conducted in English), siSwati (official)

Literacy:
definition: age 15 and over can read and write
total population: 76.7%
male: 78%
female: 75.6%

GOVERNMENT

Country name:
conventional long form: Kingdom of Swaziland
conventional short form: Swaziland

Data code: WZ
Government type: monarchy; independent member of Commonwealth
Capital: Mbabane; note - Lobamba is the royal and legislative capital
Administrative divisions: 4 districts; Hhohho, Lubombo, Manzini, Shiselweni
Independence: 6 September 1968 (from UK)
National holiday: Somhlolo (Independence) Day, 6 September (1968)

Constitution: none; constitution of 6 September 1968 was suspended 12 April 1973; a new constitution was promulgated 13 October 1978, but was not formally presented to the people; since then a few more outlines for a constitution have been compiled under the Constitutional Review Commission (CRC), but so far none have been accepted

Legal system: based on South African Roman-Dutch law in statutory courts and Swazi traditional law and custom in traditional courts; has not accepted compulsory ICJ jurisdiction

Suffrage: NA years of age

Executive branch: Swaziland

chief of state: King MSWATI III (since 25 April 1986)
head of government: Prime Minister Barnabas Sibusiso DLAMINI (since 16 October 2008)
cabinet: Cabinet recommended by the prime minister and confirmed by the monarch
elections: the monarchy is hereditary; prime minister appointed by the monarch from among the elected members of the House of Assembly

Legislative branch:

bicameral Parliament or Libandla consists of the Senate (30 seats; 10 members elected by the House of Assembly and 20 appointed by the monarch; members to serve five-year terms) and the House of Assembly (65 seats; 10 members appointed by the monarch and 55 elected by popular vote; members to serve five-year terms)

elections: House of Assembly - last held on 20 September 2013 (next scheduled for September 2018)

election results: House of Assembly - balloting is done on a nonparty basis; candidates for election nominated by the local council of each constituency and for each constituency the three candidates with the most votes in the first round of voting are narrowed to a single winner by a second round

Judicial branch: High Court, judges are appointed by the monarch; Court of Appeal, judges are appointed by the monarch

Political parties and leaders: Convention for Full Democracy in Swaziland or COFUDESWA [Sabelo DLAMINI]; Ngwane Socialist Revolutionary Party or NGWASOREP [leader NA]; People's United Democratic Movement or PUDEMO [Mario MASUKU]; Swaziland Communist Party or SWACOPA [Mphandlana SHONGWE]; Swaziland Democratic Alliance (represents key opposition parties) [Jerry NXUMALO]; Swaziland Federation of Trade Unions or SFTU [Jan SITHOLE]; Swaziland Liberation Front or FROLISA [leader NA]; Swaziland National Front or SWANAFRO [leader NA]; Swaziland Youth Congress or SWAYOCO (included in PUDEMO)
note: political parties are banned by the constitution promulgated on 13 October 1978; illegal parties are prohibited from holding large public gatherings

International organization participation: ACP, AfDB, C, CCC, ECA, FAO, G-77, IBRD, ICAO, ICFTU, ICRM, IDA, IFAD, IFC, IFRCS, ILO, IMF, Intelsat, Interpol, IOC, ITU, NAM, OAU, OPCW, PCA, SACU, SADC, UN, UNCTAD, UNESCO, UNIDO, UPU, WHO, WIPO, WMO, WTrO

Diplomatic representation in the US:
chief of mission: Ambassador Mary Madzandza KANYA
chancery: 3400 International Drive NW, Washington, DC 20008
telephone: (202) 362-6683
FAX: (202) 244-8059

Diplomatic representation from the US:
chief of mission: Ambassador Gregory L. JOHNSON
embassy: Central Bank Building, Warner Street, Mbabane
mailing address: P. O. Box 199, Mbabane
telephone: [268] 404-6441 through 404-6445
FAX: [268] 404-5959

Flag description: three horizontal bands of blue (top), red (triple width), and blue; the red band is edged in yellow; centered in the red band is a large black and white shield covering two spears and a staff decorated with feather tassels, all placed horizontally

ECONOMY

Surrounded by South Africa, except for a short border with Mozambique, Swaziland depends heavily on South Africa from which it receives more than 90% of its imports and to which it sends 60% of its exports. Swaziland's currency is pegged to the South African rand, effectively subsuming Swaziland's monetary policy to South Africa. The government is heavily dependent on customs duties from the Southern African Customs Union (SACU), and worker remittances from South Africa supplement domestically earned income. Subsistence agriculture employs approximately 70% of the population. The manufacturing sector has diversified since the mid-1980s. Sugar and wood pulp were major foreign exchange earners; however, the wood pulp producer closed in January 2010, and sugar is now the main export earner. Mining has declined in importance in recent years with only coal and quarry stone mines remaining active. Customs revenues plummeted due to the global economic crisis and a drop in South African imports. The resulting decline in revenue has pushed the country into a fiscal crisis. Swaziland is looking to other countries, including South Africa, for assistance, but continues to struggle to meet its monthly payroll and fund government programs. With an estimated 40% unemployment rate, Swaziland's need to increase the number and size of small and medium enterprises and attract foreign direct investment is acute. Overgrazing, soil depletion, drought, and floods persist as problems for the future. More than one-fourth of the population needed emergency food aid in 2006-07 because of drought, and more than one-quarter of the adult population has been infected by HIV/AIDS, as of 2013.

GDP (purchasing power parity):
$6.259 billion (2013 est.)
country comparison to the world: 164
$6.259 billion (2012 est.)
$6.354 billion (2011 est.)
note: data are in 2013 US dollars

GDP (official exchange rate):
$3.807 billion (2013 est.)

GDP - real growth rate:
0% (2013 est.)
country comparison to the world: 198
-1.5% (2012 est.)
0.3% (2011 est.)

GDP - per capita (PPP):
$5,700 (2013 est.)
country comparison to the world: 154
$5,800 (2012 est.)
$6,000 (2011 est.)
note: data are in 2013 US dollars

Gross national saving:
10.1% of GDP (2013 est.)
country comparison to the world: 132
13.4% of GDP (2012 est.)
4.5% of GDP (2011 est.)

GDP - composition, by end use:
household consumption: 86.2%
government consumption: 21.5%

investment in fixed capital: 10.1%
investment in inventories: 0%
exports of goods and services: 57.4%
imports of goods and services: -75.3%
(2013 est.)

GDP - composition, by sector of origin:
agriculture: 7.6%
industry: 47.8%
services: 44.6% (2013 est.)

Agriculture - products:
sugarcane, cotton, corn, tobacco, rice, citrus, pineapples, sorghum, peanuts; cattle, goats, sheep

Industries:
coal, wood pulp, sugar, soft drink concentrates, textiles and apparel

Industrial production growth rate:
0.4% (2013 est.)
country comparison to the world: 161

Labor force:
424,100 (2011 est.)
country comparison to the world: 158

Labor force - by occupation:
agriculture: 70%
industry: NA%
services: NA%

Unemployment rate:
40% (2006 est.)
country comparison to the world: 191

Population below poverty line:
69% (2006)

Household income or consumption by percentage share:
lowest 10%: 1.7%
highest 10%: 40.1% (2010 est.)

Distribution of family income - Gini index:
50.4 (2001)
country comparison to the world: 18

Budget:
revenues: $1.274 billion
expenditures: $1.316 billion (2013 est.)

Taxes and other revenues:
33.5% of GDP (2013 est.)
country comparison to the world: 73

Budget surplus (+) or deficit (-):
-1.1% of GDP (2013 est.)
country comparison to the world: 64

Fiscal year:
1 April - 31 March

Inflation rate (consumer prices):
6.1% (2013 est.)
country comparison to the world: 175
8.9% (2012 est.)

Central bank discount rate:
6.5% (31 December 2010 est.)
country comparison to the world: 52
6.5% (31 December 2009 est.)

Commercial bank prime lending rate:
8.5% (31 December 2013 est.)
country comparison to the world: 101
8.75% (31 December 2012 est.)

Stock of narrow money:
$421.6 million (31 December 2013 est.)
country comparison to the world: 162
$403.3 million (31 December 2012 est.)

Stock of broad money:
$1.142 billion (31 December 2013 est.)
country comparison to the world: 166
$1.138 billion (31 December 2012 est.)

Stock of domestic credit:
$763.3 million (31 December 2013 est.)
country comparison to the world: 158
$762.9 million (31 December 2012 est.)

Market value of publicly traded shares:
$203.1 million (31 December 2007)
country comparison to the world: 105
$203.1 million (31 December 2007)
$199.9 million

Current account balance:
-$1.5 million (2013 est.)

country comparison to the world: 61
$53 million (2012 est.)

Exports:
$1.603 billion (2013 est.)
country comparison to the world: 147
$1.681 billion (2012 est.)

Exports - commodities:
soft drink concentrates, sugar, wood pulp, cotton yarn, refrigerators, citrus and canned fruit

Imports:
$1.545 billion (2013 est.)
country comparison to the world: 171
$1.578 billion (2012 est.)

Imports - commodities:
motor vehicles, machinery, transport equipment, foodstuffs, petroleum products, chemicals

Reserves of foreign exchange and gold:
$801.4 million (31 December 2013 est.)
country comparison to the world: 143
$741 million (31 December 2012 est.)

Debt - external:
$609.5 million (31 December 2013 est.)
country comparison to the world: 172
$604.8 million (31 December 2012 est.)

Stock of direct foreign investment - at home:
$NA

Stock of direct foreign investment - abroad:
$NA

Exchange rates:
emalangeni per US dollar -
9.575 (2013 est.)
8.2031 (2012 est.)
7.3212 (2010 est.)
8.42 (2009)
7.75 (2008)

ENERGY

Electricity - production:
496 million kWh (2010 est.)
country comparison to the world: 163

Electricity - consumption:
1.058 billion kWh (2010 est.)
country comparison to the world: 150

Electricity - exports:
0 kWh (2012)
country comparison to the world: 215

Electricity - imports:
564 million kWh (2011 est.)
country comparison to the world: 77

Electricity - installed generating capacity:
149,000 kW (2010 est.)
country comparison to the world: 164

Electricity - from fossil fuels:
59.7% of total installed capacity (2010 est.)
country comparison to the world: 134

Electricity - from nuclear fuels:
0% of total installed capacity (2010 est.)
country comparison to the world: 207

Electricity - from hydroelectric plants:
40.3% of total installed capacity (2010 est.)
country comparison to the world: 59

Electricity - from other renewable sources:
0% of total installed capacity (2010 est.)
country comparison to the world: 142

Crude oil - production:
0 bbl/day (2012 est.)
country comparison to the world: 147

Crude oil - exports:
0 bbl/day (2010 est.)
country comparison to the world: 208

Crude oil - imports:
0 bbl/day (2010 est.)
country comparison to the world: 144

Crude oil - proved reserves:
0 bbl (1 January 2010 est.)
country comparison to the world: 209

Refined petroleum products - production:
0 bbl/day (2010 est.)
country comparison to the world: 211

Refined petroleum products - consumption:
4,567 bbl/day (2011 est.)
country comparison to the world: 171

Refined petroleum products - exports:
0 bbl/day (2010 est.)
country comparison to the world: 146

Refined petroleum products - imports:
4,761 bbl/day (2010 est.)
country comparison to the world: 155

Natural gas - production:
0 cu m (2011 est.)
country comparison to the world: 211

Natural gas - consumption:
0 cu m (2010 est.)
country comparison to the world: 211

Natural gas - exports:
0 cu m (2011 est.)
country comparison to the world: 210

Natural gas - imports:
0 cu m (2011 est.)
country comparison to the world: 81

Natural gas - proved reserves:
0 cu m (1 January 2013 est.)
country comparison to the world: 209

Carbon dioxide emissions from consumption of energy:
1.024 million Mt (2011 est.)

COMMUNICATIONS

Telephones - main lines in use:
48,600 (2012)
country comparison to the world: 164

Telephones - mobile cellular:
805,000 (2012)
country comparison to the world: 160

Telephone system:
general assessment: a somewhat modern but not an advanced system
domestic: single source for mobile-cellular service with a geographic coverage of about 90% and a rising subscribership base; combined fixed-line and mobile cellular teledensity roughly 60 telephones per 100 persons in 2011; telephone system consists of carrier-equipped, open-wire lines and low-capacity, microwave radio relay
international: country code - 268; satellite earth station - 1 Intelsat (Atlantic Ocean) (2009)

Broadcast media:
state-owned TV station; satellite dishes are able to access South African providers; state-owned radio network with 3 channels; 1 private radio station (2007)

Internet country code:
.sz

Internet hosts:
2,744 (2012)
country comparison to the world: 158

Internet users:
90,100 (2009)
country comparison to the world: 162

TRANSPORTATION

Railways:
total: 297 km; note - includes 71 km which are not in use
narrow gauge: 297 km 1.067-m gauge

Highways:
total: 2,896 km
paved: NA km
unpaved: NA km

Ports and harbors: none
Airports: 18
Airports - with paved runways:
total: 1
2,438 to 3,047 m: 1
Airports - with unpaved runways:
total: 17
914 to 1,523 m: 7
under 914 m: 10

MILITARY

Military branches: Umbutfo Swaziland Defense Force (Army), Royal Swaziland Police Force
Military manpower - availability:
males age 15-49: 242,398
Military manpower - fit for military service:
males age 15-49: 140,299

Military expenditures - dollar figure: $23 million
Military expenditures - percent of GDP: 1.9%

TRANSNATIONAL ISSUES

Disputes - international: Swaziland has asked South Africa to open negotiations on reincorporating some nearby South African territories that are populated by ethnic Swazis or that were long ago part of the Swazi Kingdom

IMPORTANT INFORMATION FOR UNDERSTANDING SWAZILAND[1]

Official Name: Kingdom of Swaziland

PROFILE

Geography
Area: 17,363 sq. km. (6,704 sq. miles); slightly smaller than New Jersey.
Major cities: Mbabane (capital, pop. 60,000), Manzini (principal commercial city, pop. 65,000).
Terrain: Mountainous plateau to savanna.
Climate: Near temperate to tropical.

People
Nationality: *Noun and adjective*--Swazi(s).
Population: 1,128,814.
Annual growth rate: -0.41%.
Ethnic groups: African 97%, European 3%.
Religion: Zionist 40% (a blend of Christianity and indigenous ancestral worship), Roman Catholic 20%, Muslim 10%, other (includes Anglican, Baha'i, Methodist, Mormon, Jewish) 30%.
Education: *Years compulsory*--none. *Attendance*--65% primary and 44% secondary. *Literacy*--81.6%.
Health: *Infant mortality rate* (2007)--70/1,000. *Life expectancy*--40 years. The prevalence of HIV in Swaziland's adult population is 39%, the highest in the world.
Work force: *Agriculture and forestry*--21.4%; *construction*--6.1%; *distribution*--10.5%; *finance*--8.3%; *manufacturing*--20.1%; *mining and quarry*--1%; *services*--32.6%; *transport*--2.9%.

Government
Type: Monarchy.
Independence: September 6, 1968.
Constitution: On July 26, 2005, King Mswati III ratified Swaziland's constitution. This is Swaziland's first constitution in over 30 years. It went into effect February 8, 2006.
Branches: *Executive*--monarch (head of state), prime minister (head of government), cabinet (appointed by the king at the recommendation of the prime minister). *Legislative*--Parliament consisting of the House of Assembly (65 members: 55 elected, 10 appointed by the king) and Senate (30 members: 10 appointed by the House of Assembly, 20 appointed by the king). *Judicial*--a dual court system of traditional courts under chiefs and a Roman-Dutch system comprising magistrates courts, High Court, Supreme Court (formerly Court of Appeals).
Administrative subdivisions: 4 regions, 9 municipal governments, and 55 tinkhundla centers (traditional administrative units).
Political parties: None registered, though the new constitution does not forbid parties.
Suffrage: Universal after 18.

Economy
GDP (2008): $2.7 billion.
GDP real growth rate (2008): 2.4%.
Gross national income per capita (2008): $2,285.
Inflation (2008): 12.6%; (2009): 7.5%.
Natural resources: Coal, quarry stone, timber, talc.
Agriculture (8.3% of GDP): *Products*--sugarcane, corn, citrus fruits, livestock, wood, pineapple, tobacco, rice, peanuts.

[1] This section based on the US and Swaziland government materials

Manufacturing (28.2% of GDP): *Types*--sugar refining, light manufactured goods, wood pulp, textiles, processed foods, consumer goods.
Trade (2008): *Exports*--$1.57 billion: soft drink concentrates, sugar, pulp, canned fruits, cotton yarn. *Major markets*--South Africa (80%), EU (10%), Mozambique (10%). *Imports*--$1.58 billion: chemicals, clothing, foodstuffs, machinery, motor vehicles, petroleum products.

PEOPLE

The majority of the population is ethnic Swazi, mixed with a small number of Zulus and non-Africans. Traditionally Swazis have been subsistence farmers and herders, but some now work in the growing urban formal economy and in government. Some Swazis work in the mines in South Africa. Christianity in Swaziland is sometimes mixed with traditional beliefs and practices. Most Swazis ascribe a special spiritual role to the monarch.

The country's official languages are SiSwati (a language related to Zulu) and English. Government and commercial business is conducted mainly in English.

HISTORY

According to tradition, the people of the present Swazi nation migrated south before the 16th century from what is now Mozambique. Following a series of conflicts with people living in the area of modern Maputo, the Swazis settled in northern Zululand in about 1750. Unable to match the growing Zulu strength, the Swazis moved gradually northward in the 1800s and established themselves in the area of modern or present Swaziland.

They consolidated their hold under several able leaders. The most important was Mswati II, from whom the Swazis derive their name. Under his leadership in the 1840s, the Swazis expanded their territory to the northwest and stabilized the southern frontier with the Zulus.

Contact with the British came early in Mswati's reign, when he asked British authorities in South Africa for assistance against Zulu raids into Swaziland. It also was during Mswati's reign that the first whites settled in the country. Following Mswati's death, the Swazis reached agreements with British and South African authorities over a range of issues, including independence, claims on resources by Europeans, administrative authority, and security. South Africans administered the Swazi interests from 1894 to 1902. In 1902 the British assumed control.

In 1921, after more than 20 years of rule by Queen Regent Lobatsibeni, Sobhuza II became Ngwenyama (lion) or head of the Swazi nation. The same year, Swaziland established its first legislative body--an advisory council of elected European representatives mandated to advise the British high commissioner on non-Swazi affairs. In 1944, the high commissioner conceded that the council had no official status and recognized the paramount chief, or king, as the native authority for the territory to issue legally enforceable orders to the Swazis.

In the early years of colonial rule, the British had expected that Swaziland would eventually be incorporated into South Africa. After World War II, however, South Africa's intensification of racial discrimination induced the United Kingdom to prepare Swaziland for independence. Political activity intensified in the early 1960s. Several political parties were formed and jostled for independence and economic development. The largely urban parties had few ties to the rural areas, where the majority of Swazis lived. The traditional Swazi leaders, including King Sobhuza II and his Inner Council, formed the Imbokodvo National Movement (INM), a political group that capitalized on its close identification with the Swazi way of life. Responding to pressure for political change, the colonial government scheduled an election in mid-1964 for the first legislative council in which the Swazis would participate. In the election, the INM and four other parties, most having more radical platforms, competed in the election. The INM won all 24 elective seats.

Having solidified its political base, INM incorporated many demands of the more radical parties, especially that of immediate independence. In 1966, the U.K. Government agreed to discuss a new constitution. A constitutional committee agreed on a constitutional monarchy for Swaziland, with self-government to follow parliamentary elections in 1967. Swaziland became independent on September 6, 1968. Swaziland's post-independence elections were held in May 1972. The INM received close to 75% of the vote. The Ngwane National Liberatory Congress (NNLC) received slightly more than 20% of the vote, which gained the party three seats in parliament.

In response to the NNLC's showing, King Sobhuza repealed the 1968 constitution on April 12, 1973 and dissolved parliament. He assumed all powers of government and prohibited all political activities and trade unions from operating. He justified his actions as having removed alien and divisive political practices incompatible with the Swazi way of life. In January 1979, a new parliament was convened, chosen partly through indirect elections and partly through direct appointment by the King.

King Sobhuza II died in August 1982, and Queen Regent Dzeliwe assumed the duties of the head of state. In 1984, an internal dispute led to the replacement of the Prime Minister and eventual replacement of Dzeliwe by a new Queen Regent Ntombi. Ntombi's only child, Prince Makhosetive, was named heir to the Swazi throne. Real power at this time was concentrated in the Liqoqo, a supreme traditional advisory body that claimed to give binding advice to the Queen Regent. In October 1985, Queen Regent Ntombi demonstrated her power by dismissing the leading figures of the Liqoqo. Prince Makhosetive returned from school in England to ascend to the throne and help end the continuing internal disputes. He was enthroned as Mswati III on April 25, 1986. Shortly afterwards he abolished the Liqoqo. In November 1987, a new parliament was elected and a new cabinet appointed.

In 1988 and 1989, an underground political party, the People's United Democratic Movement (PUDEMO) criticized the King and his government, calling for democratic reforms. In response to this political threat and to growing popular calls for greater accountability within government, the King and the Prime Minister initiated an ongoing national debate on the constitutional and political future of Swaziland. This debate produced a handful of political reforms, approved by the King, including direct and indirect voting, in the 1993 national elections.

Although domestic groups and international observers criticized the government in late 2002 for interfering with the independence of the judiciary, parliament, and freedom of the press, significant improvements have been made concerning rule of law over the past few years. Swaziland's Court of Appeals resumed hearing cases in late 2004 after a two-year absence in protest of the government's refusal to abide by the court's decisions in two important rulings. In addition, the new constitution went into effect in early 2006, and the 1973 proclamation, which, among other measures, banned political parties, lapsed at that time.

GOVERNMENT AND POLITICAL CONDITIONS

On July 26, 2005 King Mswati III ratified Swaziland's constitution. It went into effect February 8, 2006. This is Swaziland's first constitution in over 30 years.

According to Swazi law and custom, the monarch holds supreme executive, legislative, and judicial powers. In general practice, however, the monarch's power is delegated through a dualistic system: modern, statutory bodies, like the cabinet; and less formal traditional government structures. The king must approve legislation passed by parliament before it becomes law. The prime minister, who is head of government, and the cabinet, which is recommended by the prime minister and approved by the king, exercise executive authority. At present, parliament consists of a 65-seat House of Assembly (55 members are elected through popular vote; 10 are appointed by the king) and 30-seat Senate (10 members are appointed by the House of Assembly, and 20 are appointed by the king). House of Assembly elections were last held on September 19, 2008. King Mswati III appointed a new cabinet on October 24, 2008.

For local administration Swaziland is divided into four regions, each with an administrator appointed by the king. Parallel to the government structure is the traditional system consisting of the king and his advisers, traditional courts, 55 tinkhundla (sub regional districts in which traditional chiefs are grouped), and approximately 360 chiefdoms.

Swaziland is a member of the Southern African Customs Union (SACU), with which the U.S. began negotiating a free trade agreement in May 2003. The other members of SACU are Botswana, Namibia, Lesotho, and South Africa.

Principal Government Officials
Head of State--King Mswati III
Head of Government--Prime Minister Sibusiso Barnabas Dlamini
Deputy Prime Minister--Themba Masuku
Minister of Economic Planning--Prince Hlangusempi
Minister of Public Service--Mtiti Fakudze
Minister of Natural Resources and Energy--Princess Tsandzlle
Minister of Education and Training--Wilson Ntshangase
Minister of Health--Bennedict Xaba
Minister of Agriculture--Clement Dlamini
Minister of Information and Communication Technology--Nelisiwe Shogwe
Minister of Justice and Constitutional Affairs--Ndumiso Mamba
Minister of Public Works and Transport--Ntuthuko Dlamini
Minister of Tourism and Environment--Moford Sibandze
Minister of Home Affairs--Chief Magwagwa Gamedze
Minister of Commerce, Industry, and Trade--Jabulile Mashwama
Minister of Foreign Affairs and International Cooperation--Lutfo Dlamini
Minister of Local Government and Housing--Pastor Lindiwe Gwebu
Minister of Sports Culture and Youth Affairs--Hlobsile Ndlovu
Minister of Labour and Social Security--Patrick Magwebetane Mamba
Minister of Finance--Majozi V. Sithole

Permanent Representative to the United Nations--Joel Musa Nhleko
Ambassador to the United States--Ephraim M. Hlophe

Swaziland maintains an embassy in the United States at 1712 New Hampshire Avenue, NW, Washington, DC 20009 (tel: 202-234-5002; fax: 202-234-8254). Swaziland's UN Mission is located at 408 East 50th Street, New York, NY 10022 (tel: 212-371-8910; fax: 212-754-2755).

ECONOMY

Rank	158th
Currency	lilangeni (SZL), South African rand (ZAR)
Fiscal year	1 April - 31 March
Trade organisations	WTO, SADC, SACU
	Statistics
GDP	$6.344 billion
GDP growth	0.3%
GDP per capita	$5,807
GDP by sector	agriculture: 8.2%, industry: 46.9%, services: 44.9% (est.)
Inflation (CPI)	6.1%
Population below poverty line	69%

Labour force	457,900
Labour force by occupation	agriculture: 70%
Unemployment	40%
Main industries	Coal mining, wood pulp, sugar, soft drink concentrates, textile and apparel
Ease-of-doing-business rank	124th
	External
Exports	$2.049 billion f.o.b.
Export goods	soft drink concentrates, sugar, wood pulp, cotton yarn, refrigerators, citrus and canned fruit
Main export partners	South Africa 59.7%, EU 8.8%, US 8.8%, Mozambique 6.2% (2004)
Imports	$2.076 billion f.o.b.
Import goods	motor vehicles, machinery, transport equipment, foodstuffs, petroleum products, chemicals
Main import partners	South Africa 95.6%, EU 0.9%, Japan 0.9%, Singapore 0.3% (2004)
	Public finances
Public debt	$703.1 million
Revenues	$1.006 billion
Expenses	$1.488 billion
Economic aid	recipient: $104 million

The **economy of Swaziland** is fairly diversified, with agriculture, forestry and mining accounting for about 13 percent of GDP, manufacturing (textiles and sugar-related processing) representing 37 percent of GDP and services – with government services in the lead – constituting 50 percent of GDP.

Swaziland ranks as a lower middle income country, but it's estimated that 69% of the population lives in poverty. Most of the high-level economic activity is in the hands of non-Africans, but ethnic Swazis are becoming more active. Small entrepreneurs are moving into middle management positions. Although 70% of Swazis live in rural areas, nearly every homestead has a wage earner. The past few years have seen wavering economic growth, which has been exacerbated by the economy's inability to create new jobs at the same rate that new job seekers enter the market. This is due in part to the country's population growth rate, which strains the natural heritage and the country's ability to provide adequate social services, such as health care and education. Overgrazing, soil depletion, drought, and floods are persistent problems.

Nearly 60% of Swazi territory is held by the Crown in trust of the Swazi nation. The balance is privately owned, much of it by foreigners. The question of land use and ownership remains a very sensitive one. For Swazis living on rural homesteads, the principal occupation is either subsistence farming or livestock herding. Culturally, cattle are important symbols of wealth and status, but they are being used increasingly for milk, meat, and profit.

Swaziland enjoys well-developed road links with South Africa. It also has railroads running east to west and north to south. The older east-west link, called the Goba line, makes it possible to export bulk goods from Swaziland through the Port of Maputo in Mozambique. Most of Swaziland's imports were shipped through this port. Conflict in Mozambique in the 1980s diverted many Swazi exports to ports in South Africa. Swaziland mainly uses the port today for exports of sugar, citrus, and forest products, with future usage of the port expected to increase. A north-south rail link, completed in 1986, provides a connection between the Eastern Transvaal rail network and the South African ports of Richard's Bay and Durban.

The sugar industry, based solely on irrigated cane, is Swaziland's leading export earner and private-sector employer. Soft drink concentrate (a U.S. investment) is another large export earner, followed by wood pulp and lumber from cultivated pine forests. Pineapple and citrus fruit are other important agricultural exports.

Swaziland mines coal and diamonds for export. There also is a quarry industry for domestic consumption. In 2005, mining contributed about 0.6% of Swaziland's GDP, and predictions for the industry are mixed as coal mining is expected to increase but quarried stone production is expected to decrease.

A number of industrial firms have located at the industrial estate at Matsapha near Manzini. In addition to processed agricultural and forestry products, the industrial sector at Matsapha also produces garments, textiles, and a variety of light manufactured products. The Swaziland Industrial Development Company (SIDC) and the Swaziland Investment Promotion Authority (SIPA) have assisted in bringing many of these industries to the country. Government programs encourage Swazi entrepreneurs to run small and medium-sized firms. Tourism also is important, attracting more than 424,000 visitors annually, mostly from Europe and South Africa.

From the mid-1980s, foreign investment in the manufacturing sector boosted economic growth rates significantly. Beginning in mid-1985, the depreciated value of the currency increased the competitiveness of Swazi exports and moderated the growth of imports, generating trade surpluses. During the 1990s, the country often ran small trade deficits. South Africa and the European Union are major customers for Swazi exports.

Swaziland became eligible for the African Growth and Opportunity Act (AGOA) in 2000 and qualified for the apparel provision in 2001. AGOA created over 30,000 jobs, mostly for women, in Swaziland's apparel industry. However, the industry suffered in 2005-2006, due to both increased global competition as a result of the end of the Agreement on Textiles and Clothing (ATC) on January 1, 2005, and the strong Rand (Swaziland's currency is linked to the South African Rand at par), which reduced exports. There are an estimated 16,000 people employed in the apparel industry.

Swaziland, Lesotho, Botswana, Namibia, and the Republic of South Africa form the Southern African Customs Union (SACU), where import duties apply uniformly to member countries. Swaziland, Lesotho, Namibia, and South Africa also are members of the Common Monetary Area (CMA) in which repatriation and unrestricted funds are permitted. Swaziland issues its own currency, the lilangeni (plural: emalangeni).

Title Deed Lands (TDLs), where the bulk of high value crops are grown (sugar, forestry, and citrus) are characterized by high levels of investment and irrigation, and high productivity. Nevertheless, the majority of the population – about 75 percent—is employed in subsistence agriculture on Swazi Nation Land (SNL), which, in contrast, suffers from low productivity and investment. This dual nature of the Swazi economy, with high productivity in textile manufacturing and in the industrialized agricultural TDLs on the one hand, and declining productivity subsistence agriculture (on SNL) on the other, may well explain the country's overall low growth, high inequality and unemployment.

Economic growth in Swaziland has lagged behind that of its neighbors. Real GDP growth since 2001 has averaged 2.8 percent, nearly 2 percentage points lower than growth in other Southern African Customs Union (SACU) member countries. Low agricultural productivity in the SNLs, repeated droughts, the devastating effect of HIV/AIDS and an overly large and inefficient government sector are likely contributing factors. Swaziland's public finances deteriorated in the late 1990s following sizable surpluses a decade earlier. A combination of declining revenues and increased spending led to significant budget deficits. The considerable spending did not lead to more growth and did not benefit the poor. Much of the increased spending has gone to current expenditures related to wages, transfers, and subsidies. The wage bill today constitutes over 15 percent of GDP and 55 percent of total public spending; these are some of the highest levels on the African continent. The recent rapid growth in SACU revenues has, however, reversed the fiscal situation, and a sizable surplus was recorded since 2006. SACU revenues today account for over 60 percent of total government revenues. On the positive side, the external debt burden has declined markedly over the last 20 years, and domestic debt is almost negligible; external debt as a percent of GDP was less than 20 percent in 2006

FOREIGN RELATIONS

Swaziland is a member of the United Nations, the African Union, and the Common Market for Eastern and Southern Africa (COMESA). Swaziland was the chair of the Southern African Development Community's (SADC) Organ for Defense, Politics, and Security from September 2008 until the beginning of September 2009 and remains a member of the Organ Troika. Ten accredited ambassadors or honorary consuls are resident in the country. Swaziland maintains diplomatic missions in Brussels, Copenhagen, Kuala Lumpur, London, Maputo, Nairobi, Pretoria, Taipei, the United Nations, and Washington.

U.S.-SWAZILAND RELATIONS

The United States seeks to maintain and strengthen the good bilateral relations that have existed since the kingdom became independent in 1968. U.S. policy stresses continued economic and political reform and improved industrial relations.

The United States assists Swaziland with a number of HIV/AIDS initiatives and programs implemented through the U.S. Agency for International Development (USAID), Health and Human Services/Centers for Disease Control (HHS/CDC), the Peace Corps, African Development Foundation, the Department of Labor, and the Department of Defense (DoD). In June 2009, the U.S. and Swaziland finalized a Partnership Framework Agreement under the President's Emergency Plan for AIDS Relief (PEPFAR), increasing U.S. HIV/AIDS assistance to Swaziland to approximately $28 million per year. In October 2009, $30 million was allocated for programs pertaining to PEPFAR. On April 12, 2010 an additional $15 million was authorized for the Accelerated Saturation Initiative for Male Circumcision. These funds will be divided amongst the three U.S. Government agencies partnering under the PEPFAR framework in Swaziland: USAID ($9.25 million), HHS/CDC ($5 million), and DoD ($750,000). In addition, the U.S. supports small enterprise development, education, military training, institutional and human resources development, agricultural development, and trade capacity building. The U.S. is also the largest bilateral donor to the Global Fund, Swaziland's principal HIV/AIDS funding source. The U.S. Government sends about four Swazi professionals to the United States each year, from both the public and private sectors, primarily for master's degrees, and about five others for three- to four-week International Visitor programs. About six military members are sent to the United States for education and training purposes.

In 2003, Peace Corps volunteers returned to Swaziland after a nine-year absence. In June 2009, the U.S. and Swaziland finalized a memorandum of understanding (MOU) expanding the duties of the Peace Corps mission in Swaziland. The Peace Corps/Swaziland program, known as the Community Health Project, focuses on HIV/AIDS and provides assistance in the execution of two components of the HIV/AIDS national strategy--risk reduction and mitigation of the impact of the disease. Volunteers encourage youth to engage in appropriate behaviors that will reduce the spread of HIV; they work with children orphaned by the HIV/AIDS pandemic; and they assist in capacity building for non-governmental organizations and community based organizations.

Principal U.S. Officials

Ambassador--Makila James

Makila James was nominated for the appointment of United States Ambassador to Swaziland by President Obama. She was confirmed by the Senate on July 31, 2011 and sworn in as the United States Ambassador to the Kingdom of Swaziland on August 27, 2012.
Deputy Chief of Mission--Sarah Morrison
Peace Corps Country Director--Eileen Cronin

The **U.S. Embassy** in Swaziland is situated in the Central Bank of Swaziland building in the Mbabane city center. The address is American Embassy, 7th floor Central Bank Building, Warner St., Box 199, Mbabane, Swaziland (tel. 268-404-6441/6445; fax 268-404-1695).

TRAVEL AND BUSINESS INFORMATION

The U.S. Department of State's Consular Information Program advises Americans traveling and residing abroad through Country Specific Information, Travel Alerts, and Travel Warnings.

Country Specific Information exists for all countries and includes information on entry and exit requirements, currency regulations, health conditions, safety and security, crime, political disturbances, and the addresses of the U.S. embassies and consulates abroad.

Travel Alerts are issued to disseminate information quickly about terrorist threats and other relatively short-term conditions overseas that pose significant risks to the security of American travelers.

Travel Warnings are issued when the State Department recommends that Americans avoid travel to a certain country because the situation is dangerous or unstable.

For the latest security information, Americans living and traveling abroad should regularly monitor the Department's Bureau of Consular Affairs Internet web site at http://www.travel.state.gov, where the current Worldwide Caution, Travel Alerts, and Travel Warnings can be found. Consular Affairs Publications, which contain information on obtaining passports and planning a safe trip abroad, are also available at http://www.travel.state.gov. For additional information on international travel, see http://www.usa.gov/Citizen/Topics/Travel/International.shtml.

The Department of State encourages all U.S. citizens traveling or residing abroad to register via the State Department's travel registration website or at the nearest U.S. embassy or consulate abroad. Registration will make your presence and whereabouts known in case it is necessary to contact you in an emergency and will enable you to receive up-to-date information on security conditions. Emergency information concerning Americans traveling abroad may be obtained by calling 1-888-407-4747 toll free in the U.S. and Canada or the regular toll line 1-202-501-4444 for callers outside the U.S. and Canada.

The National Passport Information Center (NPIC) is the U.S. Department of State's single, centralized public contact center for U.S. passport information. Telephone: 1-877-4-USA-PPT (1-877-487-2778); TDD/TTY: 1-888-874-7793. Passport information is available 24 hours, 7 days a week. You may speak with a representative Monday-Friday, 8 a.m. to 10 p.m., Eastern Time, excluding federal holidays. Travelers can check the latest health information with the U.S. Centers for Disease Control and Prevention in Atlanta, Georgia. A hotline at 800-CDC-INFO (800-232-4636) and a web site at http://wwwn.cdc.gov/travel/default.aspx give the most recent health advisories, immunization recommendations or requirements, and advice on food and drinking water safety for regions and countries.

STRATEGIC ECONOMIC INFORMATION

ECONOMY AND INDUSTRY

Currency	lilangeni (SZL), South African rand (ZAR)
Fiscal year	1 April - 31 March
Trade organisations	WTO, SADC, SACU
	Statistics
GDP	$6.344 billion
GDP rank	159th (nominal) / 157th (PPP)
GDP growth	0.3% (2011 est.)
GDP per capita	$5,807
GDP by sector	agriculture: 8.2%, industry: 46.9%, services: 44.9% (2011 est.)
Inflation (CPI)	6.1% (est.)
Population below poverty line	69%
Labour force	457,900
Labour force by occupation	agriculture: 70%
Unemployment	40% (est.)
Main industries	Coal mining, wood pulp, sugar, soft drink concentrates, textile and apparel
Ease-of-doing-business rank	124th
	External
Exports	$2.049 billion f.o.b.
Export goods	soft drink concentrates, sugar, wood pulp, cotton yarn, refrigerators, citrus and canned fruit
Main export partners	South Africa 59.7%, EU 8.8%, US 8.8%, Mozambique 6.2% (2004)
Imports	$2.076 billion f.o.b.
Import goods	motor vehicles, machinery, transport equipment, foodstuffs, petroleum products, chemicals
Main import partners	South Africa 95.6%, EU 0.9%, Japan 0.9%, Singapore 0.3% (2004)
	Public finances
Public debt	$703.1 million
Revenues	$1.006 billion
Expenses	$1.488 billion
Economic aid	recipient: $104 million

The **economy of Swaziland** is fairly diversified, with agriculture, forestry and mining accounting for about 13 percent of GDP, manufacturing (textiles and sugar-related processing) representing 37 percent of GDP and services – with government services in the lead – constituting 50 percent of GDP

Economic growth in Swaziland has lagged behind that of its neighbors. Real GDP growth since 2001 has averaged 2.8 percent, nearly 2 percentage points lower than growth in other Southern African Customs Union (SACU) member countries. Low agricultural productivity in the SNLs, repeated droughts, the effect of HIV/AIDS, and an overly large[clarification needed] and inefficient government sector are likely contributing factors. Swaziland's public finances deteriorated in the late 1990s following sizeable[clarification needed] surpluses a decade earlier. A combination of declining revenues and increased spending led to significant[clarification needed] budget deficits. The considerable[clarification needed] spending has not led to more economic growth and has not benefitted the poor to the same extent as regional comparitors, although the poverty headcount has shifted slightly during the first decade of the 2000s (SHIES 2010). Much of the increased spending has gone to current expenditures related to wages, transfers, and subsidies. The wage bill today[when?] constitutes over 15 percent of GDP and 55 percent of total public spending; these are some of the highest levels on the African continent. The recent[when?] rapid growth in SACU revenues has, however, reversed the fiscal situation, and a sizeable[clarification needed] surplus was recorded in 2006/07 and 2012/13. SACU revenues today[when?] account for over 50 percent of total government revenues. On the positive side, the external debt burden has declined markedly[clarification needed] over the last 20 years,[when?] and domestic debt is almost negligible; external debt as a percent of GDP was less than 20 percent in 2006.

TRADE PARTNERS

The Swazi economy is very closely linked to the economy of South Africa, from which it receives over 90 percent of its imports and to which it sends about 70 percent of its exports. Swaziland's other key trading partners are the United States and the EU, from whom the country has received trade preferences for apparel exports (under the African Growth and Opportunity Act – AGOA – to the US) and for sugar (to the EU). Under these agreements, both apparel and sugar exports did well, with rapid growth and a strong inflow of foreign direct investment.

Textile exports grew by over 200 percent between 2000 and 2005 and sugar exports increasing by more than 50 percent over the same period. The continued vibrancy of the export sector is threatened by the removal of trade preferences for textiles, the accession to similar preferences for East Asian countries, and the phasing out of preferential prices for sugar to the EU market.

Swaziland will thus have to face the challenge of remaining competitive in a changing global environment. A crucial factor in addressing this challenge is the investment climate. The recently concluded Investment Climate Assessment provides some positive findings in this regard, namely that Swaziland firms are among the most productive in Sub-Saharan Africa, although they are less productive than firms in the most productive middle-income countries in other regions. They compare more favorably with firms from lower middle income countries, but are hampered by inadequate governance arrangements and infrastructure.

Swaziland, Lesotho, Botswana, Namibia, and the Republic of South Africa form the Southern African Customs Union (SACU), where import duties apply uniformly to member countries. Swaziland, Lesotho, Namibia, and South Africa also are members of the Common Monetary Area (CMA) in which repatriation and unrestricted funds are permitted. Swaziland issues its own currency, the lilangeni (plural: emalangeni), which is at par with the South African rand.

According to a United Nations report, Swaziland is rated a medium development country, ranking 113 out of 174 graded states. (South Africa stands at 101). It is believed that globalisation will provide for a more equitable climate, shifting the present balance where one fifth of the world's population in high income countries has 86% of the world GDP, 82% of export markets, 68% of foreign direct investment and 74% of telephone lines. Conversely, the bottom fifth of the population in the poorest countries has just 1% of the GDP.

Within the SADC region, Swaziland is rated third in human development and eighth in terms of economic competitiveness in Africa.

During the 1990's 80% of direct foreign investment to developing countries, including east and central Europe, went mostly to China.

FORECAST

A deficit of E337.2 million is estimated for 2000/01, representing 4% of the GNP against the previous period's 3.8%. There is little recourse to domestic funding and the continued financing of budget deficits from foreign sources will create adverse external debt service implications.

TRADE AGREEMENTS

Swaziland is party to a number of regional and international trade agreements including:

THE RAND MONETARY AREA

Through this agreement the national currency, the Emalangeni (E) - singular Lilangeni (L) - is on a par with the South African Rand.

THE SOUTHERN AFRICA CUSTOMS UNION

This agreement between Swaziland, South Africa, Botswana, Lesotho and Namibia allows for the free movement of goods between member countries, enabling each to receive its due share of the customs pool generated by commodities imported from non-member countries. The imminent finalising of renegotiating the SACU presents Swaziland with the major challenge of diversifying her revenue base, particularly in the light of poor economic performance.

The Cotonou Agreement (post-Lome Arrangement)
was signed in June 2000. This will eventually replace Lome as an agreement between the 15 European Union (EU) countries and the 70 African, Caribbean and Pacific (ACP) countries, which provides for export commodities originating from ACP states to enter EU countries free of customs and other duties.

European Union-South Africa Free Trade Agreement
This provides for reduced tariffs on goods exported from Europe into South Africa and although not directly involving Swaziland, has an impact on the country: through the SACU, Swaziland can also benefit from lower priced imports but the EU-SAFTA also creates competition for local exporters.

Southern African Development Community
Swaziland is a member of SADC, an association of 11 Southern African states, whose objective is to sustain regional collaboration in order to promote economic growth and improve general conditions for the various populations. The other members are Angola, Botswana, Lesotho, Malawi, Mozambique, Namibia, South Africa, Tanzania, Zambia and Zimbabwe.

The Preferential Trade Area/Common Market for Eastern and Southern Africa

The PTA/COMESA which represents 19 countries from as far north as Ethiopia. The organisation aims to promote cooperation between member states in all areas of economic activity. Other objectives are to achieve better standards of living, to encourage close relations between members, and to promote Africa's development. The PTA/COMESA provides for preferential trading terms between member states. A Free Trade Agreement between the COMESA countries is to be introduced and a customs union is under discussion.

WORLD TRADE ORGANISATION

Swaziland is a founder member of this organisation which was established on 1 January 1995 to replace the General Agreement on Tariffs and Trade (GATT). The WTO is an international organisation which administers the global trade rules agreed in the Uruguay Round of Multilateral Trade Negotiations. These are an improved version of the original GATT rules and clarify and reinforce the original trading directive.

GENERAL SYSTEM OF PREFERENCE

The GSP provides for goods which originate from developing countries to be imported into many industrialised countries at reduced customs levies. These countries include EU member states, the United States of America, Canada, Japan and Australia.

Swaziland's economy is further aided through her membership of the following organisations:

African Development Bank
The Commonwealth
International Monetary Fund
Organisation of African Unity
United Nations
World Bank

SWAZILAND STRATEGY AND OPPORTUNITIES[2]

The Minister of Finance Senator Martin Dlamini has presented the 2015/16 National budget with emphasis on a strong and resilient economy, macroeconomic stability, private sector competitiveness, expanding trade and industry, agricultural modernisation and enhancing natural resource management. Extracts from the Budget Speech are included below.

This is the second budget of the 10th Parliament of the Kingdom of Swaziland. The budget is not just a collection of numbers as printed in the Budget Estimates Books, but also a reflection of the values and aspirations of the Government and the nation at large.

MILESTONES

Despite the various recent challenges including the loss of AGOA, the Kingdom has achieved significant milestones in its socio-economic transformation over the recent years. To highlight a few:-

i) Universal Primary Education now covers Grades 1 to 7, thus reaching the target we set ourselves in the Constitution;

ii) Anti-Retroviral Therapy take up has more than doubled since 2009, with about 105,000 people with HIV accessing free treatment;

iii) The proportion of Swazis with access to clean water has increased to 76 percent; and

[2] Swaziland: Budget Speech 2015/16

iv) Our business and economic environment has generally improved, thanks to improved fiscal conditions and reforms, coupled with peace and security. This augurs well for our future economic growth prospects.

CHALLENGES

The challenge going forward is to consolidate our past achievements and to ensure that we sustain this growth trajectory towards the desired social and economic transformation of the Kingdom. “Kungako sitsi lamaphakelo alonyaka, atawuba yincenye yesisekelo sentfutfuko yelive”.

This Budget is a continuation of our journey towards Vision 2022. To quote the Programme of Action, we aim for a Swaziland where ‘all citizens are able to sustainably pursue their life goals, and enjoy lives of value and dignity in a safe and secure environment.” The theme for the 2015/16 Budget is therefore “Achieving more with less spending: sustaining economic growth and protecting social development.”

The budget will focus on implementing priority development programmes over the next year and medium term, within a tightly constrained resource envelope. The main focus will be on education, health and agriculture; new roads; and measures to create the right conditions for private sector investment.

This Government believes that the Swazi nation can together build a future that is prosperous, just, and secure.

ECONOMIC PERFORMANCE AND OUTLOOK

International developments

As a small open economy, the prosperity of Swaziland to a large degree is influenced by the strength of the global economy. At present, the world economy faces an uncertain future, and is still grappling with overcoming the effects of the recent global financial crisis. The world economy is expected to continue to grow modestly. According to the recent IMF’s World Economic Outlook, global economic growth was estimated at 3.3 percent in 2014, and stabilising at 3.7 percent over the medium term. This rate remains below the average recorded in the decade prior to the 2008 global crisis. On a positive note, the recent decline in international oil prices is good news for domestic inflation and trade prospects.

Regional developments

Projections indicate that the Sub-Sahara Africa’s economy will continue to grow. Growth is projected at 4.9 percent in 2015, rising to 5.2 percent in the medium term. We need to work harder to benefit from this strong regional growth.

South Africa is the destination for 63 percent of our exports. In 2014, the South African economy is projected to have grown by only 1.4 percent, against a target growth of 2.5 percent. Growth will be sluggish at 2.3 percent in 2015, increasing to 2.8 percent in the medium term. Their performance presents a significant challenge for our economy and reminds us of the need to diversify into other markets.

Domestic Developments

Real GDP Growth

On the domestic front, preliminary estimates indicate a slower pace of economic activity over the past year. Real GDP growth slowed down to 2.5 percent, in 2014 from an estimated growth rate of 3.0 percent in 2013. This slowdown has been largely due to a weak performance in mining and manufacturing sectors. The mining sector contracted by 23 percent in 2014, compared with growth of 19 percent in 2013. Falling commodity prices in the international market, and internal administrative issues were behind this weak performance. The manufacturing sector slowed down to 1.3 percent in 2014 from 1.9 percent the previous year. This stemmed from weakened performance in the textile industry, labour disputes and falling commodity prices in the sugar industry.

On the other hand, the 2.5 percent overall growth was supported by robust agricultural and construction sectors. Improved weather conditions and targeted interventions in the agricultural sector, under the LUSIP and food security programmes were the main drivers for growth in agriculture. The construction sector also remained buoyant, driven by major capital projects including the construction of roads, Information Technology and Biotechnology Parks, and the International Convention Centre and Hotel.

Over the medium term, the objective of Government as per the Programme of Action 2013-2018 is to attain real GDP growth of at least 5 percent per year. This is the minimum level of growth that could achieve the desired social economic transformation by 2022. Taking steps towards this goal will require continued implementation of economic reforms identified in the Investor Road Map.

Balance of Payments

Swaziland's balance of payments continued to reflect strong performance in 2014 according to data for the first half of the year. The current account surplus more than doubled in the first half of 2014 compared with the year before. The current account surplus for the two quarters ending June 2014 stood at E1.2 billion. The trade surplus and high SACU receipts were the main factors contributing to the increase in the current account surplus.
22. Exports increased strongly, by 29 percent in the first two quarters of 2014 compared to the same period the previous year, whilst imports increased by a lower 13 percent over the same period. Our strong performance stems from the depreciating exchange rate during 2014, and is an encouraging sign of economic vitality.

BUDGET STRATEGY FOR 2015/16

His Majesty the King in His Speech from the Throne this year, counselled to 'save for rainy days during good years'. Given our difficult fiscal circumstances, these are our priorities for Budget 2015/16:

i) **A strong and resilient economy**, with a particular focus on macroeconomic stability, private sector competitiveness, expanding trade and industry, agricultural modernisation and enhancing natural resource management;

ii) **Enhancing human capital**, with increased focus around access and quality of healthcare and education, and enhancing the welfare of the vulnerable;

iii) **Enhancing service delivery**, through improving institutional governance, transparency and accountability;

iv) **Strategic infrastructure rehabilitation and expansion**, focusing on roads, railway, aviation, water and sanitation, tourism and rural development.

This budget strategy is aimed at sustaining economic growth, employment and poverty reduction. The strategy also ensures that Government facilitates the private sector as directed by His Majesty the King in His Speech from the Throne, by implementing measures that improve efficiency and lower the cost of doing business.

REVENUE AND EXPENDITURE FOR 2015/16

Revenue and grants

Total revenue including grants for 2015/16 is estimated at E14.6 billion compared with an estimated E14.8 billion in 2014/15. In GDP terms, this is a drop of three percentage points. SACU receipts have fallen from E7.4 billion in 2014/15 to E6.9 billion in 2015/16, a reduction of around E560 million. SACU receipts are again expected to decline further in 2016/17, as Swaziland will be required to effect a sizeable repayment during 2016/17, as indicated by the SACU Secretariat. External grants will amount to E270 million, a reduction from last year, as one-off European Union grants for agricultural developments fall.

Expenditure

Expenditure is estimated at E15.9 billion, including payments for public debt and other statutory obligations, which amount to E1.0 billion. Total expenditure for 2015/16 thus represents an additional E646 million above the appropriated level for 2014/15. The estimated budget deficit, of E1.3 billion, will be financed by a mixture of external loans to projects, of around E450 million net, and additional domestic borrowing of around E1 billion. This is a sustainable budget in difficult circumstances. A variety of revenue and expenditure measures have led us to a responsible budget for 2015/16, that prepares us for a difficult year in 2016/17.

Revenue Measures

Government is proposing various revenue measures. These will assist Government in mobilizing additional resources for protecting essential services, while SACU revenues fall in the medium term.

These initiatives include an amendment of the Income Tax regulations, including removal of the tax allowance exempting gains on the disposal of business assets. However, the amendments would also reduce taxation on medical aid for the private sector.

Other initiatives intended by the Income Tax Order include the introduction of taxation of residents on their worldwide income. Currently, residents are taxed depending on source, meaning that tax is imposed on income generated within Swaziland only. This has a limitation in that there is a growing trend of Swazi residents (including individuals and companies) earning income beyond our borders. Increasing tax justice is an idea whose time has come. Our neighbours, including South Africa, have already shifted from source-based taxation to world-wide taxation.

The VAT Refund Agreement between Swaziland and South Africa is ready. From the 1st of April 2015, residents simply declare the VAT of their purchases at any of our border posts, and Government receives the revenue from South Africa. This replaces the current arrangement where declaring residents are charged twice, and must retrieve refunds from South Africa, often months later. The projected additional revenue from increased declarations is over E120 million per year. I would urge all Swazis to declare their purchases, so that vital funding for Government services can be secured.

Furthermore, Government plans to review the Customs and Excise Act; and accommodate a number of modernization initiatives aimed at enhancing revenue collection and improving our Doing Business rank. I am pleased to observe that the SRA is introducing the accreditation of preferred traders. SRA will reward those taxpayers who have a proven record of tax compliance, by issuing certificates of accreditation which grants faster treatment at our borders. Lessening delays in the declaration, clearance and release of goods, and the ability to prepay, will reduce the cost of doing business in Swaziland. Upgraded trade software, which allows electronic signature and documentation, will reduce barriers to trade.

Appropriation

This budget concerns "Achieving more with less spending: sustaining economic growth and protecting social development."

By virtue of the responsibility entrusted to me as Minister of Finance, I now present to this Honourable House, the Budget Estimates for financial year 2015/16, as follows:

1. Revenue plus grants: E14,606 million;
2. Appropriated recurrent expenditure (excludes Statutory): E11,737 million;
3. Capital expenditure: E3,217 million;
4. Total expenditure: E15,952 million; and
5. Deficit: E1,346 million.

Conclusion

There is a higher ambition than merely to stand superior in the world. It is to step down, and lift mankind a little higher than where they are. This Budget is a tough Budget. However, it has tried to focus our meagre resources towards those areas that will lift up Swazis a little higher than where they are currently.

POLICY, PLANS AND PRIORITIES

Poverty Reduction Strategy & Action Plan

PRSAP 2007 is aimed at reducing poverty by more than 50% by 2015 and eradicating poverty by 2022 through:

macro-economic stability and accelerated economic growth;
empowering the poor to generate income and reduce inequalities;
fair distribution of the benefits of growth through fiscal policy;
human capital development;
improving the quality of life for the poor;
improving governance and strengthening institutions.

A key aim of PRSAP is to attract more FDI inflows as well as to promote domestic investment through:

reducing the cost of doing business;
improving competitiveness;
developing and implementing a new set of investment incentives that are budget neutral; and
revising Foreign Direct Investment legislation to bring it into line with modern practices.

Private Sector and Growth

The Ministry of Commerce, Industry and Trade (MCIT) aims to create employment opportunities for the rural population, by decentralising industrial activities to rural areas, and help reduce poverty. The private sector is seen as the main engine of growth, with Government facilitating the process by creating an enabling environment. The decentralisation programme seeks to promote business linkages for small and medium-sized enterprises (SMEs).

Investment Policy Developed

Investment policy has not been expressed in a single comprehensive statement but an Investment Policy has been prepared and approved by Cabinet. Now awaits.

AECOM (2009) Swaziland Investment Policy report states "Several policies exist that relate in one way or another to investment. The Ministry of Commerce, Industry and Trade's National Policy on the Development of Small and Medium Enterprises (SMEs) is one such policy. Published policies also exist on agriculture, energy, transportation, mining, education, telecommunications, public debt, and privatisation, to name but a few. Investment policy exists in Swaziland, although it may not yet be publicly expressed in a formal investment code. For example, foreign investors are guaranteed certain rights as expressed in the law that set up the Swaziland Investment Promotion Authority (SIPA). At other times, policy is espoused through membership in trade blocs such as the Southern Africa Customs Union (SACU); the Southern African Development Community (SADC); and the Common Market for Eastern and Southern Africa (COMESA). These yield substantial benefits to Swaziland and to Swazi companies, as do agreements such as African Growth and Opportunity Act (AGOA), which encourages clothing and other manufacturers to take advantage of the access that is offered to the United States (U.S.) market."

NATIONAL EXPORT STRATEGY

The NES 2006 has a vision to achieve sustainable economic growth through enhanced competitiveness, value addition and export diversification in targeted sectors, and a strong Public Private Partnership (PPP) contributing to the prosperity of the people. Swaziland's trade policy objectives are:

to expand the export base and ensure an increased mix of exports, thus reducing the reliance on the sugar industry as the main foreign exchange earner;
to strengthen the existing relationships with current markets to ensure that Swaziland takes full advantage of preferences offered by these markets;
to enhance market access for exports from Swaziland through branding and improved product quality;
to improve trade facilitation through the establishment of strong public-private partnerships; and

to pave the way for technological innovations that will enhance the competitiveness of Swaziland's exports by ensuring the use of low cost production methodologies that do not compromise the national objective of employment creation.

Investor Survey

The Central Bank of Swaziland (CBS), the Swaziland Investment Promotion Authority (SIPA) and the Central Statistical Office launched the first 2010 Foreign Private Capital and Investor Perception Survey in February 2010.

Economic Diversification Study

The Government of Swaziland with the assistance of the African Development Bank conducted an Economic Diversification Study to determine how diverse the Swaziland Economy is. The study has been completed and to be presented to Cabinet.

Investor Road Map

The Investor Road Map is a summary and implementation framework that relates to improvements that need to be undertaken in the country, with an ambitious target of being amongst the top 60 countries in terms of the World Bank Ease of Doing Business rankings, as per His Majesty's launching remarks in April 2012. The Investor Road Map documents administrative, procedural and Regulatory barriers that may hinder investment in Swaziland and presents a total of 16 objectives that have been presented in order to guide the investment reform process in the country. The Investor Road Map is Government's commitment in addressing the challenges faced by Swaziland regarding the business climate. Overcoming same will mean increased economic activity that will improve the livelihoods of all, including the profitability of our private sector.

Brand Swaziland

The launch of the Investor Road Map coincided with the launch of a national brand. This national brand is envisaged and it is supreme over and is used in communicating Government's promise to improve the investment climate. Moreover, the national brand is meant to address and improve the national image locally, regionally as well as globally. In a nutshell, the brand signifies the promise by Government to the region and the world to make it easier to do business in Swaziland, thus it is called Swaziland; Africa's New Promise.

Royal Science and Technology Park

The Royal Science and Technology Park (RSTP) was commissioned by His Majesty King Mswati III and he appointed a Board of Directors. The Board has since conceptualized the essential and desired characteristics of the RSTP. The RSTP will have a number of components including research facilities, meeting areas, centres of excellence, a biotech plant with incubators of researchers and business persons wishing to take advantage of the Park. The investor will have the freedom to choose from different types of buildings which best suit the specific of industry and business and all working space, from business office units of 3000m^2 – 5000m^2 factory buildings, are to be roomy and surrounded by the eco-environment. Targeted industries under the RSTP are Pharmacueticals, Agro-processing, Manufacturing and Assembly, etc.

INVESTMENT PROMOTION

INSTITUTIONS

MCIT

The Ministry of Commerce, Industry and Trade is responsible for internal trade regulation, promotion of foreign and domestic investment, awarding licences to new businesses, registration of companies, intellectual property rights, domestic and export trade promotion and policy analysis. It is responsible for the sector, including formulating, implementing, and monitoring the industrial development policy, conducting industrial studies and surveys, establishing industrial estates, as well as development / expansion and sale of industrial land.

SIPA

The Swaziland Investment Promotion Authority is established by the Swaziland Investment Promotion Act 1998. SIPA's Mission is to "Promote and facilitate foreign direct and local investment in Swaziland, with the objective of creating the wealth necessary to enhance the Social and Economic Development of the Kingdom and its people."

SIPA Statutory Objects

The SIPA objectives set out in the Investment Promotion Act are:

to attract, encourage, facilitate and promote local and foreign investment in Swaziland;
to initiate, coordinate and facilitate the implementation of government policies and strategies on investment;
to provide a one-stop information and support facility to local and foreign investors; and
to advise the Minister on investment policies, strategies, proposals and suitable incentives for investors.

SIDC

Swaziland Industrial Development Corporation is a private development finance company formed as a joint venture between the government and several international and local financial institutions. The main objective of SIDC is to assist incoming companies by financing joint ventures, equity participation, asset leasing, and providing factory shells. It offers assistance in project appraisal and identification of local or foreign joint venture partners. It provides financial services including equity finance and medium-term and long-term loans at competitive interest rates and leasing of factory buildings, mostly at the Matsapha Industrial Estate. Participants in SIDC: Government of Kingdom of Swaziland 34.9%, German Investment and Development Company (DEG) 22.1%, International Finance Corporation (IFC) 13.7%, Commonwealth Development Corporation (CDC) 10.9%, Netherlands Development Finance Company (FMO) 10.2%, French Development Finance Institution (PROPARCO) 5%, Standard Bank of Swaziland 1.6%, Nedbank (Swaziland) Limited 1.6%.

SME Policy and MCIT, SEDCO, SIPA

The National Policy on the Development of SMEs defines small enterprises as having assets of E50,000 to E2m (US$6500- 260,000), 4 -10 employees, and sales of up to E3 million (US$395,000). Medium enterprises have assets valued at E2-5m (US$260,000-650,000), up to

50 employees, and sales of up to E8 million (US$1,040,000). (E = symbol of Swaziland's currency Lilangeni (SZL).

At policy level, the SME Unit (6 staff members) in MCIT is responsible for researching and proposing changes to existing policy or developing new policy related to SMEs in such areas as finance and training. The Small Enterprise Development Company (SEDCO) (70 staff members) promotes provides business development services such as training on business management and registration of start-up ventures. SEDCO operates eight small industry estates and rents workshops to small business owners. The SME Development Unit / Domestic Investment Department in SIPA provides extensive support to SMEs as well as operating a linkages programme to help establish business relationship between SMEs and larger enterprises.

STA

The Swaziland Tourism Authority is responsible for the development of tourism. The National Tourism Development Plan indicates that new investment in tourism infrastructure is needed. The Government is seeking to greater cooperation between SIPA and STA to identify specific needs in this area.

Swaziland Sugar Association

Under the 1967 Sugar Act, the SSA is a statutory body representing all millers and growers and is responsible for sales and marketing of all sugar produced. It controls two thirds of the industry and is among the largest sugar exporters in Africa.

Swaziland Electricity Company

The Swaziland Electricity Company (SEC) provides uninterrupted power supply for major business users and all others including household electricity needs. The electricity supply is linked regionally to the electricity supply network known as the Southern African Power Pool which enables the country to obtain power at reliable and cost effective tariffs.

INVESTMENT AND EXPORT INCENTIVES

Swaziland and foreign investors may avail of incentive schemes.

FACTORY SHELLS

The Government provides additional support to qualifying investments and industries by making available competitively priced factory shells. This infrastructure eases the start-up hurdles for investors who are venturing into priority sectors.

This tax incentive is available to investors qualifying as a "development enterprise" in terms of issued guidelines. These tax concesion allows for a reduction of the corporate tax to a minimum of 10% for 10 years and an exemption from withholding taxes on dividends for the same period.

EXPORT CREDIT GUARANTEE SCHEME

ECGS funds are held in treasury bills and term deposits monitored by the Central Bank of Swaziland (CBS). The CBS provides a guarantee to commercial banks lending to exporters. The scheme is administered by MCIT and enables exporters to finance working capital requirements and extend better credit terms to customers. A prospective exporter submits complete viable project proposals to a commercial bank to access ECGS funds. The exporter must be registered in Swaziland and present a business plan containing budgets and cash flow projections, audited accounts for the previous period (if already in operation), and the owner's contribution (security or collateral) to financing the project, export orders contracts or letters of credit indicating the list of customers and volume of export trade anticipated, and any other information considered material or relevant by the bank. The ECGS covers 75% of the loan in the case of pre-shipment applications, and 85% in the case of post-shipment applications. The maximum guarantee to any one exporter is E2.5m (US$320,000). Interest is charged at the prime interest rate per annum and the CBS charges a premium of 0.53-2.33%, depending on the length and type of credit. The scheme is not widely used as few SMEs are involved in exporting and the scheme's conditions are considered onerous.

REPATRIATION OF PROFITS

The liberalized foreign exchange mechanisms also allow full repatriation of profits and dividends of enterprises operating in the country. Repatriation is also allowed for salaries of expatriate and capital repayments.

FIVE YEAR WORK PERMITS AND VISAS

These are available for expatriate Directors, Senior Management and key technical personnel of new enterprises.

INVESTOR PROTECTION

Investments in Swaziland are protected from undue expropriation under the Swaziland Investment Promotion Act of 1998. In addition, Swaziland is a member of Multilateral Investment Guarantee Agency (MIGA) of the World Bank which provides for added legal protection of investments.

EPZS, FREEPORTS AND OTHER SPECIAL ECONOMIC ZONES

There are no Export Processing Zones (EPZs) in Swaziland. WTO (2009) states that the creation of export processing zones was consider but were found not to be viable.

TAX INCENTIVES

The corporate tax rate is 27.5% for all companies. There is provision for unlimited carrying forward of losses for set off against future assessable income.

Development Approval Order: The Development Approval Order Notice, 2000 provides that in furtherance of the Income Tax Order of 1975, the Minister for Finance is empowered to issue development approval status to an investor which gives a concessional corporate tax rate of 10% for a period of 10 years. An investor that obtains this concession may be exempted from withholding tax on dividends during the 10 year tax period. The grant of a development approval order is only applicable to approved new investment, business or development enterprises in manufacturing, mining, international services and tourism and which will not unfairly compete with existing Swazi companies. Swaziland and foreign investors are eligible to apply for this incentive but the application must be made by a company incorporated in Swaziland.

Human resources training rebate: On approval by the Commissioner of Taxes 100% of training costs is permitted to be written off against tax liabilities.
Duty Free Imports: Capital goods imported into the country for productive investments are exempt from import duties. Raw materials imported into the country to manufacture products to be exported outside SACU are exempt from import duties. The Department of Customs and Excise is responsible for monitoring this concession and determining any refund due. Refunds are normally issued as duty credits.
Initial depreciation allowance on new plant and machinery brought into use is 50% of cost.
Initial allowance on used machinery housed in a building that qualifies for an initial allowance, and not previously used in Swaziland, and not replacing other machinery is 50% of depreciated value.
Initial depreciation allowance on new industrial buildings (which includes hotel and company financed housing for employees) is 50% of cost.
Annual depreciation on cost of industrial buildings and on improvements to industrial buildings is at the rate 4% per year.

INTERNATIONAL TRADE & EXPORT PROMOTION

TRADE PROMOTION UNIT

TPU within MCIT is the national focal point for trade promotion. The unit supports enterprises by promoting goods on world markets, identifying new export products and market opportunities, and helping enterprises participate in regional and overseas trade fairs and exhibitions by paying for the shipment costs of the exhibits and for the exhibition space. TPU is responsible for issuing certificates of origin under SADC, COMESA and GSP, while the Department of Customs and Excise issues certificates of origin for AGOA trade.

IMPORT PERMIT AND EXPORT LEVY

Under the Import Control Order of 1976 and Legal Notice No. 60 of 2000, 15 broad categories of products are subject to import permits issued by the Ministry of Finance: arms, automotive parts, drugs, electrical appliances, gold and other precious metals, mineral fuels, mineral oils, specified agricultural products (i.e. wheat, flour, dairy products, maize, and rice), used clothing, used earthmoving equipment, used footwear, used motor vehicles, used textiles, used tyres and tyres casings, and wild animal products. Import licensing is used to monitor the flow of licensed goods mainly for health, safety, and environmental reasons. Any individual, firm or institution may apply for an import permit, which is valid for one year (renewable for another year). Applications for import permits are submitted to the Import Permit Committee. First-time applicants must present a certificate of incorporation, memorandum and articles of association, trading licence, tax clearance certificate, original pro forma invoice for the articles to be imported, and most recent bank statement, and must agree to inspection of their premises. Subsequent applications need to be accompanied only by the current trading licence, tax clearance, and pro forma invoices. At the time of importing goods the importer must produce an invoice, bill of entry, bill of lading, and any other relevant documents. An administrative charge is levied on import permit goods.

A sugar export levy is charged on all sugar exported from Swaziland to countries outside of SACU members (Botswana, Lesotho, Namibia, and South Africa).

Under the Swazi Economic Empowerment Initiative, a portion of sugar sold by the SSA in the regional market is reserved for local traders. The process is meant to assist traders develop exporting skills and experience.

ACCESS AND ADMISSION OF FOREIGN INVESTORS

FOREIGN INVESTMENT & CAPITAL MOBILITY

Constitution

Section 59(4) provides that foreign direct investment shall be encouraged subject to any law regulating investment.

National Treatment

The Investment Promotion Act provides for non-discriminatory treatment of investors and investment which means foreign investors are granted national treatment. There are no policies or practices that discriminate against foreign investment, and companies can be 100% foreign-owned. Foreign investment faces minimal screening, but is restricted from providing essential utilities e.g. water and electricity.

Any person, whether a citizen of Swaziland or not, may freely, and without restriction on ownership, make an investment in any sector of the economy, except for the following activities:

Manufacture of firearms, ammunition, chemical and biological weapons, and other defence weapons
Manufacture involving radioactive materials
Manufacture of explosives
Hazardous waste treatment or disposal
Security printing and minting.

WTO and FDI in Swaziland

WTO (2009) "Over the last few years, Swaziland has taken steps to improve the investment climate, notably through the centralisation of business processes (e.g. registration, trading licences, work permits, and factory shells identification), under the Swaziland Investment Promotion Authority. Nonetheless, in general, FDI in Swaziland has been inhibited by structural constraints, such as labour-market rigidities, and the under-developed legal, judicial, and regulatory frameworks. In total, the cost of doing business is high".

FOREIGN INVESTMENT ESTABLISHMENT, REGISTERING AND LICENSING PROCESSES

REGISTRATION AND LICENSING

All businesses operating in Swaziland must be registered. Most trades and professions are covered by specific legislation. If not registered under specific legislation, a trading firm must be licensed by MCIT under the Trading Licence Order of 1975. Any person or organisation engaged in importing or exporting goods or commodities of any nature requires a licence. Importers and exporters must be registered with the Customs and Excise Department under the Ministry of Finance. Declaration is through the Single Administrative Document (SAD) introduced in 2006, which applies to all imports and exports regardless of origin or destination. A Trade and Business Facilitation Bill, aimed at simplifying procedures for trade licensing, has been drafted.

ESTABLISHING A COMPANY

Business enterprises are typically incorporated as a company under the Companies Act 2009.

Registration of Name: The investor can search and reserve his company name online. Company registration now takes only five (5) days to register a company.

Incorporation: the following necessary documents should be submitted:

- Certified Copies of identity card or Passport
- Complete the application form
- Memorandum of Articles of Association – 3 copies
- Form E/TF42 – residential address of business and application of license

The Registrar's office will endorse the Memorandum and Articles of Association and issue the Certificate of Incorporation. The process can take only five (5) days. The Registrar sends copies to the Commissioner of Taxes and Ministry of Commerce, Industry and Trade.

LEGAL SYSTEM

Swaziland is governed by an Independent judiciary that ensures protection of property and individual rights. The Companies Act of 209 governs legislation regarding the formation companies in Swaziland.

FOREIGN REGISTERED COMPANIES

A company that is not incorporated in Swaziland should submit a certified Memorandum of Association from the country of incorporation to the Registrar General.

INCOME TAX REGISTRATION

After setting up a business, the company should register with the Income Tax Department. A form is submitted along with the Company Registration Certificate and the Memorandum of Agreement and Articles of Association. The company is issued with a registration number.

VALUE ADDED TAX REGISTRATION

Taxable persons who make taxable supplies in excess of E500, 000 in any consecutive 12-month period are liable for compulsory VAT registration. Businesses below the threshold may apply for voluntary registration which may be granted at the discretion of the Commissioner General of Swaziland Revenue Authority and be issued with a VAT registration number.

ENVIRONMENT

All businesses, other than service sector businesses, are to apply for approval from the Swaziland Environmental Authority. The Authority reviews the information and determines the category in which the project should be placed, prior to issuing an Environmental Compliance Certificate.

FACTORY INSPECTORATE

Before constructing a factory, a form and cover letter requesting a permit should be submitted to the Labour Commissioner. Three copies of the factory layout must be submitted as a copy is sent to the Local Authority and to the Fire and Emergency Services. When the Factories Inspectorate approval is granted a Certificate is issued. The process takes 2-4 weeks. When the factory is completed and ready to assume operations, the Factories Inspectorate performs a final inspection to confirm that the building complies with the approved plans.

SWAZILAND NATIONAL PROVIDENT FUND

An employer with more than five employees is required to register with the SNPF and SNPF issues a company number. Registration is required before commencing business.

TRADE LICENCE

Under the Trading Licence Order of 1975 a form is submitted to MCIT which places an advertisement in the media and sets a date for a local hearing at which the applicant exhibits the Memorandum and Articles of Association (or Partnership agreement), a bank statement, and a tax clearance certificate. The Trade License is renewed annually. The renewal process does not involve the advertisement and hearing. Health certification for renewals is requested for food sellers.

BANKING

The Central Bank of Swaziland (CBS) is responsible for banking supervision. Under the Financial Institutions Act 2005 banks are required;

- to obtain a licence from the CBS before they start operations.
- conditions for obtaining a licence include: the applicant must be a company registered in Swaziland;
- the applicant must explain what activities the bank will engage in, how activities will be conducted and available resources.
- the CBS must be satisfied as to the financial integrity and history of the applicant, character and experience of management, capital adequacy, how it would benefit the community and its effect on existing banks.

Under the Financial Institutions Act 2005, a bank incorporated in Swaziland must have an initial capital in the form of paid-up shares of not less than E15m (US$2m), or paid-up shares and reserves amounting to the greater of E15m or 5% of its liabilities to the public in Swaziland.

NON- BANK INSTITUTIONS

The Financial Services Regulatory Authority (FSRA) was established through the 2011 Act of Parliament. The objective of this authority is to supervise non-banking institutions. The authority is responsible for regulating and overseeing the activities of NBIs such as Insurance and pension funds are supervised and regulated by the Office of the Registrar of Insurances and Pensions, cooperative unions, etc.

INSURANCE

The Insurance Act and the Retirement Funds Act 2005 repealed the Swaziland Royal Insurance Corporation Order 1973 and brought to an end the monopoly status of the Swaziland Royal Insurance Company with four new companies starting operations in 2008. The main line of insurance business is compulsory motor insurance. The Act opened the insurance market to foreign investors that meet these conditions:

only public companies with paid-up share capital of at least E2m (US$265,000) may apply for registration as insurers;
at least 15% of the shares of the company must be held either by natural persons who are citizens of Swaziland or by juridical persons.
at least 51% of the shares or interest of juridical persons (or, in the case of a retirement fund, of its membership) must be held by citizens of Swaziland;
at least 10% of the directors of the company must be citizens of Swaziland; and
an insurer registered in Swaziland must maintain a principal office and appoint a principal representative in Swaziland.

The Retirement Funds Act 2005 provides for the use of retirement funds policies as collateral when obtaining loans for building on Swazi nation land. The Act also required pension funds to withdraw 30% of assets from external financial markets and invest these in Swaziland.

TELECOMMUNICATIONS

The Swaziland Post and Telecommunications Corporation (SPTC) was established in 1986 under Act No. 11 of 1983. Parliament has passed the Telecommunications bill which seeks to establish an independent regulator which will open up the sector.

FOREIGN EMPLOYMENT & RESIDENCE

Foreign investors are required to use domestic labour when possible, and the process for obtaining residence and work permits for foreign employees takes seven (7) days.

WORK / RESIDENCE ENTRY PERMIT

A foreign investor submits an application to the Ministry of Home Affairs containing the following:

A completed Form, Medical certificate,
Certificate of incorporation,
list of Company Directors, list of shareholders,
Memorandum and articles of association,
Cover Letter,
two passport size photos,
Police Clearance from home country,
Certified copy of passport,
Lease Agreements.

There are several different classes of entry permits for people wishing to live in Swaziland. For investors the classes are: agriculture and animal husbandry, prospecting for minerals or mining, trade, business or non-prescribed profession, manufacturing, and prescribed professions. An application for a permit to work in agriculture and animal husbandry should be submitted to the Ministry of Agriculture and Co-operatives, to work in mining requires a mining right license from the Department of Geological Surveys and Mines, while the other classes require a Trading License.

At the time of submission to the appropriate Ministry, the applicant receives a receipt to help track the application. The Ministry forwards the application to the police to ensure that the applicant has no criminal record. Once cleared by the police, the application goes to the Training and Localisation Committee. The application is then forwarded to the Temporary Residence Permit Committee which makes a decision on the application. The committee includes officials from the Ministries of Home Affairs, MCIT, and Justice & Constitutional Affairs. MCIT is responsible for evaluating the viability of the proposed business and may require a business plan to be submitted and an interview with the applicant to discuss the proposed business.

After the Committee decision, the Ministry informs the applicant of the decision and if the application is successful a permit fee is paid. The Permit is then signed by the Chief Immigration Officer and the accounts office of the Ministry. Entry permits are granted for periods up to five years although the applicant should justify the request. This justification can be based on the level of exports or jobs to be created, or because a commercial bank refuses to provide a loan to those with only a two year entry permit. Most applicants – investors and employees – now receive a five-year permit.

FOREIGN INVESTOR ACCESS TO LAND AND PROPERTY RIGHTS

CONSTITUTION, FOREIGNERS AND LAND

Section 211(4) Subject to sub-section (5), all agreements the effect of which is to vest ownership in land in Swaziland in a non-citizen or a company the majority of whose share-holders are not citizens shall be of no force and effect unless that agreement was made prior to the commencement of this Constitution.

(5) A provision of this chapter may not be used to undermine or frustrate an existing or new legitimate business undertaking of which land is a significant factor or base.

Sub-section (5) permits access to land for a foreign investor, notwithstanding the restriction contained in sub-section (4).

ACQUIRING ACCESS TO LAND

Land for business development purpose can be Title Deed Land (TDL) obtained from the private sector, Title Deed Land obtained from the government, or Swazi Nation Land (SNL).

Foreign companies may obtain access to land in Swaziland, including SNL, which accounts for more than 50% of all Swazi land, and is allocated through customary procedures. SNL may be obtained through MCIT, but as the procedure is cumbersome investors rarely acquire SNL. There are overlapping authorities involved in SNL acquisition: the king, local chiefs, district development committees, and the Government.

An investor may obtain land in Swaziland from the Government or in the private property market. An investor proposing an agricultural project obtains agriculturally zoned land through the Ministry of Agriculture. An investor proposing a hotel or tourism project obtains land through the Ministry of Tourism. The Ministry of Local Government and Housing is the approving authority for the sale of Government Title Deed Land.

Swazi citizens may lease or purchase property on the private property market without prior Government approval. Non-citizens must obtain Government approval through the Land Management Board (LMB) prior to purchasing property in the private property market. Non-citizens may lease property in the private property market without prior government approval.

Investors proposing an industrial or commercial project on Government Title Deed Land located outside the jurisdiction of the relevant local authority acquire the land directly through MCIT. This includes plots in the major urban centers of Matsapha, Nhlangano, and Ngwenya. Investors purchase industrial zoned Government Title Deed Land within designated municipal boundaries from the relevant local authority. For instance, the Mbabane City Council sells government Title Deed Land to investors if the plot is within its jurisdiction. Even in Mbabane, however, the Ministry of Housing and Urban Development must grant final approval and the Ministry of Natural Resources & Energy establishes the selling price for government Title Deed Land.

BUILDING & LAND USE PERMIT

The Ministries responsible for land allocation are the Ministry of Housing and Urban Development. If the business is to be conducted within an urban area, permits are to be obtained from the appropriate municipality which acts as an agent of the Ministry of Housing and Urban Development.

INDUSTRIAL ESTATES

Investors may lease Government Title Deed Land or lease factory shells constructed by SIPA. Government and the private sector own property within the following Matsapha, Nhlangano, and Ngwenya industrial estates. The private sector owns property in Mbabane Industrial Site and Sidwashini Industrial Site. Investors can purchase or lease privately owned land and factory shells in all estates and sites through real estate agents or SIDC.

MCIT Industrial Estate Strategy and Master plan provides for the development of industrial estates by providing basic infrastructure, i.e. access to water and sanitary services, waste disposal, road, electricity, and telephone services. The industrial estates are designated according to the character of the industrial area (e.g. light, heavy, dry, wet, high-tech or mixed) and zoned according to the nature of the activities. The MCIT also provides serviced land to prospective investors in designated industrial estate / areas.

FOREIGN INVESTMENT OPERATIONS

EMPLOYMENT

Industrial Relations Act of 2000

The Act provides the general legal framework of operations of companies, employer to employee relations, employer, trade union and employee relations, dispute resolution mechanism and other statutory requirements.

Wages Act of 1964

The Act specifies the basic minimum wage applicable per sector, conditions of service highlighting hours of work, overtime, public holidays, annual leave among others, for each business sector.

Workmen Compensation Act of 1983

The Act specifies the requirement of manufacturing companies to acquire workmen insurance cover for all employees, in case of injury sustained at work.

BUSINESS TAXATION

VALUE ADDED TAX

Businesses operating in Swaziland are required to obtain a unique identity number for purposes of collecting VAT on behalf of the Swaziland Revenue Authority (SRA). These collected taxes are repatriated to government monthly. Under the Value Added Tax (VAT) 2012, VAT tax is applied to transactions involving imported goods at the time of importing, and is applied to sales of locally manufactured goods on the date goods are sold by the manufacturer, and is also applied to taxable services, hotel accommodation and restaurant sales. The rates are 14% on general goods and services. Exemptions include necessities, intermediate goods or plant and machinery for manufacturing, medical supplies, temporary imports, certain personal imports, water and electricity. On goods imported from outside SACU taxable value is determined by adding together (i) the value for customs duty purposes + (ii) any customs, excise and surcharge duties paid + 14% sales tax of the total amount of (i) + (ii).

INCOME TAX

Under the Income Tax Order of 1975 (King's Order-in-Council No. 21 of 1975), as amended all companies are subject to tax at a rate of 30% on taxable income. Taxable income is defined as gross income (excluding capital receipts, foreign and exempt income) less allowable deductions (including loss offsets) incurred in the process of production in the Kingdom. Additional tax concessions may be granted, at the discretion of the Minister of Finance, to new businesses considered beneficial to the economy. A branch of a foreign company is subject to a tax on Swaziland profits as if it was a domestic company. In addition a branch profits tax of 15% is charged on the deemed repatriated income.

Capital allowances: Hotel and industrial Buildings used in a process of manufacture are subject to a 4% annual allowance on the cost of the building and improvements and 50% initial allowance in the year in which the building is brought into use.

Plant and machinery: A 50% initial allowance is granted in respect of qualifying assets and annual wear and tear based on the useful life of each asset.

Other capital assets may be written down over the expected period of their useful lives.

Special allowances exist in respect of the hotel industry.

Dividends: Dividends received by or accruing to a company are exempt from normal tax. Dividends received by or accruing to an individual are taxed at special rates.

Losses: Where income is exceeded by allowable deductions, an assessed loss is created. Such loss may be carried forward indefinitely for set-off against taxable income in future years of assessment. The proviso exists that the taxpayer must continue to operate and derive income.

Foreign sourced income: Only income which has a source or deemed source in Swaziland will be subject to tax in the Kingdom. Foreign-sourced income is exempt from Swaziland tax.

Incentives: Special grants and allowances are given to creators of additional productive capacity. This is in the form of initial allowances and accelerated depreciation. Further incentives are also provided to non-resident investors to encourage foreign investment in Swaziland.

Withholding tax: Certain payments to non-residents attract withholding taxes, as follows: Entertainers and sportsmen 15% of amount paid, Contractors 10% of the payment to the non-resident, Royalties and management fees 15%.

Non-resident shareholders' tax (NRST) Payable on dividends at the rate of 12.5% of the dividend if it is paid to South African, Botswana, Namibian or Lesotho companies. The rate increases to 15% in respect of all other dividends.

SWAZILAND REVENUE AUTHORITY

The Swaziland Revenue Authority (SRA) was created through an Act of Parliament, the Swaziland Investment Promotion Act of 2008. SRA is a Category A Public Enterprise and is wholly funded by the Government of Swaziland, with the aim of collecting all Government's revenue.

- Investors can now submit their tax returns online (e-tax).

ENVIRONMENT, PHYSICAL PLANNING, HEALTH & SAFETY, CONSUMER PROTECTION

ENVIRONMENT

The Environment Management Act 2002 provides for a framework for environmental protection and the integrated management of natural resources on a sustainable basis, the Swaziland Environment Authority (to succeed the Authority established under Swaziland Environment Authority Act 1992), the Swaziland Environment Fund.

Category 1 projects: unlikely to cause any significant environmental impact;

Category 2 projects: likely to cause environmental impacts some of which may be significant unless mitigation actions are taken;

Category 3 projects: likely to have significant adverse impacts whose scale, extent and significance cannot be determined without in-depth study. Appropriate mitigation measures are identified after completing the study.

SWAZILAND STANDARDS AUTHORITY

SWASA is established by the Quality and Standards Act (10) 2003 and became operational in 2007. Its functions are to promote standards and quality in local industry, commerce, and the public sector. It is responsible for all issues regarding standards, quality, accreditation, and metrology (SQAM) in Swaziland. Swaziland continues to apply South African standards procedures and relies on the South African Bureau of Standards (SABS) and the South African National Accreditation System (SANAS) for all questions relating to standard-setting, testing, certification. There are currently no Swazi standards. SWASA does not have laboratories, and relies on credible local and international laboratories.

SPS AND TBT ENQUIRY POINTS

Swaziland accepted the Technical Barriers to Trade (TBT) Code of Good Practice in 2008 and the Quality Assurance Unit (under MCIT) is the enquiry point. The allocation of responsibilities between SWASA and the Quality Assurance Unit is yet to be clearly defined.

The national enquiry points under the WTO Sanitary and Phyto-sanitary) SPS Agreement are the Directorate of Veterinary Services (for sanitary measures), under the Ministry of Agriculture, and the Directorate of Research (for phyto-sanitary measures), under the Ministry of Agriculture.

COMPETITION POLICY & LAW

Competition Commission

Under the Competition Act 2007, the Competition Commission was established with the aim of encouraging competition in the economy. The Commission is to control anti-competitive trade practices, including prohibition of abuse of dominance, and monitor mergers and acquisitions, and monopolies and concentration of economic power. The Commission has power to carry out, on its own initiative or upon request, investigations into the conduct of business to assess abuse of a dominant position and merger impact on competition and consumers. It may take action to regulate a merger or to prevent or redress the abuse of a dominant position by an enterprise. It is to provide information for the guidance of consumers regarding rights under the Act, undertake studies and publish reports regarding the operation of the Act.

Price Controls

Price controls in Swaziland are imposed under the Price Control Order of 1973. This provides for the fixing of maximum prices for both goods and services. The Minister of Agriculture may fix maximum and minimum wholesale and retail prices for any animal or animal product sold in Swaziland. Currently, price controls are applied top bread, sugar, dairy products, gasoline, and postal and telecommunication services.

MONETARY POLICY, FOREIGN EXCHANGE AND FOREIGN INVESTORS

CMA and Exchange Control

Swaziland along with Lesotho, Namibia, and South Africa form the Common Monetary Area (CMA), under which the Swazi lilangeni (E) is maintained at par with the South African rand. The rand circulates freely in Swaziland. The CMA provides for the free flow of funds between its members with no exchange controls. The CMA countries apply virtually identical exchange control regulations to foreign exchange transactions with non-members of CMA.

Foreign Exchange

The enforcement of Exchange Control Regulations has been delegated by the Minister for Finance to CBS. Authorised Dealers are appointed by CBS to process foreign exchange transactions in accordance with conditions and limits set out in rulings issued by CBS. Residents and non-residents may hold foreign exchange accounts. Inward transfers should be registered with CBS, to facilitate possible future repatriation of capital. In practice, approval is routinely granted when required for genuine investment activity. Companies that are more than 25 percent owned or controlled by persons from outside the CMA require Central Bank approval before borrowing from Swazi sources.

There are ample foreign reserves available, and the system is generous for companies who want to import raw materials or equipment for productive purposes. There is full repatriation of profits and dividends of enterprises operating in the country. Repatriation is also allowed for salaries of expatriate and capital repayments.

PUBLIC PROCUREMENT

Promotion of Swazi Business

Regulations on Public Procurement 2008 were adopted and the Procurement Bill 2008 is before the Parliament. A maximum 15% price preference is granted to Swazi-owned and registered companies. In addition, other measures are envisaged to promote Swazi companies in public procurement. These include encouraging foreign companies to sub-contract business to Swazi companies where feasible and appropriate, dividing procurement requests into small lots that permit small Swazi companies to submit a tender, and providing training in tendering and procurement.

Swazi National Tender Board

The Regulations on Public Procurement established a single tender board, the SNTB, to replace the Central and Treasury Tender Boards. The SNTB, chaired by the Principal Secretary of the Ministry of Finance manages all tender processes. It aims to ensure compliance with the Regulations by Ministries and Departments, and approves all high value awards. A recommendation to award a contract is to be based on the best evaluated tenderer as determined by the evaluation methodology and criteria specified in the invitation document. The procuring entity should prepare a notice indicating the name of the best evaluated tenderer, the value of the proposed contract, and the evaluation ratings. The notice should be sent directly to those who submitted tenders by letter, and, where appropriate, by fax or e-mail, and published on the Government's public procurement website. The procuring entity should allow at least ten working days between the date of dispatch of the letter and publication of the notice and award of the contract.

Procurement Bill

The Procurement Bill 2008 envisages the establishment of the Swaziland Public Procurement Regulatory Authority (SPPRA) to serve as an independent regulatory body, with responsibility for policy, regulation, oversight, professional development, and management and dissemination of information on public procurement. Its functions would be to advise the Government and procuring entities on procurement policy, report on the performance and functioning of the public procurement system, and recommend changes. SPPRA would be governed by a Board of Directors composed of a non-executive chairperson and four non-executive members, with at least two members from the private sector, civil society or professional bodies, to be appointed by the Minister of Finance.

INTELLECTUAL PROPERTY

IPR Institutions

General responsibility for Intellectual Property Rights is under the Registrar-General's Department in the Ministry of Justice. This is also the contact point under Article 69 of the WTO TRIPS Agreement. Other institutions responsible for intellectual property matters are the Customs and Excise Department (Ministry of Finance), for matters related to cross border trade, and courts of law for enforcement.

International IPR

Swaziland is a member of the World Intellectual Property Organisation (WIPO) and the African Regional Industrial Property Organisation (ARIPO). It is a signatory to the: ARIPO Protocol on Patents and Industrial Designs; Paris Convention for the Protection of Industrial Property; Patent Cooperation Treaty; Berne Convention for the Protection of Literary and Artistic Works; Rome Convention for the Protection of Performers, Producers of Phonograms and Broadcasting Organisations; and Madrid Agreement Concerning the International Registration of Marks. Swaziland is also in the process of accession to the WIPO Internet treaties.

Trademark Registration

The Trade Marks Act of 1981 establishes a Registrar of Trade Marks (in the Registrar General's Office). Under the Act and Trade Marks Regulations 1989 an applicant for a trademark submits a form and attaches a mark for all goods and classes of goods to the Registrar who replies with an acceptance or objection form. The applicant prepares a proof of advertisement for publication in the Trademark Gazette. Other parties have six months to object to the trademark. If there is no objection the trademark is registered. A trade mark is valid for ten years. The registered owner of a trade mark has the exclusive right to use the mark, and any assignment or transmission of the mark must be registered by the assignee. Appeals against the Registrar's decisions may be made to the High Court. The Fair Trading Act, 2001 provides for enforcement and penalties for infringement of trade marks.

Patents

The Patents, Utility Models and Industrial Designs Act of 1997, establishes a Registrar of Patents, in the Registrar-General's Office. Patents are valid for 20 years from the time of application, subject to working of the invention. A utility model certificate is valid for seven years from the application date, but is not renewable. Registration of industrial design is valid for five years from the date of application and is renewable for two subsequent periods of five years (a total of 15 years). An application for protection of an industrial design is be filed with the Registrar and must contain a request, drawing, or other adequate graphic representations of the article and an indication of the kind of products for which the design will be used. There is no provision in the legislation for compulsory licensing in respect of industrial designs, or for the protection of new varieties of plants, pharmaceutical or chemical products or textile designs.

Copyright

Copyright is protected under Copyright Act No. 36 of 1912, Copyright (Prohibited Importation) Act No. 35 of 1918, and Copyright (Rome Convention) Act No. 1 of 1933. There is no legislation relating to geographical indications, layout-designs (topographies) of integrated circuits or the protection of undisclosed information in Swaziland. The Copyright Act 1912 covers literary, dramatic, and artistic works, performances, and sound recordings first published in any part of the Commonwealth. The term of copyright protection is the life of the author plus 50 years. The legislation does not comply with Article 9 of the TRIPS Agreement (protection of the exclusive rights of authors in relation to their literary and artistic works) and does not comply with the Berne and Rome Conventions. There are no provisions for royalties to be paid to musicians, authors or performers. A new Copyright Bill, based on the WIPO model, addresses the administration of copyright and neighbouring rights, audiovisual works, expression of folklore, and computer programs. It will establish a Copyright Society, which will be responsible for the promotion of the interests of authors, artists, and performers, and a Copyright Administrator's office in the Registrar-General's office.

INVESTMENT PROTECTION AND DISPUTE SETTLEMENT

Constitution

Section 14(1) The fundamental human rights and freedoms of the individual enshrined in this Chapter are hereby declared and guaranteed, namely

(d) protection from deprivation of property without compensation;

(2) The fundamental rights and freedoms enshrined in this Chapter shall be respected and upheld by the Executive, the Legislature and the Judiciary and other organs or agencies of Government and, where applicable to them, by all natural and legal persons in Swaziland, and shall be enforceable by the courts as provided in this Constitution.

(1) A person of whatever gender, race, place of origin, political opinion, colour, religion, creed, age or disability shall be entitled to the fundamental rights and freedoms of the individual contained in this Chapter but subject to respect for the rights and freedoms of others and for the public interest.

Section 19. (1) A person has a right to own property either alone or in association with others.

(2) A person shall not be compulsorily deprived of property or any interest in or right over property of any description except where the following conditions are satisfied

(a) the taking of possession or acquisition is necessary for public use or in the interest of defence, public safety, public order, public morality or public health;
(b) the compulsory taking of possession or acquisition of the property is made under a law which makes provision for

i. prompt payment of fair and adequate compensation; and
ii. a right of access to a court of law by any person who has an interest in or right over the property;

(c) the taking of possession or the acquisition is made under a court order.

Land

Section 211 (1) From the date of commencement of this Constitution, all land (including any existing concessions) in Swaziland, save privately held title-deed land, shall continue to vest in iNgwenyama in trust for the Swazi Nation as it vested on the 12th April, 1973.

(2) Save as may be required by the exigencies of any particular situation, a citizen of Swaziland, without regard to gender, shall have equal access to land for normal domestic purposes.
(3) A person shall not be deprived of land without due process of law and where a
(4) person is deprived, that person shall be entitled to prompt and adequate compensation for any improvement on that land or loss consequent upon that deprivation unless otherwise provided by law.
(5) Subject to subsection (5), all agreements the effect of which is to vest ownership in land in Swaziland in a non-citizen or a company the majority of whose share-holders are not citizens shall be of no force and effect unless that agreement was made prior to the commencement of this Constitution.
(6) A provision of this chapter may not be used to undermine or frustrate an existing or new legitimate business undertaking of which land is a significant factor or base.

Investment Promotion Act

The Investment Promotion Act 1998 provides for protection for investors on from compulsory acquisition, except under the following circumstances;

In accordance with applicable legal procedures;
In pursuance of a public purpose;
Without any form of discrimination on the basis of nationality, and
Upon prompt payment of adequate and fair compensation.

INTERNATIONAL AGREEMENTS AND OBLIGATIONS – TRADE AND OTHER AGREEMENTS, BITS, DTTS

Swaziland is a member of SACU, SADC, COMESA and the African Union (AU). Swaziland had preferential access to the EU market under the Cotonou Agreement, which expired at the end of 2007. Swaziland signed an interim Economic Partnership Agreement (EPA) with EU in 2009. Swaziland benefits from duty-free access to the U.S. market under the AGOA, including the special provisions on textiles and clothing, and from preferential access to the markets of most developed countries under the Generalised System of Preferences (GSP). In 2008, a Trade, Investment, and Development Cooperative Agreement was signed between SACU and the U.S and the SACU-MERCOSUR Preferential Trade Agreement has been developed over a number of years and signed by SACU Ministers in 2009.

Swaziland is trading in COMESA under a derogation allowing COMESA member states who have acceded to the FTA, to grant Swaziland preferential trade treatment without any reciprocity. Swaziland can only participate in the COMESA FTA or grant reciprocal treatment to other FTA members, with concurrence from the other SACU members, under Article 31 of the 2002 SACU Agreement. In the absence of concurrence, Swaziland's derogation has been extended several times, most recently in December 2008, for two years.

Swaziland is a member of the Multilateral Investment Guarantee Agency (MIGA) and ICSID. There is no domestic arbitration system.

SADC RELATED ISSUES

Bilateral Investment Treaties

Bilateral Investment Treaties with South Africa			
Swaziland	Partner	Date of Signature	Date of Entry into Force
	Egypt	18 July 2000	-
	Germany	5 April 1990	7 Aug 1995
	Mauritius	15 May 2000	-
	Taiwan Province of China	3 March 1998	-
	United Kingdom	5 May 1995	5 May 1995

Double Tax Agreements

Double Tax Agreements with South Africa				
Swaziland	Partner	Type of Agreement	Date of Signature	Date of Entry into Force
	Mauritius	Income & Capital	29 June 1994	
	South Africa	Income	23 Jan 2004	
	South Africa	Income & Capital	21 Dec 1972	
	Sweden	Income & Capital	19 Jan 1972	
	United Kingdom	Income & Capital	26 Nov 1968	
	Lesotho		2012	

STARTING BUSINESS - BASIC INFORMATION

The Swaziland economy is closely linked with its much larger neighbour, South Africa. Their two currencies have the same value, South Africa is Swaziland trading partner with 60% of exports and 85% of imports, and there is no customs or excise duty between the two. Swazi workers have historically travelled to jobs in South African mines, although the workforce is now being reduced, and the smaller state will probably have to generate increased work itself. Formal sector employment has grown over the period 1991-98 by 0.5% every year, substantially below the population growth at 2.7%, and so probably below the increase in available manpower. Much of the deficit has been absorbed into the informal sector, where employment increased at 2.5% per year, according to Central Bank estimates. Job turnover is large.

The Swaziland Investment Promotion Agency attempts to promote investment, and ease the procedures for approval. Growth in wealth per head has slowed from its high point through the 1980s, with foreign direct investment in manufacturing showing a noticeable fall. Much of the manufacturing industry is based on the agricultural sector where the majority of the population works - the countrys main exports include soft drink concentrates, sugar, wood pulp, and cotton yarn.

There is an attempt to develop Swazilands tourist sector, which could become a significant industry, especially in view of its success in South Africa. Political instability may limit its development, having already cost the country GSP trading preferences from the United States.

A number of plans have been advanced to improve Swazilands infrastructure. Export and import costs may fall with the proposed rehabilitation of roads and of the rail route to Mozambique, while the civil service has been subject to efficiency reviews. The telephone network is said to be limited but improving, and there are a number of Internet service providers. Electricity is provided by a parastatal.

Swaziland has a small stock exchange.

REGULATIONS GOVERNING FOREIGN INVESTMENT

Most business activities are open to foreign investors.

Swaziland is a member of the Rand monetary area, and external capital controls apply outside the members: South Africa, Swaziland, Namibia, and Lesotho. There is no capital control within the area.

Dividends and interest may be repatriated freely, after tax. However, certain fees are restricted.

LEGAL FORMS

PRIVATE COMPANY

Private companies have the following characteristics:

- they have names ending in "(Proprietary) Limited",
- they are limited by share capital,
- they have no more than fifty members,
- they restrict the right to transfer shares,
- they may not invite the public to acquire shares or debentures in the company, and
- they must be registered.

PUBLIC COMPANY

Public companies have names ending in "Limited", and have no restriction on share transfer. They must:

- be limited by share capital,
- have at least seven members, and
- be registered.

FOREIGN COMPANY

Foreign companies must register with the Registrar of Companies, and are regulated by the Companies Act. They can operate through a subsidiary or a branch. In the latter case, they must be registered as an external company.

PARTNERSHIP

Partnerships are restricted to twenty persons or legal entities, except for some recognised professionals.

Other forms include sole traders, and trading trusts.

PROCEDURES FOR INVESTMENT

REGISTRATION OF COMPANIES

The first stage is to get approval of the proposed name from the Registrar of Companies. Names should not be already in use, nor cause annoyance, nor use words like "imperial", "crown", and so on.

Then the Memorandum of Association should be submitted to the Registrar, with

- the name of the company,
- the address of the registered office,
- the objectives,
- statement of whether the liability is limited, and
- the amount of the share capital.

For a limited company, the Articles of Association should also be included. Sending them is optional for a company with unlimited liability.

For foreign company, documents showing the overseas incorporation are also required.

Sole traders and partnerships must also register.

A license fee is payable, of:

- Emalangeni 20 if the share capital is no more than E10,000,
- E40 if the share capital is above E10,000 but no more than E30,000,
- E100 if the share capital is above E30,000 but no more than E50,000, and
- E200 if the share capital is above E50,000.

LABOUR CONSIDERATIONS

Work permits are generally awarded if expatriates have skills not locally available.

The Employment Act (1980) regulates the contract of employment.

The Wages Act (1964) regulates the wages and conditions of employment. The Minister of Labour sets minimum wages and standards for certain industries, such as the motor industry, transportation, mining, retail, hotel and catering, and agriculture.

The Industrial Relations Act (1980) concerns collective negotiation of terms of employment as well as establishment of a Labour Court. The Court assists in the settlement of trade or other contract disputes.

Employees may form labour organisations. Recognition is gained by registration with the Commissioner of Labour.

TAXES

Corporation tax is 37.5% (one source reports 30%). Mining companies are taxable at rates of 27% then 37% above taxable income of E20,000. Some expenditures are tax deductible.

Dividend tax is 15% generally. Companies incorporated in Botswana, Lesotho, or South Africa pay 12.5%. Non-residents pay withholding tax at the same rates.

Tax on interest is 10%.
Personal income tax is progressive from 0% to 39%.
Sales duty is 15%, and 20% on liquor and cigarettes.
Other taxes include stamp duty, sugar export tax, mineral rights tax, and casino tax.
There are double taxation agreements with South Africa and the UK.

INVESTMENT INCENTIVES

There are a number of incentive schemes.

SWAZILAND INDUSTRIAL DEVELOPMENT COMPANY LIMITED

Direct joint participation in the project may occur through the Swaziland Industrial Development Company Limited (SIDC), a limited company which provides finance to the private sector, and takes part in projects judged to be viable and well managed. Priority is given to schemes which:

- provide permanent employment,
- generate foreign exchange,
- utilise local resources,
- encourage linkage with existing industries,
- upgrade human resource skills,
- transfer appropriate technology, and
- promote local entrepreneurship.

The SIDC in principle only finances new projects, and does not refinance. The involvement is restricted to:

- 50% of the projects financial requirements,
- 35% of the companys equity,
- loans for fixed assets with terms up to 10 years, and
- financial services.

EXPORT CREDIT GUARANTEE SCHEME

The scheme provides credit to small and medium sized exporters, and is funded in part by the Government, and in part by banks and investment income.

OTHER INCENTIVES

Special tax allowances may be given to large scale investors, those training Swazi citizens, and those classified as "development" enterprises.

New manufacturing enterprises may be given a five year tax exemption, subject to the cumulative taxable income in the period less remuneration paid to Swazi citizens being below 150% of the value of the fixed assets.

Industrial machinery qualifies for a 50% write-off in the year the asset is brought into use. Industrial plants and hotels also have an initial 50% allowance, and then 4% annual allowance.

CONTACT ADDRESSES

Ministry of Finance
POB 443, Mbabane
Telephone: 42141 Telex: 2109

Central Bank of Swaziland
POB 546, Mbabane
Telephone: 43221 Telex: 2029-2108 Telefax: 45417-42636

The Swaziland Investment Development Corporation
P.O. Box 866
Mbabane
Telephone: (00268) 43391/43
Fax: 45619

Ministry of Commerce, Industry & Tourism Trade Promotion Unit
P.O. Box 451
Mbabane
Tel: (0268) 43201/41808/9
Tlx: 2232 WD
Fax: (0268) 43833

Swaziland Industrial Development Co. Ltd
Operations Department
Corner Tin & Walker Street
P.O. Box 866
Mbabane
Tel: (268) 43391-3; 44010-2
Tlx: 2052 WD
Fax: (268) 45619

COMMUNICATIONS

POSTS & TELECOMMUNICATIONS

The Swaziland Posts and Telecommunications Corporation was established in 1986 under Act No. 11 of 1983 which regulates all SPTC activities for which the Minister of Tourism, Environment and Communications is answerable in parliament While SPTC falls into the two categories of postal and telecommunications, the Telecommunications Bill Review was approved by Cabinet during the year and once this is passed, will provide for the separation of the entities.

POSTAL SERVICES

The Postal Branch of SPTC is responsible for handling all classes of mail to and from domestic and international locations, and also provides an expedited mail and courier service and a bureaufax facility. There are about 65 post offices in the county and additional postal services are introduced to identified locations with the objective of providing facilities in line with standards laid down by the Universal Postal Union. Statutory social services objectives require the branch to deliver at least a basic service to all parts of the country. Other services include money and postal orders, and handling COD parcels. There is also a stamp bureau which serves philatelists.

TELECOMMUNICATIONS

The kingdom's telephone network is fully digital and SPTC recently installed three new telephone exchanges at Mahamba, Mahwalala and Siphocosini. Other developments include a programme to speed up the extension of the local network using optical fibre based systems and wireless local loop systems. Two optical fibre systems and three wireless local loop systems have been installed and SPTC has expanded the trunk network with optical fibre links in key areas.

With the commissioning of the cellular network towards the end of 1998, Swaziland's telecommunications system became one of the most modern in Africa. The corporation is a share holder in this venture.

The corporation provides a diversity of services including phone cards, and Internet Cafes in Matsapha, Mbabane and Manzini, and during 2000, many new innovations were introduced. These include Telecentres at strategic points which provide a complete service centre for paying bills, enquiries, service applications and fault reporting. SPTC has also introduced voice mail, a pre-paid service to help subscribers budget and a message service for people awaiting connections.

A new Internet gateway, involving investment of E6 million, now connects Swaziland direct to the United States without having to go via South Africa. This has relieved congestion and is also cheaper, more accessible and faster.

An ongoing programme includes the expansion of the rural network and the international switch to cater for telephone traffic growth; upgrading the telecommunications network to provide ISDN capability; expanding the trunk network to provide alternative routing on major routes; the provision of an Internet Hub to enable countrywide use of the service, and the installation of new exchanges where demand dictates.

THE CELLULAR NETWORK

MTN Swaziland Ltd.

MTN launched its network operations in Swaziland at the end of 1998, in partnership with the Posts and Telecommunications Corporation, following its award over other bidders of a network licence.

Since its inception, Swazi MTN has significantly developed the cellular network, and now provides in excess of 70% coverage of the country's geographical area, with over 60 retail outlets established throughout Swaziland. International roaming agreements have been signed with various operators and discussions are in hand to roam with additional networks.

Coverage presently includes all the major business centres in the country's four regions, as well as continuous coverage from the Ngwenya border, along the Mbabane-Manzini highway, and on to the Mozambique border. Coverage to other areas is also being expanded.

Products available include basic voice, with value added services such as voicemail, short message service, faxmail, calling line identification, call forwarding, waiting and holding, international dialling and roaming, and directory enquiries. MTN offers two 24-month post-paid packages, ConnectaPlan and ConnectaPlus, as well as a pre-paid option. The cellular network can also be accessed through pay phones installed around the country in areas where there is either poor or no telecommunication infrastructure.

The products and services are available at the MTN Service Centres in Mbabane and Manzini, as well as at the various retail outlets.

The grade and quality of services provided by the Swazi MTN network is of international standard and is one of the most stable on the African continent.

THE INTERNET

The Internet system has become an integral part of the communications network in Swaziland with both organisations and individuals linking into the international network. This advanced information technology is a key tool for the local business community and companies that provide Internet services, including installation, training and backup, are established. Clients are given individual E-mail addresses and, through a computer and modem, may link up to the worldwide Internet network for the cost of a local call. Corporate customers can connect entire networks via dedicated lease lines provided by SPTC with a monthly subscription payable.

AFRICA ONLINE

Previously known as UUNET Internet Africa, this company changed its name when it was acquired by Africa Online Holdings in June 2004. Launched in February 1996, the company has rapidly expanded its Swaziland network, adding a second dial-in Point of Presence (PoP) in early 1998. Africa Online specialises in providing network Internet access for corporate and institutional users, to customers as diverse as the Royal Swaziland Sugar Corporation and Ubombo Sugar in the lowveld, and Tracar, Swazi Paper Mills, Mbabane City council and UNICEF in the Mbabane-Manzini corridor. Off-the-shelf dial-up Internet access is provided for home and smaller business users with Africa's Internet Explorer packs which are distributed by leading computer shops nationwide. The market for walk-in Internet use is serviced by two Internet Cafes operated as independent ventures supplied by the company.

To meet the growing demand for Web services, Africa Online operates Internet Business Solution, a subsidiary which provides a full range of Web design and programming services. Both companies are housed at the Mbabane offices.

REAL IMAGE INTERNET

Real Image was the first company to introduce full Internet access to Swaziland in 1995 and was also the first server to provide full e-commerce enabled solutions for businesses wanting to maintain a competitive edge in the new Internet economy and take advantage of the growing Internet market.

It provides dial-up and network connective solutions, Internet consulting, electronic solutions and database integration. Training and an Internet advertising and publishing services are also provided.

The dedicated web hosting and business solutions department caters for the needs of all sizes of business development, from simple static web sits to complex and dynamic database driven e-commerce solutions. Special attention is given to network Internet connectivity to cater for this growing market segment with flexible solutions to suit any size of market segment, with flexible solutions to suit any size of network.

Real Image maintains the popular Swaziland Internet Portal Sites: www.swazi.com, www.swazibusiness.com and www.swaziplace.com to actively promote local business, tourism, traditions and culture.

A unique Real Image service is web-based e-mail which allows users to access their mail, wherever they are, through the World Wide Web with any web browser.

Real Image maintains the official government site: www.swazi.com/government/, a Swaziland business Internet directory: www.swazibusiness.com/directory/, as well as other commercial sites and publications, including the electronic edition of the Swaziland Business Year Book: www.swazibusiness.com/sbyb/

Partnered with M-Web, the global technology giant and the African business hub on the Internet, Real Image Internet is in the unique position of offering all the benefits associated with a multinational company, while having a firm and committed local support base.

THE MEDIA

The standard and range of media services in Swaziland enables even people in the most remote rural areas to have access to information. English language newspapers are circulated daily while the government-owned television and radio stations penetrate throughout the country.

RADIO

Swaziland's radio station is part of the government-run Broadcasting and Information Services department and operates from a head office and studio in Mbabane. The station was established in 1966 and runs on a semi-commercial basis.

This is the medium which reaches the most Swazis: about 95% of the population owns or has access to a radio, making it one of the most effective means of advertising and of disseminating information throughout the country. Programmes covering a diversity of topics are broadcast throughout the day on two channels in English and siSwati.

The information arm of the department provides material to other media houses and is also responsible for issuing news items to diplomatic missions outside the country via the Ministry of Foreign Affairs and Trade.

TELEVISION

The local television station is run on a commercial basis by the government-owned Swaziland Television Authority which also operates a TV and video rental arm. The station may be augmented by installing equipment which provides access to South African TV channels as well as to international programmes transmitted by satellite.

Through a specialised consultant, STVA has embarked on a market study to determine what viewers really want and ultimately increase the revenue base through increased advertising income.

MULTICHOICE SWAZILAND

MultiChoice has been dealing in digital satellite television installations and subscriptions since 1991. The organisation is based in Mbabane and serves a diversity of clients throughout the country, including hotels, pubs and clubs, multiple dwellings and individual residences. Installations are carried out at highly competitive prices and full back-up and after sales services are provided. DSTV enables subscribers to tune into a selection of channels that provide entertainment for the whole family, including movies, news, children's TV, current information, sports and music.

MultiChoice subscribers also gain access to a wide range of radio stations and a comprehensive range of music channels. Each channel is dedicated to a particular form of music and all tastes are satisfied.

At the heart of DSTV's promise is the desire to help viewers to grow. By offering such a broad spectrum of perspectives on such a wide range of subjects, subscribers are able to 'expand their view'.

THE PRESS

Several newspapers circulate in Swaziland, including two dailies. The oldest of these, established in 1897, is the privately owned Times of Swaziland which publishes daily, Saturday and Sunday editions. The Observer Group, which is owned by Tibiyo Taka Ngwane, ceased publishing its daily and a weekend editions during the year but at time of writing, steps were being taken to reinstate the newspapers.

MAGAZINES

Periodicals published in Swaziland include a bi-monthly news magazine *The Nation*, the quarterly *Farming in Swaziland* and various general and special interest journals and books.

CONSTRUCTION

PERFORMANCE

Growth in this sector again increased by 10.7% overall, a trend which may be attributed to the Maguga dam project and the upgrading of various major roads.

However, despite reduced interest rates, demand for mortgage credit was low and the value of residential buildings completed was down by 12.1% while commercial structures completed reduced by 59.3%.

In the two main centres of Mbabane and Manzini, there was an increase of 61.7% in the value of plans approved, from E34.4 million to E55.7 million.

A significant decrease in the number of industrial buildings completed - from 19 to 4 units, is expected to reverse with the construction of new factory shells at Matsapha and other areas.

Overall, government financed construction activity is increasing and planned development activities show an overall increase of 25.5% over the period 2004-2002

It should be noted that official data pertaining to private sector activities is available only for Mbabane and Manzini and the figures therefore do not reflect activity in other parts of the country.

HOUSING

The developments outlined in this sub-section do not include privately financed housing construction

The introduction of the Swaziland Building Society's Homeplan in April 1997 opened a new channel for prospective buyers although, as already noted, comparatively high interest rates continue to have a negative impact on demand for home loans.

The National Housing Board is involved in the E25 million Makholokhlo Townshhip Development Project which comprises two phases, each comprising 250 small, low cost homes, over an 18 month period from late 2004. The scheme also entails 60 undeveloped plots with infrastructure for sale.

THE URBAN DEVELOPMENT PROJECT

Once completed, this project will be a major influence in resolving the housing shortage. It is implemented under the Ministry of Housing and Urban Development and involves a World Bank loan of E100 million for the first phase and a total of E400 million for all three phases. Total expenditure is expected to reach E243 million by 2003. The UDP entails improving urban infrastructure and providing reasonable, low-cost housing for purchase, as well as upgrading existing homes. Some 4,000 plots were initially involved and the overall project is expected to run until 2006 with the loans repayable by 2014. The project will benefit about 100,000 people living in the Mbabane/Manzini corridor.

COMMERCIAL BUILDINGS

Since the mid 1980's, there has been significant development of commercial and industrial buildings, particularly in Mbabane, Manzini and Matsapha. Activity in this category is continuing with factory premises at Matsapha and other industrial areas being erected to meet present and future needs. With the advent of new investment in the pipeline, a number of new factories were being constructed at Matsapha and other industrial sites during the year, while an existing textile concern was undergoing an E10 million factory expansion.

SHOPPING CENTRES

Swaziland's shopping facilities have become increasingly sophisticated and several malls have been established around the country. The oldest centre is the Swazi Plaza in Mbabane which has been frequently extended to meet growing needs and on which an E37 million expansion project, including a multi-storey car park for 400 vehicles, was recently undertaken. Manzini has two large shopping complexes. Smaller shopping centres exist throughout the country and new developments are regularly constructed. Among these are a large centre in the Ezulwini Valley, the first facility of its kind in the area.

GOVERNMENT PROJECTS

It was announced that the proposed expansion and upgrading of the international airport at Matsapha, to be funded by the African Development Bank, would be deferred for the time being. It has also been announced that there are long-term plans to construct an entirely new airport but this has not been substantiated.

The E15.5 million rehabilitation and extension of the Mankayane Government Hospital was due to be completed towards the end of the year following some delays.

A amount of E5 million has been earmarked for staff housing at the Mhlumeni border post.

The E75 million expansion of Matsapha Industrial Site, funded by the German and Swazi governments, continued and the The E75 million expansion of Matsapha Industrial Site, funded by the German and Swazi governments, continued and the further upgrading of roads was completed, most significantly the junction near the main entrance. The development of other industrial sites remains a priority in an effort to encourage industries to locate outside the Mbabane/Manzini corridor.

ROADS

NATIONAL ROADS

Since 1993, the Swaziland government has invested substantially in the construction, upgrading and maintenance of the national road network which today ranks with the best in Africa. The main project was the rehabilitation of the 45 kilometre Mbabane-Manzini road, the main arterial route, whose upgrading into an international highway was completed in September 1998, ultimately at a cost of some E300 million. This is the country's busiest route with an estimated 15,000 vehicles using it each day. The construction of an E8 million flyover at the Matsapha roundabout, basic work for which started in 1998, has yet to take place.

The current major road projects are the Mbabane-Ngwenya dual carriageway and the Nhlangano-Mantambe, Luyengo-Sicunusa and Mhlumeni roads which have a total value of E429 million.

The Mbabane-Ngwenya route connects to the main border with South Africa and this project, which is budgeted at in excess of E100 million, will impact on all sectors of the economy.

Another project in the pipeline is the 103 km. northern main road, Mliba-Msahweni via the Madlangempisi-Msahweni road. Construction will begin in 2001 at a cost of E280.66 million. This route complements the Maguga Dam scheme and will form an important link with South Africa and Mozambique.

The new Mhlanya-Malkerns road, which deteriorated shortly after completion, was reconstructed and two access roads to the Maguga dam are being constructed.

Government is also involved in a number of community access projects which are financed by the EU Microprojects fund.

Urban Roads

These are the responsibility of the various city and town councils and are of a reasonable to high standard. In Manzini, many residential roads have been upgraded, while a road connecting the Zakhele township with the city centre was recently completed. While some access roads in Mbabane's residential areas have also been upgraded, many such areas are still served by dirt roads only. Towards the end of the year, major work on the upgrading of the access road and bridge to the bus rank and two shopping centres was completed.

DAMS

Major dams have been constructed at strategic points under the Soil and Water Conservation Project which is funded by various bodies, particularly the European Union.

The development of the Komati River basin, a joint project with South Africa implemented by the Komati Basin Water Authority, will put water resources to optimum use and involves the construction of dams in the two countries for hydro-electric and agricultural projects. The project is expected to be completed late 2001 and entails funding of around E2 billion. On the Swaziland side, the huge Maguga dam alone involves a E350 million contract which has been awarded to various companies. The adjacent Piggs Peak area is enjoying spin-off benefits through related projects such as housing developments and many jobs have been created. It is possible that another dam will be built nearby to supplement Maguga. The E21 million Komati bridge was completed under the Maguga Dam Road Joint Venture

Another imminent major dam project is the development of the Usutu River basin, expected to cost about E225 million. This entails the construction of a dam for irrigating sugar cane and banana plantations and will benefit small farmers who presently do not have irrigation .

E9.8 million has been budgeted for constructing and rehabilitating small earth dams around the country.

EU MICROPROJECTS

The European Union provides financial assistance to rural communities who are expected to provide input in terms of labour. They mainly involve water supply, access roads and bridges and educational undertakings.

CONSTRUCTION COMPANIES

The construction companies operating in Swaziland range from small local contractors to major companies which are capable of carrying out highly specialised projects. With about 20,000 people employed by the large contractors alone, this industry is a key source of work and income in the kingdom. The range of work undertaken covers small buildings, multi-story projects, roads, dams and infrastructure. The larger operations have substantial investments in the country, including sophisticated plant and machinery as well as advanced infrastructure.

Stirling Construction

This privately owned operation was established in 1987, since when it has become a major player in the construction industry. It comprises two offices, one at Mbabane and the other at Tshaneni. Stirling Construction handles diverse civil and building projects, from multi-million undertakings to small residential renovation works.

Large industrial (civil) projects, major building works and a number of joinery projects have been successfully completed. The client base is diverse and the company does work for the Swaziland government, the sugar estates, major hotel groups and numerous private clients, including parastatal organisations.

The extensive list of projects includes pre-vocational schools, the Matsapha Police College multi-purpose hall, and the upgrading and renovation of the National High School. Other recent work comprises the new power house and injection cooling water upgrade for Mhlume Sugar, changing the Ezulwini Sun Hotel rooms to time share units and upgrading the Matsapha Dry Port for Swaziland Railways, which is currently in hand.

During the past year, Stirling Construction has placed greater emphasis on civil structures.

SERVING THE INDUSTRY

Swaziland's construction industry is backed by qualified professionals, including quantity surveyors, architects and engineers as well as a diversity of manufacturers and suppliers.

Although some materials, such as glass, ceramic tiles and metal frames are imported, many supplies are made locally. These include building blocks, clay bricks, roof trusses and tiles, and paint, as well as construction sheeting and fencing materials. Stone crush and sand are supplied by the local quarries and rivers, and cement is manufactured in the country.

Barlows The Swaziland arm of this South African concern is a major supplier to the construction industry as well as to the agricultural sector. The main thrust of the business is the supply of modern Caterpillar equipment for earthmoving operations, together with the provision of technical expertise. The company, which has operated in Swaziland for 31 years, also supplies parts and workshop services at its Matsapha premises where 17 people are employed.

CONWAY NYMAN

This major supplier was established during the early 1960's primarily to provide the railway and forestry industry with wire rope and consumable supplies. The company, which has branches at Matsapha and Mbabane, has operated for nearly 40 years.

Conway Nyman deals in a full range of construction materials, industrial supplies and consumable goods with technical and back-up services across the board, and has extended its base with geotextiles for soil stabilisation and drainage, and gabions - wire baskets which are filled with stone to bank sheer drops and prevent erosion, providing an economical solution which is also labour intensive.

The company has initiated a practical and cost-effective system of water storage which benefits small-scale farmers who can be adversely affected by erratic rain patterns. The dams, which can be used for irrigation purposes, may be constructed by the farmers themselves and this strategy resulted in a 20% increase in turnover.

Conway Nyman is the sole distributor for the Ecosol housing system which provides an affordable solution to the country's housing problems. It comprises wooden prefabricated units and can be erected in a very short time span.

The company provides product training to its own staff, as well as to its clients where required, and operates

INDUSTRY

There are four industrial areas; Sidwashini is a light industrial estate on the outskirts of Mbabane. Matsapha, just off the main Mbabane/Manzini road is the principle estate and there is an established industrial area in the south. Service are provided at Ngwenya, near the South African border, and plans are in hand to develop facilities at Mpaka in the Lowveld.

The Swaziland International Trade Fair, which takes place at Manzini over two weeks in August/September each year was originally an agricultural event. It has now developed into a showcase for Swazi industry and commerce. Full details from the Swaziland Trade Fair, P.O.BOX 877, Manzini.

One of the most successful groups of companies is S.W.A.K.I. Originally founded by Natie Kirsch, the group is now equally owned by the Government of Swaziland and private enterprise. One of the member companies is the National Textile Corporation (NATEX)

Many local industries are based on available local resources and include building materials, modular furniture, canning and clothing. Swaziland also produces agricultural and industrial chemicals, gases, fertilizers, submersible pumps, electronic goods and clothing zippers. Soft drinks concentrates based on the local sugar industry are exported throughout the Southern Africa region. Confectionery producers also add value to the sugar industry and dispatch sweets and soft drink products throughout the entire region.

MANUFACTURING & PROCESSING

Swaziland's many and diverse manufacturing and processing concerns, which are predominately private sector enterprises, range from small factories to giant corporations employing several thousand people and utilising the latest technology. The categories of goods include food and beverage; clothing and textiles; timber, pulp and paper; engineering, including commercial vehicles; metal industries; plastics and chemicals.

For several years, this sector has been the leader in terms of contribution to the gross domestic product, accounting for 36.9% in 1998/9. Although production slowed down during the year under review with, growth of just 1% against 5.5% the previous year, export demand was strong, particularly for sugar based concentrates and blends, paper products, textiles and sweets. The ongoing depreciation of the Lilangeni against major currencies increased the value of exports to overseas countries.

The manufacturing sector is a major employer, second only to agriculture, and provides jobs for 26% of the work force. The majority of goods manufactured in Swaziland are exported with South Africa being the main market.

POLICY DEVELOPMENT

The Ministry of Enerprise and Employment is collaborating with the different industries in order to formulate policies and strategies in line with the international economic developments such as recessionary trends, globalisation and the liberalisation of trade. The textile industry was the first to be addressed following the development of Portugal supplying the European Union, which was previously the sector's major market.

FOOD AND BEVERAGE

Most of these industries utilise local raw materials and therefore fall into the value added category, an activity which is encouraged by Government. While these manufacturers supply local markets, their main thrust is export outlets. Domestic consumption of sugar has increased significantly as a result of these activities.

BROMOR FOODS

Bromor has been a major player in Swaziland's food industry since it established its Matsapha factory at the beginning of the industrial boom in 1986. This company, which is part of the Cadbury Schweppes Group, has grown consistently while diversifying its product base and providing many job openings. Bromor has had the ISO 9002 certificate since 1998, indicative that its products meet international standards.

Sales of soft drink concentrates, one of the major products, have consistently increased over the years. The other Bromor product is a range of jellies while a sister operation produces glace cherries and dices (cubes), and cut peel made from locally grown fruit. Sugar is a main ingredient in all these products.

The bulk of the commodities are exported to South Africa as well as to some overseas markets, including the United Kingdom and Australia.

CADBURY SWAZILAND

The world renowned Cadbury company, which has produced high quality confectionery products in South Africa since 1938, established its Swaziland operation in 1989 when the Candy World factory was commissioned at Matsapha. The venture proved to be one of the country's most successful investments, quickly growing with several expansion projects taking place. The company changed its name to Cadbury Swaziland during 1992 when a major extension to the factory was implemented, effectively doubling production.

The modern plant, which is regularly upgraded, produces a wide range of sweets, the major lines of which are Choclairs (previously Chocolate Eclairs) and Chappies. These two brands are the most popular confectionery items in Southern Africa, to where most of Cadbury Swaziland's products are exported.

A major expansion project involving investment of E12.5 million was completed and commissioned in 1996 to provide for increased production of the two major brands in order to meet market demand.

The company is a major purchaser of locally refined sugar.

Cadbury employs 475 permanent staff with an additional 100 seasonal personnel recruited during the peak period which starts in September to fulfil Christmas orders. The factory operates on a three-shift system, 24 hours a day, six days a week.

THE SWAZILAND DAIRY DEVELOPMENT BOARD

Established in 1971 under the Dairy Act No. 28 of 1968, SDDB is a public enterprise owned by the Swaziland Government. Its primary function is to develop and regulate the country's dairy industry and its involvement in commercial operations, particularly the Matsapha dairy plant, has been of a secondary nature. Thus the board was restructured to enable it to revert to its original mandate and its commercial operations have been privatised.

The restructuring programme, which entailed the separation of the Matsapha plant from the development and regulatory functions, was completed in October 2004. The following month, Parmalat Swaziland took over the dairy plant.

The restructured board is now referred to as the Swaziland Dairy Development Board and the core business is to provide development and regulatory services to the industry in a supportive socio-economic environment and from a neutral position. It is also expected to coordinate, harmonise and, where necessary, regulate the activities of all stakeholders in a cost effective manner. This development promotes local milk production, especially by smallholder farmers, and has improved the sub-sector's commercial climate.

The board also encourages investment in order to achieve a sustainable level of self-reliance in dairy products, and is responsible for encouraging competition and fair market access, regulating the import and export of dairy products based on supply and demand, and regulating the statutory activities of producers, processors and distributors. The overall objective is to achieve and maintain food security in dairy products.

The SDDB protects the interests of consumers by enforcing minimum public health and quality standards, and by ensuring that products are correctly labelled for accurate information. The board also looks after producers through loan schemes and various support services such as advice to farmers, the provision of credit, project appraisal, milk collection centres and other infrastructure.

During 2004 the effective demand for dairy products was estimated at 60.7 million litres in terms of liquid milk equivalents (LME) while milk production from the dairy herd was about 11.1 million litres. The deficit of 49.6 million litres was met through imports of dairy products and milk from the local beef herd. The level of net imported dairy products amounted to 27.5 million litres of LME compared with 24.1 million litres the previous year. This increase is great cause for concern because if it is left unchecked it will frustrate and retard the development of the local infant industry.

During 2004, the SDDB headquarters were moved from Matsapha to Liqhaga House in Manzini city.

PARMALAT SWAZILAND

Parmalat was founded in Parma, Italy more than 20 years ago and today is the third largest dairy company in the world with representation in 32 countries. The Swaziland arm was established during 2004 following the restructuring of the Swaziland Dairy Board when Parmalat took over the SDB factory at Matsapha on 1 November of that year. The local concern is 60% owned by

Parmalat Africa with the balance of shares held by Tibiyo Taka Ngwane (26%) and local farmers under government (14%).

The Parmalat products distributed in Swaziland include popular brands of fresh and long-life milk, butter, cream, various cheeses, yoghurt, emasi, and fruit juices. Among the products produced at the Matsapha plant are fresh and long-life milk, yoghurt, emasi and juices.

With access to information from a world base and with its upgraded factory, Parmalat Swaziland is able to provide dairy products of the highest quality which meet the requirements of the Dairy Board and ensure consumer satisfaction.

Milk purchased from local farmers totalled 2.3 million litres during the year under review, compared with 2.8 million litres the year before. The decline is the result of new buyers joining the market following the liberalisation of dairy product prices. Some farmers also pack and market their own milk.

The producer price of fresh milk increased to E1.22 a litre with the bonus paid for quality remaining static at 25 cents a litre. All categories of dairy farmers, whether on nation or title deed land, may remain assured of a ready market for their raw milk.

SWAZILAND FRUIT CANNERS - SWAZICAN

As a strongly export-oriented company, this operation is a major earner of foreign exchange and an important value-added industry which utilises locally produced sugar. It is the country's main pineapple grower and processor of the fruit which is canned at the Malkerns factory in the form of slices, pieces and juice concentrates. Swazican also processes and cans grapefruit and oranges grown in Swaziland in segment and juice concentrate form. These products are sold to export markets and are labelled for brands worldwide. The United Kingdom is one of the largest buyers with Swazican supplying over 25% of its canned grapefruit segments market.

Swazican is one of the largest employers in the country with an average of 2,000 people working there throughout the year and up to 3,000 during the busier season.

The jam operation, which produces a full range for the South African market, has come under increasing pressure because of rises in the local sugar price. Volumes were consequently down by 18%.

Pineapple tonnages increased in 2004 due to improved agricultural yields and the company processed 14,000 MT compared with 12,000MT the previous year. Additional citrus fruit was also available as growers produced large crops and export sales of fresh citrus were again down because of poor market conditions. 44,000 MT of citrus was processed into canned segments and juice concentrates, which exceeded the previous year by 10%.

Canned Fruit Production and Sales

	1996	1997	1998	2004
Production (Mt)	16,993	17,224	19,644	22,395
Exports (Mt)	14,668	18,977	23,557	19,205
Value of Exports f.o.b. (E'000)	53,725	68,090	94,981	75,433

Domestic Sales (Mt)	277.0	200.0	200.0	200.0

Source: Swaziland Fruit Canners

NGWANE MILLS

Since it was commissioned in 1991, Ngwane Mills has grown into a diversified staple food producer which has the capacity to satisfy the entire wheat and maize product demand for Swaziland.

The addition of a state of the art animal feeds plant to the existing wheat and maize mill has confirmed Ngwane Mills' commitment to offer the people of Swaziland and surrounding regions a range of superior quality cereal products and byproducts.

The core values of the company largely centre around the development of its staff and the upliftment of the local community. Ngwane Mills has shown its commitment to development and generates opportunities and income potential for the local community by offering pre-planting contracts to maize farmers and sub-contracts for the distribution functions to local entrepreneurs. The wheaten and maize products are milled to strict ISO standards with no compromise on quality or consistency and independent tests have proved that the products from Swaziland rank with the best in the region.

The Bakers Pride flour range has established itself as the bakers' choice in Swaziland and the majority of commercially baked goods in the country are produced from this flour. The brand also offers flexibility to the housewife who takes pride in improving the quality of life for her family.

The Top Score super quality maize meal range has brought a new dimension to maize meal standards in Swaziland: it cooks whiter, fasters and provides the family with energy for the day. Ligugu is the number one and favourite maize meal in the country and delivers the trusted formula of good quality and value for money.

Ngwane Mills prices itself in its quality management: it subscribes to high ISO standards and maintained a NOSA 4 Star rating during 2004/2000.

The company will continue to contribute towards the development of the agri-business sector in Swaziland by being a world-class processor and distributor of quality staple cereal food products.

OTHER FOOD AND BEVERAGE INDUSTRIES

These include a commercial beer producer and a soft drinks bottling factory. The concentrate for Coca Cola is also manufactured in Swaziland at a plant which supplies 15 other African countries.

Swaziland Meat Industries processes beef at its abattoir and exports to the EU, Southern Africa and other markets while a sister pork project comprises a breeding scheme and abattoir which produces fresh pork and processed products.

TIMBER, PULP AND PAPER

Although pine and gum trees are exotic to Swaziland, they are grown commercially in various parts of the country to produce raw materials for various value added industries. This sub-sector comprises a significant proportion of Swaziland's exports and forex earnings. Commodities produced in this category include unbleached kraft pulp, furniture and fittings in kit and finished form, construction materials, packaging and various types of paper.

NEOPAC SWAZILAND

Neopac has served Swaziland's industrial, agricultural and commercial sectors since 1968 when the company began producing corrugated cardboard containers.

Over the years, major expansions and plant upgrading have more than doubled production capacity to cater for increased demand and growth, and projects of this nature are ongoing.

The Matsapha based company boasts state-of-the-art printing and converting equipment, ensuring consistent quality of the numerous styles and sizes of cartons which are designed to meet individual customers' requirements.

In excess of 80% of the cartons made are supplied to local producers and manufacturers who pack their products for export to various parts of the globe.

SWAZI PAPER MILLS

From a defunct chemical plant at Matsapha which was taken over by a private company in 1987 has emerged Swazi Paper Mills which today employs about 550 people. The company has grown in several phases in the 13 years since it was established and for many years it has been the largest privately owned concern in the country.

During 1998, SPM invested in new plant, machinery and technology for the production of various types of paper and packaging materials and to increase output. Further expansion took place in March 2000 when certain machinery was upgraded to substantially increase kraft volumes.

The two tissue machines produce high quality tissue paper on contract for a leading South African company and for many applications. The kraft machines produce kraft wrapping paper for local and export markets, and kraft products are introduced as market demand dictates, the most recent being fruit wrapping, light packing paper, stationery and heavy duty wrapping for commodities such as cement and potatoes.

Swazi Paper Mills is the only manufacturer of products of this type in the region and generates foreign revenue from countries throughout the PTS and SADC. The papers are also marketed locally.

Corporate responsibility in terms of the environment is a key consideration and only recycled waste paper is utilised for the manufacture of all the products. The collection of waste paper from around the country is facilitated by outside vendors using their own vehicles. This has resulted in substantial indirect employment and greater environmental awareness. However, most of the waste paper still has to be bought from outside Swaziland in order to meet requirements.

USUTU PULP COMPANY

The story of the Usutu mill began in 1949 when the Commonwealth Development Corporation (CDC) planted 40,000 ha. Of pine trees ono the western highveld of Swaziland. When these pines started to mature, the British firm Courtaulds, in partnership with CDC, established the Usutu Pulp Company.

The new group built an 90,000 MT per annum unbleached kraft pulp mill on the Great Usutu river at Bhunya which produced its first bales in 1961. In 1988, Courtaulds decided to sell its interest in the company and this was purchased by Sappi in 1990, who subsequently increased their share to 69%.

During this period the mill steadily increased its share of the world market and the plantation area has consequently grown to about 70,000 ha which represents 4% of Swaziland's total land area. Of the total area controlled by Usutu, 12,000 ha are designated 'unplanted' and include features such as fire breaks, rocky outcrops, wetlands and indigenous forests About 66% of the planted forest is under the pinus patula species, 25% under pinus elliotii and the remainder under a mixture of pinus kesiya, pinus taeda and several other trial species.

Up to 7.5 million pine seedlings are grown each year in the centralised nursery and after six to eight months, they are transplanted in the forest. Up to 1,300 seedlings per hectare are planed with no subsequent thinning necessary. The forest produces an annual average growth rate of 25 cu. m per hectare with the pine trees reaching maturity at between 15 and 20 years.

Usutu is a major supplier of UKP, providing more than 12% of world demand. In 1998, a new E240 million digester was installed at the mill which increased annual production capacity from 180,000 to 220,000 MT while enhancing the quality of the world class pulp. The centrepiece of the upgrade is the 54 metre high digester from Kvaener pulping which incorporates the supplier's latest isothermal cooking technology.

The mill's competitive edge has continued to improve with investment in upgrading the equipment and has resulted in one of the most cost-effective and best quality wood sources.

Usutu has one of the most 'closed' mills in the world with no liquid effluent, apart from evaporator process condensate which is released into the environment, and all excess process liquids are tightly controlled within the mill. A 5,000 cu. m. storage tank is used to contain surplus wah liquids which are recycled via the evaporation plant to the chemical recovery boilers. The closed nature of the process, along with sustainable harvesting in the forest, mean that Usutu has minimal impact on the local environment.

The upgrade has reinforced Usutu's qualifications on the international market, where the pulp is used for a variety of applications, such as kraftliner, testliner, MG kraft, unbleached board, sack and wrapping grades. The pulp produced at the upgraded plant has achieved a 13% improvement and burst and tensile strength, while the new screening plant provides for higher levels of cleanliness in the pulp.

Almost 70% of Usutu's pulp is exported to Korea, Thailand and Japan with the remainder sold within Africa.

METAL & ENGINEERING INDUSTRIES

FRIDGE MASTER

"Creating value for our customers" is the maxim of this Matsapha based company and in just a decade of operations, it has captured more than 40% of the southern Africa refrigeration and freezer market. The greater proportion of products is sold under the Fridge Master label and the company began manufacturing the Kelvinator range in September.

Distribution and service agents throughout southern Africa and other African countries ensure that unrivalled sales coverage and customer service are provided. The products are also sold in Indian Ocean island countries and a distribution network in Europe is being set up, for which market a special range has been developed.

Fridge Master's comprehensive product range includes fridges from 50 to 740 litres and freezers from 90 to 275 litres, as well as gas/electric and paraffin fridges and freezers from 90 to 275 litres.

All the products are designed with conditions in their country of destination in mind. For example, special attention is given to cooler and freezer requirements for the harsh African climate.

New developments include an 80 litre bottle cooler, a wine cooler and a 280 litre double door under-counter bar fridge. These will open new markets such as catering and hospitality concerns, as well as domestic users. The company is also developing a 65 litre 12V.220V cooler box for the lucrative outdoor market.

Fridge Master's entry into the commercial market has met with unprecedented response and within months, orders worth several million Emalangeni were won for beverage coolers and ice cream freezers. Many customers were acquired on the basis of superior product performance, competitive pricing and the company's status in the domestic market, as well as its extensive customer service network.

Fridge Master has its own division which manufactures fridge components and sub-assemblies, while a product design division works on reducing costs, improving quality, adding consumer benefits and developing new products.

The main line and all the component division's factories are ISO 9002 listed with the exception of the gasket factory and tool room. However, it was hoped to have these listed by the end of 2000.

The training and development of Swazi nationals is a key concern and during the year, 20 candidates were identified for middle and senior management positions. A training and development sub-committee promotes the training of the entire workforce and develops strategies to address any shortcomings that may be identified, as well as cultivate multi-skills. Health and safety courses are compulsory.

Social welfare is another major consideration and employees enjoy such benefits as a clinic on the premises and a programme to address the need for AIDS education began in 2004. Training courses in repairing and servicing fridges are designed to alleviate unemployment. The company also provides opportunities for college students to gain practical experience during a three month industrial attachment period.

SWAZI OXYGEN

Based at Matsapha with a depot at Mbabane, Swazi Oxygen is a wholly owned subsidiary of Afrox Ltd. and stocks the complete range of products. The company is Swaziland's main supplier of industrial gases, including oxygen, acetylene and carbon dioxide shielding gases. Special gas mixtures are available on request. It is also the major supplier of medical gases and stocks related regulators and equipment.

Gases for freezing and preserving food and carbon dioxide for the manufacture of carbonated drinks are also supplied, as well as helium under the name Partigas.

Liquefied petroleum gas (LPG), under the name Handigas, is distributed throughout the country in cylinders or as bulk installations.

An extensive range of arc welding machines are supplied for both domestic and industrial use, while Metal Inert Gas and Tungsten Inert Gas machines, together with Robotics and Plasma cutters are widely used in the heavy industrial sector.

Swazox also stocks a full range of Transarc welding electrodes and accessories, together with speciality electrodes; general purpose and speciality rods; multi and single stage regulators and gas torches.

Because dealing in such products requires the highest safety standards and practices, Swazi Oxygen has invested substantially in this regard as is proud of the NOSA 5 Star status.

Other Metal & Engineering Concerns
These include manufacturers components for refrigerators and borehole pumps, steel fencing and related items, and steel and wire good for the construction industry.

PLASTIC, GLASS AND CHEMICAL INDUSTRIES

SWAZI PLASTIC INDUSTRIES

SPI, which serves the packaging needs of many local companies, is an extruder of a wide range of low and linear low density polyethylene film, and PVC electrical conduit. It provides 5-colour flexographic printing and a diverse range of packaging, including side and bottom sealed bags, punched or micro-perforated with side or bottom gussets; printed film for automatic packaging, and shrink wrap materials in sleeves, sheeting or shrouds.

All SPI products are backed by a team with over 20 years experience and technical know-how and production methods are constantly reviewed and updated.

The products are manufactured at a new, modern factory at Matsapha which was completed during 1997.

Other manufactures in this category include producers of plastic products for industrial and domestic applications, and manufacturers of soaps, detergents and other cleaning materials.

CONSTRUCTION MATERIALS

LANGA BRICK SWAZILAND

Langa Brick was initiated in the early 1980's by the late King Sobhuza II and established at Mpaka under the auspices of Tibiyo Taka Ngwane, the major shareholder at the time. Backed by the technology of London Brick Engineering, another early shareholder, Langa's uniformity and consistency of product were ensured. London laboratory tests showed that Mpaka clay has a high compressive strength, making it suitable for load-bearing brickwork.

The original company was incorporated in 1982 and the factory commissioned the following year. The first products for sale were produced in 1984.

Fortis Enterprises Limited, a Swazi company, was incorporated in 2004 for the specific purpose of purchasing the assets and business of Langa National Brickworks, which went into liquidation in 1998. Fortis was successful in its bid and officially took control of the business in November 2004.

A comprehensive range of 25 products is manufactured at the factory, including a full range of face bricks and pavers, as well as stock bricks. The staff take pride in producing items of exceptional quality, which are among the strongest available in southern Africa, and constantly strive to improve the quality and aesthetic appeal of buildings in the region.

The team is available 24 hours a day to ensure that the ever-growing customer base not only receives the service it demands and deserves, but is also kept up-to-date with new developments in the product range and within the construction industry.

CLOTHING AND TEXTILES

There are several diverse manufacturers of this nature in Swaziland producing spun yarns, fabrics and various types of clothing, including fashion items, knitwear, uniforms and protective overalls.

The clothing side of the textile sector is popular with Swazi entrepreneurs, many of whom have enjoyed success and growth in this field within local markets. During the year it was announced that a number of new concerns in this category would commence operations following effort by the Swaziland Investment Promotion Authority to encourage new operations to come to Swaziland.

TOWNS AND INDUSTRIAL SITES

MBABANE

Swaziland's administrative capital was founded at the turn of the century when Britain became a protectorate following the Boer War. Mbabane, which was granted city status in the early 1990's, is named after Chief Mbabane Kunene who lived in the area which is still known as Dalriach. The name means 'something sharp and bitter', possibly after a plant which grows in the region. Mbabane, which is set among mountainous scenery at an altitude of 1200 metres with magnificent views of the surrounding valleys, is home to all the government ministries and departments, most of the diplomatic representatives and all the local media houses.

Rapid development occurred during the 1980's and early 1990's and the city offers a high standard of modern office accommodation and excellent shopping facilities in two large complexes. The residential suburbs stretch well beyond the city centre into pleasant, scenic rural surroundings. Housing varies from simple accommodation to modern flats, town houses and large detached residences.

The roads continue to be upgraded and among the more signifcant recent projects is the rehabilitation of the road between the two shopping centres and a new bridge over the river. Construction activity has also been quite notable, particularly with the recent expansion of the Swazi Plaza which includes a multi-storey car park, additional shops and headquarters for two of the commercial banks.

Private clubs and the City Council provide a wide diversity of sporting and other social amenities

Mbabane's population is estimated at in excess of 58,000 people.

The City Council operations are being guided by a strategic plan which runs up to 2002. This covers the reduction of crime, a broader source of revenue, and improved customer services. Projects in hand include ongoing road and junction improvements, rehabilitating the market and additional street lighting.

MANZINI

Swaziland's industrial capital achieved its centenary in 1990. Known as the Hub of Swaziland, the country's first capital has a picturesque history. The city was originally known as Bremersdorp after a local trader and hotelier named Alfred Bremer who operated near the river and the local people, with typical Swazi humour, thus dubbed him KaManzini meaning "at the water". It was only during the 1960's that the name of Manzini was officially adopted.

Significant residential and commercial construction activity has occurred during recent years, particularly with the opening of Manzini's first shopping complexes in 1992 - the Bhunu Mall and the Hub. These centres serve populations from the sugar belt and other rural areas, as well as Manzini itself and preclude the need for people from the large agricultural estates to shop in South Africa.

Future strategic plans include the bus rank and the Trade Fair grounds in an effort to reduce congestion and a consultant has been appointed to make recommendations. The International Trade Fair, traditionally held in Manzini, was resurrected in 2004 following several inactive years. Other projects in the pipeline include resurfacing roads, street lights in residential areas and parking.

Manzini's communal facilities are good with plenty of social and sporting amenities available. The population is estimated at about 65,000 people.

THE URBAN DEVELOPMENT PROJECT

Both Mbabane and Manzini are undergoing extensive improvements to their infrastructures through the Urban Development Project. This entails a substantial proportion of an E100 million World Bank loan which will have particular benefits for the lower income groups living in the informal settlements that have been established around the main centres. See also Page 90.

RURAL TOWNS

Nhlangano, with a population estimated at about 6,000, is the main town in southern Swaziland and is known as "the hub of the south". It has a shopping centre, a hotel which is part of a major chain and a number of agricultural and small industrial projects. New bus rank and market projects were nearing completion towards the end of 2004. The first significant investment in the area for many years came about in 2000 with the commissioning of a textile concern which will eventually employ up to 1,000 people.

The historic northern town of Piggs Peak, which is similar in size to Nhlangano, was originally a gold mining centre although today, the main activity is timber. The Maguga Dam project on the Komati river a few kilometres from the town centre has increased the town's population by about 2,000 and is providing close to 1,000 employment opportunities. Piggs Peak celebrated its centenary in 2004.

The small, mountainous town of Siteki is the administrative centre of the Lubombo region. It has been announced that a new hotel is to be constructed in this town.

Ezulwini, although not strictly a town, is also managed by a council. This area lies in a scenic sub-tropical valley about 12 km east of Mbabane.

The small town of Malkerns, which is set in the heart of agricultural country not far from Matsapha, may be declared an urban area based on popular demand by residents..

Lobamba, situated between Mbabane and Manzini, is regarded as the kingdom's spiritual capital and home of the parliament building. It is also the site of the national stadium, the national archives and museum, the state house and the Queen Mother's residence.

MATSAPHA INDUSTRIAL SITE

Matsapha, which is located near Manzini, is the kingdom's major industrial site and the largest, most active development of its kind in Swaziland. As an entity it is also the biggest employer and the most popular choice of location with investors. During recent years, the area has undergone substantial upgrading, expansion and rehabilitation to its primary infrastructure.

A further E15 million was spent up to 2004 for the re-design and re-routing of roads, including an internal by pass road, to ease traffic flows.

The overall Matsapha expansion programme involves about E100 million with an additional 130 acres of land to be developed to accommodate new business ventures over a ten year period. Telephones, electricity, fire services and banking amenities at Matsapha have all been upgraded during recent years and the inland container depot was established at the site during 1993.

Recent developments include new factory shells to house new manufacturing industries which are locating in Swaziland.

OTHER INDUSTRIAL SITES

Nhlangano is one of the areas where investment is encouraged in order to decentralise from Matsapha and provide employment opportunities in southern Swaziland and a multi-million improvement project was recently completed.

Ngwenya to the west of Mbabane also has an industrial area which falls under government's control and industries are encouraged to locate here. A small site for light manufacturing and service industries is located at Sidwashini near Mbabane with another close to the city centre. Manzini also has an industrial site of similar size near its centre.

DEVELOPMENT ORGANIZATIONS

There are a number of organisations involved in the development of agricultural and commercial activities in Swaziland.

Tibiyo Taka Ngwane is, in its simplest form, the Swazi Nation conducting business in a free-enterprise economy with the King as Trustee. Following its establishment after Independence in 1968, Tibiyo earned the majority of its revenues from mining royalties. These funds were ploughed back into land repurchase, the establishment of business and agricultural undertakings, and partnerships with major companies and investors.

This involvement in the economic wealth of Swaziland is managed by Tibiyo in the interests and for benefit of the Swazi Nation. Tibiyo is involved in sugar, asbestos, the operation of the National Airline, construction, hotel and casinos, and brewing, to mention a few. Tibiyo is also concerned with bursaries and scholarships for students and grants to support the preservation of the National Heritage.

The **Swaziland Industrial Development Company** (SIDC) is a joint undertaking of the Swaziland Government, the Commonwealth Development Corporation (CDC), the German Finance Company for Investments in Development Finance Company (FMO), Standard Bank. The aim of the SIDC is to mobilise resources to finance private sector projects in all aspects of the economy. Priority is given to projects which provide permanent employment for Swazis, generate foreign exchange, the use of local resources and so on.

The **Small Enterprise Development Company** (SEDCO) is, in contrast to SIDC, concerned with small business and the development of local entrepreneurs. It is involved in training, advice on all commercial matters and market research.

The **Commonwealth Development Corporation** (CDC) has had a profound effect on the economy of Swaziland over a period of 40 years. It is concerned related to natural resources and to create greater income equality and the growth of skills. CDC was established by an Act of the British Parliament and maintains its own field staff who provide management skills.

FINANCIAL SERVICES

THE CENTRAL BANK OF SWAZILAND

The Central Bank of Swaziland, which is the bank of issue within the country's financial structure, was established as the monetary authority in April 1974 under the Monetary Authority Order of the same year. This empowers the bank to monitor, regulate and develop Swaziland's financial infrastructure. The Authority took on the function of a central bank in 1978 when the name was changed under the Monetary Authority (Amendment) Act of 1979 and additional powers were granted through amendment to the Acts in 1982 and 1986.

Legislative amendments to the Order of 1974, which awaited parliamentary approval at time of writing, provide the legal framework enabling the bank to adapt to the changing global environment and to incorporate new developments and financial supervision. The Securities Bill was also awaiting approval by parliament.

The bank issues the national currency, advises government, manages the country's official reserves and deals in foreign exchange markets, activities in which involve both spot trading and dealings in the forward market. The commercial banks may manage limited sums of forex, reverting to the Central Bank if necessary. CBS also provides central clearing facilities for the commercial banks.

The Bank operates The Small Scale Enterprise Loan Guarantee and the Export Credit Guarantee Schemes which assist small and medium sized Swazi businesses and exporters. See page 41.

The Swaziland Government has a capital fund which is administered by the Central Bank and into which certain surpluses have been deposited to cater for future projects. The Public Enterprise Loan Guarantee Fund provides loan guarantees to the commercial banks when granting finance to Category A public enterprises.

THE NATIONAL CURRENCY

The Lilangeni (plural Emalangeni) was issued as the national currency in September 1974 on a par with the South African Rand, bank notes for which are accepted in Swaziland. Due to the ongoing depreciation of the Rand, the Lilangeni has been dropping against the world's major reserve currencies since 1985 and during 2000 was fluctuating at around E7/US $1 and E10.5/UK Sterling although towards the end of the year, the Rand was strengthening against the pound.

THE COMMON MONETARY AREA & EXCHANGE CONTROL

The monetary arrangement between South Africa and Swaziland dates back to when both countries used British Sterling as their currency. In December 1974 this was formalised with the signing of the Rand Monetary Area (RMA) Agreement which became the Common Monetary Area (CMA) in 1986. The signatories are South Africa, Swaziland, Lesotho and Namibia.

The CMA provides for the free flow of funds between the four member countries with no exchange controls. However, generally liberal regulations apply to the rest of the world and the Central Bank continues to liberalise exchange control on a gradual basis. From January 2004, investors and pension funds were permitted to invest up to 15% of their assets outside the country while approved remittance increased by 53.4% to E1,853 million as at March 2004.

The commercial banks advise on individual allowances which vary depending on circumstances.

OTHER FINANCIAL INSTITUTIONS

Swaziland Building Society
SBS is the country's major provider of long-term mortgage lending with the main objective of providing loan finance to enable the purchase of vacant land, and the purchase and construction of housing by all sections of the community.

In order to facilitate such lending and meet the demand for housing finance, the Building Society accepts deposits and investments from individuals and organisations at highly competitive interest rates, in recognition of investor demand that these should at least match inflation.

During the 2004/2000 financial year, SBS assets increased by 17.7% to E293 million - a significant improvement over an 8% increase to E248.755 million the previous year. During the same period, mortgage loans increased by 9% to E172 million.

The continued policy of containing bad debts and controlling non-performing loans while lending prudently kept arrears at an acceptable level.

Demand for mortgage loans remained low due to such factors as expensive serviced residential land, high construction costs and interest rates, the drop in which did not stimulate demand. However, through employer supported housing schemes, SBS continued to encourage housing development in urban areas and, through the "Homeplan" loan scheme, on Swazi nation land. The Building Society is also committed to financing the E40 million required by purchasers of about 4,500 serviced plots being made available though the Urban Development Project.

In a new development, the Society now insists on mortgage insurance as a condition of lending as a means of securing a home in the event of the death of the borrower.

The general outlook is that until the economy improves and technology and innovation provide for affordable housing, demand for mortgage finance will remain low.

Swaziland National Provident Fund

The SNPF was established in 1974 as a mandatory employee savings scheme, contributions to which are a maximum of E50 a month depending on salary level, and to which employers must contribute 50%. The Funds's main purpose is to provide benefits for employed persons when they retire or if they become incapacitated. Benefits are also payable in the event of emigration, to survivors in the case of the contributor's death, and on reaching the age of 50 irrespective of employment status.

During the year, statutory contributions to the fund increased by 15% to E38.6 million while the number of registered employers was up by 4.3% to 3,054. However, there was a decline of 14.9% in net surplus income to E9.7 million. Investment income was up by 1% to E28 million. Property rentals were down by 7.3% to E3.7 million while there was a 5% improvement in other investments to E17.3 million.

Claims for the year amounted to E23.4 million, about the same as the previous year.

Following several years of speculation and a recommendation by the International Labour Organisation recommended that the Fund be converted into a Pension Fund, it has been announced that the final changeover may be effected in 2001.

SWAZILAND STOCK BROKERS

This institution provides an additional channel for individual and corporate investment and is a forum for buying and selling shares and debentures in several major organisations involved in finance, manufacturing, agriculture and tourism, among others. A unit trust enables investors to purchase stakes in a pool of local and South African companies. SSB is listed by the International Finance Corporation Review as being among Africa's most active stock markets.

TAXATION

New Legislation

Expected changes to the tax structure are in the process of being implemented under the Income Tax Bill of 1997 and the Income Tax (Amendment) Bill of 2004. This will be followed by the repealing of the Income Tax Order of 1975.

Corporate Tax

Under the new legislation, this category is to be revised downward from 37.5% to a flat rate of 30% (and ultimately even lower) in an effort to make Swaziland more competitive and to bring the country into line with other SADC states. However, it remains uncertain when this will take effect. Other proposed changes include the introduction of withholding tax for royalties and non-resident management fees, branch profits tax, and bringing the parastatals, farmers on Swazi nation land and other untaxed entities into the tax net. The five year tax exemption (tax holiday) for new manufacturing concerns will be phased out and training allowances are to be withdrawn. The latter two items have been widely criticised on the grounds that they are not conducive to encouraging much needed new investment and to upgrading the work force.

Allowances for the depreciation of machinery, vehicles and equipment apply and percentages vary depending on the nature of the item. Provisional tax is payable by companies and this is subject to various rulings. Specific rulings apply to the payment of non-resident taxes.

PERSONAL TAXATION

Under the Bill of 2004, annual incomes of up to E14,000 are to be tax exempt, compared with the present E13,000. Deductions start at 12% over that amount, rising to 33% under the Bill, against the present 39% on income over E40,000. Among proposed changes to this category is the taxation of all sources of income, including benefits in kind such as housing, vehicles and educational allowance at market value, as well as gratuities and Provident Fund pay-outs.

The tax free gratuity of up to 25% payable to expatriates at the end of their contracts is expected to fall away. Expenses which are deemed to be incurred in the course of generating an income may be tax deductible, provided they are of a recurrent and not a capital nature.

Other Proposed Legislation

Trust income is to be taxed and death duties will be introduced, although it is not certain when this will take effect. It has also been suggested that interest earned on savings be taxed at 10%.

Tax Administration

Arrangements for payment of provisional tax may be granted to companies and self-employed individuals. The Swaziland tax year runs from 1 July to 30 June. Individuals and companies are given 30 days and four months respectively to complete tax returns.

Sales Tax

This is payable on most goods and services and is charged on imported items, with the exception of food, at the point of entry. The present flat rate of 12% excludes luxury goods, such as tobacco products and alcoholic drinks which are taxed at 25%. The proposal to phase out sales tax and introduce value added tax had not been implemented at time of writing although it was announced during the year that sales tax may rise to 14%.

Other Taxes

These include graded tax - which is to be phased out - transfer, stamp and customs and excise duties and municipal rates.

COST OF LIVING

The rate of inflation recorded for 2004/2000 averaged 5.9% compared with 8% in 1998/9 and continuing the single digit trend of the past few years. Sales tax at 12% applies to most consumables, although certain basic food items are exempt, and this is included in the marked prices. However, hotels and restaurants must charge the tax in addition to the prices shown for meals and accommodation, although bar prices include tax. Services are also subject to tax at a the rate of 12%. It has been announced that sales tax may increase to 14%.

People coming to Swaziland from overseas generally find the cost of living comparatively low due to the depreciated local currency.

Groceries

The prices shown should be referred to as a guide only since they differ between brands and stores. Price differentials in some goods can be substantial and it is advisable to shop around for quality and cost. Supermarkets run regular specials which are advertised in the local press and these often give excellent value for money.

The following prices were taken from an Mbabane supermarket in September 2000. Fruit and vegetable prices are not given due to sharp seasonal fluctuations depending on availability and the source of supply.

Meat per kilogram:

Chicken E11.49
Rump Steak 29.99
Pork 20.98
Mince Beef 18.99
Bacon 250 gm 8.85

Dairy Products:

Milk 500 ml. 2.95
Butter 500 gm. 13.65
Cheddar Cheese Kg. 46.95
Cottage Cheese 250 gm. 8.25
Eggs dozen 5.90
Pure Fruit Juice, litre 6.95

Dry Goods:

Bread - Brown Loaf 2.05
Bran Flakes 500 gm 15.45
White Sugar 3 kg. 10.80
Biscuits 200 gm 7.45
Mealie Meal 5 kg 10.95
Tea Bags 100 12.95
Instant Coffee 250 gm. 34.45

Household:

Toilet Tissue 1.45
Washing Powder 1 kg. 16.45
Toilet soap 2.15
General Cleaner 750 ml 5.75
Disinfectant 500 ml 7.65

Animal Food:

Dog Biscuits 10 kg. 39.95
Tinned Food 425 gm 4.45

Domestic Staff

This category, which includes maids, nannies and gardeners, comprises a significant proportion of the informal job sector and is a vital source of income for many people. There is little legislation to protect their rights although the basic minimum wage was raised under the Regulations of Wages Order of 1995.

Minimum monthly wages are as follows:

Cook and Watchman E250.23
Gardener, Maid, Laundress, Nanny E240.45

These wages remain extremely low and conscientious employers pay substantially above the gazetted rates. Salaries also depend upon the hours worked (usually a 48 hour week), the nature of the job and duration of service. New residents and those employing domestic staff for the first time should be guided by the previous salary received and rates paid by other employers in the area.

Benefits such as meals on duty and travel allowance are often provided and are a matter for agreement between the two parties. Employers are expected to supply suitable protective clothing or overalls which remain their property.

Hotels and Restaurants

Accommodation prices and categories vary from budget to luxury levels, giving business people and tourists a wide selection of accommodation options.

A good budget priced hotel for two people sharing costs around E450 and E350 single, including breakfast while the medium category is about E600 double and E540 single, again including breakfast. In the luxury bracket costs are around E925 double and E850 single, again with breakfast.

Country clubs in rural areas offer good accommodation at very low prices and caravan parks, lodges and chalets are popular, inexpensive options for many visitors.

Some hotels offer special rates for group and conference bookings and provide packages tailored to individual clients.

Restaurant prices also vary depending on the type of establishment. A good meal for two at an average restaurant costs around E150, although some restaurants offer daily 'specials' which considerably less expensive. Top category establishments can cost E275 and upwards a couple. These prices are based on two courses and a bottle of wine plus coffee.

Vehicles

Motor vehicles are comparatively expensive in Southern Africa and have performed on a steep upward trend during the past decade, mainly due to the devalued local currency. A basic vehicle can be bought for between E46,000 and E64,000 while middle market cars range between

E76,000 and E111,000. Luxury models, which are fully or partly imported start at E250,000 while imported 4x4 models cost about E450,000. Utility vehicles start at E70,000 rising to E395,000 for top-of-the-range models.

These figures are a guide only and prices vary greatly between makes.

Petrol and Diesel

In keeping with global trends, prices of these commodities rose frequently and steeply during 2000. By September, unleaded 95 octane petrol and the 97 octane cost E3.22/litre. Diesel was E3.09/litre and paraffin, which is used for cooking and heating by many Swazis, rose to E2.10/litre. Further increases were expected at time of writing.

Housing

The average price of a low cost house is around E1250/sq m, excluding land and a small house with basic finishes, can be erected for about E62,500. This rises to about E1500/sq.m. for better finishes but can be as high as E3000/sq. m.

Land in the urban suburbs is about E160,000 a hectare although much smaller plots are available. Rentals tend

EMPLOYMENT

Population

For the past decade the country's population has grown at 3.2% in the face of almost stagnant economic growth and high unemployment. The Central Statistics Office placed the population at 912,878 for the year 1997 and this was expected to rise to 1,220,000 by 2010.

The birthrate of in excess of six infants per woman was likely to cause the population to double by 2016, according to the Ministry of Health, and this corresponds with a warning from the United Nations, emphasising the importance of establishing a formal population policy which should be designed to regularise the fertility rate.

However, the high incidence of HIV/AIDS is having an impact on these projections, while presenting a different problem. Not only does the disease generally claim the young productive, trained sector of the population, it also places enormous pressure on the already stretched health services. Between 30,000 and 40,000 AIDS related deaths are projected annually for the next 15 years and data shows that about 60% of reported AIDS cases are in the 20 to 49 year age group.

Employment

In 1991, 18.2% of employable people were without jobs and the latest figures show that this has risen to 22.7%. From 1991 to 1997, annual growth rates in the private and public sectors were just 1% and 0.7% respectively and some estimates are that up to 40% of the working age population is either unemployed or under employed. This is exacerbated with only 20% of about 10,000 school leavers absorbed into the job market each year. At time of writing, it was hoped that the efforts of the Swaziland Investment Promotion Authority would pay off, with several potential investors set to commence operations in the country and recruit staff.

The latest available data shows that during 2004, employment increased marginally by 1.5% - to 110,776 from 109,185 jobs. This was due to increases in private sector and informal employment and the establishment of four new companies that year, as well as to expansions to existing concerns.

The private sector, traditionally the largest employer, accounted for 61,003 jobs compared with 59,883 the previous year. Employment increased significantly in the transport and finance industries, and marginally in agriculture and construction. However, the overall increase would have been higher were it not for a reduction in the number of people employed in the manufacturing, mining, distribution and service sectors where redundancies were necessary.

In keeping with government's efforts to curb expenditure and contain the size of the civil service, public sector employment increased marginally from 31,891 to 32,210 jobs.

The informal sector is playing an increasingly important role in creating job opportunities and the promotion of Swazi-owned businesses remains a priority in order to relieve unemployment. This sector showed marginal growth, from 17,311 jobs in 1998 to 17,563 during the review period.

Job openings for Swazis on the South African mines, traditionally a fairly important source of income, continued to decline in keeping with recent trends, falling from 10,338 to 9,307 jobs. This is the result of lower international commodity prices, especially for gold which reached a 20 year low.

Taking into account street vendors and small holder farmers, indications are that around 270,000 people are employed or engaged in some sort of income-generating activities.

The long-term Urban Development and Maguga Dam projects, are boosting the construction industry with both direct new jobs and further opportunities through multiplier effects, while the Lubombo Spatial Development Initiative and the Lower Usuthu River Basin project will also generate a significant number of jobs once they are fully in place.

The Industrial Relations Act

Workers' rights in Swaziland are governed by the Employment and Industrial Relations Acts. The latter was amended during 1996 although certain clauses were unsatisfactory to both employers and labour unions and the Act was subsequently revised through the Industrial Relations Bill of 2000 which was passed during the year. Stipulations were that the new Act must conform with International Labour Organisation standards in order to create a more structured framework for effective industrial relations, and to ensure an ideal environment for new investors. The Act should also enable procedures to be conducted in an unbiased manner, and in accordance with International Labour Organisation conventions. At time of writing, the ILO had expressed dissatisfaction with certain clauses in the new Act and this was being discussed between the appropriate authorities.

Industry Unions

Nineteen unions are registered with the Department of Labour.

* Building and Construction Workers Union of Swaziland.
* Swaziland Union of Financial Institutions and Allied Workers.
* Swaziland Hotel, Catering and Allied Workers Union.
* Swaziland Commercial and Allied Workers Union.

* Swaziland Manufacturing and Allied Workers Union.
* Swaziland Transport Workers Union.
* Swaziland Post and Telecommunications Workers Union.
* Swaziland Mining, Quarrying and Allied Workers Union.
* Swaziland National Association of Civil Servants.
* The Association of Lecturers and Academic Personnel of the University of Swaziland.
* Swaziland Electricity Supply, Maintenance and Allied Workers Union.
* University of Swaziland Workers Union.
* Workers Union of Swaziland Town Councils.
* Swaziland National Association of Teachers.
* Swaziland Conservation Workers Union.
* Swaziland Agriculture and Plantation Workers Union.
* Swaziland Engineering, Metal and Allied Workers Union.
* Workers Union of Swaziland Security Guards.
* The Swaziland Media, Publishers and Allied Workers Union.

Only non-management personnel may belong to a union which can be established within an organisation once a recognition agreement is approved by all concerned and the number of employees wishing to be unionised meets the minimum set percentage.

Staff Associations exist at large concerns with membership comprising employees whose status falls between worker and management.

The Federation of Swaziland Employers

The FSE is an employer organisation which is recognised by businesses, organised labour, government and the international community. Its objectives are to promote and protect the interests of its members and to encourage industrial harmony, productivity and prosperity for all.

It was formed in 1964 in response to the business community's wish to be represented by one body which could also work closely with the post-independence government of 1968.

Services provided by the FSE include consultation and advice on industrial relations and other legal matters, various employment issues, training, occupational health and safety, publications and research, representation in the industrial court and general representation.

The Federation has regular contact with the media, with local and international employers and labour organisations, and with foreign governments through the diplomatic missions in the country.

The various sized and diverse concerns represented by FSE account over 70% of people employed in the country.

ENVIRONMENTAL MANAGEMENT

In recent years environmental management has become an integral component of Swaziland's development activities. Experience has taught the consequences of focusing only on production and profit while neglecting environmental protection and often, environmental problems have been left with a host country once a project has made its money and the company concerned has left. In Swaziland, environmental impact assessment is mandatory before any project may commence and this is done under the auspices of the Swaziland Environmental Authority (SEA).

The primary objective of an EIA is to identify the impact of proposed activities and to formulate mitigation plans, making it relatively simple to incorporate environmental concerns into the design of a project. Further, products for export to developed countries must be produced in an environmentally friendly manner which means there are also marketing implications.

Every developer or manufacturer implementing a project is expected to commission an EIA before starting and if identified impacts cannot be mitigated, the project may not proceed. The EIA process is effectively a decision making tool aimed at avoiding environmental problems and is a legal requirement under the Swaziland Environment Act. The EIA process caters for people or organisations who will be directly affected by a proposed project, as well as those who are interested and no-one must be adversely affected by it.

An EIA entails three key steps. The project proponent first submits a brief to the Environmental Authority for catergorisation which determines the level of the EIA required. This depends on the type of project and its location. The second step involves the assessment exercise. If a project is category 3, the proponent submits terms of reference for the executer of the EIA which must be approved by the SEA. A report which includes a mitigation plan is then ubmitted to the SEA and, if approved, a compliance certificate is issued. If a project has sensitive environmental impacts, it goes for a public review and will be approved if no substantive or relevant objections are forthcoming. In the case of serious objections, the issues are referred to the proponent for consideration and correction or there is a public hearing which is rare, the last tribunal being held in 1996.

In the case of industrial sites, SEA's interest lies in the type of industry being established, the raw materials to be utilised, the waste streams and whether they can be adquately managed. All these questions are answered through an EIA. A company should not be allowed to be established without a firm commitment on waste management otherwise hazardous wast could be dumped anywhere and such contamination is likely to affect neighbours and the ground water.

Thus the Swaziland Environmental Authority plays a vital role in protecting the country and ensuring that industries are safe and that construction projects, including roads and building developments, will not have an adverse affect.

Environmental Consulting Services

ECS provides a wide range of environmental consulting and training services to government, civil engineering and agricultural industries, and private developers. The environmental management services offered promote the principles of sustainable development and of providing a safe, healthy and regulated environment for all.

ECS's core business is environmental impact assessments, initial environmental evaluations and environmental compliance monitoring. Affiliation with local and international specialist environmental consultants enable the company to provide the spectrum of relevant services and respond to the new approach to environmental management required by government, industry and other institutions.

The company also specialises in environmental education and training, policy formulation, legal advice and research. It embraces the concept of collective responsibility in the maintenance and promotional of internationally agreed environmental standards, and endorses the aspiration to a healthier environment. ESC also aims to maintain internationally recommended standards of sound environmental practices in Swaziland and works within the framework of relevant legislation.

TRANSPORT AND FREIGHT

Swaziland's diverse transport service infrastructure is well developed and covers the spectrum of requirements for the movement of goods. Several operations specialising in various services operate within the country and are professionally run to high standards.

Transport sector regulations fall under the Ministry of Public Works and Transport, through which related bodies such as the Road Transportation Board, the Road Safety Office and the Civil Aviation Authority operate.

A protocol has been agreed upon to expand cooperation relating to infrastructure and services, and to establish, among other things, a viable and sustainable transport system. In this respect, an integrated transport policy is to be established which, among other clauses, will remove hindrances regarding the movement of people, goods and services.

AIR

Following the restructuring of the national airline, Airlink Swaziland, a South Africa based operation, was identified as a strategic partner and began operating in July 2004. Other airlines, including charter services, also operate within the country and the region, providing links between neighbouring states and international destinations, with various routing options available.

Regulations relating to private aircraft allow for the operators to fly in and out of Swaziland direct from any airfield in the country, without routing via Matsapha airport, provided the relevant authorities are notified two days in advance.

The Civil Aviation Authority at the Ministry of Transport and Communications controls this sector.

AIRLINK SWAZILAND

The airline was formed as a joint venture between the Swaziland Government (60%) and S.A. Airlink (40%) to take over the operations of Royal Swazi National Airways. It began functioning in July 2004, initially leasing Royal Swazi's Fokker F28 aircraft to link Matsapha with Johannesburg and Dar-es-Salaam. The latter route was discontinued at the end of October 2004 and the frequency of flights to Johannesburg was increased, providing better connections to the rest of Africa and the world.

In June 2000 the F28 was replaced with a Jetstream J41 and an additional service was introduced to further improve access to and from Swaziland. The airline currently operates 26 return flights between Johannesburg and Matsapha each week.

The 37 employees comprise pilots, cabin attendants, aircraft technicians and passenger handling agents. An average of 4,000 passengers and 5,000 kg of cargo are carried each month.

The airline has alliances with South African Airways, South African Express and South African Airlink, and is a member of the Voyager Frequent Flyer programme.

ROAD TRANSPORT

Swaziland's diverse industries require highly sophisticated road transport services for the movement of goods between Swaziland and neighbouring countries. Efficient movement within the country, to rail depots and the Matsapha inland clearance depot, from where export goods are railed to sea ports, is also essential.

A Memorandum of Understanding between Swaziland, South Africa, Botswana and Lesotho applies to cross border traffic and provides for high safety standards and the rationalisation of road traffic density. Operators may obtain permits, which are recognised among the countries concerned, through the Ministry of Public Works and Transport. Applications must be accompanied by a certificate of fitness for each vehicle and the permits are valid for one year or 30 return trips. An infrastructure cost recovery scheme ensures that operators pay a fair share towards road maintenance.

Although the transport of goods between other countries in the region entails separate permits, a common ruling for the SADC states is in hand which will streamline operations.

Legislation pertaining to road transportation was revised in 1997 and a new Road Transportation Bill was approved by cabinet. Clauses of particular importance include the recognition of mini-buses as a form of public transport and the provision for investigating trading patterns on the various bus routes. The legislation replaces the Act of 1963.

ROAD HAULIERS

Specialised operators move all categories of commodities internally and across borders for delivery to ports for overseas shipment and to destinations in neighbouring countries. They also move goods into the country. These companies operate fleets of reliable, modern vehicles, which are often especially designed to accommodate specific types of commodities. They run fleets of reliable, modern vehicles and maintain high standards of safety and efficiency. The larger operators have their own workshops for vehicle maintenance and repairs.

CARGO CARRIERS

Cargo Carriers which marks 40 years of operating in Swaziland during 2001, is the largest transporter of its kind in the region. The Swaziland branch initially moved sugar cane with a fleet of just three vehicles but the company soon began to transport processed cane destined for export markets and has expanded along with the sugar industry. By 1970 the local operation comprised four branches at Mhlume, Big Bend, Simunye and the then newly developed industrial site at Matsapha. Cargo Carriers subsequently diverted into other commodities, including bulk fuel, and today is the country's largest road transporter with about 145 registered vehicles.

The versatile GFLT (general freight & liquid tanker) is capable of carrying general dry goods as well as liquid petroleum products and the Swaziland registered GFLT, which operates in conjunction with Shell, realises excellent results. When Cargo Carriers was awarded the transport contract for the Simunye ethanol project in 1996, three new tankers for carrying the product to Durban for export were acquired. This investment entailed about E9.6 million and almost E4 million was subsequently budgeted for the Swaziland operation.

The ISO 9002 was successfully implemented at the Simunye branch and the other branches were subsequently upgraded to that status. This was a drive to increase operational efficiency and client service.

Cargo Carriers is geared to clients of all sizes and is involved in cross border work with several countries, including Namibia, Mozambique, Zimbabwe, Malawi and Zambia, providing a vital import and export link.

The company takes initiatives with Swazi empowerment by sub-contracting certain work to local transporters. In another development, the Big Bend branch has expanded into mechanical harvesting through a strategic partner and there is a possibility of expanding such in-field operations.

An E5 million investment in a computerised internal operations system at the Johannesburg head office has ensured even better customer service which also benefits the Swaziland clientele.

COURIER SERVICES

This secure, fast means of moving documents and parcels is available through several local concerns. They provide a door-to-door service regionally and world-wide and also handle the formalities involved in moving items between borders.

DHL

Since it was established in 1969, DHL has developed the largest international network in its field, utilising the latest technology and systems. Substantial investment has been made in both human and financial resources worldwide, ensuring excellent door-to-door service for all consignments. This service is extended to the Swaziland operation which opened in 1985, and where the company has built its reputation for reliability and speed.

DHL Swaziland's operation includes two service centres based in Mbabane and Matsapha, and a dedicated daily air charter service between Johannesburg International Airport and Swaziland.

RAILSWAZILAND RAILWAY

Swaziland Railway, which has served the country in the movement of goods for nearly 36 years, is responsible for the infrastructure, rolling stock and operation of Swaziland's 300 kilometre railway system. SR provides a vital transport link for the country's diverse import and export commodities. The railway also facilitates the passage of tourist trains from South Africa and Mozambique and offers many attractions, including competitive rates.

Swaziland Railway remains committed to customer care and measuring the degree of client satisfaction is an ongoing exercise.

THE INLAND CLEARANCE DEPOT

Eighty percent of goods moved worldwide are transported by sea and containerisation is the most widely used means of safely and conveniently storing all categories of cargo while in transit. The inland clearance depot was established at Matsapha in 1993 to serve the many export industries operating from the area and to provide both importers and exporters with an efficient, convenient service which is time and cost effective.

The depot, which operates as a dry port, is ideal for a land-locked country such as Swaziland because it incorporates all the services of a sea port, including container handling, customs clearance to facilitate through bills of lading, and a customs bonded store. These enable many of the procedures carried out at a sea port to be handled at Matsapha.

Three, six and twelve metre containers enable different sizes and configurations of goods to be accommodated. The containers are moved by road on Swaziland Railway trucks and then transported by rail to the ship.

FORMALITIES

The complex formalities and paperwork involved in moving goods across borders within and beyond the Common Customs Area are handled by companies with expertise in this specialised field.

Goods arriving in the country from outside the Common Customs Area must have import permits and declared values, with clearing documents issued by a recognised agent.

Sales tax of 12% (still expected to rise to 14%) is payable on all imported goods, with the exception of alcohol and tobacco products which are taxed at 25% . Invoices must be supplied at the point of entry where the tax is also collected, unless a sales tax registration number is presented.

Although value added tax applies in South Africa, commodities exported from that country into Swaziland are allocated zero rating provided the exporter is satisfied that the goods are destined for outside that country, and that relevant forms are complete, thus avoiding double taxation.

VEHICLE RENTAL

Rental services for different types of vehicles are available in Swaziland with the major representation at Matsapha airport. Vehicles may be hired as part of a travel package or by contacting the rental outlets direct.

Affordable Car Hire

Wholly owned by indigenous Swazis, Affordable Car Hire was established in 1996 to provide vehicles for rental, including passenger cars, pick-up trucks and micro-buses. A chauffer service is available if required. The company is able to serve a wide diversity of clients, including institutional and corporate, government, tourists and the general public.

Affordable Car Hire's vehicles may be driven to Mozambique subject to prior arrangement, and payment may be tendered in cash or through major credit cards.

REMOVALS

Swaziland's expatriate population originates from many countries world-wide and by its nature entails frequent turnover of personnel. It follows that high standards of efficiency are necessary for moving their effects in and out of the country from and to global destinations. Several removal companies with the relevant international links operate in Swaziland to serve this market which also includes the diplomatic sector.

Elliott International

Based in Johannesburg, the Matsapha branch of this family-owned firm was established in 1993 in order to provide optimum standards of service to the Swaziland clientele. The company's international links and highly specialised experience in packing and moving personal effects have resulted in Elliott's sound reputation.

The policy of providing a highly personalised service is an integral part of the company's reputation and is practised by all the people involved in the Swaziland operation.

Removals to all destinations are undertaken, including local, long-distance and all parts of the globe.

PUBLIC TRANSPORT

This sector is regulated by the Road Transportation Board under the authority of the Ministry of Transport and Communications. Buses are the major form of transport for the majority of Swazis and these services are run entirely by private operators. Permits to serve specific routes are granted annually.

There is no subsidy from government or municipalities and operators are entirely responsible for maintaining their vehicles in a fit and safe condition. Buses are checked regularly by a government vehicle examiner and if found deficient, removed from service until repaired.

Because the majority of Swazis rely on buses, efficient and safe services are essential to the economy and existing legislation still does not allow the industry to be as efficient as it should be. Permit holders do not always adequately service their routes and anomalies in the system mean that permission to operate on the same run may be withheld from a potentially efficient party. New legislation addresses this problem and introduces a number of improvements, including stricter safety regulations. However, this has not yet been enforced. Since 1997, mini-buses have been officially acceptable as a means of public transport.

Privately owned taxis play a smaller but important part in the public transport sector. Operators of these vehicles must be properly registered and possess the relevant Road Transportation Board permit.

MOTOR VEHICLES

Higher interest rates and currency depreciation increased the prices of new vehicles with a resultant drop in demand. In 2004/2000, there was a slight drop in the number of vehicles registered, from 2,470 to 2,417 units. New vehicles purchased decreased by 32.8% from the previous year to only 866 units, mostly due to less purchases by government and sales to companies dominated the market. On the other hand, the used car market increased by 31.3%, while the commercial/bus category was up 7.2%. Tractor sales totalled 34 units compared with 43 the previous year, mainly due to a shortage of finance.

The future depends on suppliers' ability to contain price increases and the possible hike from 12% to 14% in sales tax will make vehicles even more expensive.

New Registration of Vehicles in Swaziland									
	1997/98			1998/99			2004/2000		
	NEW	USED	TOTAL	NEW	USED	TOTAL	NEW	USED	TOTAL

Passenger Car	690	897	1587	469	574	1043	314	830	1144
Light Commercial	911	799	1710	649	321	970	431	352	783
Heavy Commercial and Buses	255	458	713	171	286	457	121	369	490
TOTALS	1856	2154	4010	1289	1181	2470	866	1551	2417

Source: Central Statistical Office

ECONOMIC AND SOCIAL REFORM AGENDA

1. INTRODUCTION

After a number of years of economic growth and prosperity, Swaziland now faces the challenge of slow growth, characterized by stagnating investment and a high rate of population growth and unemployment. Government revenues are falling while expenditure continues to grow in real terms.

To meet the challenge, the Government of Swaziland has announced an Economic and Social Reform Agenda (ESRA), which represents a programme of changes which can be achieved in a period of two to three years and which will have a significant beneficial effect on:-

i) **the acceleration of economic growth in order to increase national income and to alleviate poverty;**

ii) **the improvement of social services to the people so as to achieve sustainability in social welfare;**

iii) **good governance characterised by, *inter alia*, transparency, accountability, discipline and the rule of law.**

ESRA represents a key selection of actions and quantified, measurable targets which Government believes it can achieve in a two to three year time-frame within available resources. ESRA is not designed to supersede the National Development Strategy (NDS) exercise, nor does it attempt to address all activities and measures necessary to achieve the objectives of the National Development Plan. It is compatible and consistent with both.

ESRA is a Government initiative that has been prepared in consultation with all stakeholders. The main thrust of ESRA is to create an enabling environment in which the private sector will be the driving force in increasing both economic growth and individual living standards.

In setting out the selection of actions to be taken, ESRA identifies the following priority areas - fiscal policy, investment policy, private sector development, infrastructure development and public sector (including public enterprises) reform.

2. ECONOMIC AND SOCIAL PERFORMANCE

Swaziland faces a substantial economic challenge over the coming years and there is a need for urgent action. The decline in GDP growth from an average of 7% in the years 1980/81 to 1989/90 (in which the rate swung widely between 15% and 2%) to 3% in the period 1990/91 to 1994/95 is cause for concern. GDP growth in the 1990's has fluctuated from a high of 9% to less than 4%. The slowdown in growth in the 1990's has largely resulted from external factors including the severe regional drought over the period 1991/92 to 1994 and a decline in foreign direct investment resulting from the lifting of sanctions against the Republic of South Africa.

The slowdown in foreign direct investment (which was largely responsible for the economic upturn in the 1980's) has greatly weakened the growth dynamic of the Swazi economy. Of major concern for the competitiveness of the Swazi economy in future years are the deteriorating industrial relations climate and the inadequate fiscal incentives.

During the last decade, economic growth has not generated productive employment opportunities to absorb a rapidly growing labour force. The capital intensive nature of most of our investment has meant that the link between employment creation and growth in GDP has weakened. The annual increase in formal employment has averaged 3.6% while the number unemployed grew by about 10% per annum. The public sector has become the foremost creator of new jobs and this has led to a financially untenable situation.

The favourable economic conditions of the 1980's led to a significant increase in Government spending, including an expansion of the public sector payroll. Recurrent Government expenditure is currently around 25% of GDP. 75% of total Government expenditure is recurrent expenditure of which personnel expenditure accounted for around 52% in 1995/96.

Development initiatives in the agricultural sector have not generally increased production and average incomes, so that formal wage employment remains the ultimate choice for the average Swazi. The high rate of population growth (3.2%) and the poor performance of the agricultural sector has not only exacerbated the unemployment problem and worsened the income disparity between urban and rural households, but is also posing an environmental threat as cultivation is extended to marginal lands.

Expenditure on education averages around 23% of the Government Budget. The literacy rate is currently estimated at around 74% and represents a substantial improvement on 30% in 1966. Gross enrolment ratios for primary education have increased from 65% in 1968 to 100% in 1992. The net figure is, however, lower, estimated at 82%, due to high drop-out and repeater rates.

It is clear that the education system is not producing the skills required to facilitate economic growth, while the structure of education costs has distorted the pattern of demand.

Expenditure on health has averaged around 8% in recent years, but, despite the considerable progress achieved in areas of increased life expectancy and immunization rates, there are a number of indicators which are less favourable than in many other middle income countries. The high rate of population growth continues to exert pressure in terms of the demand for social services as well as compromising the quality of such services in conditions of increasingly scarce fiscal resources.

The slow-down in the growth dynamic of the Swazi economy in the 1990's has meant that since 1992/93 the growth in fiscal expenditure has exceeded that in fiscal revenue, resulting in growing fiscal deficits. There has also been a significant change in the composition of fiscal revenues over the period. Customs Union receipts (around 53% of total revenue in 1996) are the most important sources of revenue. As a result, Swaziland is extremely vulnerable to changes in the level and structure of Customs Union tariffs.

3. MACROECONOMIC POLICIES, OBJECTIVES AND STRATEGIES

The key developmental challenges for Government over the coming years are:-

- encouragement of economic growth;

- revenue diversification
- expenditure control

The Government's strategy for meeting these challenges will be:-

1. promoting sound macroeconomic management;

2. improving the efficiency of the public sector by:-

   - reforming the civil service
   - reforming public enterprises
   - improving delivery of infrastructural services
   - improving administrative procedures

3. enhancing external and domestic competitiveness of the economy through:-

   - tax reforms
   - market liberalisation
   - investment incentives
   - creating a business-friendly environment

4. addressing the social aspects of development through consensus building and achieving a common vision on development goals through the National Development Strategy.

5. encouraging private sector participation.

The actions designed under ESRA to carry out these strategies are presented in the following categories:-

- **Public Sector Reform**
- **Sector Policies and Programmes**
- **Regional Integration**
- **Statistics and Data**
- **Monitoring**
- **Matrix of Action Targets**

4. PUBLIC SECTOR REFORM

4.1. Budget and Public Expenditure

The Government Budget has moved from a surplus of E 21million in 1992/3 to an expected deficit of E 136 million in 1996/7, deteriorating further to E 151 million in 1997/8. This position could worsen following the outcome of the SACU negotiations, and Government accepts the need to diversify its revenue base and achieve better control of expenditure.

Revenue

By the end of October 1997, Government will announce a balanced strategy for revenue diversification and expanding the revenue base to replace the expected fall in customs revenue.

Government is overhauling the system of direct taxation. A new Income Tax Bill has been drafted and, by May 1997, after the current round of consultations with social partners, it will be presented to Parliament for enactment. The new Act will be effective from 1 July 1997. The

Income Tax and Customs and Excise Departments will be strengthened in order to improve their assessment capability and a study will be carried out by October 1997 to determine whether the creation of a separate Authority will be more cost-effective than the present arrangements.

In order to maximize the benefits from such assistance, Government will, by the end of June 1997, set out its policy for ensuring that aid-funded expenditure is justified and that the most appropriate funding can be secured. By the same date Government will have completed its review of aid monitoring and management arrangements.

Expenditure

An expenditure reduction policy will be submitted to Cabinet by the end of October 1997.

In the coming two years, the Auditor-General's staff will undergo enhanced training to improve its capability in scrutinizing expenditure, both for compliance with propriety and legality and for the securing of value-for-money. The Audit Bill, which will give the Auditor-General powers to engage specialist auditors for the scrutiny of the more technically-oriented activities, will be presented to Parliament by October 1997.

It is also important to ensure that liabilities for expenditure properly incurred are settled promptly by Government. Improved payment procedures will be in place by April 1997. A report on potential improvements that can be made to Tender Board activities will also be issued by the end of June 1997 and consideration will be given to the contribution the private sector might make in this area.

4.2. Public Enterprises

As the reform programme for the public enterprises progresses, there is urgent need for a policy statement on the programme. That statement will be submitted to Cabinet by May 1997.

4.3. Civil Service Reform

An appointment to the position of National Director will be made by April 1997. The Public Sector Management Programme (PSMP) framework will be reviewed and consolidated by June 1997 and the revised framework discussed and agreed upon with the civil service. In the twelve months from April 1997, the management audits will be completed and thereafter Ministries will draw up strategic plans. Revised organisational structures for five Ministries will be submitted to Cabinet by the end of that period. A number of Ministries will undergo similar organisational reviews in 1998.

To complement the PSMP, Government will, by October 1997, have examined the implications of offering voluntary retirement for civil servants aged 55 and above, and the employment of senior civil servants on a contract basis, as a measure to improve accountability for performance. The study will also review and make recommendations on reducing the compulsory retirement age to 55 and making early retirement at 45 attractive.

The Civil Service is perceived to be overstaffed and, in some areas, inefficient. The PSMP is expected to come up with a report on the perceptions by the end of December 1997.

In addition to the specific measures set out in the PSMP, Government will undertake the following in order to improve its own effectiveness and efficiency:-

i) The Prime Minister's Office will produce an overall mission statement for consideration by Cabinet by April 1997 and each Ministry will draw up its own mission statement for Cabinet approval by the end of June 1997.

ii) A programme will be drawn up by the end of December 1997, identifying Government services that should be examined for greater commercialization. Consideration will be given to using the private sector where it is more cost-effective to do so.

iii) In order to improve working relationships between Parliament, Ministers and the Public Service, and between Ministries, this area will be reviewed by the end of December 1997. By the same date, there will also be a review of Parliamentary operations that will include a code of practice for politicians. The code of practice for civil servants will be reviewed by Government by the end of August 1997.

iv) The fight against corruption will be accelerated. A report explaining the current status of the Anti-Corruption Commission will be prepared by April 1997 and a programme set out for making the Commission operational and effective.

v) The implications, particularly regarding costs, of regional and international diplomatic and trade representation, will be examined in a study to be completed by the end of December 1997. The study will also examine requisite qualifications and suitability for foreign service personnel. The capacity and capability for missions to represent Government at international meetings will also be examined. An up-dated foreign policy document will be prepared at the same time.

vi) A consultancy study of the operations of the Civil Service Board, to determine an appropriate role for it in the future, and whether it is necessary to have a separate mechanism to deal with the grievances of civil servants, will be carried out by the end of December 1997. The conclusions of that study will assist in the finalisation of the Public Service Commission Bill in June 1998.

vii) In order to have a streamlined civil service where the emphasis is on increased productivity and performance assessment, the Salaries Review Commission will be constituted to examine public sector pay and benefits, identify ways of retaining qualified nationals and introduce a pay system which is more closely linked to productivity. This exercise will be completed by the end of January 1998.

viii) A training needs assessment will be carried out in 1997 and 1998 to determine the critical skills required to meet the new mandate of the civil service. The Swaziland Institute of Management and Public Administration (SIMPA) will be strengthened during that period to deliver the requisite training.

ix) A cost/benefit study of external travel by public servants will be completed by the end of 1997 and new criteria and procedures established. The review of Swaziland's membership of external organisations will be completed in June 1997. Both services will ensure that only properly justified travel is undertaken.

5. SECTOR POLICIES AND PROGRAMMES

5.1. Private Sector

The private sector is seen as the engine that will drive economic recovery and Government has a responsibility to provide a supportive framework, thereby facilitating growth and effective operations in that sector and encouraging new investment. After a surge in investment in the period 1987-91, there has been little foreign investment since that time and relatively little domestically sourced investment.

The Government is committed to its responsibility to create an enabling environment and will take the following action:-

i) Investment Promotion

The Swaziland Investment Promotion Authority (SIPA), a one-stop service to interested investors, will be established by the end of September 1997, following the securing of the necessary finance to support the proposed staffing. This will be facilitated by the Swaziland Investment Promotion Authority Bill that will be submitted to Parliament by the end of June 1997. By the same date, a new Investment Code, incorporating the revised investment incentives, will also be submitted to Parliament. SIPA will focus initially on:-

- resource-based industries (e.g. sugar- and timber-related);
- export oriented and labour-intensive industries
- tourism related investment
- mining

ii) Investment Incentives

Appropriate investment incentives, which are considered competitive within the region, will be published by the end of June 1997.

iii) Improved Administrative Processes.

A policy statement on improved administrative processes in the Ministry of Enterprise and Employment and the Ministry of Home Affairs will be published before the end of June 1997.

A report on the legislation and trade licensing arrangements, adversely affecting investment and business, will be completed by the end of September 1997. The existing trade licensing arrangements contain serious anomalies which will undoubtedly represent a deterrent to investment. The new Companies Bill, together with the Trade Facilitation Bill, are to provide the necessary remedies and will be submitted to Parliament by the end of September and December 1997 respectively.

iv) Financial Sector

The Insurance and Pensions Bill will be resubmitted to Parliament by June 1997, thereby creating competitive conditions. The Securities Bill will be submitted by the end of October 1997 and this will provide a legal basis for the operation and supervision of a securities market, including unit trusts.

v) Tourism Development

Swaziland lacks adequate physical and tourist infrastructures. The Government is committed to tourism development since it represents one of the biggest potential contributors to significant economic growth in the future. A small Working Group of key private sector representatives will be appointed by April 1997 and will prepare a tourism development policy and action programme, specifying the geographical and sectoral priorities, by the end of June 1997 for launching by the beginning of November 1997. A Tourism Development Board will be created by the end of December 1997 in respect of which the enabling legislation will be submitted to Cabinet by the end of October 1997. The new Board will work closely with the private sector and the Swaziland Investment Promotion Authority.

vi) Minerals Exploitation Development

A minerals exploitation policy will be prepared by the end of October 1997 after consultation with the appropriate authorities. The policy will incorporate procedural improvements to encourage existing and potential investors.

vii) Development of Small and Medium Scale Enterprises (SME's)

Whilst this sub-sector has received considerable attention and funding in view of its potential impact on economic growth, the existing efforts are fragmented. There are a number of small organizations providing business support, training or finance, or a mix of these, performance varies widely and the sub-sector lacks a coordinating unit to ensure the most efficient use of the available resources. A paper will be produced by June 1997 setting out the policy framework required for SME development and by the same date a task force will have developed a programme for empowering economically the small and medium scale enterprises. The programme will include identifying more opportunities and providing increased training facilities for indigenous entrepreneurs.

viii) Industrial Relations

The recent industrial relations unrest has introduced a significant potential deterrent to investors. To assist in the achievement of harmonious industrial relations, Government will continue to promote tripartite consultations on industrial relations matters. A Labour Advisory Board meeting will be held to draw up recommendations for developing active and harmonious partnerships to improve industrial relations. Agreed proposals, which make important revisions to the 1996 Industrial Relations Act, will be submitted to Parliament by the end of June 1997.

5.2. Agriculture and Nutrition

An agricultural policy statement will be submitted to Cabinet by October 1997 and a task force will, by the end of June 1997, develop an agenda for the promotion of smallholder agriculture.

A programme of promotion and support to developing smallholder livestock and intensive agricultural production schemes and enterprises has been drawn up for 1997 and 1998. The measures include demonstration units, field days, a satellite egg production unit, a tick borne diseases control programme, research and breeding projects and expansion of veterinary services. The targets under this group include increasing smallholder broiler production by 35% per term and smallholder porker production increased from 24 to 115 tonnes by the end of 1998. The Dairy Development Study will be completed by the end of 1997.

The Integrated Tick and Tick Borne Diseases Control Policy will be submitted to Cabinet by the end of April 1997. This will reduce cattle movements to dip tanks and thereby reduce one of the major causes of soil erosion.

A report on the proposed seven year in-service and short course training programme for livestock extension staff and stock farmers will be submitted to Cabinet by the end of April 1997.

A feasibility study on the establishment of a tannery and the efficient procurement of hides and skins will be submitted to Cabinet by April 1997.

A study will also be carried out by the end of September 1997 into the feasibility of commercial grape production.

Government will also, by the end of December 1997, draw up a promotional programme to expand sugar production and value-adding industries based on sugar, pulp and other locally produced raw materials, as well as small scale horticultural and vegetable production. Particular emphasis will be placed on encouraging export oriented activities.

In 1997 and 1998, Government will bring approximately 700 hectares of communal land under irrigation for smallholder sugar cane and vegetable production. Around 10 small to medium size dams and a further 10 earth dams will be built in each of the two years. A detailed physical and socio-economic study will be undertaken on the lower Great Usuthu River Basin in 1997.

Government will expand the strategic maize storage capacity around the country from 15,500 to 27,000 tonnes by November 1998, before handing over maize procurement and storage to the National Maize Corporation and privatizing all maize milling.

A study will be carried out by December 1997 with a view to guiding Government on eliminating all structural and operational constraints to the liberalisation of trading and marketing in agriculture. Greater commercialization in agricultural development will also be achieved by the introduction of a cost recovery policy in selected services by March 1998.

A policy on the accessibility and productive use of Government farms with provision for appropriate lease arrangements to encourage agri-business will be completed by July 1998.

A policy statement on rural resettlement will be submitted to Cabinet by the end of December 1997.

A great deal of importance is attached to improving nutritional levels throughout the country. As part of the Young Child Feeding Project, at least 30% of mothers will be exclusively breastfeeding their babies between birth and six months of age by the end of 1998, compared with approximately 21% at the present time. By December 1998, 50 additional homesteads in each region will have established fruit trees and vegetable gardens.

A proposal for the establishment of the Secretariat for the Swaziland Nutrition Council which will be responsible for coordinating nutrition activities in the country will be submitted to Cabinet by June 1997.

5.3. Education and Training

An education policy statement will be submitted to Cabinet by the end of October 1997.

The main emphasis of Government efforts at primary level will be on improved quality of education, through specific projects over the coming two years. It is at the primary stage that the social rates of return are highest. At secondary level the focus will be on curriculum diversification. The inspectorate division will be decentralised by December 1997 to improve support to head teachers.

In tertiary education, Government will concentrate on training for the national manpower requirements and, in view of the disproportionately large amount spent on this compared with primary and secondary, on progressively shifting to the beneficiaries more of the costs, both in terms of scholarship fund allocations and levels of loan financing. A more effective approach will be developed for recovering outstanding loans. Proposals covering these matters will be considered by Government in June 1997. Regarding manpower requirements, a National Human

Resources Plan will be produced by March 1998, thereby enabling Government to draw up, by 31 May 1998, a policy on the matching of curriculum and pattern of enrolments with the Plan.

By the end of June 1997, Government will have issued a statement on the criteria and rules relating to the award of scholarships.

5.4. Population, Health and Social Welfare

Population

The rate of increase in the population, which is currently 3.2% per annum, is the single most serious threat to Swaziland's future economic and social welfare. The number of people in the country increases by 30,000 per annum while the number of jobs and social amenities available are growing at a much slower rate. The first step to resolving this problem is the formulation of a Population Policy which has the support of all social partners. The Government will prepare this policy document by the end of December 1997.

Efforts will be made to expand and improve the delivery of Family Planning services by introducing a community-based distribution system. The contraceptive prevalence rate is targeted to rise from 28% to 33% by the end of 1998 and a community-based distribution system introduced in 50% of each region by that date.

Government recognises the need to reorient health personnel on reproductive health issues in general and in particular for women, including those with disabilities.

Health

The Government's main objective in the health sector is to improve the health status of the Swazi people by providing services that are relevant and accessible to all. The primary health care strategy has been adopted in which the main bias is on decentralisation and strengthening of health care services, in particular in the rural areas. The second Phase of the Health Sector Study will commence in March 1997 and be completed by the end of September 1997. This will produce inter alia a five year Plan of Action and a revised National Health Policy.

Several options are to be investigated by Government to improve security in the rural clinics. The Ministry of Health and Social Welfare will prepare a programme of action which will be addressing the issue of security in these clinics by July 1997.

A major threat exists in the form of the HIV/AIDS epidemic. A national response to this is being launched and an AIDS Policy document will be drawn up by July 1997. Additional resources will be allocated to an In-School Health Education Programme and a community and home-based care programme, both to be up and running before the end of 1997. The Government aims to achieve a 33% reduction in STD-related HIV infections by the end of 1998.

With a view to improving environmental health standards, water availability will increase from 45% to 60% of the population by December 1997, and pit latrines coverage from 50% to 75%.

Medical facilities will be improved by the setting up of an ICU at the Mbabane Government Hospital by April 1997 and the rehabilitation of the Government hospitals at Mankayane and Piggs Peak by April 1998. Thereafter, and provided funds are available, one new clinic will be constructed each year. The malaria case fatality rate will be reduced by 60% by the end of December 1997 and, by the end of June 1997, a proposal will be produced for a coordinated effort to eradicate malaria or at least reduce substantially the number of cases. The child immunization rate will be maintained at 90% into the foreseeable future.

By the end of December 1997, Government will draw up a plan to integrate and rationalise public and private health service provision which will improve the quality of care and increase Government revenue.

A special training programme to improve the quality of medical care will be drawn up by December 1997.

Social Welfare

The Government is conscious of the need to provide social welfare services to the physically and mentally disabled, the destitute and the aged. A Social Welfare Policy will be presented to Cabinet by the end of 1997.

Legislation to strengthen the policy on disability will be proposed by the end of June 1997. Government has embarked on a process of formulating the Disabled Act and this is expected to be completed by December 1997.

Gender and Disadvantaged Groups

The Government will establish a Coordinating mechanism by June 1997 to facilitate the production of a Draft Policy on Gender issues by the end of March 1998 and the preparation of legislation to back these up by October 1998. A task force will, by the end of June 1997, develop a programme to tackle gender issues.

Cabinet will consider the Convention of Elimination of all forms of Discrimination against Women, with a view to acceding to it by June 1997.

Youth

A programme for reviewing child protection legislation will be drawn up by December 1997. The Swaziland National Committee on Children will be re-established by May 1997.

A task force will draw up a programme, by the end of June 1997, which will include youth development as well as operationalising the Government's sports policy.

5.5. Public Order and Internal Security

In order to ensure an up-to-date legal system on the basis of which the economic and social programmes and targets should be premised, a study will be carried out by December 1997 on whether the Law Reform and Development Commission should be reactivated.

Government will undertake as a matter of urgency the strengthening of the Director of Public Prosecution's and the Attorney-General's Offices by December 1997 and further investigate how training and supervision can be improved for judicial officers and the police.

A review of the dual legal system is to be carried out by December 1997 to facilitate the strengthening and consolidating of the judiciary system in the country.

Government will consider a task force report on crime prevention and detection by the end of June 1997.

5.6. Housing and Community Amenities

Improving access to shelter for all income groups is a key priority of the Government. The main aims are to provide or improve basic infrastructures which are affordable especially to the urban poor and in particular where costs are to be recovered. The Urban Development Project, which includes the upgrading of the infrastructures of Mbabane and Manzini, will continue and be well towards completion by the end of 1998. A housing policy statement will be drawn up by the end of March 1998. The Physical Planning and Development Control Bill will be submitted to Parliament by the end of March 1998 and a National Physical Development Plan will be finalized by the end of December 1998. The Sectional Titles Bill will be submitted to Parliament by March 1998.

The introduction of a 99 year leasehold tenure on Swazi Nation Land and peri-Urban areas has been a major achievement of recent policy reform. A study will be carried out by March 1998 on extending this 99 year leasehold concept to facilitate financing and development of housing on Swazi Nation Land. A booklet on the concept of the 99 year lease will be circulated by the end of September 1997.

A report on housing finance for low income households will be issued by the middle of December 1997 and thereafter it is hoped that more financial institutions can be induced to enter the housing market.

In order to strengthen the capacity of local authorities to manage the urban areas, a new Urban Government Bill will be submitted to Parliament by the end of September 1997.

5.7. Infrastructure

In pursuit of creating an enabling environment, certain infrastructural improvements will be carried out over the coming two years.

i) Energy

A high priority is to provide a sound energy policy framework and an appropriate investment programme to address the increasingly serious shortfalls in power supply. Terms of reference will be prepared by April 1997 for a study which will, inter alia, draw up an investment programme which will meet the needs of the economy. The 1963 Electricity Act will be amended by October 1997 to facilitate competition in the generation, transmission and distribution of electricity.

The Swaziland Electricity Board will install a fourth feeder line (132 kV) from ESKOM by July 1998 and a system strengthening programme will be completed by the end of 1997. After the updating of the 1987 feasibility study in January 1998, construction of an inter-connector between Swaziland and Mozambique will commence.

A rural electrification study to identify and prioritize rural areas for connection to the grid will be completed by the end of June 1997.

A consolidated Petroleum Bill will be drafted with particular emphasis on addressing the price of petroleum products in an attempt to minimize import costs. The Act will also deal with issues affecting regulation and deregulation of the petroleum industry.

ii) Rail Transport.

Swaziland Railways will embark on a rehabilitation programme of the East-West line from Matsapa to the Mozambique border. Eighty kilometres of line will be rehabilitated by the end of

December 1998. This links with the Maputo harbour upgrading project and, the substitution of this route for the traditional ones through South Africa will facilitate a reduction in import and export transport costs. For work to commence on time, it will be necessary to conclude financing arrangements before June 1997. Subject to finance being available for which Government assistance is required, a dry port development at Matsapa is expected to be completed by September 1997. The project will involve an increase in stacking space and the acquisition of modern and faster cranes.

iii) Roads

The improvement of strategic local and regional roads will be the Government's contribution to facilitating greater economic activity and a district roads programme will improve communications in the rural areas. Main roads will be improved at the rate of 60 kms a year, district roads at 100 kms a year, the periodic maintenance of proclaimed (gazetted) roads will be undertaken at the rate of 400 kms per annum, and routing maintenance provided to the entire road network. These measures represent an acceleration of the existing programme. Further, to reduce vehicle overloading and its destructive effect on road surfaces, an overloading control programme will incorporate a permanent weighbridge at Matsapha which should be completed by June 1997.

The capacity of local contractors will be enhanced through training (three training courses available each year) and incentive arrangements (to be in place by August 1997) in order that the development of the local contracting industry is encouraged. Approximately 25 graduate engineers will undergo the necessary on-the-job training in order to integrate Swazi engineers into the Government's Roads Department.

Measures to reduce the number of road accidents include an accident investigative programme to be in place by June 1997, the improving of all major accident blackspots by March 1998 and a public road safety education programme throughout the two year period. A 1997 amendment to the Road Traffic Act, to be presented to Parliament by June 1997, will allow higher fines to be imposed for road traffic offences.

In view of the high accident rate in Swaziland, Government will explore the possibility of offering mandatory First Aid training to public transport drivers by June 1997. In the medium to long term, Government will review the implications of making First Aid training a prerequisite for drivers' licensing.

Some institutional change in Government's roads management function is expected to take place in the coming two to three years. By June 1997 an organizational structure and the setting-up procedures for a proposed Roads Authority will be submitted to Cabinet with a view to the legislative and administrative actions taking place over the subsequent two years. Simultaneously, a programme which will include a review of road user charges will commence by June 1997 with a view to providing more resources for adequate road maintenance.

A proposal on the management and maintenance of feeder roads is to be presented to Cabinet by the end of May 1997.

iv) Air

Design and tender documents for the upgrading of Matsapha airport, which will involve a new terminal building, a cargo building, an aircraft parking apron, a VIP lounge and new access roads, will be completed before the end of 1998. Funding is yet to be identified for the project.

A complete updating of the 1968 Act will be presented to Parliament by August 1997 in order to meet international standards and a satellite communications system will be installed by December 1998.

v) Telecommunications

The modernisation programme for Swaziland Posts and Telecommunications will be presented to Cabinet by May 1997. By the end of March 1998, it aims to have provided 5000 new urban and peri-urban connections and a further 1000 for the rural network. By June 1998, the national network will be fully digital and the fault rate will be reduced from 2.5 to 1.5 faults per customer per annum. There will be an optical fibre link on the Mbabane-Manzini interconnection. A policy on telecommunications, which will include strategic partnerships for value-added services (cellphones, data networks etc) will be submitted to Cabinet by the end of May 1997 and the enabling legislation sent to Parliament by the end of July 1997, with a view to introducing a cellphone system by the end of October 1997 as part of a customer-responsive telecommunications network.

vi) Water

The legal and institutional framework for water resources will be revamped in order to increase coverage and achieve an equitable distribution, at the same time encouraging conservation. The 1967 Water Act will be redrafted by June 1997 thereby facilitating the creation of a new National Water Authority, of which the implementing arm will be the Department of Water Affairs, thus bringing under one umbrella all the present water agencies. The new Act will also strengthen procedures for monitoring water usage and pollution control.

The Swaziland Water Services Corporation will complete the expansion of the treatment works at the Matsapha industrial estate by December 1997 and will upgrade the Mbabane pumping works by December 1998.

Three projects are in place for increasing the supply of potable water to the rural areas. These are the Japanese Grant Aid Project, the Rehabilitation Project and the Water Relief Fund Programme which are expected to be completed in December 1997, March 1998 and December 1998 respectively. These projects promote the principle of self-reliance and the recipient communities will bear all the operational costs and contribute 50% of capital costs over a period of ten years, as well as being trained to manage their respective systems.

The Maguga Dam project, a joint Swaziland/South Africa venture on the Komati River which will provide irrigation for around 7,000 hectares of land, is expected to commence by April 1997 with the building of housing and access roads. Construction of the dam itself is expected to start by October 1998. In order to coordinate the downstream development part of the project, the Komati Basin Development Authority will be established by the end of May 1997. The Authority will draw up a development plan by the end of November 1997.

The viability of another potential project, in the Usuthu Basin, which could provide a substantial amount of irrigable land for small farmers growing cane near to the Ubombo Mill, is being re-examined. The feasibility study is to be completed by December 1997, and most of the required funding has been identified. The European Union has pledged at least E120 million for this project which will provide an additional 14,000 hectares of irrigable land. If feasibility is positive, construction work is planned to commence by June 1998.

5.8. Environment

For the protection of the environment, a National Environment Action Plan will be drafted by April 1997 to deal with the urban, rural and industrial environmental problems. An Environmental Programme will then be put into effect by the end of November 1997. This will include the drafting of a National Land Policy by the end of December 1997. For this exercise, a facilitator will be appointed by April 1997. The National Land Policy will address land use and land tenure policies. In the meantime, the Government will consider the creation of a Directorate of Lands by the end of June 1997.

All environmental legislation will be reviewed in 1997 and the 1996 Regulations on Environmental Audit, Review and Assessment, which provide guidelines on the inclusion of environmental concerns in project planning, will be updated in 1997. A National BioDiversity Plan will be finalized by November 1997.

The Government will, by June 1997, develop a policy on the management and conservation of wildlife, which will include the issues of environmentally sustainable tourism and the impact of nature reserves and game parks on adjacent communities. A National Desertification Action Plan will be drawn up by 31 December 1997 to set out the measures to combat the threat of extensive soil erosion.

5.9. Information Services

An information policy statement will be submitted to Cabinet by the end of September 1997.

The Ministry of Public Service and Information has the responsibility of disseminating news and other information to the Swazi Nation in a way that is educative, informative and entertaining. To achieve a high standard of delivery, the Ministry is carrying out a number of projects, including the rehabilitation of the Educational Broadcasting Unit, the Radio Services Improvement Project and the upgrading of studio and engineering equipment. It is expected that these will be completed by the end of 1997. To provide a guide to itself and other media organizations, the Ministry will prepare a media policy by the end of December 1997.

A review of the operations of the Swaziland Television Broadcasting Corporation and the Swaziland Information and Broadcasting Services will be carried out by 30 June 1997.

In recognition of the importance of information on the operations and activities of Government, there will be established a proactive, coordinated information programme by April 1997.

6. REGIONAL INTEGRATION

6.1. Transport and Communication

The Transport, Communication and Meteorology Protocol, signed by Southern Africa Development Community (SADC) member states, defines cooperation in railways, roads, ports, shipping, air transport, telecommunication, postal services and meteorology. With the introduction of the Maputo Development Corridor Programme and the Lubombo Initiative, the Government will give consideration in the coming two years to extending road and rail networks to exploit the potential economic benefits of the Corridor. Quarterly progress reports on the development of the Corridor will be discussed at Cabinet level.

In order to keep abreast of the current demands of the private sector, Government is reviewing the present cross-border arrangements, in particular the number of hours for which the border posts are kept open and the visa requirements. A report on both border hours and visas is expected by June 1997.

6.2. Fuel and Energy

Government has recently signed the SADC Energy Protocol which sets out areas of cooperation in the energy sector. The Southern African Power Pool has been adopted by SADC member states and will promote energy trading and power pooling. Cooperation in petroleum and coal resources is being developed as is cooperation in other energy sub-sectors and these arrangements are expected to be finalized by August 1997.

6.3. Water Resources Management

The Protocol on shared watercourses binds the SADC member states in the development of common river basins and all related utilization. Swaziland is conducting a joint venture with the Republic of South Africa in the Development of the Komati River Basin which is seen as an integral part of the recently established Maputo Development Corridor project. A major part of this venture, the Maguga Dam project has commenced. with the building of the access roads and the housing at Piggs Peak. Construction of the dam itself will commence in October 1998.

7. STATISTICS AND DATA

7.1. General

Problems have been encountered in the collection and analysis of statistics and data and a study will be done by 30 September 1997 in order to improve the system of National Accounts to meet Government's data needs.

A study will also be carried out by the end of December 1997 to establish the feasibility of an autonomous Swaziland National Statistics Authority.

7.2. National Research

In order to provide the statistical and analytical information necessary for national development planning, a national research capacity in the form of the National Research Council was created in 1972. To take into account the importance of science and technology, the Council is to be reorganized by the end of December 1997 and established by Act of Parliament as the National Research, Science and Technology Council. Sectoral subcommittees will devise appropriate research programmes for which existing facilities, mainly at the University of Swaziland and Malkerns Research Station, will be used.

8. MONITORING

The monitoring of progress on the ESRA programme will be carried out by the Policy Analysis Unit in the Prime Minister's Office. A standardized reporting format will be used by each Ministry in order to report progress on a monthly basis and identify any problem areas for the Cabinet's attention. Cabinet will receive quarterly reports on progress. Government Ministries are committed to meeting the targets set out in ESRA.

ECONOMIC ASSISTANCE TO SWAZILAND

US ECONOMIC ASSISTANCE

Historical, Political, and Economic Background

In the early years of its colonial rule, the British expected that South Africa eventually would incorporate Swaziland, which is completely surrounded by South Africa. However, as South Africa intensified its apartheid policies after World War II, the British increased investments in education, medical care, and agriculture in an effort to help prepare Swaziland for independence. Swaziland gained independence in 1968 as a constitutional monarchy. King Sobhuza II, who reigned from 1921 to 1982, assumed absolute power in 1973. He was succeeded by his son King Mswati III in 1986. In October 1993 a parliament was elected.

Today, the principal ethnic group is the Swazi, and the official languages are English and siSwati.Swaziland is among the more prosperous countries in Africa. The cattle, mining, and sugar industries account for the bulk of Swazi wealth. While most of the high-level economic activity is in the hands of non-Africans, indigenous Swazis are becoming more active as small entrepreneurs and are moving into mid-management positions. The majority of Swazis are subsistence farmers, and approximately 17,000 work in the South Africa gold and platinum mines. Almost every homestead has someone employed for wage income, and in recent years, new entrants into the labor pool have exceeded the number of new jobs created. This, coupled with South Africa's economic downturn, drought, and an alarmingly high population growth rate have resulted in a prolonged recession. To address these problems, after the October 1993 elections, the king formulated a national development plan that encouraged active participation to identify priority needs in both the private and public sectors. The government has accomplished little in the past year to increase transparency, accountability, or responsiveness to citizens' needs. Political parties are still banned but the labor movement has become more vocal, strident, and visible in pressing for reform and change.

Pre-1993 economic growth was led by investment, and a large part of the foreign investment came to Swaziland because of sanctions against South Africa. Since South Africa achieved majority rule, no major investment projects have been completed in Swaziland. The government's main concern now seems to be to ensure that existing investors remain in Swaziland.

Status of Swaziland's Education Reform

Increasingly the Kingdom of Swaziland recognizes the need to improve education in order to achieve sustainable economic development. Key objectives include ensuring universal primary education, reorienting primary curriculum toward practical subjects that will enable school leavers to move easily into employment opportunities within the country, and training teachers. Impressive gains have resulted from investments in education by the government and donors. The school system's capacity has expanded to the point where virtually all Swazis receive some primary education. Since 1968, the percentage of all primary school teachers that meet Swaziland's standard qualifications has increased from about 69 percent to nearly 100 percent. The government determined that investments in quality and efficiency are needed to improve the human resource base and cope with expanding enrollments, and the government is concentrating on the need to produce school leavers who can assume productive roles in the formal and non-formal economic sectors.

USAID Assistance to Swaziland

USAID's assistance to basic education in Swaziland has been substantial, starting with the Primary Curriculum Development Project (1975-82) and the Teacher Training Project (1983-89). Given the requirements of economic growth and the government's timely promulgation of and demonstrated commitment to sound educational policies, USAID began the Education Policy, Management, and Technology (EPMT) project in 1989. EPMT provides the education sector with technical advice and training required for sustained implementation of reforms already adopted by the Ministry of Education.

Technical assistance and training focus on management training for headmasters, criterion-referenced testing, and contract administration. Short-term technical assistance focuses on continuous assessment, interactive radio instruction pilot testing, guidance, finance and budget, human resources, and logistics management.

All 500 primary head teachers and Grades 1-3 classroom teachers have received in-country training through this project, and 32 trainers of teachers and head teachers have also been trained in-country. The core component, continuous assessment, has been implemented in Grades 1-3 nationwide. The project will introduce the continuous assessment program to Grade 4 in January 1996.

With USAID project assistance the Ministry of Education convened a National Education Symposium in May 1994. At this event, the planning ministry paid respect to the education ministry's budget management capability by permitting it to determine on its own which programs to cut, if necessary. The Ministry of Education has used many of the planning tools developed by the project to present a compelling case for education reforms.

SELECTED PROJECTS

Education Policy, Management and Technology Project (EPMT) 645-0230

Purpose

To improve the quality and efficiency of basic education.

Nature of project assistance

Project funds support technical assistance, training, and limited amount of commodities, including materials, supplies, equipment and vehicles, limited research, and costs for monitoring and evaluation. The project supports four masters degree candidates at U.S. universities, six internships at state testing authorities in the United States, and in-country courses, seminars, and workshops.

Funding level and duration

$7.1 million in project assistance
1989-96 (amended: 1992, 1994)

Contract mechanisms

Institutional contract with IIR

Current status

The project is moving towards achieving its goal, with most components completed. The USAID Mission is closing in September 1995.

Indicators of progress in Swaziland

System-Level Impacts

Policy Level

Teacher housing equitably distributed

Institutional Level

Data from the MIS and the planning model used to make key decisions, including budget allocations, allocation of teaching posts, and teacher housing
Plans developed to reduce the number of teaching posts by 400; MIS data used to make these decisions
Early data on the impact of continuous assessment and head teacher management training suggest success

Student-Level Impacts

Quality/ Efficiency

Repetition rate in Grade 1 declined from 21.1% in 1992 to 17% in 1994

Other Donors with Programs in the Education Sector

European Community
Sweden
UNESCO
United Kingdom

THE WORLD BANK ASSISTANCE

Swaziland, a British protectorate from the 1880s until independence in 1968, is perhaps the nearest there is to a traditional African monarchy. Political parties were banned when the constitutions was suspended in 1973. King Mswati III was crowned in April 1986. In October 1986, the King appointed Sotsha Dlamini, as prime minister. An election of a new parliament was held in November 1987. The current prime minister, Sibusiso Dlamini, was appointed in July 1996. The majority of the people in the Kingdom are ethnically Swazi.

ECONOMY

Swaziland is a small landlocked country with an economy based largely on agriculture and agro-industry. Sugar, citrus, and wood pulp are the major sectors, and asbestos and coal are the major minerals. Subsistence agriculture, practiced mainly in the Middleveld and Lubombo plateau, employs about 60 percent of the population. Soft drink concentrate, wood pulp, and sugar are the main exports.

The Swazi economy is heavily dependent on South Africa from which it receives 83 percent of its imports and to which it sends 74 percent of its exports. Average real gross domestic product (GDP) grew at over 6 percent between 1968 and 1993. However, political change in South Africa has eroded some of Swaziland's advantage in attracting foreign capital, on which much growth has depended in the past and GDP growth has averaged about 3% during 1995-99.

POLITICS

Swaziland has a monarchy with a bicameral parliament consisting of the House of Assembly and the Senate. The King launched a review of the electoral system in 1991. This review resulted in the rejection of a multiparty system and recommended that the traditional electoral system tinkhundla be retained but reformed to allow for a two-stage legislative election, including a secret ballot at the second stage. The King may legislate by decree. The majority of Swazis are rural and tend to support the continuation of the monarchy, though in recent years there has been some movement toward reform.

DEVELOPMENT PICTURE/DONOR COORDINATION

Donor coordination is handled through the UN Development Program's Round Table Conference. However, donor interest in and financing to Swaziland is declining. The only substantive presence in Swaziland is the European Union, with which the Bank maintains informal coordination on its activities.

THE WORLD BANK GROUP'S ROLE

Swaziland became a member of the World Bank and International Development Association (IDA) in 1969. Cumulative commitments to date amount to $100 million for 17 IBRD loans and $8 million for two IDA credits. Currently, only one remaining loan (the Urban Development Project) is active. Cumulative commitments from the International Finance Corporation (the Bank Group's private sector lending arm) to Swaziland amount to US$39 million for seven investments. Swaziland has also received technical assistance from the Multilateral Investment Guarantee Agency (MIGA). MIGA, the Bank Group affiliate that provides investment marketing services to developing member countries, participated in a number of regional strategy workshops to promote foreign investment in tourism, and several organizations in Swaziland are using IPAnet, MIGA's on-line electronic clearinghouse for international investment information.

CONTACTS

Mr. Fayez Omar
Country Director
P.O. Box 12629
Hatfield 0028, Pretoria
Republic of South Africa
Tel: (27-12) 342-3111
Fax: (27-12) 342-5511
E-mail: fomar@worldbank.org

MINERAL AND MINING SECTOR: STRATEGIC INFORMATION

SWAZILAND

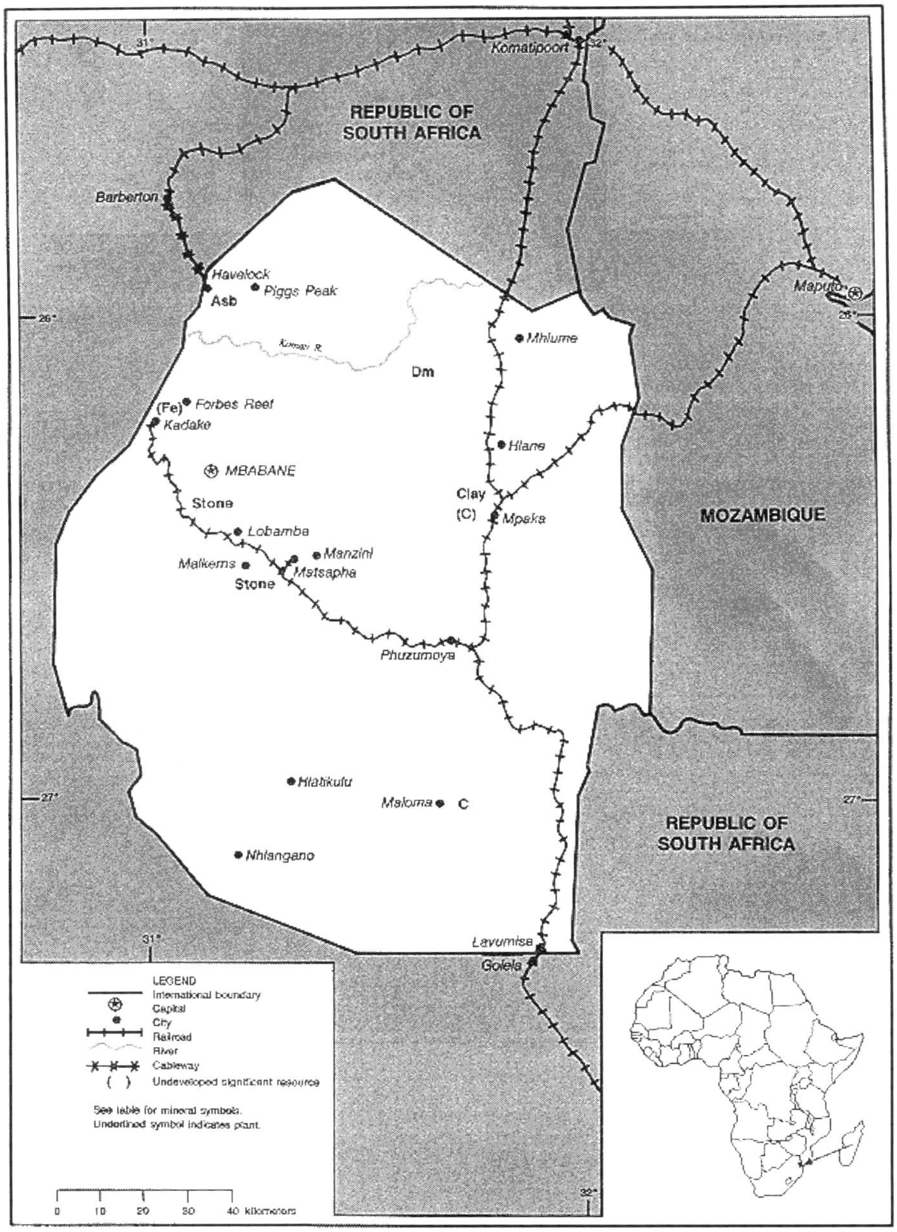

GEOLOGY AND MINING

Swaziland's diverse and ancient rock structures of Swaziland contain many minerals with economic potential. The country's mining sector dates back to ancient history and the dormant iron ore mine in the western Ngwenya mountains, which is now a tourist attraction, is the oldest in the world. Mining there ceased in 1975 and in more recent years the sector has faced mixed fortunes.

Minerals are vested in the King in trust for the nation with mining royalties paid to Tisuka Taka Ngwane, a trust established for the nation by King Sobhuza II in 1976.

The Monarch, in consultation with Libandla (which loosely translated means "meeting"), selects a Minerals Committee to advise on issues pertaining to mineral exploration and exploitation. The Commissioner of Mines is responsible for receiving applications for prospecting licences and mining rights which are passed on to the Minerals Committee for the granting of such rights. A Negotiations Committee ensures that lease terms provide for optimum utilisation of natural resources.

The country is 100% mapped at a scale of 1:50,000 and remapping was recently carried out.

PERFORMANCE

Since the closure of the Dvokolwako diamond mine in 1997, performance has been erratic and the mining sector performed below expectations during 2004/2000 with a 1.4% decline in revenue to E118.5 million. This is largely attributed to a 44.8% reduction in the production of quarried stone to 250,193 cu. m.

ASBESTOS

Production of asbestos reduced by 17% to 22,912 MT, mainly due to the closure of the underground operation. However, due to the declining rand and improved international prices, revenue was marginally up by to E57 million from E56.8 million. The main export markets are the Far and Middle East, Europe, and South Africa. Following the closure of an automotive friction materials manufacturer in 2004, there are no domestic buyers of asbestos. It is predicted that anti-asbestos campaigns in the UK and South Africa will have an adverse affect on asbestos prices in the future.

COAL

Although there are large untapped deposits of coal in the country, cost implications have so far detracted investment in mining them and the Maloma Mine, which produces high quality anthracite, is presently Swaziland's only operative coal mine. Following two years of steep upward performance, there was only a 4% increase to 426,299 MT in 2004/2000 against 410,021 MT in 1998/9 and 203,115 MT the year before. Export receipts registered an insignificant increase of 1.5% to register E51.7 million. Coal is an important component in the economy as there are sufficient identified reserves for well into the 2020's.

The Maloma mine produces eight-ash, a higher quality product than the ten-ash previously produced.

QUARRIED STONE

Due to the completion of the major Mbabane-Manzini highway, production for 2004/2000 reduced by 44.8% to 250.193 MT while sales were down by 21.1% to register E9.76 million. However, prospects for this sector are good as with major road construction in hand, including the Mbabane-Ngwenya, Nhlangano-Lavumisa and Luyengo-Sicunusa roads.

SAND AND SOAPSTONE

Excavation of these minerals is strictly controlled under the Mineral and Environmental Authority Act of 1992 in order to prevent environmental damage and rigid penalties apply to anyone violating the legislation. These commodities are not included in total mining revenue although it is estimated they generate income in excess of E7 million each year.

OTHER MINERAL DEPOSITS

Deposits of kaolin, talc and silica have been identified in Swaziland and investigations to determine the viability of mining these resources are ongoing. There was little or no activity with gold, of which there are deposits in the north-west of the country. Deposits of green chert have been located in the Malolotja/Ngwenya but there is resistance to their excavation because of the environmental implications.

GROUND WATER EXPLORATION

The Department of Geological Survey and Mines has been extensively involved in an exploration project designed to put subterranean water resources to optimum use. Exploration of this nature is necessary to determine ideal sites for clinics, schools and other social services.

MINERALS

All mineral resource are held in trust by the King. Gold and tin were the first minerals mined in Swaziland but it was not until the establishment of the Havelock Asbestos Mine at Bulembu in the north that mining became a major industry. Havelock has recently commenced restructuring its operations to extend its productive life. The Ngwenya Iron Ore Mine is closed but visits to the ancient working can be arranged through Swazi Trails. Coal is mined at Mpaka in the Lowveld and industrial diamonds are being recovered at Dvokolwako and Hlane. Other resources are clay and crushed stone quarrying for the construction industries and industrial minerals.

Mining has declined in importance in Swaziland in recent years. In 2009, the mineral industry was not a significant contributor to the country's GDP.

Some of Swaziland's minerals were of economic importance, including coal, diamond, gold, kaolin, and silica. Other minerals, such as arsenic, copper, nickel, manganese, and tin, either occur in small deposits or the quality was so low as to render them uneconomical to produce. Coal occurs in eastern Swaziland and was exploited at the Maloma Mine of Maloma Colliery Ltd. The Maloma Mine was Swaziland's only official mine in 2009 (Swaziland Investment Promotions Authority, 2009).

The Government announced that the Swaziland Electricity Co. was planning a 120-megawatt hydroelectric plant and had invited submissions from engineering firms for feasibility and pre-design studies (van der Merwe, 2009).

PRODUCTION

Information on the mineral industry of Swaziland was not readily available. Production of anthracite coal decreased, although the reason for the decrease was not reported. Quarried stone production was estimated to be about the same as in 2008. The quarrying of stone was for domestic consumption, and production depended on local demand. Xstrata plc of Switzerland operated a ferrovanadium plant at Maloma with a capacity of 2,400 metric tons per year. Production of ferrovanadium in 2009 was estimated to be about the same as in 2008. Data on mineral production are in table 1.

TABLE 1
LESOTHO AND SWAZILAND: PRODUCTION OF MINERAL COMMODITIES[1]

Country and commodity		2005	2006	2007	2008	2009[e]
LESOTHO[2]						
Fire clay[e]	cubic meters	15,000	15,000	15,000	15,000	15,000
Diamond	carats	52,036	231,324	454,014	450,000	450,000[3]
Stone, quarry products:[e]						
Dimension	square meters	1,000	1,000	1,000	1,000	1,000
Gravel and crushed rock	cubic meters	300,000	300,000	300,000	300,000	300,000
SWAZILAND[4]						
Coal, anthracite	metric tons	222,000	310,570	241,283	174,807[r]	170,000[3]
Ferrovanadium	do.	345	491	500	500	500
Stone, quarry products	cubic meters	567,000	534,688	207,535	240,997[r]	240,000

[e]Estimated; estimated data are rounded to no more than three significant digits. [r]Revised. do. Ditto.
[1]Table includes data available through May 31, 2010.
[2]Reported data from Lesotho Department of Mines and Geology.
[3]Reported figure.
[4]In addition to the commodities listed, modest quantities of crude construction materials (brick clay and sand and gravel), kaolin, pyrophyllite
(talc), and soapstone are produced, but output is not reported quantitatively, and information is inadequate to make reliable estimates of output.

SWAZILAND MINING DEPARTMENT

The Mining Department has a staff complement made of a Government Mining Engineer, Inspector of Mines, Inspector of Explosives, a Mining Technician, a Secretary, a Senior Clerical Officer, an Archivist, an Assistant Librarian, a Technical Assistant, Driver/Messenger and a Cleaner.

The Commissioner of Mines; who is also a member of the Minerals Management Board is the day to day administrator of the minerals sector. The Commissioner is authorised in terms of the Constitution to administer provisions of all mining legislation, a custodian of all geo-scientific data and / or information and may publish same.

The technical support staffs are responsible for the implementation and monitoring of reconnaissance, prospecting, mining programmes and rehabilitation activities in terms of the legislations and any mining lease agreements that the Minerals Management Board enters into with mining investors. The Department liaises with the Geological Survey Department with respect to prospective mineral deposits that may be evaluated for quality and quantity in order to inform prospective investors in the sector on the availability of minerals.

Mandate

The Mining Department is responsible for the administration of the mining and minerals industry in the Kingdom of Swaziland. The responsibilities involve the enforcement of the provisions of the Constitution; legislation namely: Mines and Minerals Act No. 4 of 2011, Diamond Act No. 3 of 2011, Explosives Act, Mines; Works and Machinery Regulations, Mines and Quarries (Safety) Regulations.

The mandate also includes an enforcement of the terms and conditions of mineral rights leases or licences issued through the Minerals Management Board for reconnaissance, prospecting and mining.

Objectives

The objectives of the Mining Department are to:

implement and continuously review the National Mining Policy to achieve the National Development Strategy (NDS), Sectoral Development Plans (SDP's) and the Poverty Reduction and Action Programme (PRSAP) goals;
establish, administer and maintain a modern, effective and visionary regulatory framework to govern the mining industry in the Kingdom of Swaziland that shall be custodian of an effective organisation;
enhance socio-economic, financial and other benefits to all Swazi Stakeholders arising from the exploitation of mineral resources;
establish more stringent social safeguards and improved fiscal management and achieve equitable sharing of the financial and development benefits derived from mineral extraction between investors and all Swazi stakeholders;
establish measures and initiatives for better environmental management in collaboration with other Agencies responsible for such;
advise on and disseminate all geo-scientific data related to the mineral resources of the country;
govern and provide professional guidance on matters of mine exploration, exploitation, health, safety, mine waste disposal and environmental control of pollution arising from mining activities;
formulate and provide technical guidelines, performance standards for mining, mineral processing, metallurgical operations and advise Government accordingly to ensure the international competitiveness of the mining sector;
regulate mining and the mineral industry through issuing of relevant mining permits or licences;
receive applications for reconnaissance, prospecting and mining licences for both large and small scale operations;
collate monthly mineral production returns from the mining industry;
collate monthly returns on the acquisition, storage and use of explosives;
control the manufacture, transportation, storage, usage, disposal/destruction, sale, importation, exportation of explosives;
implement the Kimberley Process Certification Scheme; provide for the control of import and export of diamonds;
provide for the control of production, processing, possession, purchase, sale and conveyance of diamonds;
provide secretarial services for the Minerals Management Board; and
promote optimum minerals development by encouraging value addition or downstream development and metallurgical processing in the country where possible.

Sections

- Regulatory and Inspectorate

  Mining
  Explosives
  Machinery and equipment
  Environment and surveying

- Minerals Development

  Information storage and distribution
  Administration / financial / training of small scale miners
  Secretariat – Minerals Management Board

Small Scale Mining

The Government of the Kingdom of Swaziland (GoS) realised that small scale mining (SSM) operations may provide additional or alternative rural livelihoods opportunities for Swazi Citizens. The GoS intervened in a way so that some minerals and mineral deposits or occurrences are reserved exclusively to be exploited by indigenous Swazi Citizens. The obligation for the SSM to exploit the minerals in an economically and environmentally sustainable manner is an obligation that must be enforced by the department.

The SSM sector is new and must be adequately regulated; the GoS has embarked on a project to train existing and aspiring small-scale miners. The educational exercises deal with themes including licensing, environment, health & safety, finance, taxation, reporting and labour laws.

Legislation

The GoS is in the process of reviewing mining legislation that will be in line with the Constitution, National Development Strategy, National Mining Policy, Southern African Development Community (SADC) Mining Protocol, amongst other guiding frameworks. In the first phase of the review, a National Mining Policy was formulated and subsequently approved. The second phase has involved the formulation of a mining legislation and the output is a Mines and Minerals Act No. 4 of 2011 and the Diamond Act No 3 of 2011. The review exercise is continuing with the Mines Health and Safety legislation, Explosives Control legislation and regulations. It may be mentioned that the reviewing exercise is ongoing and the final output is expected in 2012.

5. Technical Support
Technical advice and support is extended to reconnaissance, prospecting, mining and quarrying projects in the country. The support may be on a statutory obligation or at a professional level but the effort is dispatched for the sustainable exploitation of minerals and mineral aggregates for the benefit of the investor and the Swazi Nation. The mandatory support includes health and safety inspections accorded to all projects, and professional support is extended for designs in new projects or upgrades of designs already in use.

6. Application for Prospecting or Mining Rights
Minerals are vested to iNgwenyama of Swaziland in trust for the Swazi Nation. The Minerals Management Board advises iNgwenyama on the overall management of minerals and making of grants, leases or other dispositions conferring rights or interests in respect of minerals or mineral

oils in Swaziland.
Key requirements to obtain mining rights:

- Completed application form of the type of licence sought;
- Proposed programme of mining operations outlining mining forecasts of production and input costs;
- Capital investment forecast, cash flow projections and financing plans;
- Financial guarantees;
- Proposed programme of value addition or downstream development anticipated;
- Technical report on mining experience;
- Proposed programme of mining operations i.e. environmental impact assessment (EIA), comprehensive mitigation plan (CMP);
- Latest financial audited reports;
- Other pertinent requirements are on the respective application forms.

6.1 Establishment of Minerals Management Board
A Minerals Management Board (MMB) is established in terms of the Constitution. The MMB consists of the Commissioner of Mines, mine engineer, economist, legal practitioner and three other persons all of whom, including Chairperson, are appointed by the iNgwenyama on the advice of the Minister responsible for minerals.

The Commissioner is the only legally authorised person in terms of the Constitution to administer the provisions of all mining legislation. As a member of the MMB; the Commissioner must synthesise all geo-scientific data and / or information from Geology Department and Mining Department for the use by the MMB when adjudicating mineral rights applications.
The data set or information is for use by the MMB which ensures that the iNgwenyama receives holistic advice on mineral occurrences, reconnaissance, prospecting, mining or exploitation, processing, availability of mineral resources and the operations of the mining industry at large in the Country. Some operational information on geology and mining matters must be availed to the Minister for disseminating to Cabinet, Parliament and Public when necessary through the Commissioner of Mines.
There are applications to prospecting or mining for gold, coal, diamonds, kaolin and iron ore concession in various parts of the country.

6.2 Procedure for acquiring a prospecting right, mining right or concession
1. An application is lodged to the Commissioner of Mines stating the type of right sought; reconnaissance, prospecting or mining.
2. The Commissioner of Mines acknowledges receipt of the application and then appraises the contents, suitability and relevance of the project at the targeted area and makes a report based on the specific requirements, which are tabulated on each type of application.
3. The Commissioner of Mines then forwards the application to the Minerals Management Board for consideration.
4. The Minerals Management Board considers the application and then invites the project proponent to motivate his project in a form of a presentation.
5. The Minerals Management Board; after the presentation, evaluates the application using a criteria developed within the legislative framework and makes a recommendation and advises the iNgwenyama, accordingly.
6. The iNgwenyama makes a final decision, based on the recommendation of the Minerals Management Board and other supporting information, which may have been supplied at the time of application or presentation.
7. The project proponent is notified, in writing, of the outcome of his application.

6.3 Mining leases issued and being processed under the auspices of the Minerals Management Board

1. Roux Consolidated Investment (Pty) Limited was issued a twenty year mining lease in July 2008 to resuscitate and operate the Dvokolwako Diamond Mine at Dvokolwako.

Physical address:	3rd Floor Lilunga House Somhlolo Road MBABANE
Postal address:	P. O. Box 9 MBABANE H100 SWAZILAND
Telephone Numbers:	+268 2404 4263; +268 2404 3840
Fax Number:	+268 2404 8609

MINERAL RESOURCES OF SWAZILAND

June 2006

Geological Survey and Mines Department
P. O. Box 9, MBABANE H100
Swaziland.
Tel. (+268) 404 4263/3840
Fax. (+268) 404 8609
E-mail: siso@realnet.co.sz

In order to diversify the sources of economic development in the country Government wishes to foster development of a thriving mining industry that will contribute to sustainable economic development. Government recognises the positive contribution that mining can make as an engine for the economic development of Swaziland by diversifying the export base, widening the tax base, generating skilled employment, creating demand for local goods and services, contributing to infrastructure development, producing raw materials for local usage and acting as a catalyst for wider investment in the economy.

Government wishes to reverse the decline of the mining industry by attracting new investment in the exploration for and exploitation of mineral resources. Government recognises that to do this it must establish an enabling environment for investors that is based upon modern regulatory arrangements and competitive terms. Swaziland has to compete effectively against near-neighbours that are already established among the world's leading mineral producers, such as South Africa, Botswana, Namibia and Zambia.

Whilst Government is seeking to encourage investment by mining companies, there is also a need to ensure that mining operations are conducted responsibly. The neglect of the environment and harm to local communities as a result of mining operations is not acceptable. The intention is to ensure that Swaziland is securing the full economic and social benefits which mining development promises.

Government's policies are directed not only at large-scale mining but also at small-scale mining operations, which offer opportunities to support the rural livelihoods of the Swazi nation. Small scale mines needs to be assisted in their efforts to operate in an economically and environmentally sustainable manner. Government recognises its duty to discharge its regulatory responsibilities in an effective, even-handed and co-ordinated way. A process to establish appropriate legal and administrative arrangements and the requisite institutional capacity is in progress. The legal framework being created will ensure that Swaziland's mineral endowment is managed on a sustainable economic, social and environmental basis and that there is an equitable sharing of the financial and developmental benefits of mining between investors and all Swazi stakeholders.

The legal arrangement attempts to encourage local and foreign private sector participation in the exploration for and commercial exploitation of mineral resources, in keeping with Government's commitment to a free-market enterprise economy. Government recognises that private sector investors need to be able to operate profitably, be internationally competitive and satisfy their shareholders' and employees' expectations. To this end, Government through a regulatory framework is establishing a mining bill that will promote and maintain:

- a conducive macro-economic environment for mining investment,

- a stable and predictable regulatory environment in which investors are treated in an even-handed and transparent manner,

- access by investors to and security of tenure over areas of mineral potential, and

- a stable, predictable, competitive and fair fiscal regime.

This report outlines in brief the known mineral resources in the country. Government wishes to encourage investment in beneficiation and value adding activities to the minerals within the Kingdom of Swaziland. Government realises that, if this is achieved where possible shall ensure the industry earns higher export revenues, creates more employment, increases Government revenues, expand the linkages of the mining sector to the rest of the economy. This policy shall ensure sustainable economic development and a weapon to fight poverty in the country. Institutional frameworks is being set-up in the new dispensation to ensure that investors negotiate for the acquisition of mineral rights within a reasonable timeframe and agree to work together for mutual benefit.

The Geological Survey and Mines Department in the Ministry of Natural Resources of Energy has technical reports and bulletins together with geological maps that are available to the public with the relevant information pertaining the minerals in this report.

THE COAL DEPOSITS OF SWAZIILAND

This report gives a synoptic inventory of Swaziland well-defined coal deposits. Detail geological exploration work leading to the publication of mining feasibility studies was carried out in Mhlume, Area 1 & Area 2 (including the dormant Mpaka Mine), Area 3, Lubhuku and Maloma (with the only operating anthracite mine) coal deposits. The mineable coal reserves, projected life and employment levels in each potential coal mine are indicated below.

AREA MINEABLE EST. ANNUAL LIFE OF EST. EMPLOYMENT (Million tonnes) PRODUCTION MINE (YRS) LEVELS

Mhlume	18.4	665000	27	665
Area 1 9.1 - - - Area 2 Mpaka Mine	41.2	500 000	82	600
Area 3	20.6	500 000	41	450
Lubhuku	18.9	510 000	37	500
Maloma	35.3	600 000	58	600
Total	143.5	2 775 000	-	

Coal in Swaziland occurs in two coal zones found respectively in the Upper and Middle Ecca series of the Karoo Supergroup. The coal seams dip 50 to 80 to the east and up to twenty (20) coal seams are found in the coal-field of Swaziland.

The coal deposits of Swaziland are served by a network of tarred and gravel roads; telecommunication systems, electricity grids and most importantly they lie in close proximity with the railway line. As indicated in the report transport of the coal would only require the construction of a railway siding and loading facilities in the relevant railway station. Hence, the development of a coal mine would mean a significant growth to the railway freight and provide additional job opportunities to Swazi citizens.

The establishment of all the potential coal mines would create over two thousand (2 000) direct employment opportunities while other people could be employed in other allied industries such

as schools, shops, etc. It would be prudent for the mines to be run by joint venture entities with a strong local representation to ensure operational security, stability and sustainability.

COAL RESOURCES OF SWAZILAND

Coal has been known to exist in Swaziland for a long time. Concession maps drawn in the late nineteenth century accurately show the coal field of Swaziland.

The coal field of Swaziland forms a north - south continuous area with an average width of fifteen (I5) kilometres found on the eastern part of the country (Figure 1). The coal field of Swaziland comprises of Karoo sediments and occupies about one sixth of the 17 364 km2 area of Swaziland.

The coal field of Swaziland occurs within the Lowveld of Swaziland. It consists of low lying plains ranging between 300 and 400 metres above mean sea level and receives the least amount of rainfall in the country which averages only 700mm per annum.

COAL GEOLOGY

The coal-bearing Karoo sediments lie on the foot of the Lubombo mountain range, which forms its eastern boundary. The Karoo sediments dip to the east at 70. There are two coal zones each containing numerous coal seams. Up to twenty (20) coal seams of various thicknesses occur in the coal-field. The Upper Coal Zone and Lower Coal Zone are contained respectively, in the Upper Ecca Series and Middle Ecca Series of the Karoo Supergroup.

Coal seams of mineable thickness (at least 1 metre) are found in the Lower Coal Zone. The Main Coal Seam has been found to have a consistent lateral distribution and an average mineable thickness of three (3) metres throughout the coalfield. The mining geology is relatively difficult due to the occurrence of intrusions by dolerite dykes and sills, which are often accompanied by faulting. These igneous intrusions through coal bearing strata resulted in certain areas of the coal to be burnt, devolatized or even replaced by the dolerite.

KNOWN COAL RESOURCES

Coal Exploration activities conducted to date concentrated, on the shallow western part of the coalfield, and within the Lower Coal Zone. Limited exploration has been conducted on the coals of the Upper Coal Zone because of their inferior quality as compared to the coals of the Lower Coal Zone.

The Lower Coal Zone contains about 485.00 million tonnes of in situ coal resources of which 143 million tonnes are mineable (see table 1).

Table 1 Coal areas and reserves in million tons

AREA	ESTABLISHED (SITU)	MINEABLE	
MHLUME	> 34.0	18.4	
AREA 1	> 1 15.2	9.1	
AREA 2 (MPAKA MINE)	>	55.2	41.2
AREA 3 (SUMCOR)	>	50.0	20.6
MALOMA	>	44.2	35.3
LUBHUKU	186.4	18.9	
TOTAL (MILLION TONNES)	485.0	143.5	

COAL QUALITY

The coalfield of Swaziland consists of semi-anthracitic or lean coals and anthracite. Coals of the Upper Coal Zone are inferior quality anthracite with a high ash content compared to some of the high quality anthracite of the Lower Coal Zone.

ANALYTICAL SPECIFICATIONS OF LOWER COAL ZONE COALS

Table 2 **Analytical Specification of Lower Coal Zone Coals**

SPECIFICATION	MALOMA	MHLUME	MPAKA	AREA 1	AREA 2	AREA 3	LUBHUKU
YIELD %	75.00	84.10	75.00	83.20	73.00	90.50	78.00
MOISTURE %	1.60	1.10	1.30	1.00	1.30	1.00	1.40
ASH %	9.25	13.15	14.10	9.80	14.00	10.80	13.20
FIXED CARBON %	84.45	78.50	72.00	98.00	72.60	74.60	76.20
SULPHUR %	0.76	0.27	0.35	0.60	0.40	0.50	0.43
PHOSPHORUS %	0.01	0.01	0.01	0.01	0.01	0.01	-
ASH FUSION TEMP (0C) 1400	-	1250	1300	1250	1265	1320	
CALORIFIC VALUE (MJ/Kg)	30.00	29.00	32.00	29.89	31.53	29.70	31.39

The coalfield of Swaziland is served by an adequate system of tarred roads designed to serve both the coal and sugar industries. Swaziland has direct automatic dialling telecommunication with all neighbouring states and the world at large. Adequate electricity distribution networks already exist for any new coal mining development in the coalfield.

It will be necessary to develop adequate water storage facilities, as the coalfield of Swaziland is liable to drought. The coalfield is remote from the present administrative and industrial centres making it necessary for new townships to be constructed for any new coalmines.

Swaziland can provide most of the manpower required in a coalmine with the exception of experienced management personnel. For training of artisans and tradesmen Swaziland has the Swaziland College of Technology (SCOT), Vocational Training Institute, etc, while administrative personnel can be trained at the University Of Swaziland (UNISWA) and in other Institutes.

COAL DEPOSITS

Following are brief descriptions of Mhlume, Area 1 & Area 2 (Mpaka Mine), Area 3 and

Lubhuku coal deposits (Figure 1). Detail coal exploration information and the mining feasibility studies indicate that the coal reserves of each deposit can be increased through execution of further geological exploration in the adjacent areas.

MHLUME COAL DEPOSIT LOCATION

Mhlume Coal Deposit is located north-east of Swaziland in an area of approximately 7km2 situated in the south west of Mhlume townships. This area is found along the western edge of the sugar fields (see figure 1).

COAL QUALITY

The Mhlume Coal Deposit has high quality anthracite. The quality of raw and washed coal is shown below:

Raw coal Washed Coal

Average Washed Average Washed

Ash (%)	22.4	35	17	18
Volatiles (%)	9.2	11	9	11
Sulphur (%)	0.4	0.9	0.4	0.9
Calorific Value (MJ/kg)	25.9	21.0	28.3	27.5

MARKETS

Mhlume Coal Deposit has high quality anthracite. The calorific value of Mhlume anthracite is above that of normal anthracite, its main use would be as a smokeless fuel. South Korea and Japan are the ideal markets for washed coal. It would also be for metallurgical purposes, heating and as a source of fuel in boilers for thermal power stations.

AREA 2 COAL DEPOSIT (MPAKA MINE) LOCATION:

Area 2 Coal Deposit (Mpaka Mine) is situated in the central part of the Coalfield of Swaziland some 40 km east of Manzini (see figure 1). Coal from Area 2 Coal Deposit was mined from the dormant Mpaka Mine, which is found on the western edge of the coalfield 1 km south of the Manzini - Siteki tarred road.

COAL QUALITY

Area 2 Coal Deposit consists of semi-anthracitic coal generally referred to as lean coal because

of the relatively low volatile matter content (12 to 14/o) and high ash content (26% for unwashed coal). However, the coal from Area 2 Coal Deposit has a very high heat value (29MJ/kg) low sulphur and low phosphorus (less than 1 % for each case). Average coal quality data is as follows:

Yield (%)	75.0
Moisture (%)	1.3
Ash Content (%)	14.1
Volatile Matter (%)	12.7
Phosphorus (%)	0.01
Sulphur (%)	0.35
Fixed carbon (%)	72.0
Ash Fusion Temp. (%)	1250
Calorific Value (MJ/Kg)	29.0

MARKETS

Washed coal from Mpaka Mine, which is found within the Area 2 Coal Deposit has been successfully sold to Kenya where it was used for cement manufacturing. Some coal consignments from Mpaka Mine were sent to the Asian markets (Japan, S. Korea, etc.) where it was used for manufacturing smokeless briquettes for domestic heating and cooking. The bulk of the coal could be used for electricity power generation.

AREA 3 COAL DEPOSIT LOCATION

Area 3 Coal Deposit is located in Lubombo Region south of the dormant Emaswati Coal Mine It is in the lowveld region and the topography is relatively flat.

COAL QUALITY

The average coal quality is shown below:

Yield (%)	90.50
Moisture (%)	0.9
Ash (%)	15.1
Volatiles (%)	13.8
Sulphur (%)	0.6
Fixed Carbon (%)	76.6
Ash Fusion (0C)	1265
Calorific Value (MJ/kg)	31.53

MARKETS

Washed coal could find markets in Japan and Asia as a blend for steam coal and for metallurgical purposes. It could also be used as a smokeless fuel for domestic heating. Unwashed coal could be used for stern raising purposes.

LUBHUKU COAL DEPOSIT LOCATION:

Lubhuku coal deposit is located in the central eastern part of Swaziland - an area known as the lowveld (see attached figure 1). The western boundary of the deposit is adjacent to the Tshaneni to Lavumisa railway line

COAL QUALITY

The coal is mainly semi-anthracitic to anthracite and compares with Natal anthracite. The average coal analysis of main seam is given below:

Moisture (%)	1.4
Ash (%)	13.9
Fixed carbon (%)	76.9
Volatile matter (%)	7.7
Sulphur (%)	0.43
Calorific Value (MJ/Kg)	29.7

MARKETS

The exploitation of northern portion of the Main Coal Seam would yield 510,000 tons per annum of washed coal for 40 - 50 years. The unclean coal would be used in a thermal power station, which is under consideration.

Washed coal could find markets in Japan, South Korea and others, thus, providing a major freight for Swaziland Railway to transport the export coal through Maputo and/or Richards Bay.

SWAZILAND IRON ORE DEPOSITS

Swaziland has numerous occurrences of low grade iron ore deposits, the deposits vary in grade from 30% Fe-50%Fe with pockets of 60% Fe in some locations. These occurrences are restricted to narrow belt stretching from north western Swaziland, 10-15 km. North of the old –defunct Ngwenya iron ore mine to south eastern Swaziland (Figure 2).

The banded iron ore deposits in north western Swaziland are largely made up haematite and magnetite inter layered with quartzite and jaspilite. In the northern part, west of the Piggs Peak village the iron ore formations are of magnetiferous amphibolites (taconite)

The grades and estimated tonnages are shown in Table 2 A-C. It is clear from these Tables that the grade of the banded iron formations is much higher in the vicinity of the old Ngwenya Mine averaging around 45% with small pockets of 50%-60% 1ron. Further north the iron ore deposits are of slightly lower grade averaging around 35% iron.

Banded iron ore deposits in south central Swaziland are of a much lower grade than those occurring north western Swaziland and average about 30% Fe- 35% Fe. Generally these iron stones are made up of ferruginous lenses occurring within the sediments of the Mozaan Group. Some of the iron stones occur as enclaves within the granitoids. Table C shows the grades and tonnages of these iron stones.

Figure 2 Locality map of the dormant Ngwenya Iron Ore mine in the north-western part of Swaziland.

12

Table 3 A to C Showing grades and tonnage of iron stones in Swaziland

IRON FORMATION RESERVES

(A). WITHIN NGWENYA MINE LEASE AREA (ONE MULTIPLE HORIZON)

ORE TYPE	GRADE (%)	TONNAGE
BANDED HAEMATITE QUARTZITE - STOCKPILED SLIMES	43.70	28,019,839
BANDED HAEMATITE QUARTZITE - IN SITU IN HANGING WALL OF PITS	50.30	4,023,839
	43.70	26,551,623
SUB TOTAL	**43.70**	**58,595,301**
ORE IN SITU BELOW ECONOMIC PIT LEVELS	60.00	17,900,000
BANDED HAEMATITE QUARTZITE - IN SITU BELOW ECONOMIC PIT LEVELS		16,750,000
SUB TOTAL	**52.20**	**34,650,000**
BANDED MAGNETITE CARBONATE FORMATION IN PITS	45.10	339,498
BANDED MAGNETITE CARBONATE FORMATION OUTSIDE OF PITS	45.10	2,712,251
SUB TOTAL	**45.10**	**3,051,749**
TOTAL MINE LEASE AREA	***46.50***	***96,297,050***

NOTE: These were expected tonnages at the finalization of the medium grade contract.

The contract was fulfilled in the second part of 1978.

(B). NORTH OF MINE LEASE (2 HORIZONS)

ORE TYPE	GRADE (%)	TONNAGE
BANDED MAGNETITE QUARTZITE, NORTH EXTENSION BANDED MAGNETITE QUARTZITE, JASPILITE (NORTHERN) BANDED MAGNETITE QUARTZITE, JASPILITE (SOUTHERN) BANDED	32.60	16,556,852

MAGNETITE QUARTZITE, JASPILITE (NORTHERN)	32.00	11,651,495
BANDED MAGNETITE QUARTZITE, JASPILITE (SOUTHERN)	28.50	4,426,497
	32.00	33,140,768
		2,124,895
	28.50	
SUB TOTAL	***31.70***	***67,900,507***

13

(C). PIGG'S PEAK AND HAVELOCK AREA (4 DISTINCT BODIES)

DEPOSIT	GRADE %	TONNAGE (TO 100 m DOWNDIP)
NOTTIGNHAM PEAK	35.00	170,000,000
GENERALLY BANDED MAGNETITE QUARTZITE WITH SURFACE OXIDATION		
MIDWAY BANDED HAEMATITE QUARTZITE	35.00	30,000,000
MHLATANE TACONITE	35.00	46,000,000
IRON HILL	62.00	50,000
MASSIVE HAEMATITE	45.00	2,500,000
ENRICHED BANDED HAEMATITE QUARTZITE BANDED HAEMATITE QUARTZITE	35.00	45,000,000
IRON HILL SUB-TOTAL	**35.40**	**47,550,000**
PIGG'S PEAK SUB-TOTAL	***35.00***	***293,550,000***

(D). SOUTHERN SWAZILAND (3 SEPARATE DEPOSITS).

ORE TYPE	GRADE (%)	TONNAGE
MALOMA TACONITE	30.00	100,000,000
(METAMORPHOSED FERRUGINOUS SHALE OF PONGOLA SYSTEM)		
GEGE TACONITE	30.00	50,000,000
(METAMORPHOSED FERRUGINOUS SHALE OF PONGOLA SYSTEM)		

MKHONDO VALLEY	30.00	10,000,000
IRON FORMATIONS (HIGHLY METAMORPHOSED)		
SUB-TOTAL	***30.00***	***160,000,000***

GRAND TOTAL 36.00 617,747,557

14

GOLD OCCURRENCES IN NORTH WESTERN SWAZILAND

Gold occurrences were discovered over a hundred (100) years ago in north western Swaziland between Motshane and Horo (Fig 3). The gold occurrences in Swaziland are all found on the western side of the iron ore formations.

Gold mining activity was only recorded after 1910 at that time only 130,000 ounces had been produced and prior to this date it can only be assumed that a similar amount was produced.

The most productive areas in north western Swaziland at the time were: Pigg's Peak, Forbes Main Reef, Wyldsdale, Daisey and Gobolondo and most of the gold mining activity in these locations (Table3) occurred between 1882 and 1914 and between 1920 and 1967 irregular small mining activity was recorded.

Table3 shows estimated reserves and grades and from these figures it is fairly obvious that there is still enough gold in the ground for future mining and the grade is very encouraging.

Fig.3. Map of Swaziland showing the Barberton Greenstone belt and the location of gold deposits and occurrences (modified after Wilson 1982) and the road network.

Table 4. Summary of gold deposits in Swaziland

Locality	Deposit Name	Brief Deposit /Reef description	Estimated in situ reserves (t)	Average grade (g/t)	Recommended Mining method
Northern Hhohho	Daisy (Horo) deposit	Reef varied between 6.1-18.3m wide Auriferous quartz veins occur in quartz- sericite-fuchsite schists, biotite schsists, amphibolites and foliated granite	46 300 tailings and dumps not included	5.4	Open cast / stoping and selective mining
Hhelehhele	Wyldsdale	Pervasive 10mm smoky quartz veins in deeply weathered granodiorite and amafic schists	331900	5.4	Open cast may be up to 60m

Hhelehhele	Lufafa	Disseminated sulphides in ferrugenous shale of the Moodies Group	1 652 700	1.3	Open cast up to 60m / adits
Hhelehhele	Lomati	Brecciated carbonate and mafic schists	9 331 possible reserve 12 444kg Au	11.9	Stoping without pillars
Hhelehhele	Kobolondo	Almost vertical quartz veins dipping at about 78° towards the south along a shear parallel to a granodiorite plug	Not encouraging	1.2-2.62	Open cast up to 60m / Stoping without pillars
Pigg'sPeak towards Bulembu	Pigg's Peak	Single sub-vertical horizon of massive chert with a strike length of 6km	75 000 plus small amounts of Au in mine dumps and tailings	5.0	Underground method / Stoping with backfill
North east of Bulembu	Devils Reef	Gold lode within a ferrugenous and manganese wad exceptionally rich but not extensive	Information not available	1.27kg/t	Stoping without pillars
Malolotja Nature Reserve	Forbes Main Reef	Reef being an auriferous quartz vein steeply dipping at 65° towards the south	Detailed mapping required	47.5	Stoping with cement and backfill
Same as above	Waterfall	High grade obtained within a vein with a strike length of 0.91m	Detailed study recommended	11.9	Stoping with cement and backfill
Same as above	Avalanche	Acid reef ranging from 1.5-2.75m wide		4.3	Stoping without pillars
Same as above	Ivanhoe	Auriferous quartz vein in talcose and siliceous carbonate schists	6 000	8.5	Open pit
Same as above	She	Ore body was 1.5-3.4m wide striking east- west with a strike length of 457.2m dipping at 45°-	25 000	6.6	Open cast

		70° towards the south			

DIAMOND OCCURRENCES IN SWAZILAND

Diamond is hosted in a kimberlite and in Swaziland this rock type is found at Dvokolwayo. Other diamond deposits occur as fluvial deposit at Hlane and Mlawula Game Reserves. The quantity of ore in these deposits is not known.

DVOKOLWAYO KIMBERLITE

LOCALITY

The diamond bearing kimberlite pipe is located in the Dvokolwayo area some 65km from Manzini some 2km north of the Mbuluzi River (Fig. 4). It is accessed from Manzini through the northbound MR6.This dormant a 66kv power line from Swaziland Electricity Board and automatic exchange telephone line with international dialling service mine, which is under watchful eye of the army for security.

GEOLOGY

The Dvokolwayo kimberlite pipe is intruded into the Mliba granodiorite and forms a vertical pipe-like structure. Initially, at surface the pipe occupied some 2.8Ha whereas at 50m depths it occupied 3.4ha signalling size increase at depth. However at 120m depths it decreases. Presently the kimberlite has been mined up to depths of 72m.

GRADE

During previous mining operations by Trans Hex the Dvokolwayo Kimberlite produced diamonds, which were 80% industrial grade and 20% gem quality.

RESERVES

The present pit geometry is 600m in length, 160-180m in width; the kimberlite is some 60m wide. The pipe may still be mined and could still be paying to depths of 450m. This converts to

5million tons of *insitu* ore.

HLANE ALLUVIAL DEPOSIT

LOCALITY

The richest and most extensive alluvial diamond deposit in Swaziland is confined to the Hlane Game Reserve. This is some 30km to the east of the Dvokolwayo kimberlite pipe (Fig. 4). Geological reserves may be found beyond the Hlane game reserve to the south and north.

GEOLOGY

The Hlane alluvial deposit occurs within the red beds near the top of the Karoo sediments. The most occurrences are found in conglomerate/gravel horizons. The sediments dip 10-12° to the east. The main diamond bearing sediments crop out in a 5km north-south trend along the

Mbuluzane River (Howthorne et al.). Diamond bearing Red Beds were established at 170m depths some 1.2km to the east of the banks of the Mbuluzane River.

QUALITY

Diamonds in the conglomerate are moderately sorted, of small size (average 0.008 carats) and include a high percentage of well-formed crystals.

RESERVES

Diamonds are present in sufficient quantities to warrant detailed investigation of the deposit

(Howthorne, et al.). The deposit has not been quantified.

Table 5. Summary of diamond and other mineral resources in Swaziland

Diamond	Dvokolwayo	5 million tons	20% gem, 80% industrial quality	Dormant mine
	Hlane	Feasibility study recommended		
DIMENSION STONES	Mololotja Greenchert	Feasibility study recommended		
	Granites and rhyolites	Feasibility study recommended		
Barite	Londosi	286 000 tons	Industrial grade	Dormant mine
Talc	Forbes Reef/ Sicunusa	Feasibility study recommended		
Kaolin	Mahlangatsha	700 000 tons	Cream white to pinkish in colour	Dormant Mine
Silica	Madinda Hills	230 000 tons	76% SiO2	Never been exploited
Ball Clays	Lubhuku	Feasibility study recommended		
	Langa			In production

IMPORTANT LAWS AND REGULATIONS

THE DIAMONS ACT, 2011

AN ACT

ENTITLED

AN ACT to implement the Kimberly Process Certification Scheme and provide for the control of production, processing, sale, purchase, import and export of diamonds and other incidental matters.

ENACTED by the King in Parliament.

PART I PRELIMINARY PROVISIONS

Short hue and Commencement

I. (I) This Act may be cited as the Diamonds Bill, 2011 (2) This Act shall come into force on the date of publication.

Interpretation

2. In this Act, unless the context otherwise indicates -

„authorized representative means a person authorized in terms of section 35 of this Act;

"business premises", in relation to a holder of a licence or permit, means premises of the holder of a licence or permit of which particulars of the location have been endorsed on the licence in terms of this Act;

"Commissioner" means the Commissioner of Mines appointed in terms of the Constitution Act, 2005;

"contractor" means a person with whom a producer or a holder of a licence or permit has entered into an agreement to win or recover or to prospect for diamonds on behalf of the producer or a holder of a licence or permit, but does not include an agreement of employment or an agreement with an individual for the rendering of services by that individual personally;

"controlling interest", in relation to a company, means -

(a) direct or indirect beneficial ownership of 50 per cent or more of the issued share capital of the company by a person, acting singly or in concert with any other person; or

(b) direct or indirect control by a person, acting singly or in concert with any other person, of 50 per cent or more of the voting power in respect of the issued shares of the company; or

(c) the direct or indirect power by a person, acting singly or in concert with any other person, to appoint or remove the majority of the directors of the company;

„crushed diamond‶ means a diamond derived from a diamond which has been subjected to a process of crushing such that it has been rendered into fragments, splinters or particles, but does not include diamond powder;

"country of origin" means the country where a shipment of rough diamonds has been mined or extracted;

„cutter‶ means a holder of a diamond cutting licence;

"Exporting Authority" means the authority or body designed by a Participant from whose territory a shipment of rough diamonds is leaving and which are authorized to validate the Kimberly Process Certificate;

"dealer" means a holder of a diamond dealer's licence;

"diamond Valuator" means a person who holds a degree in gemology and appointed as such in terms of this Act;

"diamond‶ means a natural mineral consisting essentially of pure crystallized carbon in the isometric system with a hardness on the Mohs (scratch) scale of 10, a specific gravity of proximately *3.52* and a refractive index of2,42;

"diamond inspector" means a diamond inspector designated as such under this Act;

"diamond powder" means a powder derived from a diamond which has been subjected to a process of polishing or crushing;

"diamondiferous concentrate" means the end product of the treatment process of diamond bearing host rock or sediment through a heavy mineral concentration system, prior to removal of the diamonds by X-ray, hand sorting or other means;

"fragment" means a part of a diamond separated from the main stone in the course of diamond cutting and of so irregular a shape and small a size as to be unsuitable for cutting;

"Importing Authority" means the authority or body designed by a participant into whose territory a shipment of rough diamonds is imported to conduct all import formalities and particularly the verification of a companying Kimberly Process Certificates;

"Kimberley Process" means the international certification arrangement for rough diamonds adopted under the Interlaken Declaration;

"Kimberley Process Certificate" means a certificate issued under section 19 of this Act

"licence" means a diamond dealer's licence, diamond cutting licence, diamond tool-making licence or diamond research licence under this Act;

"holder of a licence" means a dealer, cutter, tool-maker or researcher; "Minister" means the Minister responsible for mines and minerals; "parcel" means one or more diamonds that are packed together and that are not individualized;

"Minister" means the Minister responsible for mines and minerals;

"parcel" means one or more diamonds that are packed together and that are not individualized.

"parcel of mixed origin" means a parcel that contains rough diamonds from two or more countries of origin, mixed together;

"Participant" means a state or a regional economic integration organization for which the Certification Scheme is effective;

"permit" means a permit issued in terms of this Act;

"polished diamond" means an unset diamond, including a synthetic diamond, which has undergone various manufacturing processes resulting in a gemstone which is of acceptable cut by international standards and is marketable as a polished diamond without undergoing any further manufacturing process;

"polishing", in relation to an unpolished or polished diamond, means the sawing, cutting, cleaving or dividing in any manner, faceting or altering of that diamond;

"possess" includes keeping, storing or having in custody or under control or supervision;

"processing" in relation to rough diamonds, means polishing, sawing, cutting, setting, cleaving or dividing in any manner, faceting or altering of that diamond with the view to enhancing the value of the diamond;

"producer" means a person who is in terms of the Mines and Minerals Act, 2010 entitled to win or recover diamonds, but does not include the holder of a prospecting licence;

"prospecting" means prospecting as defined in the Mines and Minerals Act, 2010; prospecting licence□ means an prospecting licence issued under the Mines and Minerals Act; „researcher" means the holder of a diamond research licence;

"restricted area" means -

(a) an area where diamond mining is carried out;

(b) an area of land in respect of which a licence or permit has been issued under this Act;

(c) an area in which bulk sampling for diamonds in terms of a prospecting licence or a mineral deposit retention licence is being carried out;

(d) an installation, equipment used for mining of or prospecting for diamonds;

(e) a place where processing of diamondiferous concentrate, or processing of gravel with the intention of recovering diamonds, takes place;

(f) business premises; or

(g) an area declared to be restricted by the Minister by notice in the Government Gazette;

"rough diamond" means a diamonds that are unworked or simply sawn, cleaved or bruted and fall under the Relevant Harmonised Commodity Description and Coding System 7 102.10,7102.21 and 7102.31;

"Kimberly Process Certificate" means a certificate issued under Part 111 of this Act;

"synthetic diamond" means a man-made diamond which has the same chemical, physical and optical properties as a natural diamond;

"tool-maker" means the holder of a diamond tool-making licence or permit Contemplated in section 23 of this Act;

"unpolished diamond" means a diamond in its natural state or a synthetic diamond which has, after the production, not been altered in any manner, and includes a crushed diamond and a partly processed diamond, but does not include any unpolished diamond set for industrial purposes in any tool.

PART II CONTROL OF IMPORT AND EXPORT OF DIAMONDS

Export of rough diamonds

3. (1) A person shall not export a rough diamond without -

(a) an export licence issued under this Act;

(b) a Kimberley Process Certificate issued under this Act; and (c) a Diamond Value Certificate issued under this Act.

(2) Subsection ***(1)*** shall not apply in respect of diamondiferous concentrate or any sand, soil, clay, gravel, stone, rock or mineral, which may contain rough diamonds.

(3) A person who contravenes this section commits an offence and shall on conviction be liable to imprisonment for a period not exceeding ten (10) years or to a fine not exceeding one hundred thousand (E100, 000.00) Emalangeni or both.

1mport of rough diamonds

4. (1) A person shall not import a rough diamond without an import licence issued under this Act and a Kimberley Process Certificate issued by the Exporting Authority.

(2) A person who contravenes this section commits an offence and shall on conviction be liable to imprisonment for a period not exceeding ten (10) years or to a fine not exceeding one hundred thousand (E100, 000.00) Emalangeni or both.

Export or import of diamond to from participants

5. (1) A person shall not export or import a diamond from a person who or a country of origin which is not a participant in the Kimberly Process Certification Scheme.

(2) A person who contravenes this section commits an offence and shall on conviction be liable to imprisonment for a period not exceeding ten (10) years or to a fine not exceeding one hundred thousand (El00, 000.00) Emalangeni or both.

Polishing, crushing or setting of rough diamonds

6. (1) A person shall not polish, crush or set a rough diamond without a licence issued under this Act.

(2) A person who contravenes this section commits an offence and shall on conviction be liable to imprisonment for a period not exceeding ten (10) years or to a fine not exceeding one hundred thousand Emalangeni (El00, 000.00) or both.

Conveyance of rough diamonds

7. (1) A person shall not convey, by any means, a rough diamond from a restricted area to any other place without a permit or a Kimberley Process Certificate issued under this Act.

(2) A person who contravenes this section commits an offence and shall on conviction be liable to imprisonment for a period not exceeding ten (10) years or to a fine not exceeding Emalangeni one hundred thousand (El00, 000.00) or both Sale, barter, purchase or receipt of rough diamonds

8. (1) A person shall not sell or barter a rough diamond unless that person is -

(a) a holder of a licence or

(b) a holder of a permit; or

(c) an authorized representative of a person referred to in paragraph

(a) or (b) and acting within the scope of duty as an authorized representative.

(2) A person shall not receive or purchase a rough diamond unless that person is -

(a) a holder of a licence; or

(b) a holder of a permit; or -

(c) an authorized representative of a person referred to in paragraph

(a) or (b) and acting within the scope of duty as an authorized representative.

(2) A person who contravenes this section commits an offence and shall on conviction be liable to imprisonment for a period not exceeding ten (10) years or to a fine not exceeding Emalangeni one hundred thousand (El00, 000.00) or both.

Import and export of polished diamonds

9. (1) A person shall not import or export a cut or polished diamond which is not set into jewellery, tool or implement unless -

(a) such diamond has been exhibited and sealed for export in the presence of the Commissioner in the prescribed manner; and

(b) a satisfactory statement of account of the possession of the diamond is submitted to the Commissioner; and

(c) that person holds an import and export licence.

(2) A person who contravenes this section commits an offence and shall on conviction be liable to imprisonment for a period not exceeding ten (10) years or to a fine not exceeding Emalangeni one hundred thousand (El00, 000.00) or both.

Approval of business premises

10. (1) A person who intends to apply for a licence or permit under this Act in respect of which such licence or permit require business premises shall first request the Commissioner for approval of the business premises.

(2) The Commissioner may approve or disapprove the utilization of business premises for an activity the applicant seeks conduct under a licence or permit.

Processing, research and tests of diamonds

11. (1) A cutter, tool-maker or holder of a permit shall not polish or crush a diamond or set a rough diamond in a tool, implement or other article or permit any such process to be conducted elsewhere other than on.

(a) the approved business premises; or
(b) such other premises as the Commissioner may approve on application in writing by such cutter, tool-maker or holder of a permit.

(2) A researcher shall not conduct analysis or tests in connection with a rough diamond or permit research or tests to be conducted on behalf of a researcher, elsewhere than on.

(a) the premises of the researcher; or
(b) such other premises as the Commissioner may approve on application in writing by the researcher.

(3) A person who contravenes this section commits an offence and shall on conviction be liable to imprisonment for a period not exceeding ten (10) years or to a fine not exceeding Emalangeni one hundred thousand (El00, 000.00) or both.

Valuing and sealing of rough diamonds

12. (1) A holder of a licence or permit shall not dispatch or sell a rough diamond to a processor, cutter, tool-maker, researcher or holder of a permit or to an authorized representative of such person unless that diamond is valued and sealed in a tamper resistant container.

(2) The market value of a rough diamond shall be determined by the Diamond Valuator taking into account-

(a) the value agreed upon between the seller and the buyer; and
(b) international market prices for such diamonds, at the time of the sale.

(3) The rough diamond after evaluation in terms of this Ac, shall and before being released for sale or disposal, be packed in a parcel and sealed in tamper resistant container in a manner prescribed under this Act.

(4) A holder of a licence or authorized person who otherwise disposes of a rough diamond shall deliver and the person who receives or purchases that diamond shall take deliver) of the diamond in a parcel sealed as prescribed under this Act.

(5) Where the sale or disposal of a rough diamond contained in a sealed parcel referred to in subsection (3) is subsequently cancelled or rescinded, the sealed parcel shall he returned to the holder of a licence or authorized person.

(6) A person who contravenes this section commits an offence and shall on conviction be liable to imprisonment for a period not exceeding ten (10) years or to a fine not exceeding Emalangeni one hundred thousand (El00, 000,00) or both.

Records of diamond transactions

13. (1) A producer, contractor, sub-contractor, holder of a diamond prospecting licence, holder of a permit or holder of a licence under this Act shall, at the approved business premises, keep or cause to be kept a register, in which shall be entered particulars in respect of the rough diamonds.

(2) A holder of a diamond prospecting licence or a holder of a permit under this Act shall keep or cause to be kept the register from such time as the holder of a licence has first won, recovered or found rough diamonds in accordance with the terms and conditions of the licence or permit.

(3) An entry referred to in subsection (1) shall be made within twenty four (24) hours after the occurrence of the event.

(4) A person required to keep a register in terms of subsection (1) shall, within fourteen (14) days after the end of each month, transmit or deliver to the Commissioner a true copy of such register kept in respect of that month and a solemn declaration in writing of the truth and correctness of the record.

(5) A person required to keep a register in terms of subsection (l) shall retain such register for a period of at least five (5) years after the date on which the last entry was recorded.

(6) A person who contravenes this section commits an offence and shall on conviction be liable to imprisonment for a period not exceeding ten (10) years or to a tine not exceeding Emalangeni one hundred thousand (El 00, 000.00) or both.

Security check of persons employed in diamond activities

14. (1) A holder of licence or permit under this Act shall not permit an employee or another person to engage in an activity or operation of or on behalf of such holder of a licence or permit which is related to diamond activity unless -

(a) such holder of a licence or permit has performed a security check on such employee or other person; and

(b) the results of such security check indicate that such employee or other person is suitable to be engaged in such activity or operation.

(2) If at any time an employee or another person referred to in subsection (l) has, pursuant to a security check referred to in subsection (l) (a) become unsuitable to be engaged, the holder of a licence or permit on whose behalf such activity or operation is being carried out, shall ensure that such employee or other person stops the engagement.

(3) A person who contravenes this section commits an offence and shall on conviction be liable to imprisonment for a period not exceeding ten (10) years or to a fine not exceeding Emalangeni one hundred thousand (El 00000.00) or both.

Restricted areas

15. (1) A person shall not enter a restricted area unless that person is-

(a) a member of the Royal Swaziland Police Service:

(b) an Inspector of Mines;

(c) the Commissioner;

(d) a Diamond Valuator;

(e) a Labour Inspector; or

(f) a staff member or public officer authorized by the Commissioner in writing, to enter, reside, travel or work at the restricted area.

(3) A person who intends to enter a restricted area shall apply to the Commissioner for a permit to do so.

(4) A permit shall specify the restricted area, or part thereof, for which it is granted.

(5) A restricted area shall be demarcated by the display of adequate signs to be a restricted area.

(6) A person who contravenes this section commits an offence and shall on conviction be liable to imprisonment for a period not exceeding ten (10) years or to a fine not exceeding Emalangeni one hundred thousand (El 00, 000.00) or both.

Diamonds found or picked up by chance

16. (1) A person who finds or picks up a diamond at any place, shall forthwith deliver that diamond to the Commissioner of Police or to the nearest police service Station Commander or Commissioner of Mines who shall keep it in a safe place.

(2) The Commissioner of Police or Station Commander shall within twenty-four hours upon receipt of the diamond deliver the diamond to the Commissioner of Mines who shall within twenty-four hours cause the found or picked up diamond to be tested for authenticity.

(3) A person who claims ownership of the found diamond shall produce proof of ownership to the Commissioner of Mines and the Commissioner of Police.

(4) Where the Commissioner of Mines and the Commissioner of Police -

(a) are satisfied that a person is the owner of the diamond referred to in subsection (1) or is entitled to be in possession of the diamond, the Commissioner of Police shall deliver that diamond to such person; or
(b) are not satisfied, the Commissioner of Police shall cause a notice to be published in the Gazette and in the newspapers circulating in Swaziland calling upon any person who may be the owner of that diamond or entitled to be in possession to prove ownership or right of possession.

(5) Where no proof to the satisfaction of the Commissioner of Mines and the Commissioner of Police of the ownership or right of possession is furnished within twenty-one (21) days after the date of publication of the two notices referred to in subsection (4)(b) the diamond in question shall be forfeited to the State.

(6) Where the State is satisfied that the diamond found or picked up in the circumstances contemplated in subsection (l), the State may reward the person who found or picked up that diamond.

(7) A person who contravenes this section commits an offence and shall on conviction be liable to imprisonment for a period not exceeding ten (10) years or to a fine not exceeding Emalangeni one hundred thousand (El 00, 000.00) or both.

PART III KIMBERLY PROCESS CERTIFICATION

Exporting and 1mporting Authority

17. (1) The Commissioner of Mines shall designate a unit in the Office of the Commissioner of Mines as the Exporting and Importing Authority.

(2) The Authority shall be composed of a Diamond Valuator and other officers as the Commissioner may consider necessary.

Functions of the Exporting and Importing Authority

18. The Exporting and Importing Unit shall be responsible for-

(a) processing a Kimberly Process Certificate;

(b) validating and issuing a Kimberly Process Certificate;

(c) liaising with Importing Authorities of other countries;

(d) inspecting rough diamonds shipments or consignments before export;

(e) inspecting and opening contents of shipments or consignments upon delivery; and

(I) any other duty as may be assigned by the Commissioner in respect of import and export of diamonds.

Application for a Kimberley Process certificate

19. (1) An application for a Kimberley Process Certificate for the export of rough diamonds shall be made to the Commissioner in the manner prescribed under this Act.

(2) An application for a Kimberley Process Certificate shall be accompanied by a valid licence or permit to possess rough diamonds.

Contents Kimberley Process Certificate

20. (1) A Kimberley Process Certificate for the export of rough diamonds shall be designed by the Commissioner and shall be -

(a) in the English language;

(b) tamper and forgery resistant; and

(c) in a manner prescribed by the Commissioner under this Act,

Kimberley Process Certificate Signatories

21. The signatories to the Kimberley Process Certificate shall be the-

(a) Governor of the Central Bank;

(b) Commissioner General of the Swaziland Revenue Authority; and

(e) Commissioner of Mines,

Duration of Kimberley Process Certificate

22. (1) A Kimberley Process Certificate for the export or import of a rough diamonds shall be valid for sixty (60) days from date of issue.

PART IV LICENSING

Kinds of licences or permits

23. The kinds of licences or permits that may be granted under this Act are licences or permits to authorizing the holder to-

(a) possess rough diamond;

(b) sell or dispose of rough diamond which is in the lawful possession of that person;

(c) receive or purchase rough diamond which is in the lawful possession of a person from whom it is to be received or purchased;

(d) export rough diamond;

(e) import rough diamond;

(1) polish rough diamond or crush or cut or set a rough diamond in a tool, implement or other article;

(g) possess diamondiferous concentrate outside a restricted area;

(h) export diamondiferous concentrate;

(i) remove sand, soil, clay, gravel, stone, rock or mineral from a restricted area;

(j) export sand, soil, clay, gravel, stone, rock or mineral which it is reasonably believed may contain diamonds;

(k) enter, reside, travel, work or be in, or to visit a restricted area, subject to a condition contained in such permit;

(1) convey rough diamond from one place to another;

Application for a licence

24. (1) An application for a licence or permit under section 23 shall be made to the iNgwenyama in terms of the Mines and Minerals law in force and in the manner prescribed.

(2) The iNgwenyama shall not grant an application unless -

> (a) the business premises upon which the activities for the intended licence are approved by the Commissioner; and
> (b) the applicant meets the requirement for the intended licence or permit as prescribed for a holder of a licence or permit under this Act and the Mines and Minerals law.

Duration of licence

25. (1) A licence granted under this Act shall he valid for one year and may be renewed.

(2) An application for the renewal of a licence shall be made within three months before the date on which such licence expires.

Transfer of licence

26. (1) The Commissioner may, on application by the holder of a licence or permit, authorize by endorsement on the licence or permit any person who is able to carry on such diamond operations for the remaining term of such licence or for any lesser period.

(2) A person to whom a licence or permit has been transferred in terms of sub-section (1) shall furnish a fresh recognizance in the prescribed manner.

(3) A person to whom a licence or permit has been transferred in terms of sub-section (1) shall for the purposes of this Act be the holder of a licence or permit for the remaining term of the licence, or for such lesser period.

Cancellation suspension of licence

27. (1) The Commissioner may cancel a licence or permit forthwith, suspend a licence for a specified period or refuse to renew a licence or permit.

(2) A licence shall not be cancelled, suspended, renewed, refused unless the Commissioner is satisfied that the holder of a licence or permit -

(a) is or has at any time either before or after the commencement of this Act been engaged in illicit trade in diamonds or other precious stones in contravention of this Act or any other law relating to precious stones whether in Swaziland or elsewhere, or is suspected of assisting or having assisted in such trade either in Swaziland or elsewhere;
(b) has been convicted of any offence of which dishonesty is an element and sentenced to a term of imprisonment exceeding six months without the option of a fine or to a fine exceeding Emalangeni five thousand (E5,000) or its equivalent whether in Swaziland or elsewhere, if such conviction in the opinion of the Commissioner renders the holder of a licence or permit unfit to carry on the diamond operation authorized by the licence issued to the holder of a licence or permit;
(c) has failed or is unable to comply with any of the provisions of this Act; or
(d) has failed to comply with a condition imposed in respect of the licence issued under this Act.

Return of cancelled licence

28.(1) A holder of a licence or permit shall return the licence or permit which has been cancelled or suspended under this Act to the Commissioner within seven days after the notification of such cancellation or suspension.

(2) A person who contravenes this section commits an offence and shall on conviction be liable to imprisonment for a period not exceeding one (1) month or to a fine not exceeding Emalangeni one thousand (El ,000.00) or both.

Display of licence at business premises

29. (1) A holder of a licence or permit shall display and keep displayed in some conspicuous place on the licensed premises -

(a) the original licence; and

(b) a list of the persons employed in the licensed premises.

(2) A person who contravenes this section commits an offence and shall on conviction be liable to imprisonment for a period not exceeding one (1) month or to a fine not exceeding Emalangeni one thousand (El,000.00) or both.

Approval of machinery

30.(1) A person, other than a holder of a licence or permit or an employee acting in the course of employment with such holder of a licence or permit who intends to erect or operate a machine designed or adapted for diamond cutting shall obtain written permission from the Commissioner,

(2) A person who contravenes this section commits an offence and shall on conviction be liable to imprisonment for a period not exceeding one (1) year or to a fine not exceeding Emalangeni five thousand (E5,000.00) or both.

PART IV MONITORING

Inspectors

31. (1) The Commissioner may designate a competent public officer as a diamond inspector.

(2) The Commissioner may at any time revoke a designation made under subsection (1).

(3) A diamond inspector designated under subsection (I) shall be issued with an identity card.

(4) Where a Diamond Inspector exercises power or performs a duty in terms of this Act, the diamond inspector shall, at the request of the person affected, produce an identity card.

Duties of inspectors

32. (I) A diamond inspector or authorized officer may, at all reasonable times, enter upon any licensed premises for the purpose of-

(a) inspecting the licenced premises;

(b) ascertaining whether the provisions of this Act are complied with:

(c) giving directions and taking steps to enforce provisions of this Act: and

(d) obtaining such information as the diamond inspector or authorized officer may deem necessary.

(2) For the purposes of this section, “authorized officer” means a person authorized by the Commissioner in writing to conduct inspections.

Search

33. (1) A diamond inspector or police officer of appropriate rank may-

(a) at any reasonable time enter upon and search any licensed premises and may require from the holder of a licence the production of any document or record;

(b) inspect any document or record and make copies of and extracts from, any record required to be kept under this Act;
(c) demand for the production of, and inspect, any diamonds in the possession or under the control of the holder of a licence; and
(d) demand from the holder of a licence or any employee or other person in his employ for information relating to the record in subsection (l) (a) and such diamonds or any other diamonds received by the holder of a licence.

(2) A person who obstructs or hinders a diamond inspector or police officer from the performance of functions in subsection (1) commits an offence and shall on conviction be liable to imprisonment for a period not exceeding ten (10) years or to a fine not exceeding Emalangeni one hundred thousand (El 00, 000.00) or both.

Seizure

34. A diamond inspector or police officer may seize a diamond, machinery, register, document or thing which may be used as evidence under this Act.

Registration of representatives

35. (1) A holder of a licence or permit who intends to appoint another person as an authorized representative, shall apply to the Commissioner on the prescribed form for the registration of that person.

(2) The Commissioner may conduct investigation regarding an application for registration as an authorized representative.

(3) The Commissioner may grant or refuse an application for registration as an authorized representative within 30 days from the date of receipt of the application and shall notify the applicant in writing of the decision.

(4) The Commissioner may, in granting a registration, attach terms and conditions reasonably necessary under the circumstances.

(5) The Commissioner may by notice in writing to the holder of a licence at any time -

(a) cancel or vary any condition determined under subsection (4): or

(b) impose any additional condition in respect of the registration of such authorized representative.

(6) Anything done by an authorized representative before the cancellation or variation of an) condition under subsection *(5)(a)* or the imposition of any condition or further condition under subsection ***(5)(b),*** shall remain valid.

(7) An authorized representative acting within the scope of the prescribed duties shall, on request produce the certificate of registration to such person for inspection.

(8) The Commissioner may on reasonable grounds -

(a) suspend the registration of an authorized representative for such period as the Commissioner ma) determine; or

(b) cancel the registration of an authorized representative with effect from such date as the Commissioner ma) determine; and

(c) the reasons for such suspension or cancellation shall be communicated in writing to the holder of a licence and the authorised representative.

(9) A holder of a licence or permit who has appointed a registered authorized representative shall, upon termination of such appointment, inform the Commissioner in writing of such termination.

(10) A holder of a licence or permit who terminates the appointment of an authorized representative shall, within 30 days after having ceased to be such, return the certificate of registration to the Commissioner.

(11) A person who contravenes this section commits an offence and shall on conviction be liable to imprisonment for a period not exceeding six (6) months or to a fine not exceeding Emalangeni five thousand (E5,000.00) or both.

PART V MISCELLANEOUS

Non-disclosure of information by an employee

36. (1) An employee shall not disclose information or record or document to a person other than a person who is authorized under this Act.

(2) A person who contravenes this section commits an offence and shall on conviction be liable to imprisonment for a period not exceeding ten (10) years or to a fine not exceeding Emalangeni one hundred thousand (El 00000.00) or both.

Preference of purchase of goods and services

37. (1) A holder of a licence shall, in the conduct of the operations under the licence, and in the purchase, construction and installation of facilities, give preference, to the maximum extent possible consistent with safety, quality, efficiency and economy, to-

(a) materials and products made in Swaziland: and

(b) service agencies located in Swaziland and owned by Swazi citizens or bodies corporate registered under the Companies Act.

(2) A holder of a licence shall, in the operations under the licence, conduct training programs in consultation with the Commissioner for the benefit of employees that they may qualify for advancement.

(3) The Commissioner may suspend or cancel a licence issued under this Act where there is reasonable proof that the holder of a licence does not comply with the provisions of this section.

False statements

38. A person who makes a statement knowing it to he false or causes to he made a statement, which is false commits an offence and shall on conviction be liable to imprisonment to a term not exceeding one (1) year or a [me not exceeding Emalangeni ten thousand (El 0, 000.00) or both.

Falsifying records

39, A person who knowingly makes or causes to be made or connives at the making of a false entry in a record required to be kept under this Act or who prevents the making of a correct entry therein commits an offence and shall on conviction be liable to imprisonment to a term not exceeding one (1) year or a [me not exceeding Emalangeni ten thousand (El 0. 000.00) or both.

Indemnity of officers

40. A public officer or any other authorized officer shall not beheld personally liable for anything done or omitted to be done in good faith in the performance of duties under this Act.

Regulations

41. The Minister may make regulations for carrying into effect of this Act and may provide (a) the maintenance of discipline and the good order and well-being of the diamond industry;

(a) the type of licence or permit;

(b) the type of an application to be made under this Act;
(c) the type of a notice to be issued or published under this Act;
(d) the terms and conditions attaching to any licence or permit provided for under this Act;
(e) the nature of an endorsement to be made on a licence or permit under this Act.
(f) the returns to be furnished by holder of a licence or permit holder;

(g) prescribing anything which in terms of this Act is to or may he prescribed;

(i) design and contents of a Kimberly Process Certificate; and

(j) the terms and conditions pertaining to the Kimberley Process Certification Scheme.

PROCEDURES FOR APPLYING AND HANDLING APPLICATIONS FOR RECONNAISSANCE, PROSPECTING AND MINING LICENCE IN SWAZILAND.

1. A person who seeks to acquire a mineral right must submit a letter of intent to the Commissioner of Mines stating the desire to acquire a mineral right.

2. The letter of intent to acquire to a mineral right must be in one standard A4 paper size written on one side including the name of the person, or company, type of mineral right sought (reconnaissance, prospecting or mining right) and the mineral(s) of interest.

3. On receipt of the letter of intent, the Commissioner of Mines shall issue an Application Form to the person for the mineral activity required, namely; reconnaissance, prospecting or mining.

4. The applicant shall supply the required information in the Application Form and return the completed Application Form to the Commissioner of Mines.

5. On submission of a completed Application Form, the Commissioner of Mines shall issue a Reference Number to the applicant for ease of reference and subsequent enquiry by the applicant.

6. The Commissioner of Mines shall present the application to the Minerals Management Board for consideration.

7. The Minerals Management Board appraises the application taking into consideration of the attachments.

8. On satisfactory assessment of the application, the Minerals Management Board invites the applicant to come and motivate the application.

9. The Minerals Management Board makes an opinion of the project proposed based on the information supplied in the application form, presentation, motivation and other references made regarding the proposed project.

10. The Minerals Management Board recommends the most comprehensive project proposal to *iNgwenyama* for consideration for a grant of a mining right

11. Each applicant shall be notified in writing of the outcome of the application within twenty (21) days after appearing before the Minerals Management Board.

PROCEDURES FOR HANDLING APPLICATIONS FOR RECONNAISSANCE, PROSPECTING AND MINING LICENCE. In terms of Section 214 of the Constitution of Swaziland 2005, the Minerals Management Board hereby adopts the following processes for execution of its task.

OBJECTIVE

The objective of this arrangement is to ensure that the applicant submits all pertinent information at the initial stage to enable a speedy processing of application(s).

There shall be standard forms that shall be used for mineral rights applications. These forms state all specific attachments that are required with each application.

1. MINERAL RIGHTS APPLICATIONS REQUIREMENTS

(a) all applications for mineral rights must be made on the prescribed forms which are obtainable from the Commissioner of Mines;

(b) each application for mineral right shall be accompanied by the prescribed fees for each type of mineral;

(c) all applications for mineral rights that are submitted must include the attachments listed on the application forms; failure to provide the information requested on the forms shall result in rejection of the application;

(d) all applications for mineral rights are addressed to the Commissioner of Mines for appraisal before consideration by the Minerals Management Board. In order to facilitate a speedy evaluation of applications and onward processing of grants there is a requirement for specific attachments with every application form. The attachments differ with the type of licence as itemised below: -

1.1 Application for Reconnaissance

An application for a reconnaissance licence shall be accompanied by the following attachments: - (a) a proposed work programme of reconnaissance operations;

(b) a costed Project Brief;1 (c) a statement of financial resources available to the applicant to carry out the proposed reconnaissance operations under the licence and to comply with conditions of the licence; (d) a statement of relevant experience and technical resources available to the applicant to carry out the proposed reconnaissance operations under the licence and to comply with conditions of the licence;

1 Project Brief as required by the Swaziland Environmental Authority for purposes of the Environmental Management Act 2000 in order to categorise a project for Environmental Impact Assessment (EIA), Comprehensive Mitigation Plan (CMP) and Environmental Compliance Certificate (ECC).

(e) a statement that specifies the applicant's proposals with respect to employment and training of citizens of Swaziland;

(f) applicants and directors of companies that have applied for a mineral right licence will be subjected to a vetting process through ITC or similar agents to ensure /establish their historical background;

(g) any other information that the Commissioner of Mines may reasonably require for the consideration of the application by the Minerals Management Board.

1.2 Application for Prospecting Licence

An application for a prospecting licence shall be accompanied by the following attachments: - (a) a proposed work programme of operations; (b) a costed Project Brief; (c) a statement of financial resources available to the applicant to carry out the proposed operations under the licence and to comply with conditions of the licence;

(d) a statement of relevant experience and technical resources available to the applicant to carry out the proposed operations under the licence and to comply with conditions of the licence;

(e) a letter of guarantee on the funding of the project or letter of comfort on the financing of the project from a credible financial institution/financier in addition to the financial statement;

(f) a statement that specifies the applicant's proposals with respect to employment and training of citizens of Swaziland;

(g) a declaration that applicant shall endeavour to procure local goods and services;

(h) applicants and directors of companies that have applied for a mineral right licence will be subjected to a vetting process through ITC or similar agents to ensure /establish their historical background;

(i) any other information that the Commissioner of Mines may reasonably require for the consideration of the application by the Minerals Management Board.

1.3 Application for Mining Licence

An application for a mining licence shall be accompanied by the following attachments: -

(a) a proposed programme of mining operations, that shall outline mine forecasts, operation plans

(b) a proposed programme of options for minerals beneficiation or value addition;

(c) a costed Project Brief;

(c) a statement of financial resources available to the applicant to carry out the proposed operations under the licence and to comply with conditions of the licence; (d) a statement of relevant experience and technical resources available to the applicant to carry out the proposed operations under the licence and to comply with conditions of the licence;

(e) a letter of guarantee on the funding of the project or letter of comfort on the financing of the project from a credible financial institution/financier in addition to the financial statement;

(f) applicants and directors of companies that have applied for a mineral right licence will be subjected to a vetting process through ITC or similar agents to ensure /establish their historical background;

(g) a statement regarding the mineral deposits in the area of land over which the licence is sought that includes details of all known minerals as well as possible mineral resources;

(h) a statement that specifies the applicant's proposals with respect to employment and training of citizens of Swaziland;

(i) a declaration that applicant shall endeavour to procure local goods and services;

(j) a statement that specifies the applicant's proposals with respect to community development;

(k) any other information that the Commissioner of Mines may reasonably require for the consideration of the application by the Minerals Management Board

2. CONSIDERATION OF APPLICATIONS

The Minerals Management Board shall not recommend a reconnaissance licence or a prospecting licence, or a mining licence unless it is satisfied that – (a) the area of land over which the licence is sought is reasonable having regard to the applicant's proposed programme of operations; (b) the applicant has adequate - (i) financial resources; (ii) technical competence and (iii) relevant industry experience to carry out the proposed programme of operations; (c) the applicant has submitted a costed project brief in the prescribed form; (d) the applicant's proposals with respect to the procurement of local goods and services are acceptable; (e) the applicant's proposals with respect to community development are acceptable; (f) the applicant's proposals with respect to employment and training of citizens of Swaziland are acceptable; (g) any other information that the Commissioner of Mines may reasonably require for the consideration of the application by the Minerals Management Board. (h) the proposal of the applicant with respect to the local beneficiation and value addition of minerals is acceptable

3. CONSIDERATION OF APPLICATIONS FOR MINES DUMPS.

(a) The Minerals Management Board shall not recommend a licence that would confer a right to work a mine dump on land that is the subject of another mineral right unless –

(i) the holder of that other mineral right has been given a reasonable opportunity to comment on the application; and,

(ii) the Board has satisfied itself that the holder of the other mineral right would not be substantially

disadvantaged if the licence were to be recommended for granting; (iii) where sub-section (a) applies, the Minerals Management Board may –

1. impose special conditions in a licence to work a mine dump; and

2. amend the existing mineral right to impose new terms and conditions, for the purpose of ensuring that the operations permitted under the mineral rights concerned can proceed with the minimal disturbance to the operations of the other.

(b) any other information that the Commissioner of Mines may reasonably require for the consideration of the application by the Minerals Management Board.

4. APPLICATION OF ENVIRONMENTAL LAWS AND REGULATIONS

The grant of a mineral right shall require compliance with the environmental laws and regulations.

(a) submission of the relevant Project Brief is a pre-requisite in order for the Commissioner of Mines and the Swaziland Environmental Authority (SEA) to assess and classify the project according to the Environmental Management Act;

(b) an Environmental Impact Assessment (EIA) shall lead to a Comprehensive Mitigation Plan (CMP) which shall be used to regulate the management of the environment where the grant is made.

4.1 Requirement for Environmental Compliance Certificate

A mineral right shall not be granted unless and until – (a) the Commissioner of Mines has received from the Applicant an Environmental Compliance Certificate (ECC); and (b) the ECC has been endorsed by the Environmental Authority where required under the environmental laws and regulations.

4.2 Environmental bond

There shall be no prospecting licence, or mining licence granted unless and until the applicant for such a licence has provided a bond or other financial security to the Commissioner of Mines in accordance with this section. The holder of a prospecting licence or a mining licence shall provide the Commissioner of Mines with –

(a) a bond; or

(b) some other form of financial security that is satisfactory to the Minerals Management Board that shall be sufficient to cover the costs associated with the implementation of the environmental and rehabilitation obligations set out in the site rehabilitation and mine-closure plans of the holder of the licence;

(c) the form and amount of the bond or other security specified in (a) shall be determined by the Minerals Management Board having regard to the characteristics of the particular project;

(d) there shall be progressive or concurrent site rehabilitation where feasible before the programme of work is completed;

(e) the amount secured by the bond or other financial security may be reduced by an amount determined by the Minerals Management Board if part of the environmental and rehabilitation obligations set out in the site rehabilitation and mine-closure plans are completed during the term of the licence; (f) the bond or other financial security specified in (a) shall be released to the holder when all the environmental and rehabilitation obligations set out in the site rehabilitation and mine-closure plans have been completed to the satisfaction of the Commissioner of Mines;

5. THE OFFICE OF THE COMMISSIONER OF MINES

These procedures suggest that an office of the Commissioner of Mines is established, which shall consist of mine engineers, an inspectorate and other officers as well as operational budgets, as the Commissioner of Mines may consider necessary. The Commissioner of Mines is also custodian of other ancillary Acts and Regulations namely Explosives Act and the Mines, Health and Safety Act. He is responsible for private sector mineral exploitation and civil works that relate to mining. The Commissioner of Mines gives executive direction to the Mining Department.

5.1 Functions of the Commissioner of Mines

The Commissioner of Mines shall –

(a) receive applications for appraisal, assess for completeness and present to the Minerals Management Board for assessment and consideration;

(b) upon receipt of an application for a mineral right made in accordance with these procedures, the Commissioner of Mines shall, within 30 days, submit the application together with a written report of appraisal on it to the Minerals Management Board;

(c) upon receipt of an application for the renewal of a mineral right made in accordance with these procedures, the Commissioner of Mines shall, within 14 days, submit the application together with a written report of appraisal on it to the Minerals Management Board;

(d) the Commissioner of Mines shall, within sixty days of the receipt of an application for a reconnaissance or a prospecting or a mining licence, and thereafter at thirty-days intervals, notify the applicant of the measures being taken regarding consideration of the application;

(e) issue mineral rights licences that have been granted by iNgwenyama under the auspices of the Minerals Management Board;

(f) ascertain whether the provisions of these procedures and the terms and conditions of any mineral rights and minerals agreement are being complied with;

(g) give directions and to take steps necessary to enforce the provisions of these procedures and the terms and conditions of mineral rights and minerals agreement to recommend to the Minerals Management Board suspension or cancellation of Mineral Rights Licences;

(h) maintain a Register of Mineral Rights Licences granted by iNgwenyama under the auspices of the Minerals Management Board;

(i) obtain information necessary for the administration of these procedures; and

(j) perform such other functions and exercise as are specified in these procedures and directed that by the Minerals Management Board.

CONDUCT BY APPLICANTS

(a) applicants shall not lobby any Board Member for purposes of influencing or inducing the outcome or expediting the processing and consideration of their application;

(b) applicants shall not make any bribe, offer, undertaking or promise to a Board Member this shall lead to disqualification of the Applicant.

NATIONAL ENERGY POLICY

3.1 COAL

3.1.1 OVERVIEW

Coal is the only naturally occurring fossil fuel in the country. The coal reserves, defined as "run-of- mine" reserves, amount to 207.6 million tonnes, while the probable and potential reserves are estimated to be at least 1 billion tonnes. Swaziland therefore holds large resources that are untapped.

At present the Maloma Colliery is the only operating mine. Maloma exports all of its production, which fluctuates considerably due to market conditions. In 2000, the production was 228,000 tonnes compared to the 1998 level of 410,000 tonnes. Another mine, EmaSwati Coal Mine based at Mpaka, was closed mainly due to the low international coal prices around 1990-1992. Other potential mining areas are at Mhlume, Hlane, Lubhuku, St Philips and Mpaka Area 3.

The coal reserves consist of semi-anthracite and anthracite coal, which have a high energy content and low content of volatiles and sulphur. While anthracitic coal can be used for power generation, it is presently more valuable if sold for industrial purposes. Domestic anthracitic coal is therefore exported for use in the metallurgical and cement industries, while cheaper bituminous coal is imported from South Africa for use as a fuel. In 1999, imported bituminous coal amounted to 243,000 tonnes.

While the anthracitic coal has good characteristics for use in the metallurgical industry, when used as a fuel it has some limitations, such as poor ignition characteristics and clinkerisation of ash. The most appropriate indigenous coal that could be used in industry, as well as for power generation, is semi-anthracite, which constitutes the greater part of the national coal reserves. However, both the anthracite and semi-anthracite coals would require retrofits to boilers, stoves etc if they were to be used locally.

Most of the bituminous coal imported from South Africa is used in the sugar and pulp industries and to a lesser degree in households. In some cases coal is used for combined heat and power generation within the industries. Import of coal is mainly done directly by the industries.

While the export of the indigenous coal is beneficial to the overall economy of Swaziland, there is a need to review its use for energy purposes within the country. This would have advantages with regard to employment, particularly in the mining sector, security of energy supply and establishing a local market to sustain the mines. Domestic anthracitic coal is also less polluting than imported bituminous coal in terms of sulphur emissions. However, coal is one of the most polluting fuels with high emissions of CO_2. There are therefore both advantages and disadvantages regarding the increased use of coal. The benefits of coal use must therefore be weighed against the global and local environmental consequences. Another important question is national security of energy supply. If investments are to be made for intensified use of indigenous coal it must be ascertained that the supply actually is available and will continue to be in the longer term.

Local coal could potentially be used for the following industrial purposes: gasification plant fuel, cement and ceramics kiln fuel, thermal power generation fuel, in the manufacture of carbides and electrodes, and as a reductant in the ferro-alloy industry. Such industries are not yet present in Swaziland. For household purposes it should be noted that coal used indoors can cause health problems and local environmental problems. However, the local anthracitic coal is a low smoke fuel compared to imported low quality bituminous coal and therefore not as damaging to both health and the local environment.

The lack of a Mining Policy in Swaziland in the past has been a hindrance in the development of the mining industry in general. Once the Mining Policy is in place, there may be some interesting possibilities for an increased use of Swaziland's coal resources. However, these must be weighed carefully against the drawbacks, which include health considerations, global and local environmental effects and costs.

3.1.2 MAIN ISSUES

From an energy point of view, the key policy issues in this sector include the need to:

- Establish the real costs and benefits of expanded coal use in the country and if feasible, ensure a conducive and enabling environment so as to encourage development and investment in the coal industry in Swaziland;

- Ensure that the environmental damage resulting from the use of coal is monitored and kept to a minimum;

- Maximise skills and expertise from returning employees in the coal mining industry; and

- Improve production in local coal mines.

3.1.3 SUBSTITUTING IMPORTED COAL FOR INDIGENOUS COAL

Use of indigenous anthracite and semi-anthracite coal could enhance energy security of supply, benefit balance of payments and reduce local pollution. However, indigenous coal is more expensive and requires investment in retrofitting of boilers, stoves etc. If such equipment can be produced in Swaziland this may also benefit local employment in the manufacturing industry and the use of returning miners' expertise and skills in increasing coal mining operations.

Government will conduct a cost-benefit analysis regarding increased use of indigenous coal in the industry and households taking due consideration of the environmental and health consequences.

The use of clean coal technologies will in particular be assessed by all stakeholders involved in the utilisation of coal.

3.1.4 ESTABLISHMENT OF A COAL-FIRED THERMAL POWER STATION IN SWAZILAND

Swaziland today imports electricity from South Africa at a relatively low unit price, making indigenous electricity generation less favourable from a purely economical point of view. However, the present surplus of generating capacity in South Africa is expected to diminish in the coming years. In the medium term, import prices for electricity may increase significantly, thereby making local power generation more attractive. The establishment of a power station may also allow Swaziland to be an active player in the SAPP with the potential to sell power in the regional market. The 400kV line and electricity network strengthening has made it possible to import and export electricity within the SADC region.

A number of feasibility studies have been carried out by the private sector regarding the establishment of a coal-fired thermal power station. However, these studies focused on commercial and financial interests rather than the social, economic and environmental interests of the country.

A feasibility study on the establishment of a coal-fired thermal power station will be conducted.

This study shall include strategic considerations such as increased security of supply and the question of mining semi-anthracite coal from the now closed coal mine and from other potential sites. This study shall also assess the environmental and social aspects and the involvement of locals in the mining industry. Government, in co-operation with the private sector, could jointly conduct the study.

3.1.5 POTENTIAL FOR COAL-BED METHANE

There are no known coal-bed methane reserves in Swaziland but there may be need for further investigation to ascertain if such additional energy resources could be available. A barrier for such an investigation is the costs involved.

The resource potential for coal-bed methane and its use for energy purposes will be investigated.

3.1.6 PRICING AND TAXATION OF COAL

Currently, prices are not regulated and there are neither incentives nor levies or extra taxation for using coal for energy purposes. Pricing mechanisms , if developed, could be powerful instruments used to support policies on the use of coal and the type of coal used.

Government will investigate the appropriateness of various pricing incentives and taxation so as to encourage the use of clean coal technologies.

Studies on the potential uses of local coal may facilitate the implementation of policies. Means of implementing this policy could include approaches such as stimulating mechanisms whereby the use of clean coal technologies is rewarded and regulations whereby the use of dirtier technologies is restricted.

3.1.7 TIME-FRAME FOR COAL UTILISATION

Since Swaziland's known resources of coal could cover more than 500 years of production, the need for future coal supply and present consumption are not in conflict.

Government will facilitate sustainable and expedient utilisation of the coal resources by private sector interests, in line with sustainable human development goals articulated in the NDS.

There is a need to provide a conducive environment for investments in coal mining and the establishment of coal based local enterprises. The Mining Policy will address these concerns and hence make it easier for prospective investors to undertake mining operations. Local coal mines will be encouraged to increase production, especially for export. In addition, it is necessary to keep an up-to-date data system to monitor the coal resources.

3.2 PETROLEUM PRODUCTS

3.2.1 OVERVIEW

Swaziland holds no known reserves of oil. All petroleum products are imported from the Republic of South Africa through five international oil companies: Shell, BP, Engen, Total and Caltex. The petroleum products are imported via rail and road and in most cases distributed from the storage depots in Matsapha. Presently, there are two main suppliers of LPG and a number of suppliers of lubricating oils.

The Government considers the supply of petroleum products to be of strategic importance. Therefore prices of petrol, diesel and illuminating paraffin are subject to regulation. Petrol and diesel are significant inputs in the production process and are a livelihood for many local businesses in public transportation. The price of illuminating paraffin on the other hand is monitored because it is a fuel for low-income groups. The market sets prices of the other petroleum products such as lubricating oil, jet fuel, heavy fuel oil and LPG. The price of LPG is at present not regulated even though mainly low-income households use it.

With regard to pricing of petroleum products the global trend is to leave the pricing to market forces. For Swaziland the situation is that all petroleum products are presently imported from South Africa where there is a regulation of product prices. The In-Land-Bonded-Cost (IBLC) of the product to the port of Durban, deemed to be purchased from Bahrain and Singapore, influences the cost of landed fuel at Matsapha (import parity).

Additionally, Government imposes the following taxes and levies: Fuel Tax, Sales Tax, Customs and Excise Duty, Fuel Oil Levy and MVA (third party insurance). The profit margins for the industry and retailers, other costs related to handling, transportation and storage of the products are added, finally giving the retail price at the pump. The main influences on the calculated prices are the international oil prices and the exchange rate between US $ and the Lilangeni. The same pricing model (IBLC) is used in all SACU Member Countries.

The Ministry monitors international pricing conditions as well as each product's slate position on a monthly basis. Proposals for changes in the prices of regulated products are discussed and recommended by the Fuel Pricing Committee. The Committee comprises representatives from Government Ministries, the petroleum sector and consumer interests. The Fuel Price Controller, in consultation with the Minister for Natural Resources and Energy, approves prices based on the Committee's recommendations. One of the roles of the Ministry is to protect the interests of consumers and to ensure access to affordable petroleum products.

The number of retail stations is controlled through the Petrol Rationalisation Committee. The committee has the objective of controlling the number of retail outlets so as to maintain economic viability in the industry while also encouraging high service standards for the consumer and public. The committee achieves its role through a Service Station Rationalisation Plan (RATPLAN), which is a five-year-plan. The RATPLAN is not a legal document but an agreement amongst the five companies and Government on the sharing and location of sites and the number of retail outlets.

The Ministry will embark on the process of updating, amending and consolidating existing pieces of legislation on petroleum to produce an all-embracing and comprehensive Petroleum Act. Relevant legislation includes the Fuel Oil levy Act of 1980, the Price Control Order of 1973, and the Petroleum legislation of 1959. In addition, a draft bill has also been completed, to establish an Energy Regulatory Authority primarily for the electricity sector. However, it is intended that regulation of the petroleum sector will be incorporated at a later date.

Security of supply especially for petroleum products continues to be a problem. Current petroleum fuel storage capacity stands on average at 5-7 days. This is considered to be very low compared to other countries and a cause for concern because Swaziland, as a landlocked country, has few alternative options in case of major supply disruptions, which could for example be as a result of accidents in refineries, natural disasters etc.

In 1990, the Ministry embarked on a prefeasibility study concerning strategic fuel depots and a feasibility study on ethanol blending using the molasses from the three sugar mills in the country. There is therefore a need to conduct studies that will investigate the viability of establishing strategic stocks for the country, including the site, size and organisational structure. The possibilities for blending petrol with ethanol or other biofuels also needs to be investigated.

There are large natural gas resources in the region that have been discovered and are being exploited. The Ministry, through regional and international forums, will explore opportunities for taking advantage of this energy resource for the diversification of energy supplies to the country.

3.2.2 MAIN ISSUES

The challenges for the petroleum sector include the following:

- Regulation of the petroleum industry;

· Ensuring adequate product availability in rural areas while not undermining the oil industry's economic competitiveness;

· Ensuring stable and reliable product availability for the country's various economic sectors;

· Achieving regional competitiveness and fair pricing of petroleum fuels;

· Encouraging meaningful and sustainable participation of locals in the industry;

· Ensuring that jobs, particularly on the forecourts, are not jeopardised and that new jobs are created; and

· Ensuring adequate commercial storage of petroleum products.

3.2.3 REGULATION OF THE PETROLEUM INDUSTRY

The Government regulates the petroleum industry in the country, i.e. petrols, diesel and paraffin. All companies importing and distributing petroleum products must be registered with the Ministry. The retailing of petroleum products is regulated through the RATPLAN. Pricing is regulated using the SACU In-Bond-Landed-Cost (IBLC) model.

Swaziland's petroleum market is closely linked to SACU, which implements the system of regulating petroleum product prices according to the IBLC formula. This formula is undergoing review in order to make it relevant for today's trading environments as well as to improve its transparency.

Price regulation shall be maintained in the short term and will be subject to review so as to ascertain its appropriateness and relevance in the longer term.

Government will closely monitor the oil market and pricing issues in practice and evaluate the need for revised regulation of the petroleum product prices. The procedures for price regulation will be reviewed in the proposed Petroleum Act. In the longer term the liberalisation of the petroleum market will be considered subject to regional developments. The Government, in collaboration with the Oil Industry and SACU and/or SADC Member States, will also strive to work towards a pricing mechanism that reflects the true costs of importing products into the country. Meanwhile the Government will consider if regulation of oil prices shall only apply to the wholesale prices and let the local market determine the retail prices.

Government will investigate deregulation options in the medium to long term.

The regulatory framework will be monitored and reviewed on a regular basis or in the event of a significant development in the regional or international environment. Government will investigate the regulation of other petroleum products. The regime of price regulation in Southern Africa will need to be taken into account.

The Ministry is presently the regulator on petroleum prices, however the regulatory function may be transferred to the proposed Energy Regulatory Authority (ERA) at a future date.

3.2.4 MARKETING AND DISTRIBUTION

The Service Station Rationalisation Plan (RATPLAN) intends to secure availability of oil products around Swaziland by regulating the number of outlets while taking economic development of the oil industry into consideration.

Regulation of service stations and fuel outlets by means of the Rationalisation Plan will be maintained, and modifications to the Plan will be effected every five years.

For effectiveness of the RATPLAN, Government will ensure that newcomers in the market also comply. In future, trading licenses for petroleum wholesale and retail should be obtained from the Ministry of Natural Resources and Energy in order to improve governance of the sector. This will be reflected in the proposed Petroleum Act, including legalising the RATPLAN. In the meantime, closer co-ordination between the Ministry of Enterprise and Employment and the Ministry when issuing licenses for petroleum marketing is necessary.

Since access to modern energy services in rural areas is one of the key objectives of the energy policy, means to improve suppiy and distribution of petroleum products in rural areas should be investigated.

Government in collaboration with the oil industry (including LPG suppliers) will develop effective means of ensuring adequate access to petroleum products.

Government will work closely with local businesses involved in the petroleum industry especially the dealer councils and associations.

3.2.5 COMMERCIAL FUEL STORAGE FACILITIES

The oil industry's storage facilities are located in Matsapha. Normally the storage holds supply for 5-7 days of operations, while dealers hold 2-3 days of supply. At present there are limited possibilities to expand the storage facilities in Matsapha. These stocks are maintained to secure smooth operation of the supply chain under normal circumstances. In case of major disruptions in the oil supplies, these stocks may not be adequate. This is a critical issue because, being a landlocked country, Swaziland has few alternative supply routes for fuel in case of supply problems.

Government will require commercial companies to store a minimum quantity of stocks to ensure fuel availability.

An appropriate minimum will be determined in collaboration with the oil industry taking into consideration the costs involved.

3.2.6 PROCUREMENT

Procurement of oil products for commercial use is a natural part of the industry's activities, which may be best taken care of by the companies in the market. Government's interests are in ensuring good product quality so as to protect local consumers and also encouraging diversity of product sourcing.

Government will put in place quality control measures that will ensure that marketers of oil products adhere to agreed product specifications - including environmental considerations - and that these conform to regional and/or international standards.

Government needs to carefully consider in the future investigating means and ways to participate and get involved in the procurement of this product. This could be done in the most cost-effective manner in partnership with one of the players in the industry.

Government will ensure diversification of the sources of petroleum products imported into the country so as to enhance security of supply as well take advantage of competitively priced fuels available in the international markets.

The establishment of a refinery has also been debated on several occasions; however the size of the local market and the logistical problems in exporting from the refinery, as well as the huge investment costs do not favour such an idea at present. However, in the medium to long term, the establishment of a refinery may be an option and this position will be reviewed when the need arises.

3.2.7 INVOLVEMENT OF LOCALS

Today, all oil companies are foreign international companies trading as local companies. More local involvement in the industry could be achieved through the development of programmes to assist interested locals in entering the market. Other opportunities include increased involvement of locals in providing services to the industry such as the maintenance of dispensing and other technical systems.

Government will ensure the oil industry increases the involvement of locals.

Government is also considering the establishment of a national oil company responsible for the strategic stockholding, in co-operation with the oil industry.

3.2.8 USE OF INDIGENOUS BIOFUELS

There are some plants that can be grown specifically for oil extraction to use a biofuel, e.g. maize. rape seed, sunflower seed, jathropa cursas, and euphorbia. Some of the oils can directly substitute petroleum fuels like paraffin and diesel, although blending with other fuels is the predominant method of using biofuels. It is technically feasible to produce ethanol from molasses, a by-product of sugar manufacturing. There are presently two companies in the country producing ethanol from molasses.

Ethanol can be used as a supplement for petroleum; but it must be ensured that the petrol meets the required specifications for the country's vehicles. The use of ethanol will have positive environmental effects and also benefit the balance of payments and economic development in the industries concerned. Ethanol blending with petroleum takes place in some countries and many of the technological problems have been resolved. The commercial introduction of this option in the local market is therefore the main issue.

Government will conduct further investigations on blending ethanol with petrol with a focus on introducing products in the local markets.

It is envisaged that a small-scale demonstration project will be commissioned in consultation with vehicle dealers and the oil industry, before embarking on a full-scale scheme, if this option is found appropriate.

3.2.9 PRICING AND DISTRIBUTION OF LIQUEFIED PETROLEUM GAS (LPG)

The LPG market is not regulated, as is the case for other petroleum products; and the suppliers and dealers are not part of any stakeholder group. The price for LPG varies considerably across the country. It is to a high degree used in the urban and peri-urban areas by low and middle income households; the distribution to remote areas is costly.

Government will monitor pricing of LPG products more closely and will facilitate a closer dialogue between herself, suppliers and dealers.

The need for price regulation of LPG will be investigated. Government will also ensure the distribution of information on the safe use of LPG.

3.3 ELECTRICITY

3.3.1 OVERVIEW

Electricity supply and use is one of the most important themes within the energy sector in Swaziland. The organisational infrastructure, the technical performance, and delivery mechanism are just a few of the challenges the sector faces.

The mission for the Swaziland electricity supply industry is to provide affordable and accessible electricity to meet social and economic needs, in a financially and environmentally sustainable manner, while optimising the use of national energy and infrastructure resources.

The global trend is liberalisation of the electricity sector. The objectives of this liberalisation are that electricity should be produced more efficiently and traded in competitive markets and thus result in lower tariffs. New investments and new players could also be attracted to the business. This situation puts specific emphasis on how the sector should be regulated and how the existing utilities shall be reorganised in order to survive in the new environment with increased competition.

Swaziland's electricity supply is to a high degree dependent on imported electricity from South Africa. This is a cause for concern with regard to security of supply since almost all supplies come from one source. Increased utilisation of local energy resources – hydro, coal, biomass, solar and wind - could alleviate this problem. However, the situation today is that electricity imports are relatively cheap due to excess capacity in the region. Therefore new technologies may seem uneconomic in the shorter term. In the longer term the regional excess capacity is expected to diminish and imports prices may therefore increase making other supply alternatives more attractive.

Also, Swaziland faces challenges regarding the security, reliability and quality of supplies as the local electricity supply often experiences power cuts. This is a consequence of a combination of poor weather conditions with excessive lightening and a weak power grid with little reserve capacity. The country has for a long time been supplied from three 132 kV lines. The integration of the 400 kV transmission line will now improve the power supply situation.

Another important question is the extension of electricity supply. Only about 20% of the population are connected to the grid and there is a huge gap between the urban and rural households with regard to connection. On average 40-50% of urban households are connected, whereas in rural areas only about 5% of the households are connected. Access to electricity is considered an important part of the standard and quality of life and alleviation of poverty. Social and economic consequences of extended supply must therefore be carefully considered and evaluated against each other.

Further extension of the electricity supply is not only a technical problem. The major problem is that extending the grid into sparsely populated areas is uneconomic from the utilities point of view, because the electricity consumption is too low compared to the grid extension and maintenance costs.

In 1999 electricity counted for 10% of Swaziland's total energy consumption. Of the total electricity consumption of 988 GWh, 15% is consumed by the households, 14% by the agricultural sector while industry, commerce and services account for 71%. Most of the electricity consumed in industry can be attributed to a small number of large companies.

The Government owned Swaziland Electricity Board (SEB) has monopoly on the import, distribution and supply of electricity through the national grid. SEB operates according to the Electricity Act of 1963 and the Public Enterprises (Control and Monitoring) Act of 1989.

In addition to the electricity supplied from SEB, some of the major industries produce electricity for their own industrial consumption and for their company towns. These companies are connected to the national grid but do not sell the generated electricity to SEB.

As described in figure 8, the total electricity supply in Swaziland in 1999 amounted to 1,100 GWh. Of this 639 GWh (58.1%) was imported from South Africa by SEB. 196 GWh (17.8%) was produced from domestic hydro power plants, mainly operated by SEB. SEB also produced 1.4 GWh (0.1%) from their diesel generator. The industries produced 264 GWh (24.0%).

In the National Development Strategy it is stated that future options for the development of the Swaziland electricity supply industry shall be identified and options for competition and private sector participation shall be investigated.

Swaziland is a party to the SADC Protocol on Energy of 1996 and a member of the Southern African Power Pool (SAPP). The SAPP enables SEB to trade freely within the Power Pool with respect to purchase of bulk power and energy.

The SADC Energy Protocol states that the members of SADC shall strive towards an integrated power system that would be productively used and optimally managed in an environmentally sound manner.

The protocol sets forth the following guidelines for regional integration and co-operation: electricity trading and power pooling shall be promoted within the SAPP; integrated resource planning in the electricity sector shall be promoted; a regional electricity master plan shall be developed; and common regional standards, rules and procedures relevant to generation, transmission and distribution of electricity shall be promoted, particularly in areas where the region holds a comparative advantage.

The electricity infrastructure shall be developed and utilised in an environmentally sound manner, and electricity projects shall be subject to environmental impact assessments in conformity with agreed standards. Universal and affordable service to all citizens and the importance of quality customer service in national electricity policies shall be emphasised.

3.3.2 MAIN ISSUES

There are therefore many challenges facing Swaziland's electricity sector. These may include:

- The globalisation trend in the world towards liberalising energy markets with consequences on ownership, re-organisation and investment;
- Ensuring reliability and quality of power supplies;
- Inefficiencies in the Electricity Supply Industry;
- Introduction of a regulatory framework capable of securing a market oriented electricity supply industry, which at the same time attracts new players and investments;
- Increased use of indigenous energy resources for electricity generation, thereby contributing to the security of supply;
- Securing development of the sector in an environmentally sustainable manner;
- Ensuring continuing increase of quality and reliability of electricity supply;
- Affordability of electricity supply for consumers;
- Increasing access of electricity throughout the country; and
- Increasing cost reflectivity and transparency of electricity tariffs.

3.3.3 RESTRUCTURING OF THE ELECTRICITY SUPPLY INDUSTRY (ESI)

As in many countries in the region, the ESI in Swaziland is undergoing major reforms that intend to liberalise the industry and allow more effective private sector participation.

Presently, the legislation and regulation of the Swaziland ESI is based on the 1963 Electricity Act. This Act is considered amongst all parties to be outdated and not reflective of recent developments in the ESI. Government's objectives for the ESI, among others, are to:

- Improve quality and reliability of supply;
- Facilitate economic development by increasing access;
- Attract/ facilitate private sector involvement in the ESI;
- Mobilise finance;
- Increase commercialisation/customer orientation in the ESI;
- Reform the legal and regulatory framework;
- Improve ease of connection and reduce costs;
- Increase public acceptability;

- Enhance security of supply; and
- Ensure consistency with international trends.

In March 1998, Cabinet made a decision to corporatise the utility and establish an independent regulatory authority. The aim of the restructuring process is to facilitate the commercialisation of the ESI through a new legal framework and regulatory reform. This will allow private participation and third party access, enable the monitoring of performance and allow reform and transparency in pricing. In this context corporatisation means the transfer of SEB from a Governmental parastatal to a company operating under the Companies Act.

Following Government's decision, a review of the 1963 Electricity Act was undertaken and new Electricity and Energy Regulatory Authority Bills will be in place in the short term. The legal status of SEB will evolve in stages in line with Government's Privatisation Policy. The initial corporasitation will not affect the ownership, as the new company will remain fully owned by Government. An independent Energy Regulatory Authority, once in place, will be responsible for the monitoring and controlling of the industry and the issuing of licences. In the initial stages, it will regulate the electricity industry; in the future its mandate will be expected to cover the whole energy sector. Realising that Swaziland is a small country, steps would be undertaken to ensure that, before the electricity market is unbundled, the market will be developed to sustain itself and to make sure that the energy supply is not neglected.

Government will continue with the present restructuring process and will investigate the various commercialisation opportunities for the electricity supply industry.

A timetable for restructuring will be put in place in the short term, with clear objectives and targets and procedures for review and monitoring. Through the restructuring of the electricity supply industry Government will ease the way for attracting investments to the power sector. This process will also identify opportunities for the involvement and empowerment of locals.

3.3.4 ELECTRICITY INFRASTRUCTURE

Prior to 2000, electricity was imported from South Africa through three 132 kV lines with a total capacity of 96 MW. Subsequently a 400 kV transmission line between Mozambique and South Africa through Swaziland has been established, adding 250MW to the capacity. Although the 400 kV line was built with the intention of supplying power from Eskom to an aluminium smelter in Maputo, it also contributes to Swaziland's security of supply, as SEB is tapping power from the line.

The integration of the 400 kV line into the national grid will improve the quality of supply to industry. Power outages within this sector, even for a short period, can result in huge losses of production. This situation is improving as a result of the ongoing system-strengthening programme. Later on this improvement will also be realised in households once the system integration project is finalised and further upgrading of the national grid has taken place.

The Government has also been encouraging the development of industrial areas in selected areas outside the Manzini-Mbabane corridor. It is necessary that the electricity infrastructure be geared to support this objective.

Government will continue to facilitate improvement of the electricity supply infrastructure and thus improve the energy supply service.

This will also be beneficial to the industrial sector as part of the overall strategy for attracting investment.

3.3.5 PRODUCTION

In 1999, the domestic electricity production amounted to 460 GWh. SEB produced 190 GWh from the hydropower plants at Edwaleni, Ezulwini, Maguduza and Mbabane. A privately owned hydro plant also produced 6 GWh, and SEB produced 1.4 GWh from their diesel unit. Installed capacity of the SEB hydro plants is 41 MW and the diesel units add 9.5 MW.

The remaining electricity production came from independent producers, mainly from the major industries Ubombo, Mhlume and Simunye sugar mills and the pulp industry. Together these four companies produced 264 GWh, 27% of the electricity consumed in Swaziland, thus contributing considerably to the overall supply.

For the sugar mills the electricity produced is mainly based on bagasse and coal. The pulp industry utilises black liquor, a by-product in the pulp production process, together with wood waste and bark. All electricity produced is co-generated with steam for industrial processes, and is used for their own industrial purposes and for supply to the nearby company towns. At present there are no arrangements for selling self-generated electricity to the grid, but this will in future be facilitated with the coming of new legislation for the sector.

The restructuring of the electricity supply industry will also facilitate access to the market for third party producers by creating a level playing field and as such pave the way for increased security of supply. An important feature within the production sector could also be the utilisation of domestic coal in power production as dealt with under Section 3.1 on Coal.

Government will ensure there are clear guidelines for opening access to the national grid.

Increased utilisation of indigenous energy resources for electricity will improve security of supply, create job-opportunities and stimulate the economic growth. Due to the relatively low import prices at present these opportunities are more relevant in the medium term.

Government will carry out investigations and promote efficient and environmentally sound technologies for the utilisation of indigenous resources for electricity production.

3.3.6 HYDRO POTENTIAL, WIND AND SOLAR ENERGY

As mentioned above, SEB produces the major part of hydro-based electricity in Swaziland. SEB's hydro-based installed capacity is 40.5 MW.

Additional capacity could come from the Maguga Dam. The Maguga power plant could, once developed, operate with a capacity of 19 MW in peak periods.

There is a modest potential for run-of-river plants particularly in the scale of less than 1MW, which might be suitable for local off-grid solutions possibly in combination with other stand-alone technologies.

Electricity generation from solar photovoltaic is increasingly gaining ground in many countries. Some of these systems are grid connected and can be integrated into facades of buildings. The costs however, remain very high compared to traditional electricity technologies. But the costs are decreasing and for the time being, solar photovoltaic is a realistic alternative to supply isolated areas with distances too long and costly for the normal grid.

World wide, wind electricity generation has been growing rapidly in recent years. In many cases wind turbines provide a significant input to traditional energy sources and are becoming increasingly economically attractive. The competitive situation of wind energy is dependent on the wind conditions and the alternative supply costs.

Activities are being carried out in Swaziland to gain further information on the solar and wind resources to help evaluate their economical viability.

These renewable energy resources are necessary from an environmental and security point of view. However, economically these technologies must be able to compete with traditional energy sources, which for the time being are relatively cheap in Swaziland, otherwise they will have to be subsidised. Swaziland's economic situation may not favour large scale subsidies, however direct subsidies alongside other ways to support the development of renewable energy sources, will be required.

The Kyoto Protocol, and the subsequently developed instruments for investments in cleaner energy options, may support the establishment of such systems in Swaziland and thereby subsidise the sector. Indirectly, investments in clean technology systems in Swaziland will reduce the need for coal based electricity produced in other countries and be beneficial both to the regional and global climate.

Renewable energy solutions and other IPP technologies can also be supported by Public Service Obligations (PSO), which is a levy imposed on the users of an electricity grid. Such provisions are common in other liberalised electricity markets. The initiatives on restructuring the electricity sector are also a possibility to create an environment to facilitate the entry of new technologies into the supply system.

Government will support programmes promoting the utilisation of renewable energy resources for electricity production.

Government will establish and support demonstration plants aimed at promoting the utilisation of the various technologies.

Another, often overseen, indigenous energy resource is the generation of heat and power using waste incineration. Use of landfill gas is also a possibility in the future. In the longer term when waste collection, disposal, and treatment of waste is more developed and the quantities justify it, the possibilities for utilising these resources should be further evaluated.

3.3.7 INDEPENDENT POWER PRODUCERS (IPP)

Independent Power Producers (IPPs) refer in general to private firms or other entities that produce energy for sale to the national grid and/or for own purposes. The existing local generators within the sugar and pulp industries could be developed into IPP's if they also delivered power to the grid. Presently, the installed capacity of independent industrial production plants is approximately 50MW.

These industries may be able to increase their production of electricity in order to be self-sufficient or to sell electricity to the national grid if the playing field is level. The following benefits could be achieved: increased efficiency of energy conversion and use; increased diversity of electricity supplies; job creation; reduction in electricity imports; and a reduction of harmful emissions.

There is a huge potential for the use of indigenous resources in the production of electricity and process heat in Swaziland. The large coal reserves represent the most obvious resource but also bagasse and wood waste could be utilised further. Feasibility studies are being considered on establishment of plants for further utilisation of bagasse.

From the viewpoint of security of supply and local employment, utilisation of these resources is desirable. However, the viability of production of electricity is highly dependent on the prevailing electricity prices in the region, which for the time being are rather low. It is therefore difficult for IPPs to compete with the low import prices SEB obtain from South Africa.

Since the low import prices are caused by an over capacity in South Africa, which is expected to diminish over the coming years, prices in the longer terms are expected to increase and thereby making production from IPP generators more financially viable.

The challenge today for Swaziland is to establish a regulatory framework that enables the establishment of IPPs, but at the same time realising that the establishment of such generators is at present not financially attractive without incentives.

It is possible that development of IPP's which utilise renewable energy resources can benefit from the international initiatives related to the agreements on the Kyoto Protocol being developed by the UNFCCC. Part of this agreement is to develop mechanisms to support environmental friendly electricity production. The Clean Development Mechanism (CDM) may support IPP solutions, which from a narrow economic point of view are less economically viable. The CDM guidelines are currently being developed.

Government will create an enabling environment to allow the establishment of IPPs in the country and support projects to be implemented.

The private sector will be the driving force in the establishment of IPPs. The licensing procedures for IPPs will ensure the company fulfils specified social responsibilities, as defined by the proposed Energy Regulatory Authority.

The potential for IPPs will regularly be reviewed. An important aspect of this programme will be exploring the potential of utilisation of CDM or similar funds with environmental objectives. A secretariat within the Government will be established to provide information on procedures and developments under the CDM programme.

3.3.8 TARIFFS

Electricity prices to consumers differ considerably based on consumption patterns and requirements. However, the price the consumer pays does not necessarily reflect the true costs of supplying the power. Recent tariff studies indicate that domestic consumers pay less than the actual costs of electricity service, whilst commercial and industrial consumers are being overcharged (compared to the costs of supplying them). The electricity tariff in the country is uniform for domestic consumers. However, there is a high cost of servicing rural domestic consumers due to the low number of connections.

The situation, when some consumer groups pay more than others and the differences are not justified in real cost, is referred to as cross-subsidisation. In principle, tariffs with cross subsidies should be avoided and "true" cost reflective tariffs imposed. However, there might be good reasons for some cross subsidies. A special tariff for low-income groups (poverty tariff) would also have some social benefits.

There might also be a need to introduce more flexible tariffs reflecting the regional situation where import prices vary over the day and season. Generally, there is a need that the way tariffs are constructed and their relation to costs should be made fully transparent.

Government will ensure that electricity tariffs are fully transparent and cost-reflective.

There will continue to be a justification for some cross subsidisation for rural consumers. The options for more flexible tariffs (eg smart tariffs, poverty tariffs etc) and cost reflective tariffs will be further investigated.

THE SWAZILAND INVESTMENT PROMOTION ACT

Date of commencement: 25th March, 1998.

An act to provide for the promotion of investment in Swaziland and the establishment of an investment promotion authority and for matters incidental thereto.

Short title and commencement.

1. This Act may be cited as the Swaziland Investment Promotion Act, 1998, and shall come into force on such date as the Minister may appoint by notice in the Gazette.

Interpretation.

2. In this Act, unless the context otherwise requires —

“Authority” means the Swaziland Investment Promotion Authority established under section 3;

“Board” means the Board of Directors of the Authority established under section 7;

“enterprise” means an undertaking carrying on business or commercial activity for gain or reward in any sector of the economy;

“foreign national” means —

(*a*) a person who is not a citizen of Swaziland;

(*b*) a company incorporated under the laws of any country other than Swaziland;

(*c*) a partnership or association in which the controlling interest is held by persons who are not citizens of Swaziland;

“investment” means a contribution of capital, in cash or in kind, made by a person to a new enterprise or to the expansion or rehabilitation of an existing busi-ness enterprise or to the purchase of an existing business enterprise;

“investor” means any person, natural or juridical, who has made an investment in Swaziland and is registered under section 26 of this Act, and where the person is a foreign national, the minimum amount of the investment shall be stipu-lated by the Minister from time to time by notice in the Gazette;

“manufacturing” means the substantial transformation of tangible movable prop-erty, but does not include construction, installation, assembly, transportation, power generation, or the provision of public utility services;

“Minister” means the Minister responsible for Enterprise and Employment in Swaziland, who shall, in relation to the Authority, also be the Minister re-sponsible for the purposes of the Public Enterprises (Control and Monitoring) Act, 1989;

“simple assembly” means bringing together of components or the mixing of prod-ucts which does not result in a substantial transformation of the final product.

CHAPTER ONE ESTABLISHMENT OF THE AUTHORITY

Establishment of the Authority.

3. (1) There is hereby established the Swaziland Investment Promotion Authority (“the Authority”), which shall be a body corporate, having perpetual succession and a common seal, capable of suing and being sued in its name.

(2) The Authority may acquire, hold or alienate movable and immovable property, and, subject to this Act, do or perform all such acts or things as bodies corporate may by law do or perform.

(3) The Authority shall be a category A public enterprise for purposes of the Public Enterprises (Control and Monitoring) Act, 1989.

Objects of the Authority

4. The objects of the Authority are —

(*a*) to attract, encourage, facilitate and promote local and foreign investment in Swaziland;

(*b*) to initiate, co-ordinate and facilitate the implementation of Government policies and strategies on investment;

(*c*) to provide a one-stop information and support facility to local and foreign investors;

(*d*) to advise the Minister on investment policies, strategies, proposals and suitable incentives.

Powers of the Authority.

5. For the purpose of achieving its objects, the Authority has power to —

(*a*) hold, manage, develop, let, hire, buy or subscribe for or otherwise acquire or sell or otherwise dispose of or hypothecate or otherwise deal in immovable or movable property of any sort, open and operate banking accounts and make, draw, accept or endorse negotiable instruments in the ordinary course of busi-ness;

(*b*) make representations to any public official, person or Minister on behalf of an investor in cases where theAuthority is not satisfied with the reasons given for a negative decision;

(*c*) instruct any public official or authority to decide promptly and in accordance with written law any matter submitted to him by or on behalf of an investor or in furtherance of this Act;

(*d*) investigate complaints made by investors, enquire or cause to be enquired into the reasons for a delayed or negative decision, and report cases of laxity, inef-ficiency and ineptitude by any public official or authority in the performance of his or its duties in connection with this Act;

(*e*) with the prior written consent of the Minister (with the concurrence of the Minister for Finance), borrow such sums as it may require for its purposes and to that end mortgage, pledge or otherwise hypothecate any property as security for any such loans;

(*f*) and, generally (subject to the prior written consent of the Minister), to enter into any contract and perform any act, whether in Swaziland or elsewhere, which may be necessary for or incidental or conducive to the attainment of any of its objectives;

(*g*) commission any research or study which would facilitate the better attainment of the objects of this Act;

(*h*) appoint such committees as it may deem necessary to advise it on its func-tions.

Functions of the Authority.

6. The Authority shall —

(*a*) operate as a one-stop service for investors;

(*b*) liaise with government Ministries and departments, local authorities, or other bodies in order to facilitate investors with timely compliance with any for-malities and to help secure all necessary approvals, permits, licenses, registra-tions, land, and the fulfilment of all other requirements related to the investment process;

(*c*) recommend to the Government changes in the statutory and administrative framework relevant to the investment climate of Swaziland and to make rep-resentations regarding any changes to such statutory or administrative frame-work;

(*d*) consult widely with a view to advising the Government on strategic policies and other matters related to the improvement of the investment climate in Swaziland;

(*e*) advise on the availability of the range of incentives to eligible domestic and foreign investors and to recommend additional incentives where circum-stances warrant;

(*f*) develop and implement a favourable investment image of Swaziland locally, regionally, and extra-regionally through advertising and public relations cam-paigns, seminars, exhibitions and workshops, and any other such promotional device as may be deemed appropriate;

(*g*) undertake investment promotion initiatives in Swaziland and abroad;

(*h*) liaise with Swaziland Missions abroad in order to publicize Swaziland's investment prospects and to disseminate information on investment opportu-nities in Swaziland;

(*i*) open offices in identified strategic locations abroad for the purpose of pro-moting investment in Swaziland;

(*j*) encourage expansions and new investments by existing investors in Swazi-land;

(*k*) support local investment promotion institutions where necessary to encourage and facilitate increased local investment;

(*1*) identify partners inside or outside Swaziland for joint venture investment opportunities in Swaziland;

(*m*) liaise with local and international financial institutions for the benefit of investors;

(*n*) facilitate the employment and residence of foreign nationals as senior manag-ers, non-available experts and technical employees necessary for the success of private sector investment in Swaziland, in accordance with existing struc-tures;

(*o*) establish a data bank to provide accurate and up-to-date information on the industrial and economic environment including prevailing and projected mar-ket conditions relating to investment and on investment opportunities in Swa-ziland to potential investors or their agents;

(*p*) interpret this Act in order to achieve its aims and objectives;

(*q*) do all such things as are necessary or incidental or conducive to the functions specified in this Act.

Establishment and composition of the Board of Directors.

7. (1) There is hereby established a Board of Directors of the Authority which shall be the governing body of the Authority and shall be responsible for carrying out the objects of, and exercising the powers and functions conferred on, the Authority.

(2) The Board shall consist of not more than nine members appointed in terms of sec-tion 6 of the Public Enterprise (Control and Monitoring) Act, 1989, made up as follows —

(*a*) a chairman, who shall be appointed by the Minister from the private sector and shall possess such professional qualifications as are necessary for the achievement of the objects of this Act;

(*b*) the Principal Secretaries from the Ministries responsible for commercial enterprises, employment, economic planning, finance and agriculture or their representatives;

(*c*) four persons from organisations or institutions in Swaziland who shall be appointed by the Minister for their ability and experience in labour, business, finance or the legal or accountancy professions;

(*d*) the General Manager appointed under section 10 who shall also be the Secretary to the Board.

(3) Subject to subsection (4), a member of the Board appointed under subsections (2)(*a*) and (*c*) shall be appointed for a period of three years on such terms and conditions as the Minister may determine.

(4) In the case of the first Board appointed after the commencement of this Act, two of the members appointed under subsections (2)(*a*) and (*c*) shall be appointed for a period of two years and two of the members shall be appointed for three years.

(5) A Member, other than a Principal Secretary, may be re-appointed for only two further terms after the expiry of the initial period of appointment.

(6) The Board shall regulate its own procedure.

Procedure at meetings of the Board.

8 (1) Without prejudice to section 7(6), the procedure of the Board at meetings and any other matters relating thereto shall be governed by the provisions set out in the Schedule hereto.

(2) The Minister may, by notice published in the Gazette, amend the Schedule.

Vacation of office by Board Members.

9. A Member of the Board, other than a Principal Secretary, shall vacate his office if he —

(*a*) resigns from his office by letter addressed to the Secretary of the Board;

(*b*) becomes an unrehabilitated insolvent;

(*c*) becomes of unsound mind or becomes in any other way physically incapaci-tated;

(*d*) is absent from three consecutive meetings of the Board without leave of the Chairman;

(*e*) is convicted of an offence and is sentenced to a term of imprisonment for a period of at least three months without the option of a fine; and

(*f*) conducts himself in a manner which, in the Minister's opinion, would bring disrepute to the Board or prejudice to the activities of the Authority.

Appointment of the General Manager.

10. (1) The Minister shall appoint a person with extensive business experience as the General Manager of the Authority in accordance with the provision of section 8(1) of the Public Enterprises

(Control and Monitoring) Act, 1989, and on such terms and conditions as the Minister may determine.

(2) The General Manager shall be:

(*a*) the Chief Executive Officer of the Authority;

(*b*) appointed for a term not exceeding four years which may be renewed for not more than two further terms; and

(*c*) answerable to the Board.

Duties of the General Manager.

11. (1) The General Manager shall:

(*a*) be responsible for the day to day administration of the Authority;

(*b*) carry out or perform any duties which are expedient for the achievement of the purposes of this Act, subject to any specific or general directives of the Board;

(*c*) prepare a budget including the staff complement for the Authority for ap-proval by the Board;

(*d*) with the approval of the Board, appoint such staff of the Authority as may be necessary for the proper performance of the functions of the Authority.

(2) The salaries, wages or other remuneration of the staff shall be determined by the Board.

Termination of appointment of General Manager.

12. The appointment of the General Manager shall be terminated in the manner provided for in the Public Enterprises (Control and Monitoring) Act, 1989 where:

(*a*) he commits any of the acts specified in section 9(*a*) to (*f*); or

(*b*) he violates the terms and conditions of his appointment; or

(*c*) he fails to carry out his duties.

Appointment of Chief Financial Officer.

13. There shall be appointed a Chief Financial Officer as provided in section 8(2) of the Public Enterprises (Control and Monitoring) Act, 1989.

Duties of the Chief Financial Officer.

14. The Chief Financial Officer shall —

(*a*) keep all proper books of account and other books and records in relation to the funds, undertakings, activities and property of the Authority;

(*b*) prepare such statements of account as may be necessary to indicate the financial status of the Authority at the end of each financial year;

(*c*) cause the accounts of the Authority to be examined, audited and reported on annually by auditors appointed by the Board under section 17;

(*d*) carry out any other duties assigned to him by the General Manager; and

(*e*) be answerable to the General Manager.

Termination of appointment of Chief Financial Officer.

15. The appointment of the Chief Financial Officer shall be terminated in the manner provided in the Public Enterprises (Control and Monitoring) Act, 1989 where —

(*a*) he commits any of the acts specified in section 9(*a*) to (*f*) excluding (*d*) of this Act; or

(*b*) he violates the terms and conditions of his appointment; or

(*c*) he fails to carry out any of his duties.

Funds and assets of the Authority.

16. (1) The funds and assets of the Authority shall consist of all monies —

(*a*) received as remuneration for its services;

(*b*) appropriated by Parliament for purposes of this Act;

(*c*) donated to the Authority for purposes of this Act.

(2) The Authority shall, out of its funds —

(*a*) pay to the members of the Board such remuneration and allowances as approved by the Minister;

(*b*) pay salaries, wages and allowances to the employees of the Authority;

(*c*) pay or authorise the payment of all such sums of money as may be legally due from the Authority.

(3) The Minister shall, by notice in the Gazette, designate persons who shall be signa-tories to the funds of the Authority.

Appointment of auditor.

17. (1) A reputable firm of auditors shall be appointed in the manner provided in the Public Enterprises (Control and Monitoring) Act, 1989 as auditors of the Authority for such period as the Minister shall determine.

(2) No person may be appointed an auditor if —

(*a*) he is a member of the Board or an employee of the Authority;

(*b*) he is a partner of a member of the Board or a partner of any employee of the Authority;

(*c*) he is an employer or employee of a member of the Board or of the Authority; and

(*d*) he has any pecuniary interest in the Authority or in any of its activities.

Financial Year.

18. The financial year of the Authority shall be from the 1st April to the 31st March of the following year, unless the Minister indicates otherwise by notice published in the Gazette.

CHAPTER TWO PROTECTION OF INVESTMENT AND SETTLEMENT OF DISPUTES

Freedom of investment.

19. (1) Subject to subsection (2), any person, whether or not a citizen of Swaziland, may freely and without restriction on ownership make an investment in any sector of the economy of Swaziland.

(2) Subsection (1) does not apply to the foliowing sectors:

(*a*) the manufacture of firearms, ammunition, chemical and biological weapons, and other defence weapons;

(*b*) manufacture involving radioactive materials;

(*c*) the manufacture of explosives;

(*d*) manufacture involving hazardous waste treatment or disposal;

(*e*) security printing (currency notes) and minting.

(3) All investments shall be made, and all enterprises shall be conducted, in confor-mity with the applicable laws in force in Swaziland.

(4) The Minister may, with the approval of Cabinet and by notice published in the Gazette, increase or reduce the sectors referred to in subsection (2), but such increase or reduction shall have no retrospective effect.

Protection of investment.

20. (1) Notwithstanding anything contained in any other law, no property, or any interest in or right over property of any description which forms part of an investment shall be com-pulsorily acquired or subjected to measures which have similar effect, except where it is done:

(*a*) in accordance with applicable legal procedures;

(*b*) in pursuance of a public purpose;

(*c*) without any form of discrimination on the basis of nationality; and

(*d*) upon prompt payment of adequate and fair compensation.

(2) Where all the conditions laid down in subsection (1) are satisfied, the compensa-tion shall be determined on the basis of current market value and shall be fully transferable at the prevailing current exchange rate in the currency in which the investment was originally made, without deduction of taxes, levies or other duties except where these had previously accrued.

Investment disputes.

21. Subject to any agreement previously made in writing between the investor and the Government, in the event of a dispute arising between an investor and the government the investor may elect to submit the dispute either —

(*a*) to the jurisdiction of the High Court of Swaziland; or

(*b*) to a process of arbitration under the Arbitration Act, 1904; or

(*c*) to arbitration under the Arbitration Rules of the United Nations Commission on International Trade Law; or

(*d*) in the case of a foreign investor, to arbitration under the International Con-vention for the Settlement of Investment Disputes Between States and Na-tionals of Other States.

CHAPTER THREE GENERAL

Facilitation and non-discrimination.

22. (1) Unless otherwise required by law, the Government or the Authority shall not discriminate between investors.

(2) The Authority shall ensure that work and residence permits or trading licences are processed promptly.

(3) If the officer responsible for renewing a permit or licence fails to inform the appli-cant wtthin fourteen (14) working days of his decision, the permit or licence shall be deemed to be renewed on the terms and conditions stated in the application.

(4) The Authority shall, at the request of an investor, lodge documents for the regis-tration of a new company with the Registrar of Companies and obtain a Certification of Incorporation on his behalf.

Prevention of corrupt business practices.

23. The Authority or the Minister shall take suitable measures to prevent and control any alleged corrupt business practice, and, where necessary, recommend appropriate sanction against the offender.

Disclosure of information.

24. (1) No person shall, without the prior written consent of the Authority, publish or disclose to any person, other than in the course of his duties, the contents of any document, communication or information whatsoever, which relates to, and which has come to his knowledge in the course of, his duties under this Act.

(2) A person who contravenes subsection (1) shall be guilty of an offence and liable on conviction to imprisonment for a period not exceeding one year or a fine not exceeding one thousand Emalangeni (E1000) or both.

Exemption from personal liability.

25. No action or other proceedings shall lie or be instituted against any member of the Board or employee of the Authority for or in respect of anything done or omitted to be done in good faith in the exercise of his functions under this Act.

Register of investors.

26. (1) The Authority shall maintain a register of investors, wherein shall be shown, on the application of (and where necessary, verification by) an investor:

(*a*) the name and address of the investor

(*b*) the nature and location of the enterprise;

(*c*) the number, roles and nationality of senior managers resident in Swaziland;

(*d*) the total number of employees in Swaziland; and

(*e*) the amount of the investment by that investor.

(2) The register shall be updated annually on information supplied, and where neces-sary verified, by the investor.

Regulations

27. The Minister may, by notice in the Gazette, make such regulations as he deems neces-sary for giving effect to this Act, and may prescribe such penalties as are appropriate for the contravention of the Act provided that the penalties prescribed shall not exceed the penalty prescribed in section 24(2).

SCHEDULE

(Under section 8)

Rules and procedures of the Board.

1. The Board shall meet at least four times a year for the despatch of the business of the Authority.

2. The Chairman shall convene and preside over all meetings of the Board and shall convene a special meeting whenever requested by at least three members or by the Minister.

3. At a special meeting, only the business stipulated in a written request may be trans-acted.

4. In the absence of the Chairman, but subject to the quorum, the members present shall nominate one of them to preside at the meeting.

5. The quorum for a meeting of the Board shall be five members.

6. All decisions of the Board shall be made by a simple majority of the votes of the members present and the person presiding shall only have a casting vote where there is an equality of votes.

7. The Secretary shall keep minutes of all proceedings of the Board in a minute book which shall show all details of business transacted at each meeting.

8. The Chairman, in consultation with the Board, may invite a member of the committee under section 5(*h*) to attend and participate in a Board meeting dealing with a specific subject of interest to or affecting the work of that committee.

9. A member invited in terms of paragraph 8 shall not have the right to vote.

PRACTICAL INFORMATION FOR BUSINESS AND INVESTMENTS

DOING BUSINESS IN SWAZILAND

MARKET OVERVIEW

Swaziland is a small country (slightly smaller than New Jersey), with a population of 1.1 million. It is bordered by South Africa and Mozambique.

Swaziland's preliminary growth domestic product (GDP) numbers indicate real growth of 1.2 percent in 2009, a slowdown from the 2.4 percent growth observed in 2008. A modest recovery in GDP of 2 percent was projected for 2010. Inflation moderated to 5.4 percent at the end of 2009.

Swaziland is heavily dependent on South Africa, from which it receives more than 80 percent of its imports and to which it sends 60 percent of its exports.

Swaziland's currency is pegged to the South African Rand at par.

MARKET CHALLENGES

Swaziland is facing a serious socio-economic situation characterized by sluggish economic performance, food insecurity, poverty, high HIV/AIDS prevalence rate, and growing unemployment.

The real appreciation of the Lilangeni exchange rate against the U.S. dollar and other trading partner' currencies during 2009 reduced the value of exports destined to markets outside the Common Monetary Area.

The fiscal outlook took a dramatic downturn in 2009/10, reflecting a sharp drop in Southern African Customs Union (SACU) receipts coupled with continued growth in total government expenditure. The economy was also affected by the closure of the wood pulp company, Sappi Usuthu, at the end of January 2010.

Implementation of the final phase of the EU sugar sector reforms, coupled with a stronger Lilangeni exchange rate against currencies, notably the Euro and the US Dollar, decreased export earnings in this sector.

Swaziland performs poorly in terms of procedures and time required to do and start a business, as indicated in the World Bank Doing Business Report 2011.

MARKET OPPORTUNITIES

Suppliers of seeds, pesticides, transportation, and storage for these products could find opportunities for new sales.

Franchising opportunities for U.S. business, such as restaurants and retail shops, are plentiful in Swaziland and have been successful in the past.

The Public Procurement Regulations were published in 2008 in terms of the Finance and Audit Act of 1967, whose sole responsibility was to regulate the procurement of goods, works and services of government ministries and departments. U.S. companies could find opportunities to sell to the government.

The Financial Services Regulatory Authority Act was made law in February 2010. The Act will regulate and supervise nonbanking financial service providers including securities. The securities industry is still at its infancy.

The government, in its Fiscal Adjustment Roadmap (FAR) of 2010/11-2014/15, states that it intends to pilot a public-private partnership and privatization program. With this the government hopes to attract foreign capital and deliver services to the people, mainly in construction.

MARKET ENTRY STRATEGY

The Embassy recommends contacting the Swaziland Investment Promotion Authority (SIPA), which can help to register companies and secure premises.

The Embassy advises potential investors to visit Swaziland prior to establishing a business. Some foreign businesses partner with Tibiyio Taka Ngwane, Swaziland Industrial Development Company (SIDC), and/or SWAKI (Swaziland Kirsh Industries). See Chapter 3, Joint Ventures , for more information.

SELLING U.S. PRODUCTS AND SERVICES

USING AN AGENT OR DISTRIBUTOR

Marketing U.S. goods and services may best be accomplished through bases or agents in South Africa. The Foreign Commercial Service office at the U.S. Consulate General in Johannesburg can help U.S. businesses interested in accessing Swazi markets find agents and partners in South Africa. In addition, the following organizations are available to help foreign businesses find distributors and partners in Swaziland:

* The Swaziland Investment Promotion Authority (SIPA) and Swaziland Industrial Development Company (SIDC) can help with finding partners.
* Swaziland Kirsh Industries (SWAKI) offers local expertise to foreign businesses on a diversity of projects and can help larger enterprises not yet represented in Swaziland to establish retail outlets.
* Small Enterprise Development Company (SEDCO) helps small and medium Companies (SME's) to reach their full potential through training in business management. SEDCO also directs SME's to available opportunities.

Swaziland Investment Promotion Agency
7th Floor, Mbandzeni House
Church Street
P.O. Box 4194
Mbabane H100, Swaziland
Tel.: (268) 2404-0470/4
Fax: (268) 2404-3374
http://www.sipa.org.sz

Swaziland Industrial Development Company

5th Floor Dlanubeka Building
P.O. Box 866
Mbabane H100, Swaziland
Tel.: (268) 2404-3391
Fax: (268) 2404-5619
E-mail: sidc@africaonline.co.sz
http://www.sidc.co.sz

SWAKI
P.O. Box 1839
Manzini H100, Swaziland
Tel.: (268) 2505-2693
Fax: (268) 2505-2001

ESTABLISHING AN OFFICE

The Swaziland Investment Promotion Authority (SIPA) is a government agency created to promote, attract and assist the establishment of both local and foreign enterprises. SIPA is the logical first point of contact for a new business in Swaziland. The following are SIPA's guidelines for establishing operations in Swaziland:

1. Business Registration: SIPA facilitates the registration of the company through legal practitioners (Companies Act of 2009). Costs range between US$400– US$800 including the registrar of companies' costs.
2. Immigration: SIPA handles the applications for entry permits on behalf of the investor. Medical certificate, certificates of association, share certificates, bank statements, police clearances and two passport size photos are required. Permit fees range from US$100 for up to 12 months to US$350 for up to five years.
3. Trading Licenses: SIPA will also handle this application (Trading Licenses Order No. 20 or 1975). The cost of the license is US$700.
4. Utilities Services: Applications are handled by SIPA.
5. Environmental Compliance: All non-services related businesses are required by law to apply for approval from the Swaziland Environmental Authority, a process that SIPA fully facilitates. All waste-creating industries are required by law to undertake an environmental impact assessment.
6. Factory Inspectorate and National Provident: Law requires these registrations. The registration process is facilitated by SIPA.

Foreign investors have encountered some difficulties working with SIPA and with government regulations outside of SIPA's scope. A May 2005 study by USAID's Regional Center for Southern Africa, the "Swaziland Investor Roadmap" describes in detail the problems encountered by investors in Swaziland. The study (available at: http://mbabane.usembassy.gov/local_links.html) outlines many step-by-step procedures related to employing, reporting, locating, and operating in Swaziland.

Two common problems described in the "Swaziland Investor Roadmap" are:

1. Trading License/Entry Permit: The current procedures require a trading license to obtain an entry permit while simultaneously requiring an entry permit to obtain a trading license. In practice, an investor must negotiate with both the Department of Immigration and the Ministry of Commerce, Industry and Trade to reach an informal agreement as to which permission will be granted first.

2. Entry Permit Review: Some investors complain that the review of applications for employee entry permits can vary; thus, employers cannot predict if and when an employee will be able to work legally in the country.

The U.S. Embassy in Mbabane continues to work with SIPA and the government in general to clarify the issues raised in the "Swaziland Investor Roadmap." As circumstances change, this document will be updated accordingly.

FRANCHISING

Franchising opportunities for U.S. business, such as restaurants and retail shops, are plentiful in Swaziland. Franchises in Swaziland are mostly South African, or come to Swaziland by way of a South African entity that has purchased master franchise rights to the region, e.g. Kentucky Fried Chicken, John Deere, Bandag Tyres, FedEx, and DHL.

In the past, South African buyers have allegedly taken advantage of foreigners' ignorance of Swaziland's political independence, and illegally set up franchises in Swaziland without having proper licensing for the country. Swazi business people are thus often suspicious of new franchises in the country. Master franchise deals exclusively for Swaziland or for the region are not subject to restrictions beyond the requirements of any other business arrangement.

There are several urban centers that could support a variety of franchise types. Swazi business people are very interested in cutting their own deals with U.S. and other foreign firms for franchising rights instead of going through South Africa.

Uneasiness with South African dominance in regional franchising extends across southern Africa and can be an important impetus to U.S. firms, not only to sell Swazi franchising rights directly to Swaziland-based buyers, but to consider a Swazi franchiser for the broader region.

There are Swazis interested in becoming regional franchisers who can command the resources necessary to do so. The disadvantage of Swaziland-based franchising is the lack of a strong manufacturing base. In certain ventures, South Africa's ability to more readily provide needed supplies gives it an advantage.

DIRECT MARKETING

There are no restrictions against U.S. companies marketing their goods in Swaziland. The government's annual Swaziland International Trade Fair held the last week of August or the first week of September, welcomes international companies for marketing purposes.

JOINT VENTURES/LICENSING

A number of organizations in Swaziland can help foreign firms to pursue joint ventures. The four largest are the Swaziland Industrial Development Company (SIDC), the Swaziland Investment Promotion Investment (SIPA), SWAKI, and Tibiyo Taka Ngwane.

SIDC is a private development finance company formed as a joint venture between the government and several international and local financial institutions. The main objective of SIDC is to assist incoming companies by financing joint ventures, equity participation, asset leasing, and providing factory shells. Partners include:

* Government of Kingdom of Swaziland – 34.9 percent
* German Investment and Development Company (DEG) - 22.1 percent
* International Finance Corporation (IFC) - 13.7 percent
* Commonwealth Development Corporation (CDC) - 10.9 percent
* Netherlands Development Finance Company (FMO) - 10.2 percent
* French Development Finance Institution (PROPARCO) - 5.0 percent
* Standard Bank of Swaziland - 1.6 percent
* Nedbank (Swaziland) Limited - 1.6 percent

SIPA is a government agency which facilitates investment in Swaziland. It can help foreign businesses search for partners.

SWAKI Group of Companies is a private entity, but forms joint ventures with incoming companies to boost small to medium enterprises.

Tibiyo Taka Ngwane, a private trust fund managed by the king for the nation, is a major player in Swazi joint venture enterprises. Tibiyo invites foreign partners to either form joint venture projects or to run Tibiyo's wholly owned projects under direct management contract. Tibiyo usually expects the joint venture partner to provide leadership in technical project implementation as well as professional management. When participating in a joint venture, Tibiyo is flexible on the level of its equity stake, generally ranging between 20-50 percent. It can provide limited loan financing to the joint venture at a favorable rate. Tibiyo, when requested, also can play a facilitator role to investors wanting to set up in the country but wishing to "go it alone."

SELLING TO THE GOVERNMENT

In marketing products and services to the government, companies should not expect a steady flow of sales, but there are occasional opportunities for one-off sales of considerable size. Generally the government publishes tenders in the local media and, depending on the commodity required, occasionally in the South African media. The

U.S. Embassy in Mbabane has a fair overview of what opportunities exist. The commercial office in the U.S. Embassy welcomes the chance to direct interested American parties to the relevant authorities and actively seeks to secure fair consideration of American offers of goods and services.

After the introduction of the Public Procurement Regulations in 2008, procurement for all goods, works and services are managed by a leading procurement organization, which is the ministry responsible for health for medical and pharmaceutical products and related services; the ministry responsible for agriculture for drugs and related services for use by the Veterinary Department; the ministry responsible for transport for vehicles and mechanical plant, including heavy earth moving equipment, spare parts for vehicles and mechanical plant and services related to the foregoing; the ministry responsible for public works for all building, engineering and other works and for all consultancy services related to works procurement; Government Central Stores for all common use items which are held in stock in the Central Stores; and the Technical Secretariat for all other procurement.

Opportunities for U.S. companies to sell to government are available in medical equipment and supplies, heavy earth moving equipment, spare parts for vehicles and mechanical plant, telecommunications equipment and mining equipment.

Potential bidders pay for the right to bid at the government revenue office and then collect tender documents from Government Stores after showing receipt from the government revenue office. Bids are returned to the Swaziland National Tender Board. Bidders are invited for the opening of the bids. In some instances, a ministry can apply for a tender waiver if there are too few companies supplying a particular commodity.

The government requires three quotes to procure an item. It will issue an order to the company selected, and then the company applies for an import permit from the Ministry of Finance.

DISTRIBUTION AND SALES CHANNELS

Swaziland uses two ports for imported goods: Durban, South Africa, and Maputo, Mozambique. Swaziland has a dry port at Matsapha, near Manzini, that clears consignments coming into Swaziland via the railway line.

SELLING FACTORS/TECHNIQUES

Service plans and warranties are an important selling point in Swaziland, especially for equipment and automobiles. In order to compete with South African products, U.S. businesses should make provisions for after-sale maintenance.

English is one of Swaziland's two official languages and, as long as labeling is done professionally and instructions for use are explicit, Swazi buyers will not have a problem with the commodity.

ELECTRONIC COMMERCE

E-commerce is not widely used in Swaziland. Few individuals buy items over the internet or use credit cards. Three financial institutions in the country have introduced e-banking.

Internet scams are common in Swaziland. When dealing with Swazi companies claiming to support e-commerce, it would be best to check with local banks to confirm the validity of the transaction.

TRADE PROMOTION AND ADVERTISING

Two newspapers in Swaziland offer advertising possibilities for U.S. businesses: the privately-owned *Times of Swaziland* and Tibiyo Taka Ngwane's *Swazi Observer*. A monthly magazine, *The Nation*, at one time banned by the government, has been back in circulation for some time. Swaziland has one business journal, *The Swaziland Business Yearbook,* now in its fourteenth year.

Newspapers:
The Swazi Observer
Observer House, West Street Mbabane
Tel (268) 2404-5190, 2404-5194
Fax (268) 2404-5503
E-mail: observmb@realnet.co.sz
Website address: www.observer.org.sz

The Times of Swaziland

P.O. Box 156, Mbabane
Tel (268) 2404-1550, 2404-1551, 2404-1552, 2404-1553
Fax (268) 2404-2438
E-mail: times@realnet.co.sz
Website address: www.times.co.sz

Other Publications:
The Nation
P.O. Box 3433, Mbabane
Tel. (268) 2404-6611
E-mail: thenation@realnet.co.sz

Swaziland Business Yearbook
Published by Christina Forsyth Thompson
P.O. Box 592, Mbabane
Tel (268) 2404-3400, 2404-1839
Fax (268) 2404-3400
E-mail: cft@realnet.co.sz
Website address: http://www.swazibusiness.com/indexsbyb.html

The government owns radio and television stations which sell advertising (no website is available for the radio station). Swaziland has one privately-owned radio station

broadcasting Christian material, but has no privately-owned television stations. It is possible to advertise with South African television stations broadcasting into Swaziland.

Television
Swaziland Television Authority
P.O. Box A146
Swazi Plaza, H101
Mbabane
Tel: (268) 2404-3036
Fax: (268) 2404-2093
E-mail: info@swazitv.co.sz
Website address: http://www.swazitv.co.sz

PRICING

Pricing of commodities in Swaziland is usually inclusive of all taxes. Swaziland charges 14 percent tax on all goods sold within the country.

SALES SERVICE/CUSTOMER SUPPORT

After-sale maintenance is top priority for any sale to succeed in Swaziland. Swazis are hesitant to buy products that cannot be serviced in Swaziland, and U.S. exporters should make provisions for in-country service to promote sales. For example, although government agencies may be willing to wait up to two weeks for automobile service in South Africa, private individuals will not tolerate the inconvenience. Like western consumers, many Swazis will demand same-day or overnight service on their vehicles.

PROTECTING YOUR INTELLECTUAL PROPERTY

Protection for patents, trademarks, and copyrights is currently inadequate under Swazi law. Swaziland has an intellectual property rights regime inherited from the colonial era, under which copyrights, patents, and trademarks were more or less protected under various acts promulgated by the colonial authorities.

Patents are currently protected under a 1936 act that automatically extends patent protection upon proper application to products that have been patented in either South Africa or Great Britain. Updated patent legislation is in the pipeline. Under the new legislation, patents would be granted by the government with technical assistance from the African Regional Industrial Property Organization in Harare. Protection would be extended to pharmaceutical and agricultural chemical products.

The Trade Marks Act of 1981, although also inadequate, established registration of trademarks for a period of ten years, and may be renewed for subsequent periods of ten years. The registered proprietor of a trademark in Swaziland has the exclusive right to use the mark, and any assignment or transmission of the mark must be registered by the assignee. Appeals against the Registrar's decisions regarding trademarks may be made

to the High Court. The Fair Trading Act, 2001 also provides for pursuit and penalties in the case of violation of trademarks.

Copyright protection is addressed under four statutes, dated 1912, 1918, and 1933 under the Intellectual Property Rights Organization (WIPO) model. Swaziland does not have bilateral copyright relations with the United States.

The government has acceded to the WTO TRIPS agreement, but has not signed the WIPO internet agreement. See Chapter 6, Investment Climate Statement.

Protecting Your Intellectual Property in Swaziland:

Several general principles are important for effective management of intellectual property ("IP") rights in Swaziland. First, it is important to have an overall strategy to protect your IP. Second, IP is protected differently in Swaziland than in the U.S. Third, rights must be registered and enforced in Swaziland, under local laws. Your U.S. trademark and patent registrations will not protect you in Swaziland. There is no such thing as an "international copyright" that will automatically protect an author's writings throughout the entire world. Protection against unauthorized use in a particular country depends on the national laws of that country. However, most countries do offer copyright protection to foreign works under certain conditions, and these conditions have been greatly simplified by international copyright treaties and conventions.

Registration of patents and trademarks is on a first-in-time, first-in-right basis, so you should consider applying for trademark and patent protection even before selling your products or services in the Swaziland market. It is vital that companies understand that intellectual property is primarily a private right and that the US government generally cannot enforce rights for private individuals in Swaziland. It is the responsibility of the rights' holders to register, protect, and enforce their rights where relevant, retaining their own counsel and advisors. Companies may wish to seek advice from local attorneys or IP consultants who are experts in Swaziland law. The U.S. Commercial Service can provide a list of local lawyers upon request.

While the U.S. Government stands ready to assist, there is little we can do if the rights holders have not taken these fundamental steps necessary to securing and enforcing their IP in a timely fashion. Moreover, in many countries, rights holders who delay enforcing their rights on a mistaken belief that the USG can provide a political resolution to a legal problem may find that their rights have been eroded or abrogated due to legal doctrines such as statutes of limitations, laches, estoppel, or unreasonable delay in prosecuting a law suit. In no instance should U.S. Government advice be seen as a substitute for the obligation of a rights holder to promptly pursue its case.

It is always advisable to conduct due diligence on potential partners. Negotiate from the position of your partner and give your partner clear incentives to honor the contract. A good partner is an important ally in protecting IP rights. Consider carefully, however, whether to permit your partner to register your IP rights on your behalf. Doing so may create a risk that your partner will list itself as the IP owner and fail to transfer the rights should the partnership end. Keep an eye on your cost structure and reduce the margins (and the incentive) of would-be bad actors. Projects and sales in Swaziland require constant attention. Work with legal counsel familiar with Swaziland laws to create a solid

contract that includes non-compete clauses, and confidentiality/non-disclosure provisions.

It is also recommended that small and medium-size companies understand the importance of working together with trade associations and organizations to support efforts to protect IP and stop counterfeiting. There are a number of these organizations, both Swaziland or U.S.-based. These include:

* The U.S. Chamber and local American Chambers of Commerce
* National Association of Manufacturers (NAM)
* International Intellectual Property Alliance (IIPA)
* International Trademark Association (INTA)
* The Coalition Against Counterfeiting and Piracy
* International Anti-Counterfeiting Coalition (IACC)
* Pharmaceutical Research and Manufacturers of America (PhRMA)
* Biotechnology Industry Organization (BIO)

IP Resources

A wealth of information on protecting IP is freely available to U.S. rights holders. Some excellent resources for companies regarding intellectual property include the following:

* For information about patent, trademark, or copyright issues -- including enforcement issues in the US and other countries -- call the STOP! Hotline:

1-866-999-HALT or register at www.StopFakes.gov .

* For more information about registering trademarks and patents (both in the U.S. as well as in foreign countries), contact the US Patent and Trademark Office (USPTO) at: 1-800-786-9199.
* For more information about registering for copyright protection in the US, contact the US Copyright Office at: 1-202-707-5959.
* For more information about how to evaluate, protect, and enforce intellectual property rights and how these rights may be important for businesses, a free online training program is available at www.stopfakes.gov .
* For US small and medium-size companies, the Department of Commerce offers a "SME IP Advisory Program" available through the American Bar Association that provides one hour of free IP legal advice for companies with concerns in Brazil, China, Egypt, India,

Russia, and . For details and to register, visit:
http://www.abanet.org/intlaw/intlproj/iprprogram_consultation.html
* For information on obtaining and enforcing intellectual property rights and market-specific IP Toolkits visit: www.StopFakes.gov This site is linked to the USPTO website for registering trademarks and patents (both in the U.S. as well as in foreign countries), the U.S. Customs & Border Protection website to record registered trademarks and copyrighted works (to assist customs in blocking imports of IP-infringing products) and allows you to register for Webinars on protecting IP.
* The U.S. Commerce Department has positioned IP attachés in key markets around the world. You can get contact information for the IP attaché who covers Swaziland at: Johannesburg.office.box@mail.doc.gov .

DUE DILIGENCE

Proper due diligence should form the starting base for any business negotiation with Swazi concerns. U.S. companies should act prudently in completing due diligence reports prior to any proposed business deals.

The U.S. Department of Commerce's Foreign Commercial Services (FSC) Section at the U.S. Consulate General in Johannesburg can provide valuable background information on Swazi firms through their International Company Profile (ICP) service. Further information can be obtained by visiting www.buyusa.gov/southafrica or contacting the FCS Export Assistance Center at (+27) 11-778-4808.

LOCAL PROFESSIONAL SERVICES

Professional Associations:
Law Society of Swaziland,
High Court Building, Mbabane
Phone: +268 2404-9945
Accountants and Auditors
Kobla Quashie and Associates
Email: info@koblaquashie.co.sz

Management Consulting
Regional Excellence & Development Initiative
Email: info@redi.realnet.co.sz
KPMG Management Services
Email: kpmg@kpmg.co.sz

WEB RESOURCES

Business Yearbook http://www.swazibusiness.com/indexsbyb.html

Swaziland Industrial Development Company http://www.sidc.co.sz

Swaziland Investment Promotion Agency http://www.sipa.org.sz

Tibiyo Taka Ngwane http://ww2.tibiyo.com

Small Enterprise Development Company http://www.sedco.co.sz

LEADING SECTORS FOR U.S. EXPORT AND INVESTMENT

TELECOMMUNICATIONS EQUIPMENT - TEL

Unit: USD million

	2009	2010	2011 (estimated)	2012 (estimated
Total Market Size	44.25	65.52	n/a	n/a
Exchange Rate: 1 USD	E10.5	E7.45	n/a	n/a

Data Sources: *Above figures are unofficial sourced from SPTC annual report.*

Swaziland's telecommunications network is fully digital. Optical fiber and local loop systems have been installed and link key areas throughout the country and neighboring countries. Swaziland also introduced the wire-line broadband services along with the Next Generation Networks. The landline network is a state monopoly. A private company provides cellular phone services. Swaziland Telecommunications' Corporation has begun a project to be the second cellular provider. Swaziland plans to enhance its optic fiber connectivity with its neighbors South Africa and Mozambique to take advantage of the undersea optic fiber cables for affordable international bandwidth.

SUB-SECTOR BEST PROSPECTS

* Next Generation Network Solutions
* Optic Fiber Cables
* Cell phones
* Main Distribution Frames
* Spare parts for the equipment e.g. interface protocols

OPPORTUNITIES

As Swaziland plans the commercialization of wireless services, US telecommunications suppliers could find opportunities in this venture;

Only MTN Swaziland Ltd offers cellular service, although SPTC has begun developing wireless products. MTN's monopoly ended in 2008;

Swaziland is building an international airport which still needs to be provided with a telecommunications network.

WEB RESOURCES

Swaziland Posts and Telecommunications Corporation http://www.sptc.co.sz

AGRICULTURAL MACHINERY & EQUIPMENT - AGM

Unit: USD thousands

	2009	2010	2011 (estimated)	2012 (estimated)
Exchange Rate: 1 USD	E10.50	E7.45	n/a	n/a

Swaziland 2008 imports from the U.S. of agricultural machinery and parts thereof excluding tractors amounted to USD 899,389.14 according to the Central Statistics office. (ROE: USD2/E7.75)

Swaziland, in its fiscal adjustment roadmap, plans to diversify its economy and agriculture. The Swaziland Water and Agricultural Development Enterprise (SWADE) is implementing a project where three small holder irrigation schemes will be built in three phases at the Lower Usuthu Small-holder Irrigation Project (LUSIP). Construction of Phase 1 started in 2010 and should be fully operation in 2014. LUSIP has also a potential for a small scale hydroelectricity generation.

SUB-SECTOR BEST PROSPECTS

* Agricultural Machinery/equipment
* Irrigation equipment; drilling rigs
* Hydroelectricity generation equipment.

OPPORTUNITIES

The agro-based economy of Swaziland opens opportunities for U.S. companies who supply agricultural machinery and equipment.

U.S. investors should also look for the niche sectors that will come up as a result of the agricultural development at LUSIP e.g. food processing.

WEB RESOURCES

Swaziland Water and Agricultural Development Enterprise http://www.swade.co.sz

MEDICAL EQUIPMENT - MED

Swaziland's healthcare sector is serviced by the public health care system, which is not well equipped. A number of cases have to be referred to South Africa because of lack of equipment and expertise. Because of the cost of sending patients to South Africa, Swaziland plans to upgrade the hospitals. The government, in its Medium Term Budget Policy 2010/2011, increased it health budget to 17.5 percent which will go towards the purchasing of medical equipment and construction of hospitals and subvention of non government hospitals.

SUB-SECTOR BEST PROSPECTS

A partially government funded hospital is currently seeking tenders for equipment.

* Medical Equipment, e.g. ICU Unit and dialysis equipment
* Patient care monitors
* Chemotherapy equipment
* Imaging equipment
* Optical instruments

OPPORTUNITIES

The government, in its medium term budget policy, plans to embark on the upgrade of hospitals and to build a regional hospital on the eastern part of Swaziland. U.S. companies have an opportunity to supply medical equipment and supplies.

WEB RESOURCES

Swaziland Government /Ministry of Finance http://www.gov.sz/finance

TRAVEL AND TOURISM - TRA

Unit: USD millions

	2009	2010
Total Market Size	44.85	n/a

Data Sources: Central Bank of Swaziland

Swaziland, despite its small size, supports a strong cultural heritage and biodiversity which attracts tourists into the country. Visitors traveling to South Africa often plan a short side trip to Swaziland to experience unique traditions and an easy pace of life. Tourism is expected to grow steadily in southern Africa, and Swaziland will continue to capture a share of the regional market. In 2008 total receipts obtained from tourism amounted to USD 52.49 million (ROE USD1/E7.75). Swaziland also boasts of a range of modern hotel accommodation.

SUB-SECTOR BEST PROSPECTS

* Organize travel tours
* Research into Swaziland's biodiversity

OPPORTUNITIES

Swaziland has only one biodiversity valuation study which was undertaken in 1997 by Turpie and Albert. There is, therefore, an urgent need to ascertain the true value of these biological resources in Swaziland.

U.S. tourist organizations can organize tours direct to Swaziland and then visit the region from the country, especially after the completion of the Sikhuphe International Airport.

WEB RESOURCES

Ministry of Tourism, Communication and Environment http://www.gov.sz/tourism

Swaziland Environment Authority http://www.environment.gov.sz

COMPUTERS/PERIPHERALS - CPT

Unit: USD thousands

	2009	2010	2011 (estimated)	2012 (estimated)
Exchange Rate: 1 USD	E10.50	E7.45	n/a	n/a

According to the Central Statistics Office Swaziland imports from the U.S. of computers and peripherals in 2008 amounted to USD 3,249,143 (roe USD1/E7.75). This surge is attributed to telecommunications and electricity sectors' upgrades.

Sub-Sector Best Prospects

* Computerized billing systems for the various sectors
* Introduction of IT in high schools and tertiary institutions

Opportunities

The continued IT migration of the various sectors to computerize their establishments would see significant investment in computers and peripherals.

Web Resources

Swaziland Investment Promotion Authority http://www.sipa.org.sz

AUTOMOTIVE PARTS/SERVICE EQUIPMENT - APS

Unit: USD thousands

	2009	2010	2011 (estimated)	2012 (estimated)
Exchange Rate: 1 USD	E10.50	E7.45	n/a	n/a

Data Sources: Central Statistics Office

The automotive components sector has increased greatly with the rising of import cars. The rate of new registrations continues to climb. Imports of a variety of motor vehicles and transport from the U.S. in 2008 reached US 70, 000.00. Central Statistics office

Government is now privatizing the department that supports government's transportation services.

Sub-Sector Best Prospects

* Body parts passenger motor vehicles, motor cycles, trailers and semi-trailers.
* Electronic components
* Engine and engine components.
* Specialty equipment and spare parts for soon to be privatized government garage.

Opportunities

Swazis recognize the U.S. as the world leader in truck manufacturing, and recently Swazi buyers have been looking more seriously at U.S.-manufactured trucks.

Web Resources

Ministry of Public Works and Transport http://www.gov.sz/public works

ELECTRICAL POWER SYSTEMS - ELP

Unit: USD millions

	2009	2010	2011 (estimated)	2012 (estimated)
Total Market Size	53.38	107.32	n/a	n/a
Exchange Rate: 1 USD	E10.50	E7.45	n/a	n/a

Data Sources: *Swaziland Electricity Report 2009/2010*

South Africa's dwindling surplus of electricity for export will force Swaziland to invest in greater domestic production. Swaziland generates approximately 24 percent of its required 1.2 billion kilowatt hours of electricity and imports the remainder from South Africa and Mozambique. As demand for electricity in South Africa grows, the South African power utility, Eskom, will be less willing to sell to Swaziland.

The Electricity Company is doing a feasibility study to build a 300MW thermal power station.

The Electricity Company is implementing its rural electrification program.

While increasing its supply to the country, the electricity company continues to pay attention to the environment. Lines passing through nature reserves are constructed using underground cables and to protect the bird life flappers are installed on the lines.

SUB-SECTOR BEST PROSPECTS

* Joint ventures in the 300MW thermal power station
* Environment impact assessment contracts
* Copper sales
* Construction of 400kV integration for rural substations

OPPORTUNITIES

Feasibility studies for the 300MW thermal are at an advanced stage.

Environment assessment studies are done by private companies.

The ongoing rural electrification is planned for the four regions of the country.

WEB RESOURCES

Swaziland Electricity Company http://www.sec.co.sz

AIRPORT/GROUND SUPPORT AND EQUIPMENT - APG

Unit: USD thousands

	2009	2010	2011 (estimated)	2012 (estimated)

Exchange Rate: 1 USD	E10.50	E7.45	n/a	n/a

Swaziland is currently building a new airport that will accommodate large passenger planes. The airport is being built to serve as the country's only international airport. Swaziland is currently serviced by Matsapa Airport, which can only handle trans-Atlantic or inter-continental flights and serves largely as a charter airport for small regional carriers.

SUB-SECTOR BEST PROSPECTS

* Ground Support Equipment
* Passenger Transport Vehicles
* Luggage Handling Vehicles and Systems
* Passenger Air Bridges
* Air Traffic Control equipment
* Instrument Landing Systems and
* Safety and Security Systems Integration.

OPPORTUNITIES

The roll out of the new equipment and systems at Sikhuphe airport is a significant opportunity for U.S. companies.

Also the general maintenance of the air traffic control and its navigation services would be a great opportunity for the U.S.

WEB RESOURCES

Ministry of Economic Planning and Development http://www.gov.sz/economic planning

FOOD PROCESSING/PACKAGING EQUIPMENT - FPP

Unit: USD thousands

	2009	2010	2011 (estimated)	2012 (estimated)
Exchange Rate: 1 USD	E10.50	E7.45	n/a	n/a

Swaziland is actively pursuing investors in value-added industries which use inputs such as sugar, citrus fruit, and vegetables. For example, Swaziland is a major exporter of soft drink concentrate and imports machine parts and ingredients for this production from the U.S. These imports account for the largest regular export from the U.S. to Swaziland. The closure of the north-western Africa concentrate plant increased the market share of the locally produced product, which also sells under Common Market for Eastern and Southern Africa (COMESA).

SUB-SECTOR BEST PROSPECTS

* Start up of food processing establishments.
* Supply of ingredients for the concentrate

* Supply of equipment and upgrade of technology
* Supply of packaging

Opportunities

U.S. companies can supply equipment and technology for the beverage plant and new food processing factories.

Web Resources

Swaziland Investment Promotion Authority http://www.sipa.org.sz

AGRICULTURAL SECTORS

Swaziland's agriculture sector is dominated by sugar, citrus and canned fruit production for export. Many Swazis practice subsistence agriculture focusing on maize cultivation.

The country is historically a net importer of maize, and the quantity demanded depends significantly on unreliable rainfall. Besides subsistence production, the country meets much of its demand for agricultural products through imports from South Africa. Maize and wheat are the top agriculture products imported from the U.S. In 2008 imports of maize, rice, wheat, barley and other cereals amounted to USD 1,137,188 (ROE USD1/E7.75).

The U.S. Foreign Agriculture Service office at the U.S. Embassy in Pretoria, South Africa, can provide information on exporting U.S. agriculture products to Swaziland. The office's contact information is:

Foreign Agriculture Service
U.S. Embassy Pretoria, South Africa
Tel: +27-12-431 4235
Fax: +27-12-342 2264
Email: agpretoria@fas.usda.gov

Wheat is the only cereal with a significant import share from a country other than South Africa. Culturally, wheat is not a staple food in Swaziland. However, because of government price controls on bread and poor maize yields, people are consuming increasing amounts of imported wheat.

Rice is another grain that was not a staple food but now is consumed in large quantities Swaziland. In 2008 rice imported from the U.S. amounted to USD 2,910, 967.74. (ROE: USD1/E7.75) *Source: Central Statistics Office*

Swaziland Beef export receipts fell by 4.1 percent recording USD 4.79 million in 2009 (ROE:USD1/E10.50) drive to commercialize this industry is ongoing. *Source: Central Bank of Swaziland 2009/2010 report.*

The dairy industry in Swaziland is dominated by the informal market with only 32 percent of the total production sold to the formal market. Swaziland imported milk products, other than butter or cheese, from the U.S. in 2008 amounting to USD 248,521.55. *Source: Central Statistics office.*

Canned fruit export receipts registered USD 20.51 million in 2009 and imports of preserved fruit (excluding fruit juices) from the U.S. in 2008 registered USD 23,807. *(ROE: USD1/E7.75). Source: Central Statistics Office*

Citrus production export receipts fell in USD 8.25 million in 2009 from USD 9.57 million in 2008. Domestic sales registered USD 3.23 million (ROE: USD1/E10.50) in 2009. *Source: Central Bank of Swaziland 2009/2010 report.*

TRADE REGULATIONS, CUSTOMS AND STANDARDS

IMPORT TARIFFS

Swaziland, together with Botswana, Lesotho, Namibia and South Africa, are members of the Southern Africa Customs Union (SACU). As a Custom Union, the five countries have a common external tariff, but each country has an internal tax that applies to imports from the other member states as well from third counties. In Swaziland, this tax is the General Sales Tax (GST) of 14 percent, which is governed by the Sales Tax Act (Act No.12 of 1983).

According to a report by USAID's Regional Center for Southern Africa, entitled the "Swaziland Investor Roadmap" (available at http://mbabane.usembassy.gov), the rates of customs duty and excise duty are determined at the SACU level. The taxes collected are remitted into the SACU revenue pool from which they are distributed to the five countries in accordance with an agreed revenue sharing formula.

For a number of products, the import duty and excise tariff provides for both *ad*

valorem and specific rates of duty. The ad valorem rates of duty range from 0-40 percent. Most products originating in SADC countries are duty free. The excise tariff is contained in Part 2 of Schedule No. 1 of the Act. Excise duty is charged on both imported and locally manufactured goods, but it applies only to a limited number of consumer products, such as beverages.

TRADE BARRIERS

Transporting goods to and from Swaziland represents a challenge for traders. Swaziland has no direct sea access and a very small international airport. However, quality facilities are available nearby. The ports at Durban, South Africa, and Maputo, Mozambique, can be accessed by rail, and a dry port in Swaziland facilitates the road-to-rail connection.

Johannesburg International Airport is easily accessible by road and a new, large airport is under construction in eastern Swaziland. Swaziland's main roads are in good condition.

For information on Swaziland transportation barriers, please see a study by USAID's Regional Center for Southern Africa, entitled "Improving Transportation Logistics for Competitiveness of Swaziland," posted on the Embassy's website:

http://mbabane.usembassy.gov/local_links.html.

In addition to transportation, government procedures can hinder business in Swaziland.

There is a general lack of procedural transparency, and reliable information regarding trade and investment is not readily available. The U.S. Embassy recommends that those interested in investing in Swaziland personally visit the country.

IMPORT REQUIREMENTS AND DOCUMENTATION

Permits are required for certain imports, including all agricultural products, mineral fuels, used clothes, mineral oils, motor vehicle parts, used cars, medicinal drugs, and electrical appliances. Licensing permits issued by the Ministry of Finance are generally easy to obtain and are valid for one shipment. Goods consigned to Swaziland from outside SACU must be cleared through customs at the first port of importation into SACU. A bill of entry must be completed and submitted to customs along with copies of the supplier's invoices and a Swaziland import permit.

U.S. EXPORT CONTROLS

Swaziland's "listed" items are those that appear on the U.S. Department of Commerce Control List. These require a license to be exported to Swaziland based on the Export Control Classification Number and the Country Chart. These items are detailed on the U.S. Department of Commerce's Bureau of Industry and Security website at www.gpo.gov/bis/ear/ear_data.html

The Country Chart, which includes Swaziland, is in Part 738. The Commerce Control List is in Part 774; there are 10 categories that can be pulled up as separate files.

TEMPORARY ENTRY

There is no restriction on temporary entry of goods in transit to another country, but

importers may be charged transit rebates, which include warehousing guarantee bonds. Transit rebates ensure that goods destined for a third country leave Swaziland. Transit rebates are paid upon entry into Swaziland, and the owner of the goods applies for refund of the rebate when the goods leave Swaziland.

LABELING AND MARKING REQUIREMENTS

Only country of origin labeling is required. Swaziland has established the Standards Authority, which will introduce standards certification.

PROHIBITED AND RESTRICTED IMPORTS

Importing illicit drugs and arms of war is prohibited.

CUSTOMS REGULATIONS AND CONTACT INFORMATION

The Swaziland Revenue Authority (SRA), which opened its doors on January 01, 2011, was formed after a merger of the Customs and Income Tax departments. The SRA office administers import duties and controls.

Swaziland Revenue Authority
Imfumbe Building
Mahlokohla Street
P.O. Box 5628
Mbabane, Swaziland
Tel: +268 2406 4000

Email: info@sra.org.sz

STANDARDS

Swaziland Standards Authority (SWASA) is a statutory body formed in accordance with the Quality and Standards Act 10 of 2003. The office was opened in April 2007. SWASA is responsible for the promotion and maintenance of standardization and quality relating to commodities and the rendering of services. Its tasks include:

* serve industry, commerce and the public sector by developing, maintaining and monitoring the implementation of standards and performing conformity assessments;
* acquire, develop and publish standards, and provide testing facilities;
* acquire affiliation to relevant international bodies.

STANDARDS ORGANIZATIONS

Swaziland Standards Authority (SWASA) – A Swaziland government agency responsible for standards. Website: http://www.swasa.co.sz

SWASA has a memorandum of understanding with the South African Bureau of Standards (SABS). Website: http://www.sabs.co.za

SADC Stan – SADC Cooperation in Standardization. The Southern African Development Community (SADC) constitutes fourteen member states, and has the goal of harmonizing member countries' standards and technical regulations. It is reliant on the capacity of primarily the SABS for its operations. Website: http://www.sadcstan.co.za .

SWASA signed a memorandum of understanding with the ASTM International formerly known as the American Society for Testing and Materials. Website: http://www.astm.org

NIST NOTIFY U.S. SERVICE

Member countries of the World Trade Organization (WTO) are required under the Agreement on Technical Barriers to Trade (TBT Agreement) to report to the WTO all proposed technical regulations that could affect trade with other Member countries. Notify U.S. is a free, web-based e-mail subscription service that offers an opportunity to review and comment on proposed foreign technical regulations that can affect your access to international markets. Register online at Internet URL: http://www.nist.gov/notifyus/

CONFORMITY ASSESSMENT

SWASA is involved in conformity assessment with the South African Bureau of Standards (SABS), a South African government agency regulating standards. Website: http://www.sabs.co.za

PRODUCT CERTIFICATION

SWASA has been working on the development and adoption of close to 30 standards, 7 of which are in the process of being published in the government gazette. Given that the Swaziland did not have any national standards previously, the SWASA has been helping local companies source standards, from neighboring national standards bodies.

ACCREDITATION

SWASA has established that South African National Standards sourced from SABS are most commonly used by Swaziland companies. Another commonly used standard is ISO 9000 and some companies are in the process of implementing HACCP. So far only one company is known to be implementing ISO22000 and is accredited to the standard.

PUBLICATION OF TECHNICAL REGULATIONS

All proposed and final technical regulations will be published in the Swaziland *Government Gazette* and also SWASA's website: http://www.swasa.org.sz

LABELING AND MARKING

Labeling/marking for industrial and pharmaceutical imports has to be provided in English. Swaziland follows the Harmonized System (HS) and belongs to the Southern African Customs Union (SACU).

CONTACTS

Swaziland Standards Authority
2nd Floor Public Pension Fund Building
Mhlambanyatsi Road
Mbabane
P.O. Box 300
Eveni, H103
Tel: +268 2404 7770; Fax: +268 2404 7746
Website: http://www.swasa.co.sz

TRADE AGREEMENTS

Swaziland is currently a member state of the Common Market for Eastern and Southern Africa (COMESA). The Preferential Trade Area agreements for Eastern and Southern Africa grant Swazi goods and services preferential access to a market of over 250 million people.

The SADC Trade Protocol came into force in January 2000. This initiative is strongly supported by the World Bank, International Monetary Fund, and the African Development Bank. Under SADC, a company with operations in Swaziland can supply the entire SADC region with minimal export controls. SADC is made up of Angola,

Botswana, Democratic Republic of the Congo, Lesotho, Malawi, Mauritius, Mozambique,

Namibia, Seychelles, Swaziland, South Africa, Tanzania, Zambia and Zimbabwe.

Swaziland membership in the Southern African Customs Union (SACU), with Botswana, Lesotho, Namibia, and South Africa, allows for duty-free exchange of goods to a market of 45 million people. Goods from outside SACU require an import permit. Member countries receive due shares of the customs pool generated by commodities imported from outside the SACU. Customs revenue continues to be a major component of Swazi government receipts, until recently accounting for an estimated 60 percent of total revenue. The renegotiated SACU Agreement came into effect in July 2004.

Swaziland continues to benefit from eligibility for the African Growth and Opportunity Act (AGOA). On January 18, 2001, Swaziland was designated as the 35th AGOA eligible country. Foreign investors have taken advantage of Swaziland's AGOA-eligible status, especially in the garment manufacturing industry.

Swaziland is a signatory of the General Agreement on Tariffs and Trade. The GATT Agreement affects Swazi industry through its membership in SACU. To meet GATT obligations, South Africa, on behalf of SACU, has submitted schedules for the gradual reduction of tariffs for some commodity imports.

WEB RESOURCES

Swaziland Investment Promotion Authority – http://www.sipa.org.sz

Swaziland Standards Authority – http://www.swasa.co.sz

U.S. Commercial Service South Africa – http://buyusa.gov/southafrica/en or http://www.ussatrade.co.za

Ministry of Commerce, Industry and Trade – http://www/gov.sz/commerce

INVESTMENT CLIMATE

SWAZILAND INVESTMENT AND BUSINESS CLIMATE - STRATEGIC INFORMATION AND CONTACTS FOR STARTING BUSINESS IN SWAZILAND

Swaziland is a landlocked kingdom located in Southern Africa. Swaziland's investment climate has become less conducive to U.S. investment due to; increased government entanglement, corruption, and the higher costs involved with doing business. The official policy is to encourage foreign investment, as a means to drive economic growth but the pace of reforming the investment policies are slow. In 2012, Swaziland re-launched its 2005 Investor Roadmap aiming to improve the country's competitiveness. The roadmap details procedural, administrative and regulatory barriers that hinder investment in the country and recommends regulatory reforms. Most of the identified reforms remain unaddressed.

Increasingly, the government of Swaziland (GOS) is competing with the private sector through state owned enterprises (SOEs) or companies owned by the royal family. The implementation of the re-launched of the Investor Roadmap in 2012 is slowly progressing. The Swaziland Investment Promotion Authority (SIPA) advocates for foreign investors and facilitates regulatory approval, but lacks the political clout necessary to prevent unsolicited government and royal family interference in private business affairs. Recent positive developments include allowing for company registration online and amending the immigration laws to make it easier for foreign workers to remain in the country. In addition, the Swaziland government has prioritized the renewable energy sector and is working on a Grid Code and Independent Power Producer (IPP) Policy to create a transparent regulatory regime in this industry.

The GOS has prioritized the energy sector and is currently crafting policies to attract private investment. Swaziland imports 80 percent of its power from South Africa and Mozambique. With both South Africa and Mozambique experiencing electricity shortages, Swaziland is working on producing its own energy using renewable energy. A developed renewable energy sector in Swaziland would make the energy supply more reliable and create domestic employment. In the long term, renewable energy would also have environmental benefits and provide energy self-sufficiency for the country. Information, Communications and Technology (ICT) is also an emerging sector. Swaziland has embarked on a number of initiatives to spur the growth of this key sector such as e-governance and the construction of the Royal Science and Technology Park. The digital migration program of the Southern African Development Community (SADC) presents ICT opportunities in the country

Incentives to invest in Swaziland include repatriation of profits, fully-serviced industrial sites, provision of purpose-built factory shells at competitive rates, and exemption from duty on raw materials for manufacture goods to be exported outside the Southern African Customs Union (SACU). Financial incentives for all investors also include tax allowances and deductions for new enterprises, including a 10-year exemption from withholding tax on dividends and a low corporate tax of 10 percent for approved investment projects. New investors also enjoy duty-free import of machinery and equipment.

SOEs and the royal family's private trust are invested in many industries and distort the economy through their influence. Virtually all large-scale investments in Swaziland involve, either by law or by custom, the participation of the government and the royal family as a partner. Public sector and royal family involvement in the economy discourages private investment and encourages monopolistic behavior driving up prices and reducing competitiveness of the country. In addition, Swaziland's land tenure system, where the majority of usable land remains the property of the King "in trust for the Swazi nation," discourages long-term investment in commercial real estate and agriculture.

Swaziland's poor human rights and labor rights record has jeopardized its access to export markets and to donor support. In 2015, Swaziland lost its duty free access to the U.S. market under the African Growth and Opportunity Act (AGOA) due to continued infringements on internationally recognized workers' rights. Swaziland also remains ineligible for Millennium Challenge Corporation (MCC) support due to its poor rankings on political and civil liberties by international non-governmental organizations.

1. OPENNESS TO, AND RESTRICTIONS UPON, FOREIGN INVESTMENT

Attitude toward Foreign Direct Investment

The GOS regards foreign direct investment as a means to drive the country's economic growth, obtain access to foreign markets for its exports, and improve international competitiveness. However, the government and the royal family also exercise considerable influence in the private sector through state owned enterprises (SOEs) that compete with private companies and through government and the royal family's substantial shareholding in private corporations. All business sectors are open to foreign investment although government approval is needed. The Swaziland Investment Promotion Authority (SIPA) is charged with designing and implementing strategies for attracting desired foreign investors. SIPA is currently functional and helpful but it is not yet a one-stop-shop for foreign investors. The Swaziland Government continues its attempts to facilitate the ease of doing business in the country, but the pace of improvement has failed to keep up with other countries in the region. Foreign investors are confused by Swaziland's dual system of governance where approval is often required by traditional authorities as well as the various government ministries.

In general, there are no laws that discriminate against foreign investors. However, in practice most successful foreign investments require local partners - often the government or the royal family - to navigate the complex bureaucracy of the country. In addition, the majority of the land is owned by the king in trust for the Swazi nation and cannot be purchased by foreign investors. Foreign investors that require significant land for the enterprise therefore must engage the king directly in business negotiations. The mining sector mandates this practice by statute. The Mining and Minerals Act of 2011 stipulates that the king will acquire 25 percent of shareholding without any monetary consideration and another 25 percent shareholding in any mining enterprise will be allocated to the government. Mining companies are also expected to pay rent for the area where company mining is going on to the head of state. The Swaziland Government recognizes the significant potential of gold, iron ore, diamonds and coal and is placing renewed emphasis on the sector and is seeking foreign investors.

Other Investment Policy Reviews

Swaziland has been a World Trade Organization (WTO) member since 1995. There has been no investment policy review conducted by UNCTAD, WTO, or OECD. The GOS is continuing to work with the United States Agency for International Development (USAID) Southern African Trade Hub in reviewing and implementing the recommendations of the Swaziland Investor Roadmap, which can be found at pdf.usaid.gov/pdf_docs/Pnadw920.pdf

Laws/Regulations of Foreign Direct Investment

Swaziland's legal and regulatory environment is underdeveloped, opaque, or unpredictable. But there are no efforts to restrict foreign investment by industry standards-setting organizations. The Competition Law of 2007 stipulates anti-competitive trade practices, requirements for mergers and acquisitions and protecting consumer welfare, and provides for an institutional mechanism for implementing these objectives. The Competition Commission monitors, regulates, controls and prevents acts or behaviors, which are likely to adversely affect the climate for competition within the country.

The country's Economic Recovery Strategy identifies the need to promote strategies and reforms in order to facilitate investment. The executive regularly interferes in court administration, case allocations, and judicial decisions. In cases involving the government or royal family, investors are unlikely to receive a fair hearing. However, the courts independently rule on purely private business disputes.

The Swaziland Investment Promotion Authority (SIPA) helps navigate the laws, rules, procedures and registration requirements for foreign investors. SIPA's website is: www.sipa.org.sz/

Investors can access registration forms for their companies on this website.

Industrial Promotion

Other than the facilitation assistance provided by SIPA, there are no official government programs to attract investment.

Energy and Mining and Information Communications and Technology are two areas that the GOS is currently promoting.

Limits on Foreign Control

The only industries that have limits on foreign control are mining and real estate. According to the Mines and Minerals Act of 2011, in any mining company the king acquires 25 percent of shareholding without any monetary consideration and another 25 percent shareholding is allocated to the government. Foreigners cannot own the majority of the countries land as it remains in trust for the Swazi nation and the King and chiefs have control over its use allocation.

Privatization Program

The International Monetary Fund (IMF) has advised the Swaziland government to privatize state owned businesses, particularly the telecommunications sector and the electricity sector. In response, the Swaziland Government passed several laws, but privatization efforts remain slow. The Swaziland Communications Commission Act and the Electronic Communications Act came into effect on July 31, 2013. The Swaziland Communications Act establishes a Commission to regulate and supervise the operation of electronic communications networks and the provision of electronic communications services in the country, including the regulation of data protection in electronic communications. The SOE, the Swaziland Posts and Telecommunications Corporation (SPTC), besides being the provider of the service, was also the regulator. The Act now transfers the regulatory powers from SPTC to the Commission.

The Swaziland government is also working on producing its own electricity using renewable energy. Swaziland imports the bulk of its electricity from South Africa (80 percent) and approximately 10 percent from Mozambique. With both countries experiencing electricity shortages, Swaziland is working on producing its own energy using renewable energy. The government is currently developing a Renewable Energy and Independent Power Producers Policy with the help of the Southern African Trade Hub with the hope of incentivizing investors in this sector.

The Swaziland Energy Regulatory Authority regulates the sector, screening investors interested in establishing power generation facilities.

Screening of FDI

Any company wishing to invest in Swaziland must adopt articles of incorporation governed by the laws Swaziland. Investors are screened for credit worthiness, business ethics, and criminal records. Foreign direct investment in manufacturing may need an environmental impact assessment. Investors complain about the amount of time the screening process takes and the cost involved.

U.S. companies have complained about the approval process with the Central Bank of Swaziland for capital transfers. While the law allows repatriation of profits, there have been instances where the regulatory approval process took a significant amount of time and effort.

With the implementation of the Swaziland Investor Roadmap 2005 that was re-launched in 2012, the Swaziland Investment Promotion Authority coordinates the screening of foreign investors. The Ministry of Commerce screens trading licenses, the office of the registrar of companies does registration; and entry permits of investors and immigration and the labor office coordinate employees. The Central Bank of Swaziland reviews applications for offshore investment by companies registered in Swaziland. The reviewing authorities are generally found to be transparent. However, the various government ministries are not always responsive to investor inquiries.

The general purpose of the screening is for the government to manage risk associated with unknown foreign investors and to encourage domestic employment. According to the Companies Act of 2009, any person, company or other corporate body, aggrieved by any decision, ruling or order of the Registrar of Companies may bring the matter under review by the High Court.

At minimum, a foreign investor must supply the following documents for screening:

Certified copies of the Directors' passports or ID documents;

Residential address from the country of origin of the applicant;

Bank account details;

Police Clearance - An original copy has to be obtained from the country of origin and it must be less than six months old;

Two color passport sized photos;

Certificate of Incorporation and Memorandum and Articles of Association.

Lease Agreement.

The requirement of a lease agreement can be problematic if a lease has not been signed pending the registration of the company. Companies have avoided this by having a condition subjecting its enforceability to the company registration.

Competition Law

The Swaziland Competition Commission reviews investment and its effect on specific industries, the effect on employment, and the ability of small businesses to be competitive. All mergers and acquisitions are subject to screening and approval of the Swaziland Competition Commission.

Investment Trends

Table 1

Measure	Year	Index or Rank	Website Address
TI Corruption Perceptions index	2014	69 of 175	transparency.org/cpi2014/results
World Bank's Doing Business Report "Ease of Doing Business"	2015	110 of 189	doingbusiness.org/rankings
Global Innovation Index	2014	127 of 143	globalinnovationindex.org/content.aspx?page=data-analysis
World Bank GNI per capita	2013	USD 2,990	data.worldbank.org/indicator/NY.GNP.PCAP.CD

Millennium Challenge Corporation Country Scorecard

The Millennium Challenge Corporation, a U.S. Government entity charged with delivering development grants to countries that have demonstrated a commitment to reform, produced scorecards for countries with a per capita gross national income (GNI) or USD 4,125 or less. A list of countries/economies with MCC scorecards and links to those scorecards is available here: http://www.mcc.gov/pages/selection/scorecards. Details on each of the MCC's indicators and a guide to reading the scorecards are available here: http://www.mcc.gov/pages/docs/doc/report-guide-to-the-indicators-and-the-selection-process-fy-2015.

2. CONVERSION AND TRANSFER POLICIES

Foreign Exchange

There are no limitations on the inflow or outflow of funds for remittances. Dividends derived from current trading profits are freely transferable on submission of documentation (including latest annual financial statements of the company concerned) to the Central Bank of Swaziland, subject to provision for the non-resident shareholders tax of 15 percent. Local credit facilities may not be utilized for paying dividends.

All capital transfers into Swaziland outside the Common Monetary Area (CMA) require prior approval of the Central Bank of Swaziland to avoid problems in the subsequent repatriation of interest, dividends, profits and other income accrued. Otherwise there are no restrictions placed on the transfers.

Other than the Rand which the Swaziland Lilangeni is pegged to, Swaziland mainly deals with three international currencies; the U.S Dollar, the Euro and the Pound Sterling. There is a straightforward process of obtaining foreign currency. A resident requiring currency other than Swaziland Emalangeni (E) or South African Rand (which are accepted as legal tender with the exchange rate on a par with Emalangeni) for permissible purposes must apply through an authorized dealer and a resident who acquires foreign currency must sell it to an authorized dealer for the local currency within ninety day. No person is permitted to hold or deal in foreign currency other than an authorized dealer. Authorized dealers in Swaziland are the First National Bank of Swaziland (FNB), Nedbank, Standard Bank, and Swazi Bank.

The Lilangeni is pegged at par with the South African Rand and exchange rates are thus determined according to the Rand and the monetary policy of South Africa.

Remittance Policies

The average delay period in remitting investments is dependent on the mode of remitting funds. SWIFT transfers average a week, while other electronic transfers typically take less than a week.

If all required documents are submitted remittances in Swaziland do not exceed 60 days. The Swaziland Government does not issue dollar-denominated bonds. Otherwise there are no limitations on the inflow and outflow of funds for remittances of profits or revenue. Swaziland currency is linked to the South African Rand so has little ability to manipulate currency.

Swaziland is a member of the Eastern and Southern Africa Anti-Money Laundering Group (ESAAMLG), the assessment of the implementation of anti-money laundering and counter-terrorist financing (AML/CFT) measures in Swaziland was conducted by ESAAMLG.

3. EXPROPRIATION AND COMPENSATION

Law prohibits expropriation and nationalization. There have been no known cases of foreign owned business being expropriated. Swaziland land tenure system can be confusing for foreign investors. Approximately sixty percent of land is Swazi Nation Land (SNL), is held by the monarchy in trust for the people of Swaziland. Control of SNL is delegated to local chiefs. Settlement of disputes regarding traditionally held land could take years. There are reported cases of land disputes between foreign businesses operating on Swazi Nation Land and traditional authorities. However, since the right of ownership on SNL remains with the King, any rights are temporary and thus their involuntary relinquishment is not technically expropriation.

In 2010, there was a dispute on a 99-year lease on Swazi Nation Land with a company developing a tourist business in the southern part of Swaziland bordering South Africa. The disputed facility was a lodge and was supposed to be a trans-frontier park between Swaziland and South Africa housing wildlife. In 2010, the King tried to revoke the 99-year lease agreement with the foreign investor. The owners of the facility applied to the High Court, but a settlement was never reached because the King has constitutional immunity from lawsuits. The investors complained of their multi-million dollar investment loss.

Similarly, in 2014 a dispute emerged involving a foreign investor in the iron ore mining business. The foreign investor complained he was driven out of the country by the King's advisors and accused the government and king of destroying the business to avoid repaying a loan the company had provided the king. The mining operation closed after only three years in operation and the company complained that they lost tens of millions of USD in investment and lost earnings.

The GOS has shown no pattern of discrimination against U.S. persons.

The mining sector and natural resources sector are a high risk due to the political regulations surrounding this type of sector.

4. DISPUTE SETTLEMENT

Legal System, Specialized Courts, Judicial Independence, Judgments of Foreign Courts

Swaziland has a dual legal system consisting of a set of courts that follow Roman-Dutch law and a set of national courts that follow Swazi law and customs. This parallel system can be confusing ad has presented problems for foreign-owned businesses. Swaziland western-style courts do enforce property rights. The legal system has a western-style court system to enforce contracts and the industrial court hears industrial relations matters.

The country has various laws governing commercial or contractual laws. The Industrial Relations Act of 2000 created the Conciliation, Mediation and Arbitration Commission (CMAC) to resolve employer-employee disputes. The Company Act of 2009, which outlines commercial law; the Competition Act of 2007, which screens and approves mergers and acquisitions; and the Standards Act of 2003, which promotes quality principles and facilitates the use of standards to reduce technical barriers to trade and investment.

Intellectual property law is currently inadequate under Swaziland law. Copyright protection is addressed under four statutes dated 1912, 1918, 1933 and 1936. Swaziland inherited its intellectual property rights regime from the colonial era, under which copyrights, patents, and trademarks were somewhat protected under various acts promulgated by colonial authority.

In August 2014 a Copyright and Neighboring Bill repealing the Copyright Act of 1912 was circulated and in February 2015, the government circulated two more bills, one for the establishment of an intellectual property tribunal and the Trademarks Amendment bill amending the Trademarks Act of 1981. All these bills are still to be debated in Parliament.

The majority of investor disputes are employee-related and resolved in arbitration or the courts.

Bankruptcy

The Insolvency Act of 1955 is the law that governs bankruptcy in Swaziland. The insolvent debtor or his agent petitions the court for the acceptance of the surrender of the debtor's estate for the benefit of his creditors. Creditors need to petition with the court and provide documents supporting their claim.

Bankruptcy is only criminalized if the debtor, trustee or sole owner does not comply with the requirements of the Master or the creditor, for example if he/she fails to submit documents, declare assets; or obstructs, hinders a liquidator appointed under the Act in the performance of his functions, is guilty of an offence.

In the World Bank's, 2015 Doing Business Report", Swaziland's ranking in the category of Ease of Resolving Insolvency dropped to 80 from 77 the previous year out of 189 economies, a -3 change..

Investment Disputes

Investment disputes are not common in Swaziland. The GOS accepts international arbitration of investment disputes between foreign investors and the state. Any agreement with international investors/companies can include an enforceable clause stating where arbitration will take place and which laws will apply. Swaziland does not have a domestic arbitration body for investment disputes between companies. Swaziland is a member state to the International Centre for the Settlement of Investment Disputes (ICSID Convention) and the Multilateral Investment Guarantee Agency (MIGA).

There have been at least two major investment disputes involving foreign investors in the past ten years but none involving U.S. citizens.

The few disputes that have arisen involve a pattern of companies that are partly owned by the king and Swaziland government investing in natural resources. The pattern is that after a few years of operation or development, the foreign investors are required to relinquish their claims to ownership of the resources under non-transparent threats against them. Domestic civil society has been virtually silent with a few exceptions.

International Arbitration

The GOS accepts international arbitration.

Swaziland, as a member of the Southern African Customs Union (SACU), in 2008 SACU signed a Trade, Investment and Development Cooperative Agreement (TIDCA). There are no claims under this agreement.

Swaziland has a dual legal system consisting of Roman-Dutch law and Swazi law and customs. In addition to Western-style court system, Swazi traditional courts run parallel, which can be confusing for foreign-owned businesses. These traditional courts, in which the king is supreme authority, are available for dispute settlement. Such disputes, however, can be transferred to the formal court system at the option of the foreign investor.

The Conciliation, Mediation and Arbitration Commission (CMAC), which is governed by the Industrial Relations, Act 2000 resolves employer-employee disputes.

ICSID Convention and New York Convention

Swaziland is a member state to the International Centre for the Settlement of Investment Disputes (ICSID Convention).

The Swaziland Government accepts binding international arbitration of investment disputes between foreign investors and the state. Any agreement with international investors/parties includes a clause stating where arbitration will take place and which laws will apply.

Swaziland is not a signatory to the convention on the Recognition and Enforcement of Foreign Arbitral Awards (1958 New York Convention).

Duration of Dispute Resolution

Due to the dual legal system in Swaziland, it is difficult to approximate the duration of dispute resolutions in Swaziland. If the traditional structures are involved, as they would be in the case of natural resources or land investments, the dispute may take several years to be resolved.

General contract disputes may take up to one year to resolve in the Industrial Court, depending on the level of complexity. Anti-trust cases are relatively new but have taken several years to reach resolution. Due to the existence of the Conciliation, Mediation, and Arbitration Commission for labor disputes, employer-employee disputes are generally resolved within a few months.

Political interference is the most significant problem in local courts. Parties attempt to extend the King's constitutional immunity to all lawsuits in which his companies are an investor. The local legal profession lacks sufficient ethical standards.

In general the Swazi legal system has effectively enforced court decisions and international arbitration awards. Judgments of foreign courts are accepted and enforced. Swaziland is not a signatory of the New York Convention but ICSD membership binds the country to enforce international arbitration awards generated in that venue.

5. PERFORMANCE REQUIREMENTS AND INVESTMENT INCENTIVES

WTO/TRIMS

The GOS does not maintain any measures that are alleged to violate the WTO's Trade Related Investment Measures requirements.

Investment Incentives

Swaziland has a human resources training rebate - a rebate of 150 percent of the cost is written again tax for training. At the discretion of the Minister of Finance, the Swazi government applies a reduced tax rate of 10 percent for the first ten-year period of operation, available for businesses that qualify under the Development Approval Order. Capital goods imported into the country for productive investments are exempt from import duties. Raw materials imported into the country to manufacture products to be exported outside the SACU area are also exempt from import duties. The law allows for repatriation of profits and dividends including salaries for expatriate staff and capital repayments. The Central Bank of Swaziland guarantees loans raised by investors for the export markets. There is also provision of loss cover which company can carry over in case it incurs a loss in the year of assessment.

Research and Development

The law is silent on research and development programs.

Performance Requirements

The Ministry of Labor and Social Security requires the hiring of qualified Swazi workers where possible, even at executive positions. Foreign investors are required to apply for residence and work permits. Although they are generally awarded business people complain that the process is cumbersome. SIPA is now supervising the application of these permits for incoming foreign businesses as part of the implementation of the Investor Roadmap.

There are no government-imposed conditions on permission to invest, including tariff and non-tariff barriers. In the manufacturing sector if a company plans to label a product to export as made in Swaziland, the government requires that the local content of such export be at least 25 percent. These requirements are applied systematically.

Data Storage

The government does not follow a forced localization policy. There are no requirements for foreign IT providers to turn over source code and/or provide access to surveillance (backdoors into hardware and software or turn over keys for encryption. The technology industry in Swaziland is still at its infancy.

6. RIGHT TO PRIVATE OWNERSHIP AND ESTABLISHMENT

Foreign investors own the majority of Swaziland's largest businesses, either fully or with minority participation by Swazi institutions. There are no legal restrictions on foreign ownership that are discriminatory against foreign investors, but the government and the royal family's direct investment in industry is a practical limitation to foreign investment requiring a Swazi investor or joint venture. Both foreign and domestic private entities have a right to establish businesses and acquire and dispose of interest in business enterprises.

7. PROTECTION OF PROPERTY RIGHTS

Real Property

For titled property the Swaziland Government recognizes and enforces secured interest in property. For titled property there is a recognized and reliable system of recording security interests. Most land is the country is referred to as Swazi Nation Land and is governed by the traditional structures overseen by the king. Swazi Nation land rests with the king who appoints chiefs to oversee the use of it. The Constitution of the country protects the right to own property, but most Swazis reside on Swazi Nation Land that is not covered by this constitutional protection. The law allows for eminent domain but requires compensation. The compensation is not forthcoming in all cases.

60 percent of land does not have clear title. The chiefs as people in charge keep their own records of who owns what land.

The World's Bank ease of registering property refers to property in urban areas where there are titles for land. Swazi nation land is not titled and even lending institutions are reluctant to use it as collateral. Lending institutions can only give a loan for development on non-titled land if the borrower has titled land as collateral.

Intellectual Property Rights

Protection for patents, trademarks and copyrights is currently inadequate under Swazi law. Patents are currently protected under a 1936 act that automatically extends patent protection, upon proper application, to products that have been patented in either South Arica or Great Britain. Trademark protection is addressed in the 1981 Trademarks Act. Copyright protections are addressed under four statues, dated 1912, 1918, 1933 and 1936.

There are bills that are pending that amend the Copyright Act of 1912, and the Trademarks Act of 1981. The Copyright and Neighboring Rights Bill of 2014 will change Swaziland's intellectual property law. The Act will protect literary, musical, artistic, audio-visual, sound recordings, broadcasts and published editions. It also criminalizes illicit recording and false representation of someone else's work. The Act also gives the duration of copyright among other things. The Swaziland Intellectual Property Tribunal Bill 2015 will establish the Intellectual Property Tribunal, which will be responsible for hearing over all matters and disputes involving intellectual property in Swaziland.

The Trademarks (Amendment) Bill of 2015 is to amend the Trademarks of 1981 and bring it into compliance with provisions of the Agreement on Trade Related Aspects of Intellectual Property Rights (TRIPS), the Madrid Agreement concerning International Registration of Marks and the Banjul Protocol on Trademarks.

None of these proposed amendments are law yet.

Swaziland does not track and report on seizures of counterfeit goods.

Swaziland is not listed in USTR's Special 301 report.

Swaziland is not listed in the notorious market report.

For additional information about treaty obligations and points of contact at local IP offices, please see WIPO's country profiles at http://www.wipo.int/directory/en/ Swaziland joined WIPO in 1988. Until the bills on Intellectual Property go through parliament the current information is up to date.

Resources for Rights Holders
NAME of IP Attaché or Economic Officer: Christian Olsen
Political Economic Officer

+268 2404 6441
olsencr@state.gov

8. TRANSPARENCY OF THE REGULATORY SYSTEM

In general, the laws of the country are transparent. However, the application of the laws is inconsistent. The Competition Act came into force in 2007 and the Competition Commission Regulations came into effect in 2010. All of the regulations are publicly available.

There are no regulatory processes managed by nongovernmental organizations. Foreign investors coming into the country can join the Federation of Swaziland Employers/Chamber of Commerce on an equal basis with nationals of the country. This association is the link between the private sector and government.

Proposed laws and regulations are published in the government Gazette for public comment thirty days prior to a bill's presentation to parliament. Ministries sometimes consult with selected members of the public and private sector.

International accounting firms have branches in the country e.g. KPMG, PricewaterhouseCooper (PwC). But the legal and regulatory environment is underdeveloped, opaque and unpredictable. For instance Swaziland does not have an approved trade policy, investment policy, or industrial policy.

Proposed law and regulations are published in the government Gazette for public comment thirty days prior to a bill's presentation to parliament. Ministries at draft stage sometimes consult with selected members of the public and the private sector. There are no informal regulatory processes managed by nongovernmental organizations or private sector associations.

9. EFFICIENT CAPITAL MARKETS AND PORTFOLIO INVESTMENT

Swaziland's capital markets are closely tied to those of South Africa and operate under conditions generally similar to the conditions in that market. The government in 2010 enacted the Securities Act to strengthen the regulation of the portfolio investment. The Act was primarily to facilitate and develop an orderly, fair and efficient capital market in the country.

Swaziland has a small stock exchange with only six companies currently trading. In 2010 the Financial Services Regulatory Authority was established. This institution governs non-bank financial institutions including capital markets, insurance, retirement fund, building societies, micro-finance institutions and savings and credit cooperatives. The royal wealth fund and national pension fund invest in the private equity market, but there are otherwise few professional investors.

Existing policies neither inhibit nor facilitate the free flow of financial resources. The demand is simply not present. The Central Bank respects International Monetary Fund (IMF) Article VIII.

Credit is allocated on market terms. The Central Bank of Swaziland guarantees loans for the export market and for small businesses.

Money and Banking System, Hostile Takeovers

Swaziland's banks are primarily subsidiaries of South African banks. Standard Bank is the largest bank by capital assets and employs about 400 workers. Swaziland has a central bank system. The Central Bank's prior approval is necessary for all capital transfers into Swaziland from outside the Common Monetary Area (CMA) to avoid problems in the subsequent repatriation of interest; dividends, profits and other income accrued. Hostile takeovers are uncommon.

10. COMPETITION FROM STATE-OWNED ENTERPRISES

SOEs are active in Information and Communication Technology, Energy and Mining, and Environmental Technologies. Under the Ministry of Finance, the Public Enterprise Unit (http://www.gov.sz/) there is a list of SOEs. The Swaziland Government defines SOEs as private enterprises. They are separated in categories. Category A are those SOEs that are wholly owned by Government. Category B are those SOEs in which government has a minority interest or which monitors other financial institutions or a local government authority. These categories are further broken down to profit making SOEs but with a social responsibility; those that are profit making and developmental; those that are regulatory and those that are regulatory but developmental. SOEs are normally monopolies. For example, the power utility is an SOE and is a monopoly. The private sector (non-SOE) is the main contributor to research and developments. SOEs purchase and supply goods and services to and from the private sector and foreign firms. SOEs in Swaziland are usually monopolies and therefor the private sector cannot compete. SOEs where government is a major shareholder and has a controlling position are not subjected to the same tax burden. But the ones where government has a minority shareholder are subject to the same tax burden and tax rebate policies as the private sector. SOEs have preferential access to Swazi nation land. The Public Enterprise Act governs SOEs. The Boards review the budget before tabling it to the line ministry, which, in turn, tables it in parliament where it is scrutinized by the public accounts committee.

OECD Guidelines on Corporate Governance of SOEs

SOEs' senior managers report to the board and in turn the board reports to a line minister. The minister then works with the Standing Committee on Public Enterprise (SCOPE), which is composed of cabinet ministers. SOEs are governed by the Public Enterprises Act, which requires audits of the SOEs and public annual reports. SOEs generally practice the OECD Guidelines and Corporate Governance of SOEs in Swaziland. Government is not involved in the day-to-day management of SOEs. Boards of SOEs exercise their independence and responsibility. The Public Enterprise Unit provides regular monitoring of SOEs. SOEs submit yearly reports and financial statements to parliament. Senior SOE management reports to an independent board of directors who then report to a line minister. The line minister of the SOE appoints the board. In some cases, the allocation is politically motivated. In some cases, the king appoints his own representative as well. Generally, court processes are nondiscriminatory in relation to SOEs.

Sovereign Wealth Funds

In 1968 the late King Sobhuza II created a Royal Charter this governs the only Sovereign Wealth Fund, Tibiyo Taka Ngwane. This fund is not subject to government or parliamentary oversight and need not provide public information on assets or financial performance. The SWF known as Tibiyo Taka Ngwane publishes its annual report, but it is not required by law to do so. Similarly the SWF obtains independent audits at its own discretion.

Tibiyo Taka Ngwane in its objectives says it supports the government in fostering economic independence and self-sufficiency. The SWF widely invests in the economy and holds shares in most major industries e.g. Sugar, commercial real estate, beverages, dairy, hotel industry and transportation. For their social responsibility they pay bursaries for pupils. They do not have any legal obligations other than the vague language of investing in assets in trust for the Swazi nation. It is run as a private equity investment fund for the benefit of the King and the royal family. The Sovereign Wealth Fund and the government co-invest to exercise majority control in many instances.

Government Departments do not engage in commercial activity that has an adverse commercial impact on U.S. firms. The SWF who owns its assets is an entity managed by a board of directors, which is appointed by the king. Tibiyo Taka Ngwane invests entirely in the local economy and local subsidiaries of foreign companies. Tibiyo has shares in a number of private companies. Sometimes foreign companies can form relationships with Tibiyo especially if the foreign company wants to raise capital and if experienced can manage the project.

The government does not have jurisdiction over the SWF, which is subject only to the King's approval. The SWF usually plays a passive role. In some companies the Chief Executive Officer of the SWF sits on the board of the private company.

11. CORPORATE SOCIAL RESPONSIBILITY

Multinational enterprises in the country have robust corporate social responsibility programs, and consumers often recognize their efforts. However, smaller domestic companies are less likely to have CSR programs. The Development Approval Order which is part of the Income Tax law allows a company to apply to the minister of finance if the company plans to make significant CSR investments to be charged a reduced tax rate up to 10 percent. The Swaziland Government enforcement is sporadic but generally does not vary based on whether a company is domestic or foreign. Requirements are not waived to attract foreign investment. The government does not have corporate governance, accounting, and executive compensation standards to protect shareholders. There are not independent NGOs monitoring CSR.

OECD Guidelines for Multinational Enterprises

The Swaziland Government encourages foreign and local enterprises to follow generally accepted CSR principles.

12. POLITICAL VIOLENCE

There are few incidents of political violence against the government or private businesses but police regularly harass arrest and imprison critics of the government. Police routinely prevent meetings planned by labor unions and other organizations focused on political or socio-economic issues. There are no examples, over the past ten years, of damage to projects and/or installations.

Government critics are under increased pressure in the form of police harassment, criminal charges for sedition and related crimes, and informal harassment of family members. In addition, the low economic growth rate and lack of social protection has begun to politicize the otherwise apolitical rural majority.

13. CORRUPTION

Swaziland passed the Prevention of Corruption Act in 2007 which established the Anti-Corruption Commission. The Swaziland Public Procurement Act became law in 2010. The Swaziland Public Procurement Agency (SPPRA) was established in 2012. The SPPRA will oversee public purchasing and set up a code of conduct for public sector procurement officers to track all public funds not only for procurement but any other contractual agreement for goods, works or services. Civil society organizations accuse Swaziland's Anti-Corruption Commission of engaging in politically motivated investigations and failing to tackle genuine issues of corruption. The act disqualifies public sector workers and politicians from supplying the government.

SPPRA conducted capacity building exercise nationwide to increase knowledge and adoption of universally practiced purchasing systems with private companies. And according to section 27 of the Public Procurement Regulations suppliers are prohibited to offer gifts or hospitality, directly or indirectly to staff of a procuring entity, members of the tender board and members of the SPPRA.

Only the large multi-national companies in the country have internal controls and compliance programs. Swaziland is a signatory of the UN Anti-corruption Convention, African Union Convention on Preventing and Combating Corruption and Related Offences, and the SADC Protocol against Corruption. But Swaziland has not domesticated the UN Anti-Corruption Convention. Only the Anti-Corruption Commission that is legally allowed to investigate corruption.

Corruption is particularly prevalent in government procurement. As mentioned above the Swazi government set up the Swaziland Public Procurement Regulatory Agency (SPPRA) to provide regulation and control practice in respect of public procurement. Giving or receiving a bribe is illegal. A convicted person faces a maximum of a 100,000 emalangeni (USD 10,000.00) fine or ten years imprisonment. A convicted law enforcement officer or public prosecutor faces a maximum fine of 200,000 emalangeni (USD 20,000).

Foreign and domestic businesses have indicated that corruption and bribery requests impact profits, contracts and investment decisions for their companies.

UN Anticorruption Convention, OECD Convention on Combatting Bribery

Swaziland is not a signatory of the OECD Convention for Combating Bribery nor the UN Anticorruption Convention.

Resources to Report Corruption

Contact at government agency or agencies are responsible for combating corruption:
Thanda Mngwengwe
Commissioner
Swaziland Anti-Corruption Commission
3rd Floor, Mbandzeni House, Mbabane
+268 2404 3179/0761

anticorruption@realnet.co.sz

14. BILATERAL INVESTMENT AGREEMENTS

Swaziland does not have a bilateral investment treaty with the U.S.

Swaziland has investment agreements with the United Kingdom, Germany, and the European Union (EU). The EU concluded negotiations on an Economic Partnership Agreement (EPA) on 15 July with the Southern African Development Community (SADC) group comprising of Botswana, Lesotho, Mozambique, Namibia, South Africa and Swaziland. The SADC EPA countries are also members of the WTO.

Swaziland also has bilateral investment protection agreements with Egypt, Taiwan, and Mauritius.

Bilateral Taxation Treaties

Swaziland does not have a bilateral taxation treaty with the U.S.

15. OPIC AND OTHER INVESTMENT INSURANCE PROGRAMS

There is potential for an Overseas Private Investment Corporation (OPIC) program in Swaziland, particularly in the renewable energy industry. Here the GOS has demonstrated a commitment towards encouraging private sector investment, particularly by U.S. companies. However, OPIC has not yet signed in agreement with Swaziland.

16. LABOR

According to the Swaziland Central Statistics office the Unemployment Rate Relaxed stands at 40.6 percent whilst the Strict Definition stands at 28.5 percent. Literacy rate in 2013 was at 89 percent but there is a shortage of technically skilled labor and the country relies heavily on expatriate technicians, accountants and engineers. The youth unemployment rate is 42.3 percent. The urban areas were the hard hit as one out of five young people was unemployed and the rate stood at 44.8 percent.

Swaziland has a shortage of technically skilled labor. The engineering, accountancy, and technical sectors are a priority for the government. The Ministry of Education has listed these fields as the ones the government will sponsor. The law requires that companies to employ Swazi nationals unless they cannot find a qualified national.

The Employment Act says if the employer contemplates adjusting employment, the employer will give not less than one-month notice to the Labor Commissioner and the trade union. The employer must state the number of employees to be affected, their occupation and remuneration; the reasons for the adjustment; the effective date; financial statements and audited accounts, and opinions that have been looked into to avert the situation.

Section 34 of the Employment Act says if the services of an employee are terminated other than being fired, a severance allowance amounting to ten working days' wages for each completed year in excess of one year that he has been continuously employed by that employer.

Swaziland does not have free trade zones but supports four industrial areas. The largest is in Matsapha, located between the primary cities of Mbabane and Manzini. It has direct rail and road links. The Matsapha Industrial Estates dry port maximizes time and cost savings for importers and exporters using the ports of Durban and Richard's Bay in South Africa and Maputo in Mozambique.

Swaziland has ratified all the ILO eight core conventions; however, gaps continue to remain salient both in law and practice. The laws provide that workers, except for those in essential services, have the right to form and join independent unions, conduct legal strikes, and bargain collectively. Provisions of other laws restricting freedom of assembly and association, however, often abrogate these rights. The laws provide for the registration of unions and federations, but grant far-reaching powers to the labor commissioner with respect to determining eligibility for registration. Unions must represent at least 50 percent of employees in a work place to be automatically recognized. The law also gives employers discretion as to whether or not to recognize a labor organization as a collective employee representative if less than 50 percent of the employees are members of the organization, and allows employers to set conditions for such recognition. Collective agreements must be registered with the Industrial Court.

Labor unions are independent of the government. However, the government has refused to recognize a number of labor unions in the country, and only recently registered the primary labor federation --Trade Union Congress of Swaziland (TUCOSWA) and the two employer federations it delisted in 2012, following three years of consistent engagement by the U.S. Government, ILO, and domestic labor organizations calling for this action in support of workers' rights.

Labor unions practice collective bargaining, but there are few industry associations and bargaining is conducted largely with individual employers in the private sector.

According to the Industrial Relations Act of 2000, as amended, employees who are not engaged in "essential services" have the right to undertake peaceful protest actions to "promote or defend socio-economic interests" of workers, i.e. not to include matters of a purely political nature. Despite its legal recognition, the right to strike is strictly regulated. Strikes and lockouts are prohibited in essential services. The current list of these essential services provides for broad prohibition of strikes in nonessential sectors, including posts, telephone, telegraph, radio, and teaching, in consistent with the ILO's standard.

Additionally, the minister has the power to modify this list as deemed appropriate. The law details the steps to be followed when disputes arise and provides penalties for employers who conduct unauthorized lockouts. The law also provides for the establishment of a conciliation, mediation, and arbitration commission for dispute resolution but confers on the commissioner of labor the power to "intervene" in labor disputes before they are reported to the commission, if there is reason to believe that a dispute could have serious consequences for the employers, workers, or the economy if not resolved promptly.

The Conciliation, Mediation and Arbitration Commission (CMAC) is the organization that resolves labor disputes. Cases generally start at CMAC with mediation and arbitration. Either party can refuse arbitration and bring the case to the Industrial Court, which can also order arbitration. According to the Industrial Relations Act workers can engage in a strike action if there is an unresolved dispute. The party that intends to go on strike needs to give notice to the employer, the labor commissioner and (CMAC). CMAC should arrange and supervise a secret ballot to determine whether the majority of employees are in favor of the strike action. When disputes arose with civil servant unions, the government often intervened to reduce the chances of a protest action, which may not be called legally until all avenues of negotiation have been exhausted and a secret ballot of union members has been conducted.

Approximately 12 percent of children in Swaziland are engaged in child labor, primarily in agriculture and livestock herding.

The labor office has inspectors who inspect if companies adhere to the labor regulations, health, safety standards, and wage laws. Swaziland has been in ILO's special paragraph for failing to allow freedom of association of workers. The Minister of Labor and Social is empowered by the law to set minimum wages. In 2014, Swaziland deregistered federations in the country citing that the old industrial relations act did not provide for the registration of federations. Three federations were deregistered. This put the country in a difficult situation as registration of federations was a requirement of the ILO. In November 2014 the Industrial Relations Act was passed. The law provided for the registration of federations. The federations that were deregistered were the employers' federation, the labor federation and an indigenous business people federation. Despite the amendment to the law, none of the federations have been subsequently registered.

Labor laws are not waived in order to attract or retain investments.

17. FOREIGN DIRECT INVESTMENT AND FOREIGN PORTFOLIO INVESTMENT STATISTICS

Table 2: Key Macroeconomic Data, U.S. FDI in Host Country/Economy

	Host Country Statistical source*		USG or international statistical source		USG or International Source of Data: BEA; IMF; Eurostat; UNCTAD, Other
Economic Data	Year	Amount	Year	Amount	
Host Country Gross Domestic Product (GDP) ($M USD)	2013	3,791	2014	3,791	www.worldbank.org/en/country
Foreign Direct Investment	Host Country Statistical source*		USG or international statistical source		USG or international Source of data: BEA; IMF; Eurostat; UNCTAD, Other
U.S. FDI in partner country ($M USD, stock positions)	N/A		2013	N/A	http://bea.gov/international/factsheet/factsheet.cfm?Area=442
Host country's FDI in the United States ($M USD, stock positions)	N/A		2013	2	http://bea.gov/international/factsheet/factsheet.cfm?Area=442
Total inbound stock of FDI as % host GDP	N/A		N/A		

*Central Bank of Swaziland http://www.centralbank.org.sz

ATTORNEYS IN SWAZILAND

Mabila Attorneys
Umphohlo & Lomadvokola Street
Queengate, Mbabane
Tel: (268) 2404-2725, 2404-2497

Robinson Bertram Attorneys
Ingcongwane Building
Gwamile Stree, Mbabane
Te: (268) 2404-2953

Dunseith Attorneys
Landsdowne House
Mbabane
Tel: (268) 2404-0276

MPS Law Firm
Samora Machel Street
Mbabane
Tel: (268) 2404-3132, 2404-1177

Currie & Sibandze Associates
1st floor Development House
Swazi Plaza, Mbabane
Tel: (268) 2404-2936, 2404-2937

Maphanga Howe Masuku Nsibande Attorneys
Corner of Ben Dunn & Lomadvokola Streets
Queensgate, Mbabane
Tel: (268) 2404-2178, 2404-3860

Masina Ndlovu Mzizi & Company
President Building, Manzini
Tel: (268) 2505-2897, 2404-7654

Sigwane & Partners
Embassy House
Mbabane
Tel: (268) 2404-5360/1

WEB RESOURCES

Central Bank of Swaziland – http://www.centralbank.org.sz
Swaziland Investment Promotion Authority – http://www.sipa.org.sz
African Alliance Swaziland Securities Limited – http://www.africanalliance.com
AGOA: http://www.agoa.gov
Government of Kingdom of Swaziland: http://www.gov.sz
USAID Southern Africa Trade Hub: http://www.satradehub.org
African Development Bank Group: www.afdb.org
Country Limitation Schedule: http://www.exim.gov/tools/country/country_limits.html
Export-Import Bank of the United States: http://www.exim.gov
Overseas Private Investment Corporation: http://www.opic.gov
SBA's Office of International Trade: http://www.sba.gov/oit/
Southern Africa Global Competitiveness Hub: http://www.satradehub.org
Swaziland Industrial Development Company: http://www.sidc.co.sz
Tibiyo Taka Nwane: http://ww2.tibiyo.com
Trade and Development Agency: http://www.tda.gov
U.S. Agency for International Development: http://www.usaid.gov
USDA Commodity Credit Corporation: http://www.fsa.usda.gov/ccc/default.htm

TRADE AND PROJECT FINANCING

How Do I Get Paid (Methods of Payment) Swaziland importers utilize most of the standard payment methods available in international commerce. The most commonly used are:

* Cash in Advance
* Letters of Credit (LC),
* Bank Collections and Bills of Exchange
* Open Account
* Sales on Consignment
* International Money Transfers

American exporters should offer quotations based on the f.o.b. value at the port of export. As a general rule, such quotations should also include a statement of the actual charges for freight and insurance, plus any additional charges, to the port of delivery. Quotations are usually in terms of the currency of the country of origin. The terms of payment for imported goods vary according to the type of buyer and the buyer's access to capital.

HOW DOES THE BANKING SYSTEM OPERATE

The Central Bank of Swaziland is the monetary authority responsible for management of the country's foreign exchange reserves, administration of exchange controls, and regulation of financial institutions.

There are four commercial banks operating in Swaziland: First National Bank of Swaziland, NedBank, SwaziBank, and Standard Bank. The government-owned Swaziland Development and Savings Bank went bankrupt due to millions of dollars of unpaid loans in June 1995 and is now operating, although the Swaziland Government in its 2010/2011 Fiscal Adjustment Roadmap listed the bank as one of the institutions that will be privatized.

Each of the operating banks has at least two branches. Normal banking facilities are provided at all four banks, and interest rates on borrowing are below those in South Africa. The prime rate is 9.0 percent and the mortgage rate is 7.0 percent (January 2011). Through Swaziland's membership in the Common Monetary Area, after-tax profits can be repatriated anywhere the investor chooses. The corporate tax rate is 30 percent, and new businesses can apply for a 10-year rate of 10 percent. Dividends, subject to a withholding tax of 15 percent, are likewise freely remitted. There are no exchange regulations affecting transactions within the CMA.

Export financing is available through the Export-Import Bank but must be applied for by a Swazi partner. There are no Export-Import Bank bundling facilities in Swaziland. Project financing is available through such multilateral institutions as the World Bank and African Development Bank. In the past, resources have gone largely to infrastructure development, including roads and irrigation systems.

FOREIGN-EXCHANGE CONTROLS

Exchange controls are currently administered by the Central Bank Exchange Control Department. All international commercial transactions must be through authorized foreign exchange dealers.

U.S. BANKS AND LOCAL CORRESPONDENT BANKS

Banks with correspondent U.S. banking arrangements are:

* First National Bank of Swaziland Limited
* Nedbank
* Standard Bank

PROJECT FINANCING

Sources of Project Financing in Swaziland

Swaziland Industrial Development Company (SIDC) SIDC is prepared to take up shares, thereby providing equity finance where required. SIDC also offers medium- to long-term loans and leases factory space. SIDC will only participate in projects that are technically feasible, financially viable, and soundly managed. SIDC gives priority to projects which provide permanent employment, generate foreign exchange, and improve Swaziland's human capacity.

Swaziland Investment Development Company
P.O. Box 866
Mbabane
Tel: (+268) 404-4010/2
Fax: (+268) 404-5619
http://www.sidc.co.sz

Tibiyo Taka Ngwane

Tibiyo Taka Ngwane conducts free enterprise business on behalf of the Swazi Nation with the King serving as Trustee. Tibiyo has a portfolio of nearly 30 interests in sectors including mining, manufacturing, property, finance, agriculture, tourism, and transport. Tibiyo frequently works in partnership with major companies and international development agencies.

Tibiyo Taka Ngwane
P.O. Box 181
Kwaluseni
Tel: (+268) 518-4390
Fax: (+268) 518-4399
http://www.tibiyo.com

WEB RESOURCES

Export-Import Bank of the United States: http://www.exim.gov
Country Limitation Schedule: http://www.exim.gov/tools/country/country_limits.html
OPIC: http://www.opic.gov
Trade and Development Agency: http://www.tda.gov/
SBA's Office of International Trade: http://www.sba.gov/oit/
USDA Commodity Credit Corporation: http://www.fsa.usda.gov/ccc/default.htm
U.S. Agency for International Development: http://www.usaid.gov
African Development Bank: http://www.afdb.org
Southern Africa Global Competitiveness Hub: http://www.satradehub.org

Swaziland Industrial Development Company: http://www.sidc.co.sz
Tibiyo Taka Ngwane: http://ww2.tibiyo.com
Small Business Development in Swaziland
For a comprehensive listing of organizations in Swaziland that support small and medium business development, please refer to the OPIC/U.S. Department of Commerce publication entitled Africa, "A Guide to Business Finance for U.S. Firms." http://permanent.access.gpo.gov/lps15194/sb-guide.pdf

BUSINESS TRAVEL

BUSINESS CUSTOMS

Foreigners still largely dominate the Swazi business sector and the Swazi business community has experience with foreign businesspeople. Nevertheless, a familiarity with some Swazi social and cultural customs would be helpful to any American planning on doing business in the country.

* Although Swazi society appears open to outsiders, it is only so on a superficial level. Developing strong institutional and personal relations is possible in Swaziland but takes time. Newcomers are advised to appreciate what is and what is not considered the "Swazi way."
* Historically, there is little indigenous entrepreneurship. Swazis are accustomed to working for wages, not starting their own businesses. There is only a fledgling Swazi entrepreneurial community.
* Swazis tend to be more relaxed and easy-going in business style, both in behavior and ethics. Business is built less around principles and the honor of a person's word than on the basis of what works at the time. This can be disconcerting to some Americans.
* Quality customer service is not widely practiced. According to a Swazi businessman trained in the United States, customer service is a new idea to many Swazis and something that must be taught.
* Decision-making is not always a quick or easy process. Some Swazis may say

"yes" merely out of politeness. Traditionally, decisions are made communally, not individually. Standing against the majority is not easy. Americans should be conscious of this and not expect rapid decisions.

* Swazis tend not to be confrontational and at times not forthcoming with opinions.

Speaking one's mind, even when solicited, is not as respected as it is in the United States. This can clash with the American tendency to be very direct.

* In making business deals with Swazi partners, bargaining is common and expected. It is not an insult to try and talk somebody down in price.
* Foreign business people have noted that native Swazis can have a difficult time assuming managerial roles. One factor that impinges on their decision-making freedom is reluctance to fire workers or employees connected to the royal family.

TRAVEL ADVISORY

Please view the Consular Information Sheet for Swaziland:
http://travel.state.gov/travel/cis_pa_tw/cis/cis_1031.html

VISA REQUIREMENTS

A passport is required. U.S. citizens do not need a visa for short visits of up to 60 days for tourism and business. Permission-to-stay is initially granted for 30 days and can be renewed for a total of 60 days. For further information on visa requirements, contact the Embassy of the Kingdom of Swaziland, 1712 New Hampshire Avenue, NW, Washington, DC 20009, phone (202) 234-5002.

U.S. companies that require travel of foreign businesspersons to the United States should be advised that security evaluations are handled via an interagency process. Visa applicants should go to the following links.

State Department Visa Website: http://travel.state.gov/visa/

United States Visas.gov http://evisaforms.state.gov/SchedulingSystem.asp

Consular services for American Citizens: http://swaziland.usembassy.gov

TELECOMMUNICATIONS

Direct dialing is available to many countries, including the U.S. Cellular services are provided by one cellular provider.

Several internet service providers are available and there are several Internet cafes along the Mbabane-Manzini corridor.

Swaziland telecommunications costs, including ADSL, remain one of the highest in the world.

TRANSPORTATION

Flights from Matsapha Airport, near Manzini, link Swaziland with Johannesburg, Maputo, and Durban. Flights use small propeller planes and are fairly reliable. Good roads link Swaziland to South Africa and Mozambique.

Owning a private car is essential in Swaziland, as public transportation is not reliable or safe. Taxis and buses run in the major towns, but it is not advisable to use them. Paved roads link the main centers, but most side roads are unpaved, dusty, and uneven during the dry season and slippery during the rainy season.

Motor vehicle registration is simple, provided the car is in good working condition. All cars require a road worthiness certificate issued by the Ministry of Public Works and Transportation.

Unleaded gasoline is available but the octane rating is not as high as in the U.S. Third-party insurance is covered by a levy included in the gasoline price.

LANGUAGE

English and siSwati are the official languages, and English is the official written language. Businesspeople will have little trouble being understood by educated Swazis.

HEALTH

Medical facilities are limited throughout Swaziland. Although the Mbabane Clinic in the capital is small, it is well equipped and well staffed for minor procedures. For advanced care, Americans often choose to go to South Africa where better facilities and specialists exist. Most prescription drugs are available locally or can be imported from South Africa, but travelers are advised to bring sufficient quantities of their own required medication. A doctor's note describing the medication may be helpful if questioned by authorities.

Malaria prophylactics are recommended for travel to the lowlands of Swaziland.

Hepatitis A and Hepatitis B vaccinations are recommended. Rabies exists in all areas of Swaziland, including Mbabane. Those people who wish to walk or jog are advised to be vaccinated with HDCV.

Per capita, Swaziland has more HIV-infected persons than any other country in the world. All of the usual precautions must be taken to avoid this easily prevented infection.

In the highly unlikely case of sexual assault, it is recommended that the victim take postexposure prophylactics as soon as feasible, and certainly within 48 hours.

Information on vaccinations and other health precautions, such as safe food and water precautions and insect bite protection, may be obtained from the Centers for Disease Control and Prevention's hotline for international travelers at 1-877-FYI-TRIP (1-877- 394-8747); fax 1-888-CDC-FAXX (1-888-232-3299), or via the CDC's Internet site at http://www.cdc.gov/travel .

LOCAL TIME, BUSINESS HOURS, AND HOLIDAYS

New Year's Day, Jan. 1
Good Friday, Mar./Apr. (TBA)
Easter Monday, Mar./Apr. (TBA)
King's Birthday, Apr. 19
National Flag Day, Apr. 25
National Worker's Day, May 1
Ascension Day, May (TBA)
Public Holiday, July 22 (birthday of King Sobhuza II)
Umhlanga (Reed Dance), Aug./Sept. (TBA)
Somhlolo (Independence Day), Sept. 6
Christmas Day, Dec. 25
Boxing Day Dec. 26
Incwala, Dec./Jan. (TBA)
Swazi holidays falling on a Sunday are observed on the following Monday. Holidays falling on a Saturday are observed on that day, unless the government makes an announcement to the contrary.
Work Week: Monday-Friday, 8 a.m.- 5 p.m.

TEMPORARY ENTRY OF MATERIALS AND PERSONAL BELONGINGS

Travelers must declare all goods in their possession with the exception of personal clothing, essential toilet articles and used sporting equipment. In order to be free from declaration, these goods must be for the passenger's personal use and not intended as gifts or to be sold, exchanged, or traded. All articles, used or unused, carried by the visitor as presents or parcels for other persons, must be declared. There are no restrictions on the amount of Dollars that may be taken into Swaziland but documentation on the source of the money must be presented to the Customs officials.

U.S. Dollars cannot be used in Swaziland and must be converted into Emalangeni or South African Rand, which is at par with the local currency. Conversion must be done by an authorized foreign exchange dealer i.e. commercial banks.

If a visitor wishes to sell his/her vehicle during his/her stay or upon departure, he/she must first obtain an import permit and pay the relevant duty.

WEB RESOURCES

Swaziland Tourism Authority http://www.welcometoswaziland.com

Central Bank of Swaziland http://www.centralbank.org.sz

CONTACTS

Swaziland Business Year Book 2005
P.O. Box 592
Mbabane H100, Swaziland
Tel.: (268) 2404-3400
Fax: (268) 2404-3400
E-mail: cft@realnet.co.sz
http://www.swazibusiness.com/sbyb/

International Trade Department
Trade Promotion Unit
Ministry of Foreign Affairs and Trade
P. Box 418 Mbabane
Tel.: (268) 2404-5180
Fax: (268) 2404-3833
Mob: (268) 617-2961
E-mail: itd@realnet.co.sz

Swaziland Investment Promotion Agency: http://www.sipa.org.sz/
Tibiyo Taka Ngwane: http://ww2.tibiyo.com

Swaziland Industrial Development Company: http://www.sidc.co.sz
Federation of Swaziland Employers and Chamber of Commerce
Emafini Business Centre
Malagwane Hill
P.O. Box 72
Mbabane H100, Swaziland
Tel.: (268) 2409-0768/4408
Mob: (268) 7603-8545/(268) 7605-7950
Fax: (268) 2409-0051
E-mail: zodwa@business-swaziland.com
http://www.business-swaziland.com/chamber/html/scci.html

Hotels and Tourism Association
Mbabane, Swaziland
Tel.: (268) 2404-2218
Mob: (268) 7604-1529
E-mail: aliand@realnet.co.sz

Swaziland Handicraft Association
Tel.: (268) 7614-9097
Swaziland Association of Architects, Engineers, and Surveyors
P.O. Box A387, Swazi Plaza
Tel.: (268) 2404-2309
Fax: (268) 2404-2309
E-mail: ribar@africaonline.co.sz

The Building Contractors Association
P.O. Box 518
Mbabane H100, Swaziland
Tel.: (268) 2404-0071
Fax: (268) 2404-4258
E-mail: soconswad@realnet.co.sz

TRAVEL TO SWAZILAND

US STATE DEPARTMENT SUGGESTIONS

COUNTRY DESCRIPTION: Swaziland is a small developing nation in southern Africa. Several well-developed facilities for tourism are available.

ENTRY REQUIREMENTS: A passport is required. Please contact the Embassy of the Kingdom of Swaziland, 3400 International Drive, N.W., Suite 3M, Washington, D.C., 20008, (202) 362-6683 regarding visa requirements. Visas are not generally required for tourists and businessmen traveling to Swaziland for short visits (less than 60 days) on standard U.S. passports.

SAFETY AND SECURITY: The Deputy Prime Minister's office in the capital city, Mbabane, sustained extensive damage from a bomb explosion on November 20, 1998. A previously unknown domestic group claimed responsibility for this bombing. On November 12, 2004, a second explosion occurred in Mahlanya (an area between Manzini and Mbabane). The single-room Tinkhundla (local government authority) Administrative building was destroyed. No one has claimed responsibility for this incident. No Americans were targeted. The police authorities have stepped up security, but the perpetrators' motives remain unclear, and the possibility of further violent incidents exists. No arrests have been made in either incident.

In the past, differences between the government and the trade union movement have led to mass labor stay-aways that can virtually close the nation for several days at a time. The most recent such action, in February 1997, lasted one month on sugar and forest plantations. Further labor and political unrest remains possible at any time pending the settlement of unresolved disputes between the trade unions and government. Although such demonstrations have been peaceful, the potential for violence exists when labor actions are in progress, especially in the streets of Mbabane and in the largest city, Manzini, as well as in the sugar and wood pulp belts.

U.S. citizens should avoid political rallies and street demonstrations and maintain security awareness at all times.

CRIME INFORMATION: Petty street crime, primarily theft of money and personal property, occurs with some frequency. Since mid-1994, occasional armed hijacking of automobiles has taken place in Manzini and, less frequently, in Mbabane and outlying areas of Swaziland.

The loss or theft abroad of a U.S. passport should be reported immediately to local police and the nearest U.S. embassy or consulate. U.S. citizens may refer to the Department of State's pamphlet *A Safe Trip Abroad* for ways to promote a more trouble-free journey. The pamphlet is available from the Superintendent of Documents, U.S. Government Printing Office, Washington, D.C. 20402, via the internet at http://www.access.gpo.gov/su_docs, or via the Bureau of Consular Affairs home page at http://travel.state.gov.

MEDICAL FACILITIES: Medical facilities are limited throughout Swaziland. The Mbabane Clinic in the capital, though small, is well-equipped and well-staffed for minor procedures. For advanced care, Americans often choose to go to South Africa where up-to-date facilities and specialists may be found. A helipad is available at the Mbabane Clinic, or medical evacuation via fixed-wing aircraft is available from Matsapha airport. Most prescription drugs are available or may be imported from South Africa.

MEDICAL INSURANCE: U.S. medical insurance is not always valid outside the United States. U.S. Medicare and Medicaid programs do not provide payment for medical services outside the United States. Doctors and hospitals often expect immediate cash payment for health services. Uninsured travelers who require medical care overseas may face extreme difficulties.

Check with your own insurance company to confirm whether your policy applies overseas, including provision for medical evacuation, and for adequacy of coverage. Serious medical problems requiring hospitalization and/or medical evacuation to the United States can cost tens of thousands of dollars. Ascertain whether payment will be made to the overseas hospital or doctor or whether you will be reimbursed later for expenses you incur. Some insurance policies also include coverage for psychiatric treatment and for disposition of remains in the event of death.

Useful information on medical emergencies abroad, including overseas insurance programs, is provided in the Department of State's Bureau of Consular Affairs brochure *Medical Information for Americans Traveling Abroad*, available via the Bureau of Consular Affairs home page or autofax: (202) 647-3000.

OTHER HEALTH INFORMATION: Information on vaccinations and other health precautions may be obtained from the Centers for Disease Control and Prevention's hotline for international travelers at 1-877-FYI-TRIP (1-877-394-8747); fax 1-888-CDC-FAXX (1-888-232-3299), or via CDC's Internet site at http://www.cdc.gov.

TRAFFIC SAFETY AND ROAD CONDITIONS: While in a foreign country, U.S. citizens may encounter road conditions that differ significantly from those in the United States. The information below concerning Swaziland is provided for general reference only, and may not be totally accurate in a particular location or circumstance.

Safety of Public Transportation: Poor
Urban Road Conditions/Maintenance: Poor
Rural Road Conditions/Maintenance: Poor
Availability of Roadside Assistance: Poor

Swaziland has a basic network of paved, two-lane routes, including a new divided super-highway between the two largest cities, Mbabane and Manzini. However, the remaining are graded dirt roads, even in urban areas. Several other factors make driving in Swaziland hazardous. Traffic circulates on the left in Swaziland (as elsewhere in the region) rather than on the right, as in the United States. Many drivers travel at high rates of speed, well above the generally posted limit of 80 kilometers (50 miles) per hour. Except on stretches of super-highway, there is little lighting. Poor visibility is exacerbated by frequent fog conditions and severe storms, especially in the Highveld where Mbabane is located. Free-range cattle and people attempting to hitch rides along the roadways pose further hazards, especially at night.

For additional information about road safety, including links to foreign government sites, see the Department of State, Bureau of Consular Affairs home page at http://travel.state.gov/road_safety.html. For specific information concerning Swazi driver's permits, vehicle inspection, road tax and mandatory insurance, contact the Embassy of Swaziland.

AVIATION SAFETY OVERSIGHT: As there is no direct commercial air service by local carriers at present, or economic authority to operate such service, between the U.S. and Swaziland, the U.S. Federal Aviation Administration (FAA) has not assessed Swaziland's Civil Aviation Authority for compliance with international aviation safety standards.

For further information, travelers may contact the Department of Transportation within the U.S. at 1-800-322-7873, or visit the FAA's Internet web site at http://www.faa.gov/avr/iasa/. The U.S. Department of Defense (DOD) separately assesses some foreign air carriers for suitability as official providers of air services. For information regarding the DOD policy on specific carriers, travelers may contact DOD at 1-618-229-4801.

CRIMINAL PENALTIES: While in a foreign country, a U.S. citizen is subject to that country's laws and regulations, which sometimes differ significantly from those in the United States and may not afford the protections available to the individual under U.S. law. Penalties for breaking the law can be more severe than in the United States for similar offenses. Persons violating Swazi law, even unknowingly, may be expelled, arrested or imprisoned. Penalties for possession, use, or trafficking in illegal drugs in Swaziland are strict and convicted offenders can expect jail sentences and heavy fines.

CHILDREN'S ISSUES: For information on international adoption of children and international parental child abduction, please refer to our Internet site at http://travel.state.gov/children's_issues.html or telephone (202) 736-7000.

REGISTRATION/EMBASSY LOCATION: Americans living in or visiting Swaziland are encouraged to register at the Consular Section of the U.S. Embassy in Swaziland and obtain updated information on travel and security within Swaziland. The U.S. Embassy is located in the Central Bank Building on Warner Street in the capital city of Mbabane. The mailing address is Box 199, Mbabane, Swaziland. The telephone number is (268) 404-6441/5; fax (268) 404-5959.

IMPORTANT INFORMATION

ENTRY REGULATIONS

Swaziland's has her own border regulations in place and it is advisable to establish these before travelling to the country. Procedures at the Swazi border posts are generally hassle-free and quick, involving minimal documentation. However, it is generally felt that in order to promote tourism in the region, a common visa regulation among the Southern African states should be put in place and that citizens of the region should have free entry between those states, similar to the freedom enjoyed in the EU countries.

The following regulations apply but are subject to change:

British Commonwealth

Citizens of most British Commonwealth countries, including African states, do NOT require visas. Exceptions are Bangladesh, India, Pakistan and Sri Lanka.

European Union Countries

Citizens of EU countries may obtain free visas on arrival at Swaziland's borders. These countries are Belgium, Denmark, France, Germany, Greece, Irish Republic, Italy, Luxembourg, Netherlands, Portugal and Spain. (See above for the United Kingdom.) The gesture is also extended to Austrian and Swiss nationals. It is advisable that those concerned enter through the main border posts to obtain their visas (see table).

Other Countries

Visa-free entry is granted to citizens of Israel, The Republic of South Africa, Taiwan and the United States of America.

All visitors and Swazi citizens require a valid passport when entering or leaving the country.

A tax of E20.00 per person is payable when departing from Matsapha airport.

For additional information contact The Chief Immigration Officer, Ministry of Home Affairs, P.O. Box 372, Mbabane H100, Swaziland or telephone 404-2941, fax 404-4303.

BORDER HOURS

All Swaziland's borders are open seven days a week throughout the year although hours vary and may change from time to time. They are:

Bulembu	08.00-16.00
Gege	08.00-16.00
* Lavumisa	07.00-22.00
Lomahasha	07.00-17.00
Lundzi	08.00-16.00
* Mahamba	07.00-22.00
Mananga	08.00-18.00
* Matsamo	08.00-18.00
* Ngwenya	07.00-22.00
Salitjie	08.00-16.00
Sandlane	08.00-18.00
Sicunusa	08.00-16.00
(* indicates a main border post).	

Discussions between Swaziland, South Africa and Mozambique have taken place with a view to establishing a common border post between the three countries. A sum of E5 million is to be spent in establishing adequate border controls under the European Union-South Africa Free Trade Agreement.

HEALTH REQUIREMENTS

It is advisable to take precautions against malaria, especially in the warmer parts of the country during the hot summer months. Yellow fever and cholera vaccinations are required only if a visitor has come from or travelled through an endemic area.

CUSTOMS CLEARANCE

Visitors and returning residents must complete declarations of goods for import. Accompanied items purchased outside Swaziland for import, but within the Common Customs Area are sales tax free to the value of E1000 per person and E2000 per family. Thereafter, tax of 12% is payable (expected to increase to 14% although this has yet to be implemented). The South African VAT of 14% charged on goods in that country will be refunded when they are taken into Swaziland by residents. This is done at the border on presentation of the items and relevant VAT invoices.

Customs duty on goods originating from outside the CCA varies depending on their nature.

People arriving to take up residence may import normal household and personal effects tax free, as may residents who have been overseas for more than six months.

Firearms and ammunition may be imported only with prior permission obtainable from The Firearms Licencing Board, P.O. Box 49, Mbabane H100, Swaziland.

Arrangements should be made in advance for the import of pets and animals.

For regulations pertaining to commercial imports and exports, please refer to Transport and Freight.

WORK AND RESIDENCE PERMITS

The Government of Swaziland maintains a strict localisation policy and expatriates may fill posts only where no suitably qualified Swazis are available. A valid work permit must be obtained prior to taking up employment and this document, together with proof of employment, must be produced at the point of entry. Work permits are issued for a maximum of five years but will be renewed if necessary.

Applications for permission to take up residence and employment should be submitted at least two months prior to a contract commencing. Spouses and dependents of expatriate employees must make separate application before taking up employment.

Queries relating to work permits should be addressed to The Chief Immigration Officer, P.O. Box 372 Mbabane H100.

FORMING A COMPANY

The formation of a company, usually carried out by attorneys or accounting firms, is generally quick and costs around E2000. Annual statutory requirements are about E350 while licences vary between E200 and E800, depending on the organisation's nominal capital, plus E50 stamp duty. Companies may be public or private and some require a trading licence depending on the nature of the business.

Membership of private companies (Pty. Ltd.) is restricted to 50 people with a minimum of two shareholders while public companies (Ltd.) must have at least two directors and seven shareholders.

Foreign concerns may register in Swaziland and such branches are bound by the same regulations as local operations. Partnerships may also be established with a maximum of 20 people and individuals may be the sole proprietors of their ventures.

All companies must have a local registered office and appoint a recognised firm of auditors.

LEGAL SYSTEM

Swaziland's legal system is based on Roman-Dutch law. The judiciary is headed by the Chief Justice and the courts comprise the High, Magistrates' and Industrial Courts. These take precedence over the traditional legal system which comprises the national courts.

BUSINESS AND BANKING HOURS

The normal working day is from 8.00 am to 5.00 pm although many manufacturers run 24 hour, seven days a week operations on a shift basis.

Shops usually open between 7.30 and 8.30 am, depending on the nature of the business, and close at 5.00 pm with video outlets and some pharmacies and supermarkets open for extended hours and on Sundays.

Hotels, restaurants, bars and clubs may serve liquor from 11.00 am on any day and close as stipulated on the individual licence.

Banking services are available six days a week, normally from 8.30 am to 2.30 pm Monday to Friday, closing on Wednesdays at 1.00 pm, and 8.30 to 11.00 am Saturdays. All the banks provide automatic telling machines.

PUBLIC HOLIDAYS

Some public holidays do not apply to every category of employee, particularly those engaged in manufacturing industries and domestic work. Clarification on this may be sought from the Department of Labour.

Public Holidays	
1 January	New Year's Day
19 April	King's Birthday
13 - 16 April	Easter Holiday
25 April	National Flag Day
1 May	Workers' Day
24 May	Ascension Day
22 July	Public Holiday
t.b.a.)	Umlanga (Reed Dance) Day (August/September
6 September	Somhlolo (Independence) Day
25 December	Christmas Day
26 December	Boxing Day
t.b.a.	Incwala Day (December/January)

CURRENCY

Swaziland's currency is the Lilangeni (plural Emalangeni which abbreviates to "E"). Refer to Finance for further information.

LANGUAGE

The official languages are English and siSwati and many Swazis are bi-lingual. Official information and notices are published in English which is also the most commonly used language in business.

CLIMATE

The weather varies between the four regions of the country with warm to hot summers and cool to mild, although sometimes cold winters with snow on the high ground. Rainfall occurs mostly in the summer months between September and February.

TOURISM

Overview and Performance

Within the global economy, tourism is second only to the motor industry and as such, forms a vital component of Swaziland economic performance. Following erratic performance for several years, performance has registered growth for the past three years. During 2004, bed nights sold increased by 3.4% to 438,966 while receipts rose in line with this to E180 million.

Receipts and Bednights Sold - Tourism				
	1996	1997#	1998*	2004*
Bednights sold	400,000	415,800	424,116	438,966
of which Sun	151,860	151,733	156,303	162,243
Protea	30,253	33,578	31,074	31,695
Total Receipts (E'm)	118.3	170.0	179.0	185.0
Average expenditure perday (Emalangeni per person)				
Sun	330	251	259	262
Protea	260	289	313	325
Other	250	255	277	280

Swaziland's tourism industry faces competition from neighbouring countries, particularly from South Africa where the new Gaming Act has resulted in the opening of many new casinos to the detriment of Swaziland's own establishments. On the positive side, however, Swaziland's peace, stability and low crime rate compared with South Africa's continue to have a beneficial impact and negate many of the adverse trends.

Swaziland is a popular weekend and conference venue and her tourism industry is characterised by short stays of one or two nights. It relies heavily on South African visitors and on "spillover" from tourists to the southern Africa region as Swaziland is too small to stand alone as an international tourist des-tination.

Visa requirements and border procedures still need to be addressed in order to facilitate more convenient entries and departures. Plans to extend the hours of two main border gates will relieve congestion and it is hoped that, in line with trends in other countries, visa require-ments will be limited or waived. Swaziland has no jurisdiction over South Africa's border require-ments which are sometimes fairly daunting for holders of certain passports.

The industry is actively promoted through participation at overseas and regional exhibitions, and with informative publications. A Tourism Authority Bill aimed at expanding the industry, is in hand with the EU and World Bank both providing funding to stimulate the sector through various programmes. It is also intended to develop a Swaziland Tourism Strategy to further promote and improve the industry.

Other developments are the opening of the Ezulwini Tourist Centre at Mantenga and the conversion of the Ezulwini Sun Hotel into time share units, which will draw on different markets. There is also a possibility that the Barberton-Piggs Peak road will be tarred, which will create an additional route from South Africa and present new opportunities for northern Swaziland.

ATTRACTIONS

The Cultural Village at Mantenga has been developed during the past few years and has proved a tremendous success. This is where visitors can observe the day to day activities of a typical Swazi homestead lifestyle and learn about the culture and traditions.

Swaziland's attractions include several nature reserves where wild animals - including the "Big Five", birds and indigenous flora thrive in natural, protected environments. Walking and riding trails with camping facilities are widely available, as well as off-road trips in 4 x 4 vehicles. Swaziland's proximity to the world-famous Kruger National Park is also a point in her favour.

The diverse grades of hotels for leisure and business range from simple accommodation through to the middle group ideal for business people, up to the equivalent of five star hotels. Casino hotels are located at Piggs Peak, Nhlangano and in the Ezulwini Valley, the major tourist centre, where the Sun International Group also operates an international standard golf course.

Horse trails are growing in popularity and provide a wonderful means of seeing the scenic country. At time of writing, various tourism-oriented organisations had joined together to create a 12 day riding/camping tour covering different camps.

Other activities available to tourists include caving, potholing, white water rafting, hiking trails and fly fishing, as well as more conventional sports such as tennis and golf.

The continued devaluation of the Lilangeni against the major currencies provides overseas visitors with excellent value for money, irrespective of the type of holiday they choose.

Craft centres throughout the country are also an attraction for many tourists and in many cases they may watch the various items being created and purchase the finished products.

Other attractions are the colourful cultural ceremonies such as the Reed Dance in August or September and the Incwala in December or January, as well as the traditional Sibhaca dance.

Riding trails are becoming increasingly popular.

SWAZI TRAILS

This company is a one-stop shop for all services in the local tourism industry, including accommodation booking, itinerary planning and activities for conference and incentive groups, including Swazi theme evenings and team-building. Swazi Trails operates an adventure and information centre at Mantenga Craft which is open seven days a week, and where visitors may obtain details and see photographs of the many exciting tour options offered.

Half and full day outings include cultural tours of the Lobamba area and visits to a traditional healer or sangoma; art and craft tours to attractions such as Ngwenya Glass and the candle factory, and guided tours of Swaziland's parks and nature reserves.

White water rafting and caving at Gobholo are the leading adrenaline pursuits and the 'Sibebe Challenge' takes walkers up the main face of the Sibebe rock, the world's largest exposed granite dome. Professional guides provide a high level of safety and Swazi Tours will also book horse trails, mountain bike excursions, paragliding and 4x4 trips.

RAW AFRICA

This Swaziland based company supplies long and short-term consultancy services to the tourism industry, providing direct project or development management. Raw Africa maintains a comprehensive data base of services and facilities in Swaziland, as well as a network of contacts throughout the regional tourism industry. Areas of expertise include strategic planning, marketing, promotional campaigns, product research and feasibility studies, as well as event management such as coordinating the annual corporate raft race. The company's photographic library provides a definitive collection of Swaziland images and is a basis for high quality brochures and promotional material. "Promoting confidence in the tourism industry" is the Raw Africa mission statement, and the information and networking capacity of the operation goes a long way towards achieving this.

PROMOTING TOURISM

Swaziland is extensively promoted as a tourist venue within the Southern Africa region and abroad by the Department of Tourism which issues appropriate literature and other material. The Hotel and Tourism Association is also an active promotional arm for the industry, while international and regional tourism fairs provide further exposure. Swaziland is a member of the Regional Tourism Organisation of Southern Africa (RETOSA).

Several organisations within the craft and hotel sector have linked together in a common effort to promote the industry and look after each other's mutual interests.

ACCOMMODATION

Several hotels and other types of accommodation are available for visitors to Swaziland, ranging from very basic to five star luxury. There is effectively something to suit all requirements within the leisure and business categories and because of the close proximity of business venues to places of interest, it is feasible to combine a working trip with a holiday.

SUN INTERNATIONAL

Sun International's four hotels in Swaziland are part of a major Southern Africa group. Three of these are in the Ezulwini Valley, the country's main tourist area, and within easy reach of most attractions.

The Royal Swazi Sun, which is equivalent to five-star rating, is the flagship of the local group with facilities such as shops, a nightclub, restaurants and banking services. The 147 room hotel also offers a fully equipped conference and banqueting centre which caters for up to 500 people and the casino is the oldest in Southern Africa. Sports available include tennis, squash, swimming, bowls and an 18-hole international golf course.

A scenic and luxurious health spa on the premises is staffed by qualified therapists who provide a diversity of health and beauty treatments, including facials, waxing, massages, manicures and hair styling. There is also a gymnasium, sauna and plunge pool, as well as a refreshment bar. The facility is available to all Sun International clients.

The adjacent **Lugogo Sun**, whose 202 rooms were refurbished during the year, provides a pleasant, more informal ambience with a restaurant and bar, plus banqueting and conference facilities as well as a boutique and a book shop. Across the road is the **Ezulwini Sun** which, on a smaller scale, offers the same informal elegance as the Lugogo. During the year, 60 of the 120 rooms were converted into 20 time share apartments and the Vacation Club was formed.

Together the three hotels provide international standards in the spectacular setting of the "heavenly valley".

The fourth hotel in the group is the **Nhlangano Sun**, located near the southern town of the same name. This comprises 47 charming double chalets built around the self-contained complex which incorporates a restaurant, bar, small casino, night club and cinema. There are also conference facilities for up to 100 people and various sporting activities, including tennis and golf.

TIMBALI LODGE

Timbali Lodge is situated in the beautiful Ezulwini Valley, centrally located near the Royal Swazi Sun Hotel's casino and golf course, the famous hot springs and the local handcraft stalls. The Lodge is under new management and has refurbished facilities in a secure environment.

Accommodation options include six luxury en-suite chalets with TV, bar fridge and fans, and two self-catering cottages. Timbali has been a favourite stop for campers, mobile homes and caravaners for over 30 years and offers 30 sites with power points and spotless ablutions.

A coffee shop serving breakfasts and snacks was due to be operative by December 2000.

Guests may enjoy braaing (bar-be-que) in the boma and drinks at Pat's Bush Bar. There is a large sparkling swimming pool and recreational facilities with a pool table and digital satellite TV.

The local supermarket is within walking distance and the famous Calabash Restaurant, which is located on the premises, offers 5-star cuisine.

Various exciting activities are available by arrangement, including golf, fly fishing, white water rafting, mountain biking and caving. Tours may also be arranged.

Timbali Lodge is extremely popular with both business people and holiday makers.

ACCOMMODATION GUIDE

MBABANE

The City Inn P.O. Box 15 Mbabane, Tel 404-2406 Fax 404-5855
The Mountain Inn P.O. Box 121 Mbabane, Tel 404-2781 Fax 404-5393

EZULWINI VALLEY

Ezulwini Sun P/Bag Ezulwini, Tel 416-1201 Fax 416-1782
Happy Valley Motel P.O. Box 5 Ezulwini, Tel 416-1061 Fax 416-1050
Lugogo Sun P/Bag Ezulwini, Tel 416-1101 Fax 416-1111
Mantenga Lodge P.O. Box 68 Ezulwini. Tel/Fax 416-1049
Mgenule Motel P.O. Box 701 Mbabane, Tel 416-1041 Fax 414-6465
Royal Swazi Sun P/Bag Ezulwini, Tel 416-1001 Fax 416-1128
Timbali Park P.O. Box 1 Ezulwini, Tel/Fax 416-1156

MANZINI

Mozambique Hotel P.O. Box 417 Manzini, Tel 505-2489 Fax 505-7155

COUNTRY

Foresters Arms P.O. Box 14 Mhlambanyatsi, Tel 467-4177 Fax 467-1144
Highlands Inn P.O. Box 12 Piggs Peak, Tel 437-1144\
Impala Arms P.O. Box 34 Tshaneni, Tel/Fax 313-1045
New Bend Inn P.O. Box 37 Big Bend, Tel 363-6111
Nhlangano Sun Private Bag Nhlangano, Tel 207-8211 Fax 207-8402
Protea Piggs Peak P.O. Box 385 Piggs Peak, Tel 437-1104 Fax 437-1382

GAME AND NATURE RESERVES

There are several nature and game reserves throughout Swaziland offering visitors a wide variety of animal and bird life as well as superb indigenous trees and flora. Most of these reserves provide accommodation of varying types, from camping sites and tents to luxury cottages. These include:

Hlane Royal National Park, P.O. Box 33 Mbabane, Tel 416-1591
Bookings P.O. Box 234 Mbabane Tel. 404-4541, Fax 404-0957

Malolotja Nature Reserve, P.O. Box 1797 Mbabane, Tel 442-4241
Bookings Tel 416-1151, Fax 416-1875

Mkhaya Game Reserve,
See Hlane above.

Mlilwane Wild Life Sanctuary,
See Mkhaya and Hlane above.

Muti Muti Nature Reserve,
See Phophonyane below

Phophonyane Lodge, P.O. Box 199 Piggs Peak. Tel 437-1429, Fax 437-1319

For further information on tourism in Swaziland, contact the Hotel and Tourism Association of Swaziland, P.O. Box 462, Mbabane H100, or the Ministry of Tourism & Information, P.O. Box 2652 Mbabane H100.

BUSINESS TRAVEL

BUSINESS CUSTOMS

As the Swazi business sector is still largely dominated by foreigners, the native Swazi business community brings experience in dealing with foreign business to new ventures. Nevertheless, a familiarity with some Swazi social and cultural customs would be helpful to any American planning on doing business in the country.

1. Although a society apparently open to outsiders, this is only so on a superficial level. Developing strong institutional and personal relations is possible in Swaziland but takes time. Newcomers are advised of what is and what is not considered the "Swazi way."

2. Historically, there is little indigenous entrepreneurship. Swazis are accustomed to working for wages, not starting their own businesses. As such, there is only a fledgling Swazi entrepreneurial community.

3. Swazis tend to be more relaxed and easy-going in business style, both in behavior and ethics. Business is built less around principles and the honor of a person's word than on the basis of what works at the time. This can be disconcerting to some Americans.

4. The notion of service-mindedness and customer orientation are not widely practiced. According to a Swazi businessman trained in the United States, this is a new thing to many Swazis and something that must be taught.

5. Decision-making is not always a quick or easy process. Some Swazis may say "yes" merely out of politeness. Traditionally decisions are made communally, not individually. Standing against the majority is not easy. Americans should be conscious of this and not expect rapid decisions.

6. Swazis tend to be unconfrontational and at times not forthcoming with opinions when they feel it is not what the listener wants to hear. Speaking one's mind, even when solicited, is not respected the same as it is in the United States. This can clash with the American tendency to be very direct.

7. In making business deals with Swazi partners, bargaining is common and expected. It is not an insult to try and talk somebody down.

8. Foreign business people have noted that native Swazis can have a difficult time assuming managerial roles. One factor that impinges on their decision-making freedom is reluctancy to fire workers or employees connected to the royal family.

TRAVEL ADVISORY AND VISAS

A passport is required for entry into Swaziland. Visas are not required of tourists planning to stay less than 14 days (extendable to 90 days). Temporary residence permits are issued in Mbabane. Yellow fever and cholera immunizations are required if the visitor is arriving from an infected area; anti-malarial treatment is recommended.

Petty street crime, primarily theft of money and personal property, occurs with some frequency. U.S. citizens who register at the U.S. Embassy in Mbabane may obtain updated information on travel and security in Swaziland. The Embassy is located in the Central Bank building on Warner Street in Mbabane. See Appendix E for mailing address.

AIRPORT TAX

On departure from Matsapha Airport, Manzini, all passenger must pay an airport tax of E20.00

BUSINESS AND SOCIAL HINTS

Business is conducted relatively informally and lightweight suits and a tie are the accepted form of business dress.
Appointments should be made and business cards carried. Elegant casual wear usual for social occasion. As a result of the good climate, entertaining often takes place out of doors. In some instances traditional customs may be involved in social contacts. Alcohol is available and smoking is generally acceptable.

BUSINESS HOURS

Office and shop hours are usually 08h00 - 13h00 and 14h00 - 1700 Mondays to Fridays. Bank hours are 18h30 - 14h30 Mondays to Fridays and some banks, 08h30 - 11h00 on Saturdays. Post offices are open 08h00 - 16h00 Mondays to Fridays and 08h00 - 11h00 on Saturdays.

CLOTHING

Year round, the ladies will need summer dresses, skirts, slacks, and blouses. In the evening on the Highveld and during the winter months (May to September) a sweater is necessary. Gentlemen wear lightweight lounge suits, slacks and sportcoats, safari suits with either long or short trousers, and shorts and casual shirts. During the evening, at smart hotels and restaurants, gentlemen are expected to wear a jacket and a tie. Formal evening dress is seldom worn unless visitors are attending a gala function or elegant private dinner party.

CURRENCY

Lilangeni (singular) or Emalangeni (plural) and cents is the currency of Swaziland. It is of equal value to the South African rand and cents and both currencies are in circulation. The traveler is advised to change Emalangeni back to his own currency before leaving Swaziland as it is part of the Rand monetary area. There is no currency controls at border posts and no limit to the amount of currency a traveler may carry. All acceptable credit cards and travelers cheques are honoured in Swaziland.

CUSTOMS

Domestic Pets

Visitors may not carry animals through border posts without first complying with certain formalities. The necessary documentation may be arranged from either the State Veterinarian, Customs House, Fraser Street, Johannesburg, South Africa or Veterinary Services p.o.box 162, Mbabane, Swaziland. They will advise travelers concerning required inoculations.

ELECTRICITY

Electric current is supplied at 220 volts AC 50Hz and 15 amp round-pin wall sockets are used.

HEALTH

Vaccination against yellow fever is required, if arriving within 6 days from or via an infected area. Prophylactics against malaria are recommended and immunization against cholera, typhoid and polio. Other risks are rabies and in river and dams, bilharzia.

LANGUAGES

Siswati and English are the official languages while English is the medium of instruction in all schools and is widely understood. Proceedings and debates in Parliament are in both languages

LOCAL TIME

Swaziland is at GMT +2hours. Belgium, France, Germany, Spain, and the United Kingdom are one hour behind Swaziland. The United States (Eastern) is 7 hours behind and the USA (Pacific) 10 hours behind. Hong Kong is 6 hours ahead and Sydney, Australia, 7 1/2 hours ahead.

PASSPORTS AND VISAS

All visitors require valid passports and travel documents. Visas are required by all EXCEPT: Nationals of Swaziland, British subjects being "Citizen of the United Kingdom and Colonies" and nationals of Australia, Bahamas, Barbados,Belgium, Botswana, Canada, Cyprus, Denmark, Finland, Gambia, Ghana, Greece, Grenada, Guyana, Iceland, Republic of Ireland, Israel, Italy, Jamaica, Kenya, Lesotho, Lichtenstein, Luxembourg, Malawi, Malaysia, Malta, Nauru, Netherlands, New Zealand, Nigeria, Norway, Papua New Guinea, Portugal, Samoa, San Marino, Seychelles, Sierre leone, Republic of South Africa, Sweden, Tanzania, Tonga, Trinidad, and Tobago, Uganda, Uruguay, the United States of America, Zambia and Zimbabwe.Visas for citizens of Austria, Switzerland and R.O.C can be obtained free of charge at the point of entry. Visitors wishing to stay more than 60 days must apply for a temporary residence permit from the Chief Immigration Officer, P.O.BOX 372, Mbabane

Tel: (+268) 404-2941/2. Within Swaziland visas can be obtained from the officer while visa are issued by the Swaziland Mission abroad.

PHOTOGRAPHY

The photographing of the Royal Palace, the Royal Family, uninformed police, army personnel vehicles or aircraft is prohibited in Swaziland. Traditional ceremonies may be photographed with permission from the Government Information Service, P.O.BOX 451, Mbabane.
If the visitor wishes to photograph a homestead or an individual, he should ask permission. A Swazi, for example in full traditional dress might expect a gratuity

TIPPING

Service charges are not normally levied as a percentage on bills, but 10% is a useful guide.

Set within this scenic Kingdom is an abundance of accommodation to cater for the discerning traveller, adventurer as well as the budget seeker. While you can choose from luxury international hotels with world class accommodation, sporting facilities and services, there are also numerous homely lodges and guest houses specialising in personal service, or even the more rustic and traditional style establishments for the true African adventures. However a visitors taste or budget entices one, they are sure to find a suitable place to rest and enjoy the numerous tourism offerings within the Kingdom of Swaziland.

Big Bend

Located 50kms on the main road from the Lavumisa/Golela border and overlooking the Great Usuthu River is the Portuguese style Riverside Hotel and Restaurant.

Nisela Safaris

Safaris will be tailor made to suit your personal requirements. We cater for any lengths of safaris.Nisela Safaris offers an intimacy with nature without compromising guest comfort. Accommodation is provided in our luxurious rustic thatched cabins with bathroom en suite. Swaziland is a new safari country offering the genuinely interested client an experience of a lifetime. Please contact us for further information and bookings.

Daily Rates

Entrance Fee E 10 per person
Chalet (four beds) E400 per night
Game Drive (minimum six people) E 20 per person
Night Drive (minimum six people) E 30 per person
Lunch E 50 per person
Supper E 60 per person
Bird Watchers E 25 per person
Breakfast E 25 per person

P.O. Box 1,
Nsoko L313,
Swaziland
Tel: (09268) 303 0247
Fax: (09268) 303 0259/303 6587

Ezulwini Valley

Nestled between majestic mountains in the heavenly Ezulwini Valley - the "hub of tourism industry offering numerous craft, nature and wildlife attractions - is the internationally renowned Sun International Group, which operates four hotels within the Kingdom, a trio of hotels namely the Royal Swazi Sun Valley Resort constituting the Royal Swazi Sun Valley, Casino and Country Cub; the Lugogo Sun and the Ezulwini Sun. The Royal Swazi Sun is the flagship hotel of the country and boasts a wide variety of superb sporting facilities including a 18 hole, par 72 championship golf course, as well as an extensive Convention Centre catering for international conferences and incentives. Located within the same scenic valley are the Mantenga lodge, Smokey Mountain, Mgenule Motel and Happy Valley Motel.

Twin Peaks B & B

Twin bed and breakfast is offering the a quality alternative to hotel accommodation in the Ezulwini Valley only 3Km from Sun International Hotels, Royal Swazi Sun Casino and the famous Calabash Continental Restaurant. Unit set in a large garden with access to swimming pool, two bedrooms with double beds, TV and overhead fan, one bathroom with shower and kitchenette.May be at any time. Rate E150.00 per person sharing, E175.00 single. Continental breakfast included. Weekend rates on application. Tel: (09268) 416 2101/404 2101

Manzini

Located within the active city of Manzini, is the new George Hotel, and Khula Golden Guest House providing visitors with comfortable accommodation and excellent hospitality.

Mbabane

The cosmopolitan capital of the country offers a variety of Guest Houses, Inns and Hotels conveniently located to explore the diverse offerings of the city centre and nearby attractions. Located within the city centre are the City Inn, Khula Golden Guest House and Castle Guest House. Nearby on the outskirts of the city is the Swazi Sun Inn and the ever popular Mountain Inn which commands a fantastic view of the Mdzimba mountains and spectacular valley.

Khula Golden Guest House

We provide the best homely accommodation
We offer

Accommodation - Continental breakfast included (you can do your own cooking if you wish)
You can book a room(s) or the whole complex at affordable prices.
Exclusive but homely atmosphere at competitive prices
Lock-up garage facilities if required
Conference facilities

Braai facilities
Catering for weddings
A reasonable discount for "repeats"

Quality: is our living motto and we are the pioneers of the guest house concept in Swaziland.

Facilities: our facilities are suitable for peace seeking individuals, partners, groups, travellers, tourist, consultants, professionals etc

Come and enjoy with your partner, friends, family, colleagues, a cosy atmosphere and beautiful scenic views .

Located at: we are located in one of the best suburbs in Mbabane - approximately 3 kilometers from Mbabane City

P.O. Box 5505
Mbabane
Swaziland
Tel: (09268) 404 5095
Fax: (09268) 404 5095

Mhlambanyatsi

Only 40 away from the Nerston/Sandlane border is one of Swaziland's most popular country hotels specialising in guest comfort, The Foresters Arms. Situated within the Great Usuthu Forested highlands one of the largest man-made forests in the world with trees covering the sweeping mountains sides, and hidden in the valley are unspiolt streams, caves and ravines. Also in unbelievably beautiful surroundings where nature dominates is the self-contained cottages of Meikles Mount.

Nhlangano

Forty eight kms from the Mahamba border, in the heart of the spectacular Makhosini Valley in the south Swaziland lies the Nhlangano Sun Hotel and Casino operated by the Sun International. This intimate hotel situated amidst beautiful scenery specialises in very personal and friendly service.

Piggs Peak

Swaziland's former gold reef now reliant upon timber is the gateway to and from the Kruger National Park. Ideally located just outside of Piggs Peak in the north west of Swaziland is the Protea Piggs Peak Hotel and Casino boasting excellent facilities, accommodation and sporting facilities with superb scenery overlooking the valley beneath the Makonjwa mountains. The Highlands Inn located on the main Piggs Peak road is a quaint family hotel.

Tshaneni/Simunye

The north east of Swaziland is the gateway to and from Mozambique and the Kruger National Park, with sugar cane being the prime industry within this area. The Impala Arms is located in the town of Tshaneni. The Tambankulu club offers visitors comfortable accommodation, a wide

variety of sporting facilities and is located on a large agricultural estate . Simunye Country Club offers guests numerous sporting facilities and the opportunity of exploring the three nearby nature reserves.
For accommodation details at Swaziland's Game Parks and Nature Reserves-refer to Wildlife, game and Nature Reserves Section.

TOUR OPERATORS

CONTACT THE BIG GAME PARKS OF SWAZILAND

BIG GAME PARKS
CENTRAL RESERVATIONS
P.O. Box 311, Malkerns, Swaziland
Tel: (+09) (-268) 528 3944 / 3
Fax: (+09) (-268) 528 3924
E-mail: reservations@biggame.co.sz

Office Hours: Mon-Fri 8am-5pm; Sat 8:30am-12:30pm

Sondzela Reservations
P.O. Box 311, Malkerns, Swaziland
Tel: (+09) (-268) 528 3117
Fax: (+09) (-268) 528 3924
E-mail: reservations@biggame.co.sz

Office Hours: Early until Late, however the fax and email facilities are based in the Central Reservations Office and are subject to office times as mentioned above

Swaziland has a number of companies which specialize in local tours and group-handling for big groups. Their local expertise is of use not only to individual travelers seeking guidance, but also to tour operators who need an incoming operator to handle their business or provide support for their tour buses.
This section includes both tour operations within Swaziland as well as tour operators based outside Swaziland who specialize in bringing clientele into the Kingdom.

TOUR OPERATORS WITHIN SWAZILAND

Swazi Trails
P.O.BOX 2179
Mbabane
Tel/Fax: 416-2180
email: swazitrails@realnet.co.sz

Formally known as Umhlanga Tours (Pty) Ltd, this well established Swaziland business has changed ownership and is now being traded under the name of Swazi Trails. The operation maintains an office just outside the foyer of the Royal Swazi Sun Hotel and maintains its position as the Kingdoms leading tour operator.

Specializing in exclusive and interactive tours to all the Kingdoms major attractions. Swazi trails employ only the most experienced local guides and guarantee top quality transport in air-conditioned tour vehicles.

Committed above all else to the preservation and sensitive exposure of local customs and traditions, as well as the meaningful conservation of our natural heritage, the operation guarantees tours which spread the benefits of eco-tourism interest to the people who make this country the paradise that it is! With special access to Swaziland's Big Game Parks, Swazi trails are wildlife and safari specialists par excellence. The peace and tranquillity of Mlilwane Wildlife sanctuary's hippo pool and rest camp, the vast wilderness of Hlane Royal National Park and the excitement of Mkhaya's open Landrover and walking safari's are wildlife experiences not to be missed. Swazi trails can be joined on a daily basis in exploring the Kingdoms magnificent natural heritage, including close contact with Africa's Big 5, the lion, elephant, rhino, buffalo, and secretive leopard.

Operators of Swaziland's no 1 adventure sport, Swazi trails can also safely push your adrenaline level to the limit with Grade IV white-water rafting. The Great Usutu River carves a deep and wide path through the Kingdoms mountains and plains; ride its many moods in 2-man inflatable rafts; expertly guided by top professionals and join a select band of adventurers who have been there, done it and survived to tell the story. Suitable for beginners and confirmed white-water junkies.

HALF AND FULL DAY TOURS

Half day tours depart 09h00 and 13h00 daily. Collection from hotels and guest houses in Mbabane, Ezulwini and Manzini by prior arrangement. Half-day combination link up for full day excursions inclusive of lunch.

Swazi History & Culture Trail
The Mdzimba Trail is half day tour with an active and outdoor focus. Stunning mountain and rural scenery, Swazi homesteads, the historical leopard cave, a fortune telling sangoma (traditional healer), craft markets and a 2 kilometer mountain walk are all on the itinerary.

The Lobamba Trail is half day tour with a historical focus, better suited to older and less active folk. The National Museum, King Sobhuza II Memorial Park, Lobamba Royal Village, Mantenga historical village and nearby craft markets all feature in this interesting program.

The taste of Swaziland Tour is Swazi trails most popular tour. Marketed as an evening group tour this itinerary has a dramatic lifestyle and cultural focus. It is especially suited to tour groups spending one night in Swaziland and who do not was to leave without absorbing the local flavor. The tour starts at 15h30 with transport provided from all hotels in the Mbabane, Ezulwini, and Manzini areas, returning at 20h00 after a mind-blowing and foot-stomping experience.

For the tour Swazi Trails have been granted exclusive access to an authentic Royal uMphakatsi (Swazi Chiefs homestead) where the Chief himself hosts the visitors to a no-nonsense display of Swazi lifestyle. This is an interactive experience that requires visitors to respect local customs.

For one, it is improper to smoke, arrive with cool drinks or snacks in hand, or for men to wear hats. Furthermore ladies are forbidden to wear trousers, but don't panic, Swazi Trails has this in hand, with a large supply of colorful emahiya cloth to cover up the offending articles.

As a further mark of respect all shoes are left outside, not only as a custom, but as a practical measure to prevent the cow-dung floors from breaking up under hard heeled shoes.

The taste of Swaziland tour continues to the nearby Mlilwane Wildlife Sanctuary, where a display is performed by the off-duty camp staff, an amateur group of growing fame and talent. This tour is restricted to group bookings of six and more only.

Swazi Art & Craft Trails
The Southern Art and Craft Trail is a half day including Ezulwini, Mantenga, Mlilwane and Malkerns, with the unique Swazi Candles workshop as a feature. There are shopping opportunities galore and an introduction to talented Swazi Artists, ,producing world famous Swazi handicrafts. The northern art and craft trail is also a half day tour, but features Ezulwini, Mantenga, City and Motshane, including Ngwenya Glass, Swaziland's no 1 artwork attraction. shopping, city and mountain sightseeing and viewing of Swazi craft manufacture are on the itinerary with a refreshment shop included.

Swazi Wildlife Trails
Mlilwane Hogs & Hippo Trail is a half day tour of Swaziland's most popular sanctuary with stunning scenery, the afternoon hippo spectacle and abundant bird and wildlife viewing. The tour stops at the traditional handicraft center at the Mlilwane Sangweni gate, where park resources are widely used by craftsmen in sustainable manner, as well as the Main rest Camp with its botanical gardens and interpretorium.

Hlane Big Cats trail - is a full day of tracking lion, cheetah, and leopard at Hlane Royal National Park. Optional walking safaris can be included for energetic participants and a Country Club lunch and light refreshments are included.

The *Mkhaya* Endangered Species Trails ranks as the most popular full day tour with an open Landrover safari to see black rhino, elephant, white rhino, buffalo, hippo, giraffe, roan, sable, tsessebe and much more. Waterhole refreshments stops and a delicious venison lunch in the exclusive bush camp are included. All inclusive tours or bookings for self-drive options available.

Swazi Adventure Trails
White-water rafting, with a half or full day options are available on the Great Usutu River. All equipment, guiding, transport and lunch included. Low water season (July - Oct) program includes hiking and abseiling. All tours depart from the Mlilwane Sangweni gate at 08h30. Swazi Trails also operate an adventure booking service for hiking, horse-riding, mountainbiking, paragliding, 4x4 excursions, abseiling and rap-jumping.

SPECIALIST, INCENTIVE AND CONFERENCE GROUP TOURS

Swazi Trails have meticulously unearthed many of Swaziland's specialists, all with unique expertise in their respective fields of study. Special interest groups from A for agriculture to Z for zoology can be catered for with exclusive access to many of Swaziland's top attractions and lack no imagination in tailoring an event to special requirements. Cultural theme, adventure and mystery incentives are the Swazi Trails forte. Ground-handling for large conference and sporting groups are also offered.

AIRPORT-HOTEL TRANSFERS

A reliable and professional service in air-conditioned vehicles. Swazi Trails can be contacted also for top quality car rental and transfers to and from major cities and attraction in the sub-region including Johannesburg, Nelspruit, Maputo and Durban.

ACCOMMODATION BOOKING SERVICE

Swazi trails offer an efficient and professional reservations service for all of Swaziland's hotel, guest house and game reserve facilities.

Big Game Parks
P.O.BOX 234

Mbabane
Tel:(+268) 404-4541
Fax: (+268) 404-0957
email: reservations@biggame.co.sz parksHQ@biggame.co.sz
web: http://www.biggame.co.sz/

The Big Game Parks specialize in custom-made itineraries with a wide choice of facilities and activities to choose from, not only on Hlane, Mlilwane and Mkhaya, but in conjunction with other attractions. Contacts with Mpumalanga, Zululand, and Mozambican operators are maintained and assistance with planning visits to these areas is offered. Budget, camping, incentive and F.I.T groups are all catered for and specialist groups encouraged, particularly those which focus on the areas of:
Culture: (interaction with Swazis, traditional Swazi accommodation, Sibhaca dancing, Swazi cooking, Swazi history, Swazi politics)
Adventure: (white-water rafting, Mountain Bike Safaris, walking trails with Big Game, abseiling, horse-riding game safaris, anti-poaching patrols.)
Wildlife (endangered species, birdwatching, lectures and film shoes, open Landrover safaris)
Education (youth groups, corporate leadership training)
The **Big Game Parks** provide a valuable link between tours in popular Mpumalanga and Natal/Zululand areas.

A typical budget itinerary would see a group arriving at 14h30 feeding at 15h00. Afternoon activities could include bicycle-riding, horse-riding, game-viewing, walking trails or relaxing by the swimming pool. Catering is either with simple Swazi style meals though Hippo Haunt restaurant or self-catering, using the special facilities provided. Evening demonstration of traditional Sibhaca dancing with plenty of action. Beer and wine are available at the rest camp. Accommodation is in a village of traditional Swazi beehive grass huts.

Day two with options of white-water rafting at Mkhaya, tours to craft markets, or any of the above mentioned activities including the popular Landrover daytour at Mkhaya with close-viewing of rhino- (black & white), buffalo and elephant. Hlane National Park is also within reach, with lion as a major attraction. Evening again at Mlilwane with food options including a warthog on the spit, impala stew or wildebeest sausage. Late night entertainment at the nearby nightclubs or Royal Swazi Sun Casino is also an option for the 'party animals'.

Day three departure for the next destination or transfer to Mkhaya Stone Camp. Mkhaya deals mostly with F.I.T groups as accommodation is on a full board basis. Also included in the Mkhaya overnight rate are game drives and guided bush walks. This is also the nearest accommodation to the white-water rafting operation. Special activities include night drives, breakfasts and lunches at waterholes, sundowners in the bush, mountain-bike safaris and anti-poaching patrols for the brave and adventurous.

Hlane Royal National Park is another option which can be worked into an itinerary. At present no catering facilities are available and a group needs to be self-catering. Hlane is home to the only prides of lion in Swaziland and also supports the largest herds of game including elephant and giraffe. Hlane is highly recommended as a top birdwatching area in the Lowveld. Contact the Big Game Parks for a quotation, including transport, itineraries with local tour operators, car hire, aircraft charter, helicopter charter and contacts with other organisations in Swaziland.

Eco-Africa Safaris
c/o Phophonyane Lodge
P.O.BOX 199

Piggs Peak
Tel: (+268) 437-1319, 437-1429, 437-1579

Swaziland Safaris
P.O.BOX 33
Mbabane
Tel/Fax; (+268) 416-2366

A number of professional stables offer riding and hacking tours including mountain tracking and cross country

Ezulwini Stables
Private Bag, Ezulwini
Tel: (+268) 416-1001
Telex: 2014WD

Hawane Stables
Timbuti Farm
Tel: (+268) 442-4109

Meikles Mount (Residents)
P.O.BOX 13
Mhlambanyatsi
Tel: (+268) 467-4110

Mlilwane Stables
P.O.BOX 234
Mbabane
Tel: (+268) 416-1591/2/3
Fax: (+268) 416-1594

Foresters Arms
P.O.BOX 14
Mhlambanyatsi
Tel: (+268) 467-4177

Sun International (Residents)
Private Bag
Ezulwini
Tel: (+268) 416-1001

Nyanza Stables
Malkerns
Tel: (+268) 528-3090

Piggs Peak Hotel
P.O.BOX 485
Piggs Peak
Tel: (+268) 437-1104

TOUR OPERATORS IN SWAZILAND

Sun International
P.O.BOX 784487
Sandton
2146
South Africa
Tel: (+27) 11 783-8660
Durban: Tel: (+27) 31 304 9237
Capetown: Tel: (+27) 21 21 5978

"Sunscape" packages offering the Royal Swazi Sun, Lugogo and Ezulwini Sun and Nhlangano Sun at better than normal rack rates. Guests with their own transport may drive themselves or alternatively the "Air scape" plans out of Johannesburg, Durban and Capetown include airfares.

Protea Hotels
P.O.BOX 6482, Roggebaai, Cape 8012
South Africa
Tel: (+27) 11 484 1717
Toll Free: (+27) 0800 11 9000
Tlx: 4 20420
Fax: (+27) 11 484 2752

Protea "Price Breakers" offer very special rates Sunday to Thursday or a minimum of two consecutive nights at the Protea Piggs Peak Hotel and Casino.

MEMBERS OF SUPER NATIONAL HOTELS

Drifters
P.O.BOX 48434, Roosevelt Park 2129, South Africa
Tel: (+27) 11 888 1160
Fax: (+27) 11 888 1020

Drifters offer a four day trip ex Johannesburg driving to Malolotja Nature Reserve for hiking. There are scheduled departure dates throughout the year.

Wydah Tour c.c
P.O.BOX 987
Pinegowrie 2123,
South Africa
Tel: (0711) 781-2093/3/4/5
Fax: (0711) 781-2096

Specializing in adventure tours, white-water rafting and wildlife safaris to Swaziland. Operating from Johannesburg with various itineraries.

Go Africa Tours
P.O.BOX 93064, Yeoville 2143
Johannesburg
Tel: (+27) 11 487 1254
Fax: (+27) 11 487 2789

COMBINATIONS WITH SWAZILAND

Umhlanga Tours

Tour 5RSKP luxury Tour
5 days/4 nights (2 nights at the Royal Swazi Sun Hotel). Visits to traditional Craft Market, Sangoma Visit. Full day tour of scenic Malkerns Valley, Swazi Candles, Mlilwane Wildlife Sanctuary. Day 3: Depart for Kruger National Park via scenic Piggs Peak, Half board at Karos Kruger Lodge. Tour includes bush lunches in the park, buffet dinners at the Karos Kruger Lodge, entrances and airport transfers.

Tour 5SZ Royal Experience
5 days/4 nights. 2 nights with breakfast at the Ezulwini Sun Hotel. Sundowner Safari at Mlilwane Wildlife Sanctuary. Full day tour of Ngwenya Glassworks, Sangoma visit and Ngwenya Iron Ore mine, lunch at Malkerns and visit to Swazi candles and Mantenga craft center. Day 3: Depart for Zululand via Grand Valley, game viewing, overnight and breakfast at Itala Game reserve. Early game drive, leave for Shakaland, dinner, overnight and breakfast at luxury traditional huts. Transfers to and from Matsapha, Richards Bay or Durban Airport.

Tour 3PP
3 days/2 nights half board at the Protea Piggs peak hotel. Day 2 is a full day in the Kruger National Park including game drive, lunch at a bush camp and entrances. Evenings spent at the Casino or enjoying the peace of the mountains. Airport transfers

Tour 4SKP
4 days/3 nights, two night at the Ezulwini Sun hotel, half board. Day 2: Full day tour of Houses of Parliament, Museum, Swazi village, Malkerns crafts. Lunch en-route. Day 3: Depart for Kruger National Park, lunch at a bush camp, dinner and overnight at Lower Sabie. Skukuza or Berg en Dal camp. Dinner under the stars. Day 4: Return to Swaziland to the airport or fly from Nelspruit to Johannesburg. Optional road transfer to Johannesburg International Airport.

Tour 4SZ
4 days/3 nights
2 nights at Mkhaya Game Reserve on full board basis. Game drives, meals at the central Stone camp, evening game spotting, bush walks. Overnight in luxury tents. Day 3: Depart for Zululand passing through the sugar cane and rolling hills of the magnificent area. Overnight at Shakaland. Day 4: Airport transfer to depart from Durban.

Tour 4SM
4 days/3 nights in Swaziland and Mocambique
Day 1: Overnight, dinner and breakfast at the splendid Royal Swazi sun Hotel. Day 2: Depart for Mocambique, scenic drive through the Lowveld to Maputo. Overnight and breakfast at the magnificent Polana Hotel, shellfish supper in Maputo. Day 3: City tour to include the museums, craft and fish markets, Eiffel Iron House, Cathedral and gardens. Lunch en-route and return to Swaziland. Dinner, overnight and breakfast at the Royal Swazi Sun Hotel, Tour includes airport transfers and crossing border taxes. Clients must obtain their own visas for Mocambique, with assistance provided by Umhlanga Tours.

Tour 4LS
4 days/3 nights
Overnight and breakfast at Lugogo Sun Hotel. Day tout at Protea Piggs Peak Hotel. Overnight, breakfast and lunch at Lugogo Sun Hotel. Visit to craft centers, game viewing at Mlilwane wildlife sanctuary, fireside braai. Overnight and breakfast at the Lugogo Sun Hotel. Airport transfers.

Tour 3HP
3 days/2 nights at Hawana Park
This is an adventure tour, sleeping in 4 bedded, log chalets, horse-riding, mountain climbing, hiking in Malolotja, bush braais. Tour included all meals, fees and entrances.

Tour 7MF
7 days/6 nights
3 nights at the Mountain Inn, 3 nights at the Foresters Arms hotel - Half board. Includes full day tours of Swaziland Crafts, Mkhaya Game reserve. Visits to Mlilwane, Malkerns and Mbabane. Tour includes airport transfers, 3 lunches and entrances.

Comair
P.O.BOX 7015, Bonaero Park, Johannesburg 1622, South Africa
Tel: (+27) 11 973 2911
Fax: (+27) 11 973 3913, 973 1659
Telex: 7 46738
From Johannesburg regular flights to Swaziland to interconnect with Umhlanga Tours for any of the above tours

Special Interest Tours
Whatever the specific special interest, contact one of the operators, in Swaziland for a suggested program. This could cover wildlife, flora, bird watching, agriculture or any one of a number of commercial interests.
When communicating with the tour operator of your choice, please indicate the exact nature of the interest to be followed, the number of persons in the party and something about their background, and the amount of time available.

SUPPLEMENTS

U.S. AND COUNTRY CONTACTS

U.S. EMBASSY TRADE-RELATED CONTACTS

Coopers & Lybrand Chartered Accountants
Suite 108, 2nd Floor
Development House, Swazi Plaza
P.O. Box 569
Mbabane, Swaziland
tel (268) 42861/2/3, 46450/1
fax (268) 45015

Ernst & Young, Swaziland
P.O. Box 210
Mbabane, Swaziland
tel (268) 42015/6/7
fax (268) 45012

Matsapha Industrial Sites
P.O. Box 401
Manzini, Swaziland
tel (268) 86678
fax (268) 86678

Royal Swazi National Shipping Corporation Ltd
P.O. Box 1915
Manzini, Swaziland
tel (268) 53471/2, 53788
fax (268) 53820

Swaki (PTY) Ltd.
Liqhaga Building 4th floor, Nkoseluhlaza St.
P.O. Box 1839
Manzini, Swaziland
tel (268) 52693
fax (268) 52001

Swazi Business Growth Trust (SBGT)
Mr. Norman W. Buckham
Embassy House, 1st Floor
Mbabane, Swaziland
P.O. Box 78
Eveni, Swaziland
tel (268) 44705/44716
fax (268) 44783

Swaziland Industrial Development Council (SIDC)
Mrs. Lura Xaba, Senior Operations Executive
Dhlantubeka House 5th Floor
P.O. Box 866
Mbabane, Swaziland
tel (268) 43391/2/3, 44010/1/2
fax (268) 45619

BUSINESS COUNCILS

Federation of Swazi Employers (FSE)
Mr. Musa Hlophe, Executive Director
P.O. Box 777
Mbabane, Swaziland
tel (268) 40768
fax (268) 46107

Swaziland Chamber of Commerce and Industry
Mr. Harvey Bird, Executive Director
P.O. Box 72
Mbabane, Swaziland
tel (268) 44408
fax (268) 45442

GOVERNMENT

Central Bank of Swaziland
P.0. Box 546
Mbabane, Swaziland
tel (268) 43221/5, 42161
fax (268) 45417/42636

Department of Customs and Excise
Private Bag
Mbabane, Swaziland
tel (268) 48147

Ministry of Enterprise and Employment
P.O. Box 451
Mbabane, Swaziland
tel (268) 43201
fax (268) 44711

Ministry of Finance
P.0. Box 443

Mbabane, Swaziland
tel (268) 48145/9
fax (268) 43187

Ministry of Tourism and Communications
P.0. Box 58
Mbabane, Swaziland
tel (268) 46420
fax (268) 46438

Small Enterprises Development Company Limited (SEDCO)
P.0. Box A186, Swazi Plaza
Mbabane, Swaziland
tel (268) 43046, 42811
fax (268) 40723

Tibiyo Taka Ngwane
P.0. Box 181
Kwaluseni, Swaziland
tel (268) 84390, 84306/7/8
fax (268) 84399

Trade Promotion Unit (TPU)
Ministry of Enterprise and Employment
P.0. Box 451
Mbabane, Swaziland
tel (268) 45180/2
fax (268) 43833

Mr Meshack M L Shongwe
Director Public Policy Co-ordination Unit and
Acting Government Spokesman
Office of the Prime Minister
PO Box 395 Mbabane
Kingdom of Swaziland
Tel: (+268) 403993/401432 or (+268) 6064003
Fax: (+268) 403943/44073
E-mail: ppcu@realnet.co.sz

Ministry of Agriculture:
Principal Secretary: moac-hq@realnet.co.sz
Forestry Department:
minagfd@realnet.co.sz

Ministry of Economic Planning & Development
Statistics Section:ep_cso@realnet.co.sz

Ministry of Natural Resources & Energy
Energy Department:
nergyswa@realnet.co.sz
Geological Survey & Mines:

Director:
geoswz_dir@realnet.co.sz

Laboratory:
geoswz_lab@realnet.co.sz

Computers:
geoswz_com@realnet.co.sz

Library:
geoswz_lib@realnet.co.sz

Ministry Of Education
National Examinations Council:
examscos@realnet.co.sz

Ministry Of Housing And Urban Development
Principal Secretary:
minhouse@realnet.co.sz

Ministry Of Finance
Principal Secretary: minfin@realnet.co.sz
Public Enterprise Unit:
farmers@realnet.co.sz

Ministry of Public Works & Transport
Water Resources Branch

Laboratory:
wrb-lab@realnet.co.sz
Hydrology:
wrb-hydr@realnet.co.sz
Engineering:
wrb-eng@realnet.co.sz

wrb-wcon@realnet.co.sz

Roads Department:
mopwt_rd@realnet.co.sz

National Meteorlogical Service:
weather@realnet.co.sz

Treasury:accgensz@realnet.co.sz

Swaziland Information & Broadcasting Services: sbisnews@realnet.co.sz

Swaziland National Library Service
Senior Librarian: nomkhwa@realnet.co.sz

Department of Labour:
deptlab@realnet.co.sz

Komati project coordination unit:
komatpcu@realnet.co.sz

COMMERCIAL BANKS

Barclays Bank of Swaziland Limited
P.O. Box 667
Mbabane, Swaziland
tel (268) 42691, 42869
fax (268) 43413/4

First National
Head Office
P.O. Box 261
Eveni, Swaziland
tel (268) 45401/2/3
fax (268) 44735

Nedbank
P.O. Box 68
Mbabane, Swaziland
tel (268) 43351/5
fax (268) 44060

Standard Bank
International Trade Center
P.O. Box A294 Swazi Plaza
Mbabane, Swaziland
tel (268) 46587/89/92
fax (268) 45899

U.S. GOVERNMENT

United States Embassy Mbabane
Commercial Officer
Central Bank Building, Warner Street
P.0. Box 199
Mbabane, Swaziland
tel (268) 46441
fax (268) 45959
U.S. and Foreign Commercial Service
American Consulate General
P.0. Box 2155
Johannesburg, South Africa
tel (27) 11-442-3571
fax (27) 11-442-3761

Trade Promotion Coordinating Committee (TPCC)
Trade Information Center
Washington, D.C.
tel (800) USA-TRADE

U.S. Dept. of State
Office of the Coordinator for Business Affairs
Washington, D.C.
tel (202) 746-1625
fax (202) 647-3953

U.S. Dept. of Commerce
Debra Rogers
Swaziland Desk Officer
tel (202) 482-5148
fax (202) 482-5198
e-mail rogers@usita.gov

U.S. Dept. of Agriculture
Foreign Agricultural Service
Trade Assistance and Promotion Office
tel (202) 720-7420

AFR/WASHINGTON, D.C. DIRECTORY

OFFICE OF THE ASSISTANT ADMINISTRATOR (AFR/AA)

Assistant Administrator (Acting)	Valerie Dickson-Horton, Patricia Dixon	202-712-0500
Deputy Assistant Administrator	Keith Brown, Julia Simpson	202-712-0500
Deputy Assistant Administrator	James T. Smith	202-712-0230
Deputy Assistant Administrator	Barbara Smither, Valerie Dickson-	202-712-0500

	Horton, Julia Simpson,	
Special Assistant	Wade Warren	202-712-0500

Based in Washington, D.C. this office directs and supervises the activities of the Bureau and the USAID Missions in Africa, and currently includes the Acting Assistant Administrator and two Deputy Assistant Administrators.

OFFICE OF SUSTAINABLE DEVELOPMENT (AFR/SD)

Director	**Thomas Park**	**202-712-1660**

The Office of Sustainable Development is responsible for:

Leading the Bureau's strategic thinking in key technical areas;
Supporting the Bureau and Africa Missions by providing analytical and technical assistance related to country programs; and
Coordinating with donors and partner organizations to promote social and economic development.

OFFICE OF DEVELOPMENT PLANNING (AFR/DP)

Director	**James T Smith**	**202-712-0230**

This office assumes the lead in defining the overall policy, program and procedural framework within which the country programs are designed and implemented, plays an active role in identifying and addressing cross-cutting issues, assures necessary budget support and collaborates with all relevant USAID/W offices to:

Develop and monitor the Africa Bureau strategy for providing assistance to Africa;
Manage an efficient, effective and responsive budget allocation system; and
Provide outreach in support of the Africa program.

AFRICA BUREAU REGIONAL OFFICES (WASHINGTON, D.C.)

OFFICE OF WEST AFRICAN AFFAIRS (AFR/WA)

Director Erna Kerst 202-712-0220

OFFICE OF EASTERN AFRICA AFFAIRS (AFR/EA)

Director James Anderson 202-712-0410

OFFICE OF SOUTHERN AFRICA AFFAIRS (AFR/SA)

Director	**Carol S. Palma**	**202-712-4790**

NGO'S IN *SWAZILAND*

□**Save The Children Fund (SCF)**
PO Box 472, Mbabane
Tel: +268 45181/42573
Fax: +268 44719
e-mail: childsav@realnet.co.sz

□**Council of Swaziland Churches (CSC)**
Tel: +268 53628 / 53931
CSC Drought Relief Department
PO Box 1095, Manzini
Tel: +268 57997
Fax: +268 55841
e-mail: drelief@realnet.co.sz

□**Women's Resource Centre (WRC)**
PO Box 3573, Manzini
Tel: +268 55772
Fax: +268 55771
e-mail: wrcumtapo@iafrica.sz

□**World Vision International**
PO Box 2870, Mbabane
Tel: +26844117
Fax: +26846467
e-mail: wvswa@realnet.co.sz

□**Caritas**
PO Box 660, Manzini
Tel: +26856900/4
Fax: +26852338
e-mail: caritas@realnet.co.sz

□**Lutheran Development Service**
PO Box 388, Mbabane
Tel: +26842562
Fax: +26843870
e-mail: lds@realnet.co.sz

□**Swaziland Farmers' Development Foundation**
(SFDF)
PO Box 549, Manzini
Tel: +26854114
Fax: +268 54114
e-mail: stocksi@realnet.co.sz

□**Baphalali Swaziland Red Cross**
PO Box 377, Mbabane
Tel: +268 42532 / 48462 / 49242

□WORLD UNIVERSITY SERVICE OF CANADA
PO BOX 1574 MBABANE
TEL: +268 45100
FAX: +268 45363
E-MAIL: WUSCSWAZ@REALNET.CO.SZ

DIPLOMATIC MISSIONS IN SWAZILAND

REPUBLIC OF CHINA

Embassy of the Republic of China
Warner Street, Mbabane.
P.O. Box 56, Mbabane H100.
Phone 404-2379, Fax 404-6688.
E-mail: chineseembassy@iafrica.sz
Ambassador: Mr. George Jin-gou Chang

GERMANY:

Embassy of the Federal Republic of Germany -
Liaison Office
2nd Floor Dhlan'ubeka House, Mbabane
P.O. Box 146 Mbabane H100.
Phone and Fax 404-3174
Liaison Officer: Mrs. Angelina Topfer

MOZAMBIQUE:

Embassy of the People's Republic of Mozambique
Princess Drive, Mbabane.
P.O. Box 1212, Mbabane H100.
Phone 404-3700, Fax 404-3692, Telex 2248 WD.
Ambassador: Mr. Jacito Januario Maguni

SOUTH AFRICA

The South African High Commission
The New Mall, Mbabane
P.O. Box 2597, Mbabane H100.
Phone 404-4651, Fax 404-6944.
E-mail: sahc@iafrica.sz
High Commissioner: Mr. Walter Seate

UNITED KINGDOM:

The British High Commission
Allister Miller Street, Mbabane.
Private Bag, Mbabane H100.
Phone 404-2581. Fax 404-2585.
High Commissioner: Mr. Neil Hook

UNITED STATES OF AMERICA

Embassy of the United States of America
Central Bank Building, Mbabane H100
Phone 404-6442, Fax 404-5959.
E-mail: usembswd@realnet.co.sz
Ambassador: Mr. Gregory Lee Johnson

CONSULAR OFFICES

Republic of Cyprus:
P.O. Box 1019, Mbabane H100.
Phone 404-2650/404-1138. Fax 404-0328.
E-mail: dandbexport@iafrica.sz
Hon. Consul: Mr. Basil Athenides

Denmark & Norway
CDC Building, Johnson Street, Mbabane.
P.O. Box 815, Mbabane, H100.
Phone 404-3547, Fax 404-3548
Hon. Consul: Mr. Per Sonne Noddeboe.

Italy:
Italian Consulate
219 Tenbergen Street, Manzini.
P.O. Box 928 Manzini, M100.
Phone 505-2436, Fax 505-2436.
Hon. Consul: Mr. Marzio D'Orsi.

Netherlands:
Consulate of the Netherlands
Business Machines House, Gilfillan St, Mbabane
P.O. Box 1205, Mbabane, Swaziland.
Phone 404-5178, Fax 404-4006.
E-mail: bsn@realnet.co.sz
Hon. Consul: Mr. Frederik Oostergetel.

Portugal:
Portuguese Consulate
Portuguese Club, O.K. Road, Mbabane.
P.O. Box 855, Mbabane, Swaziland.
Phone 404-6780, Fax 404-6770.
Hon Consul: Mr. Carlos E. De M. Lopes.

INTERNATIONAL ORGANISATIONS IN SWAZILAND

European Union:
Delegation of the Commission of the European Union,
Lilunga House, Mbabane.
P.O. Box A36, Swazi Plaza, Mbabane H100.
Phone Phone 404-4769, Fax 404-6729.
Resident Advisor: Mr. Aloys Lorkeers

The United Nations:
United Nations Development Programme
Lilunga House, Mbabane.
P.O. Box 261, Mbabane H100.
Phone 404-2301, Fax 404-5341
Coordinator & UNDP Representative:
Ms. Elizabeth Luanga

United Nations Children's Fund (UNICEF)
Lilanga House, Mbabane.
P.O. Box 1859, Mbabane H100.
Phone 404-3725, Fax 404-5202.
Representative: Mr. Alan Brody

World Health Organisation
The New Mall, Mbabane
P.O. Box 903, Mbabane H100.
Phone 404-4268, Fax 404-4566.
Representative: Dr. Therese Lesikel

United Nations High Commission for Refugees
Liaison Office, Phone 404-3414
Senior Liaison Officer: Ms. Neimah Warsame

SWAZILAND MISSIONS ABROAD

During 2000, the Swaziland Embassy in Korea was relocated to Malaysia and became a High Commission while the High Commission in Canada was closed. The other Swaziland missions are:

Belgium:
Embassy of the Kingdom of Swaziland
188 Avenue Winston Chruchill
1180 Brussels.
Phone 00322-347-5725, Fax 00322-347-4623
Ambassador: Dr. Thembayena Dlamini

Republic of China
Embassy of the Kindgom of Swaziland
No. 9 Lane 62 Tien-Mu West Road
Taipei, Taiwan.
Phone: 00886 2 2873, Fax 6189.
Ambassador: Mr. Mathendele Dlamini.

Denmark:
Embassy of the Kingdom of Swaziland
Kastelsvej 19, DK-2100 Copenhagen.
Phone 00 4535 426111. Fax 00 4535 426300.
Ambassador: HRH Prince David

East Africa:
High Commission of the Kingdom of Swaziland

Silopark House, Mama Ngina Street,
P.O. Box 41887, Nairobi, Kenya.
Phone 00254 3 339231. Fax 330540.
High Commissioner: Mr. Solomon Dlamini

Malaysia
High Commission of the Kingdom of Swaziland
Menara Lion Building Level 22, Suite 22.03.3 (A)
50 450 Kuala Lumpur.
Phone 603 2162511, Fax 2633326
High Commissioner: Mr. Mabili Dlamini

Mozambique:
Embassy of the Kingdom of Swaziland
Av. do Zimbabwe 608, P.O. Box 4711, Maputo.
Phone 065281 492451. Fax 492117.
Ambassador: Mr. Mr. Mthunzi Dlamini

South Africa:
Swaziland High Commission
715 Government Avenue, Acadia 0083, Pretoria.
Phone: 344-1917, Fax 343-0455.
High Commissioner: Mr. Mpumelelo Hlophe

Consulate of the Kingdom of Swaziland
Braamfontein Centre, 23 Jorissen Street
P.O. Box 41887, Johannesburg 2000.
Phone 403-2050, Fax 403-7473
Consul: Mr. Christian Mkambule

United Kingdom:
Swaziland High Commission
20 Buckingham Gate, London SW1 E6LB
Phone 630-6611, Fax 630-6565
High Commissioner: Rev. Percy Mngomezulu

United Nations:
Permanent Mission of the Kingdom of Swaziland to the United Nations,
408 East 50th Street, New York, N.Y. 10022.
Phone 371-8910. Fax 754-2755.
Representative: Mr. Clifford S. Mamba

United States of America:
Embassy of the Kingdom of Swaziland
3400 International Drive, Washington DC 20008.
Phone 202-362-6683. Fax 202-244-8059.
Telex Swazi 64435.
Ambassador: Mrs. Mary M. Kanya

For further information contact the Ministry of Foreign Affairs & Trade,
P.O. Box 451, Mbabane H100. Swaziland. Phone 404-2661.

BUSINESS IN SWAZILAND

Swaziland has an open, market-oriented economy which encourages private investment and free-enterprise and is committed to actively participating in the global environment through actively seeing new markets and investors.

BUSINESS CONTACTS

Swaziland Investment Promotion Authority (SIPA) provides a one-stop information and support facility to local and foreign investors.

PO Box 451
Mbabane
Tel: (+268) 403201
Fax: (+268) 404711

Swaziland Industrial Development Company (SIDC) assists investors in securing finances for the industrial, mining, agribusiness, tourism, commercial and service sectors.

Ministry of Foreign Affairs and Trade
Trade Promotion Unit
PO Box 2652
Mbabane
Tel: (+268) 404 5180

CULTURAL CENTRES IN SWAZILAND

ALLIANCE FRANCAISE - SWAZILAND

PO Box A266 - Swazi Plaza, Mbabane, Swaziland
Tel: +268 43667
Fax: +268 48340
E-Mail: afs@realnet.co.sz

BRITISH COUNCIL - SWAZILAND

Private Bag - Mbabane Swaziland
Tel: +268 42918, 43101, 43103
Fax: +268 42641
E-Mail: general.inquiries@bc-swaziland.bcouncil.org

UNITED STATES INFORMATION SERVICE - AMERICAN CULTURAL CENTRE

PO Box 199 Mbabane Swaziland
Tel: +268 42 059 / 42445
Fax: +268 45 846
Internet - Mail: usismbao@realnet.co.sz

UNITED STATES INFORMATION SERVICE - LIBRARY

PO Box 199 Mbabane Swaziland
Tel: +268 42 059 / 42445

Fax: +268 45 846
Internet - Mail: usismbal@realnet.co.sz

USEFUL ADDRESSES

AIRLINES

Royal Swazi National Airways
P.O.BOX 939, Manzini,
Matsapha Airport,Tel: (+268) 518-6155/ 518-6087,Fax: (+268) 518-6156

Mbabane:
Swazi Plaza, Tel: (+268) 404-3486/7, Fax: (+268) 404-5984

Johannesburg:
Tel:(+27) 11 616 7323 Fax: 11 616 7757

Kenya:
P.O.BOX 58716, Nairobi, Tel: (+254) 2 210670

Zambia:
P.O.BOX 35384, Lusaka, Tel: (+260) 1 224451

Zimbabwe:
212, C & J Centre, king George Rdm Avondale, P.O.BOX AY 249, Amby Tel: (+263) 4 333582
Fax: 4302432

Tanzania:
P.O.BOX 22636, Dar-es-Salaam, Tel: (+255) 1 111357 Fax: (+255) 1113182 Tlx: 41436

Air Zimbabwe:
P.O.BOX 81, Harare, Zimbabwe Tel: (+263) 4 737011 Tlx: 4548

Air Botswana: P.O.BOX 92, Gaborone, Botswana, Tel: (+267) 52812 Tlx; 2413

Aero Zambia:
ZNIB House, Dedan Kimathi Road, Lusaka, Zambia. Tel:(+260) 1 226192, Fax: 1 226147

LAM
(Linhas Aereas de Mocambique) Matsapha Airport, Tel: (+268) 404-4782/404-0769 Tel: JHB
(+27) 11 331 6081

Comair:
P.O.BOX 7015, bonaero Park, JGB 1627 Tel: (+27) 11921 0222 Fax: 11973 3913

Scan Air Charter:
P.O.BOX 1231, Manzini, Matsapha Airport: Tel: (+268) 518-4474/518-4331 a/h 505-2673 Fax:
518-6340

Steffen Air Charter Services:P.O.BOX 1, Big Bend, Swaziland Tel/Fax: (+268) 363-6531

CLUBS

Havelock Mine Club
Private Bag, Bulembu Tel: 437-3211

Mananga Club
Private Bag, Big Bend

Manzini Club
Siteki Road, Manzini Tel: 505-2254

Mbabane Club
Allistar Miller street, Mbabane, Tel: 404-2285

Rotary Club of Mbabane
P.O.BOX 481, Mbabane

Royal Swazi Golf Club
P.Bag Ezulwini, Tel: 416-1001, Fax: 416-1606

Siteki Club
Private Bag, Siteki

Southern Swaziland Country Club
Private Bag, Nhlangano Tel: 207-8376

Swaziland Automobile Club
P.O.BOX 237, Mbabane

Swaziland Flying Club
P.O.BOX 487, Manzini, Tel: 518-4372

Usutu Country Club
Private Bag, Mhlambanyatsi, Tel: 467-4156

DIPLOMATIC REPRESENTATION

Swazilands diplomatic representation abroad Missions

Swaziland Permanent Mission to the United Nations
408 East 50th Street, New York, NY 10022
Tel: (212) 371 8910/1 Fax: (212) 754 2755

Kingdom of Swaziland Mission to the EC
P.O.BOX 8, 188 Avenue Winston Churchill, 1180 Brussel, Belguim
Tel:322 347 4771 Fax: 322347 6723

High Commision of the Kingdom of Swaziland, London, UK
20 Buckingham Gate, London SW1E 6LB
England tel: 44 171 630 6611/2/4
Fax: 44 171 630 6564

High Commission of Kingdom of Swaziland, Kenya, E.Africa
P.O.BOX 41887, Nairobi, Kenya Tel: 00254 2 339 231/2/3 Fax: 330540

Swaziland Embasy to the Peoples Republic of Mocambique
PO.BOX 4711 , Maputo, Mocambique Tel: 492451/491721/4911656 Fax: 492117

Embassy of the Kingdom of Swaziland Washington D.C USA
3400 International DR., NW Suite #3m
Washington 20008 USA
Tel:(202) 362 6683/4/5 Fax: (202) 244 6059

Consulate of the Kingdom of Swaziland Republic of South Africa
23 Jorissen Street, Braamfontein Centre 6th Floor, P.O.BOX 8030, Johannesburg 2000, South Africa
Tel: (011) 403 2036/7472 Fax: (011) 403 7473
715 Government Toad, Pretoria, Republic of South Africa Tel: (012) 342-5782/3/4 Fax: 342 5682

High Commission of the Kingdom of Swaziland, Ottawa, Canada
130 Albert Street, Suite 1204, Ottawa, Ontario KIP 5G4 Canada Tel: (613) 567 1480 Fax: (613) 567 1058

Embassy of the Kingdom of Swaziland Copenhagen, Denmark
Kastelevej 19, Third Floor, DK - 2100, Copenhagen, Denmark
Tel: (45131) 426111 Fax: (45131) 426300

Embassy of the Kingdom of Swaziland Seoul, Korea
K.P.O BOX 1427, Seoul, Republic of Korea
Tel: (822) 744 0263/4 Fax: (822) 744 0265

HONORARY CONSULATES ABROAD

Greece
Honorary Consul of Swaziland
88 Drossopoulo Street, Athens 04, Greece
Tel: 8655 342 Telex:21 -4231

Korea
Samwhan Corporation
98-20, Wooni-Dong, Chongro-Ku, Seoul, South Korea. Tel: 082 2 7402714 Fax: 082 2 7421849, 7440608

Japan
Honorary Consul General
1 Kanda Izumi-cho, Chiyonda-ku, Tokyo 101
Tel: 03 3864 2111/ 386 42139

Spain
C.Mare Nostrum, 22 Majadahonda Madrid, Spain Tel: 00341 6385211

China
Honorary Consul General of the Kingdom of Swaziland
3F No 2 Sec 1. tunhwa Sard, Taipei, Taiwan, Republic of China.P.O.BOX 24-333, Taipei, Taiwan, R.O.C
Tel: (02) 776801 Fax: 7513577

Italy
Honorary Consul General, Via del Carso, 262, Rome
Tel: 0039 667896481 Fax: 0039 66796201/3

Germany
Honorary General, D4 Dusseldorf 1, Worringer stre. 59, West Germany

Switzerland
Honorary Consul General, 1 Seadya Gaon Street, Rehavia, Jerusalem 92267, Israel
Tel: 0972 2 5632071
Fax: 0972 2 5635377

Canada
111 Echo Drive Suite, 270 Melaren Street, Ottawa, Ontario K2P OM3

Denmark
Standuejen 100, Hellerup, Denmark Tel: 626500 (0) 6517259 (h)

Luxembourg
I.T.C, Place de Nancy 6, L2212 Luxembourgh, Grand - Duche de Luxembourg Tel: 454397 Fax: (352) 44 0354

EMBASSIES & HIGH COMMISSIONS RESIDENT IN SWAZILAND

United Kingdom
The British High Commission
Private Bag, Mbabane, Swaziland Tel: (+268) 404-2581/6 Fax: 404-2585

Germany
Liason Office, Tel/Fax: \9+268) 404-3714
Mozambique
High Commission of the Republic of Mozambique
P.O.BOX 1212, Mbabane, Swaziland, Tel: (+268) 404-3700, Fax: 404-3692

South Africa
The South African High Commission
P.O.BOX 2597, Mbabane, Swaziland Tel: (+268) 404-4651, FAx: 404-6944

INTERNATIONAL TELEPHONE DIALLING CODE +268

China
Embassy of the Republic of China, P.O.BOX 56, Mbabane, Swaziland Tel: 404-2379 Fax: 404-6688

United States of America
Embassy of the United States of America, P.O.BOX 199, Mbabane, Swaziland Tel: 404-3547, Fax: 404-3548 Tlx: 2018WD

Italy
The Italian Consulate, P.O.BOX 928, Manzini, Swaziland, Tel: 505-4368, Fax: 505-4622

Portugal
Portuguese Consulate, P.O.BOX 855, Mbabane, Swaziland, Tel: 404-6780, Fax: 404-6770

Netherlands
Consulate of the Netherlands,P.O.BOX

1025, Mbabane, Swaziland Tel: 404-5178, Fax: 404-4006

Cyprus
Republic of Cyprus, P.O.BOX 1019, Mbabane, Swaziland Tel: 404-2650, 404-1138, Fax: 404-0328

ADDRESSES OF INTERNATIONAL ORGANISATIONS

Commonwealth Development Coporation
P.O.BOX 133, Mbabane, Tel: 404-2051, Fax: 404-5185

Delegation of the Commission of the European Union
P.O.BOX A36, Swazi Plaza, Mbabane, Tel; 404-4769, Fax: 404-6729

United Nations Development Programme (UNDP)
P.O.BOX 261, Mbabane Tel: 404-2301/3, Fax:; 404-5341

United Nations Childrens Fund
P.O.BOX 1859, Mbabane, Swaziland Tel: 404-3725, Fax: 404-5202

World Health Organisation
P.O.BOX 903, Mbabane, Swaziland Tel: 404-4268, Fax: 404-4566

United Nations High Commission for Refugees
P.O.BOX 83, Mbabane, Tel: 404-3414 Fax: 404-4066

GOVERNMENT AND MUNICIPAL OFFICES AND OFFICIAL BOARDS

Ministry of Agriculture and Co-operatives
P.O.BOX 162, Mbabane, Tel: 404-2731

Attorney General
P.O.BOX 546, Mbabane, Tel: 404-2807

Ministry of Commerce and Industry
P.O.BOX 451, Mbabane, Tel: 404-3201 Fax: 404-3833

Department of Customs & Excise
P.O.BOX 489, Mbabane, Tel: 404-5370

Ministry of Education
P.O.BOX 39, Mbabane, Tel: 404-2491

Minsitry of Finance
P.O.BOX 443, Mbabane, Tel: 404-8145

Ministry of Foreign Affairs
P.O.BOX 451,Mbabane, Tel: 404-2431

Department of Immigration
P.O.BOX 372, Mbabane Tel: 404-2941

Ministry of Justice
P.O.BOX 924, Mbabane, Tel: 404-6010

Department of Labour
P.O.BOX 198, Mbabane, Tel: 404-3521

Ministry of Tourism, Environment and Communications
P.O.BOX 2652, Mbabane Tel: 404-4556

Ministry of Works
P.O.BOX 20, Mbabane, Tel: 404-2321

Manzini City Council
P.O.BOX 418, Manzini Tel: 505-2481

Mbabane City Council
P.O.BOX 1,Mbabane Tel:404-2611

Post & Telecomms Corp
P.O.BOX 125, Mbabane Tel: 404-2341

Registar of Companies
P.O.BOX 460, Mbabane Tel: 404-3041

Swaziland Business Growth Trust
Embassy House, Mbabane Tel: 404-4705

Small Enterprises Development Company
P.O.BOX A186, Swazi Plaza, Mbabane Tel: 404-3046

Swaziland Cane Growers Association
P.O.BOX 273, Mbabane, Tel: 404-3561

Swaziland Chamber of Commerce
P.O.BOX 72, Mbabane, Tel: 404-4408

Swaziland Citrus Board
P.O.BOX 343, Mbabane Tel: 404-4266

Swaziland Industrial Development Company
P.O.BOX 866, Mbabane TEl: 404-3391, Fax: 404-5619

Swaziland National Archives
P.O.BOX 946, Mbabane Tel: 416-1276

Swaziland National Trust Commission
P.O.BOX 100, Lobamba, Tel: 416-1151

Swaziland Railway
P.O.BOX 475, Mbabane Tel: 404-2486

Swaziland Sugar Association
P.O.BOX 445, Mbabane, Tel: 404-2345/6

Swaziland Tourist Office
P.O.BOX 338, Mbabane, Tel: 404-4556 Fax: 404-2774

Tibiyo Taka Ngwane
P.O.BOX 181, Kwaluseni, Tel: 518-4390, Tlx: 2116WD, Fax: 518-4399

Department of the Treasury
P.O.BOX 38, Mbabane, Tel: 404-2041

Department of Veterinary Services
P.O.BOX 10, Mbabane,Tel: 404-2731

TOUR OPERATORS

Eco-Africa Safaris
P.O.BOX 199, Piggs Peak TEl: 437-1319

Swaziland Safaris
P.O.BOX 33, Mbabane Tel/Fax: 416-2366

Swazi Trails (Umhlanga Tours)
P.O.BOX 2197, Mbabane Tel/Fax: 416-2180

ASSOCIATIONS

Hotels and Tourism Association of Swaziland
P.O.BOX 462, Mbabane, Tel: 404-2218, Tlx: 2010WD Fax: 404-4516

SATOA (Southern African Travel Organisers Association
P.O.BOX 675, Gerrards Cross, Bucks SL9 8YS, United Kingdom

ASA (Arbeitsgemeinschaft Sudliches Afrika)
Postfach 909, 7140 Ludwigsburg, Germany

SATOA (Southern African Travel Organisers Association)
P.O.BOX C27, Clarence Street, Sydney, NSW, Australia

IATA TRAVEL AGENCIES

Inter Tour Travel Services
P.O.BOX 741, Mbabane, Tel: 404-2672, Fax: 404-5250

Connections Travel Services
P.O.BOX 73, Mbabane, Tel: 404-2101, Fax: 404-6120

The Travel Centre
P.O.BOX 1741, Manzini, Tel: 505-2983, Fax: 505-3829

Ultra Travel
P.O.BOX 4009, Manzini, Tel: 505-2237, Fax: 505-2137

HOTELS

MBABANE
City Inn

P.O.BOX 15
Mbabane
Tel: (+268) 404-2406, 404-2034
Fax: (+268) 404-5393
28 rooms

Situated in the city Centre, close to all amenities, fronted by the popular "Pablo's" restaurant and snack bar. Just two minutes walk from the delights of the handicraft market with its colorful array of curios and souvenirs in soapstone, wood and grass. The Swazi Plaza and the Mall are just round the corner and facilities for bowls, squash, tennis and golf are nearby at the Mbabane Club.

Khula Golden Guest House
P.O.BOX 5505
Mbabane
Tel: (+268) 404-7323

Well signposted from Allistar Miller Street is the Khula Golden Guest House which offers reasonably priced accommodation in a homely atmosphere. The guest house offers continental breakfast, lock up parking facilities, a swimming pool and a braai area plus self-catering facilities. Each room has an en suite bathroom and the Khula Guest House is located on an elevated position overlooking Mbabane city. They also have extensive conference facilities as well as specializing in Engagement and Wedding celebrations.

Mountain Inn
P.O.BOX 223
Mbabane
Tel: (+268) 404-2781; 404-2776
Fax: (+268) 404-5393

60 rooms with private bathroom radio and television
Situated just one and a half kilometers from Mbabane city Centre, the Mountain Inn, commands a view of the Highlands and looks down the Ezulwini Valley into the very heart of Swaziland. All rooms have radios, telephones, televisions and private bathrooms. There is a lovely swimming pool and the Friar Tuck Restaurant with an a la carte menu. The mountain Inn also has two large conference rooms which accommodate 130 people and four smaller rooms for 40 and 20 persons.

MHLAMBANYATSI

Foresters Arms Hotel

P.O.BOX 14
Mhlambanyatsi
Tel:(+268) 467-4177; 467-4377
Fax: (+268) 467-4051
email: forestersarms@iafrica.sz

24 rooms with private bathroom en suite and satellite television with video channel. There is a sauna and conference facility. Gloriously set in its own scenic, timbered 95 hectares estate in the mountains and forests. Just 27 kilometers from Mbabane, on newly tarred roads, this beautiful country hotel enjoys clean, fresh mountain air and has imaginatively and individually furnished rooms with bow windows overlooking the sparkling swimming pool. The charming dining room

offers breakfast, lunch, teas, and candle-lit dinner. The Foresters Arms is famous for its Sunday Lunches and breakfasts and lunches may be also enjoyed on the open-air terrace. Evening entertainment, in the form of Swazi traditional dance, can be provided on request and special dinner/dance function can be arranged for groups.

The surrounding countryside may be explored on foot or on horseback; the hotel has horses for hire. The nearby Usuthu Club has a 9 hole golf course, tennis, bowls and squash and excellent sporting equipment for all of these is available from the hotel. There is fishing for trout and bass in well-stocked dams and rods for hire. The Foresters Arms has a tandem cycle and mountain bikes for the use of guest.

After a day of just relaxing or exploring the exhilarating mountain countryside, unwind infront of a log fire in the quaint "olde Worlde' pub, the cosy lounge or the candle-lit dining room.

Meikles Mount

P.O.BOX 13
Mhlambanyatsi
Tel: (+268) 467-4110
8 self contained cottages

Escape to your own dream thatched cottage in a world where mountains, forests, streams and waterfalls dominate the landscape. Escape to walk through lush woods beside winding streams or climb to the hill tops for magnificent views over the Usutu Forest, Mlilwane and Lobamba, This is the world of Meikles Mount.

The fully equipped cottages are positioned to take advantage of the view and for privacy. Each has an individual, trained cook-maid in attendance and food is obtainable from the estate shop. Cottages have one, two or three double bedrooms and all are self-contained small houses with lounge, kitchen, bathrooms, carport, patio and barbecue area. Recreational facilities are provided but the key to a stay at Meikles Mount is complete relaxation in superb surroundings.

EZULWINI

Sun International Resorts - Swaziland

Internationally renowned resort group Sun International operates four hotels in the Kingdom of Swaziland. A trio situated in the beautiful Ezulwini Valley consisting of the Kingdoms flagship hotel, the Royal Swazi Sun,as well as the Lugogo Sun and the Ezulwini Sun hotels. This resort complex provides a world of fun and excitement, with a range of varied entertainment, with a range of varied entertainment, many sporting facilities, restaurants and bars. The fourth is the intimate Nhlangano Sun Hotel & Casino in the South-western corner of the country. For tailor made itineraries and service excellence, these leading resort hotels are your perfect choice:

Royal Swazi Sun Hotel, Casino and Country Club

Private Bag, Ezulwini, Swaziland
Tel: (+268) 416-1001/ 416-1450
Fax: (+268) 416-1859
Email addresses: swazisun@realnet.co.sz
Internet address: http://www.swazi.com/swazisun/

Situated in idyllic surroundings on the sweeping slopes of the Ezulwini Valley, and surrounded by majestic mountains is the flagship of Swaziland's hotel industry; the Royal Swazi Sun. The Royal Swazi Sun is a fine example of unrivalled luxury at its best, this superb hotel has a colonial

atmosphere of elegance, charm and relaxation.
Rooms: 147 rooms with facilities to international standards. All 126 double rooms, 14 family rooms and 7 deluxe suites are tastefully decorated and have air-conditioning, heating, bath, shower, TV, radio, telephone, hairdryers and 24 hour inroom dining service. Each room has spectacular views of sweeping mountains, lush gardens surrounding the pool terrace and the rolling of the golf course.
Three superb restaurants offer a wide variety of fine cuisine, ranging from lavish buffets served at breakfast, lunch and dinner to evening dining in the a la carte restaurants. Sip a quiet drink in the plush lounge, ,or enjoy exotic cocktails at the poolside while watching the sunset.
From an elegant casino, fine dining and entertainment, exclusive world class Health Spa, magnificent 18 hole championship golf course, bowling greens, floodlit tennis courts and squash courts, boutiques, to the nearby craft markets and tourist attractions - the Royal Swazi Sun Resort has it all!
The Royal Swazi Sun Convention Centre offers a 505 seat auditorium and a 600 seat banqueting hall. This magnificent venue is fully equipped with the most up-to-date conference facilities.

Lugogo Sun Hotel

Private Bag, Ezulwini, Swaziland
Tel:(+268) 416-1101 ; 416-1550
Fax: (+268) 416-1111

Swaziland's most beautiful valley holds yet another secret, the Lugogo Sun Hotel. Part of the heavenly Royal Swazi Sun Valley resort situated in the Ezulwini Valley and barely a minutes drive from the Royal Swazi Sun hotel.
Rooms: 202 with facilities to international standards.
All 199 spacious rooms and 3 suites offer informal yet sophisticated luxury, and have air-conditioning, heating, 2 double beds, bath, shower, TV, radio, telephone,and hairdryers. The Lugogo Sun hotel has the highest number of hotel rooms in the Kingdom.

The Ilanga restaurant offers a wide variety of tempting carvery and buffet dishes, adjoined by the Sportmans Bar, an intimate English-style pub. This popular hotel boasts a splendid swimming pool, outdoor terrace area, and traditional Swazi Boma. The Swazi village is close to the Lugogo and offers traditional arts and crafts, including some of the finest wood carvings. Guests at the Lugogo have access to all facilities offered at the Royal Swazi Sun Valley. These includes the restaurants, bars numerous sporting facilities, Casino and inter hotel transport. The Lugogo Sun has a small conference room which accommodates 45 people.

Ezulwini Sun Hotel

Private Bag, Ezulwini
Tel: (+268) 416-1201; 416-1650
Fax: (+268) 416-1782

Lying between the majestic Lobamba and Mdzimba Mountains is the Ezulwini Sun Hotel, forming art of the Royal Swazi Sun Valley resort, consisting of the Royal Swazi Sun and Lugogo Sun.
Rooms: 120 with facilities to international standards. The Ezulwini Sun has 120 attractively decorated spacious rooms, with 2 double beds, air-conditioning, heating, bath, shower, TV, radio, telephone and hairdryers. Views from all the rooms are spectacular, across the pool terrace, gardens and into the valley which becomes the Royal area of Lobamba.
The hotel is a major attraction to the international tourist market, providing visitors with a further

option to the Royal Swazi Sun and Lugogo Sun as favored high quality tourist destinations. The decor is a melange of refreshing colours of blue and white, highlighted with turquoises and soft coral pinks carried throughout the hotel creating an evocative Caribbean theme.
The Valley Blues open plan restaurant and bar offer a variety of entertainment and international cuisine. The Ezulwini Sun has its own swimming pool, outdoor terrace, tow all-weather tennis courts, volley ball court and pharmacy. The professionally run Ezulwini Stables are adjacent to the hotel providing tuition and the chances to explore the picturesque Ezulwini valley on horseback.
The Ezulwini conference room accommodates 60 persons and guest again have full access to the facilities of the Royal Swazi Sun Valley resort.

Mantenga Lodge

P.O.BOX 68
Ezulwini
Tel: (+268) 416-1049; 416-2515/6
Fax: (+268) 416-2168

26 rooms with private bathroom en suite, television (M-Net) video channel, and telephone.

Mantenga Lodge is set in one of Swazilands most note beauty spots in the Ezulwini Valley. Centrally situated along the Manzini - Mbabane corridor the Lodge provides an ideal base from which to explore the whole of Swaziland. For the business men it allows easy access to the industrial and commercial centers while providing a charming country Lodge base to return to at the end of the day.

From the rooms which are tastefully furnished to ensure your comfort the guests have a wonderful view of the surrounding mountains and valleys. Mantenga Lodge has its own intimate restaurant providing "a la carte" cuisine in a relaxed atmosphere. Lunches are also served daily on the terrace which overlooks a sparkling pool. The bar provides an ideal watering hole where the guests all meet and mingle.

The lodge has a fully equipped conference center which caters for up to eighty people. Mantenga Lodge borders a wildlife reserve and all the major tourist attractions are in close proximity. Add to the above the fact that the Lodge has a reputation for its personal and friendly service and it is no wonder that Mantenga Lodge has fast become one of the most popular places in which to stay when visiting Swaziland.

Smokey Mountain Village

P.O.BOX 21
Ezulwini
Tel: (+268) 416-1291/3
Fax: (+268) 404-6465
18 self contained chalets. The grassed peaks of Sheba's Breasts overlook the green roofed chalets in a forest clearing. Smokey Mountain Village is just that, a village atmosphere, for those who prefer quiet and privacy to the bustle of a hotel. The chalets area is arranged around a sparkling pool and have three, four, five and six beds with all the necessary equipment for self-catering. There is also an "a la carte" restaurant, The Gourmet Grub, and a cheery "English" pub boasting a roaring log fire in winter. The best of both worlds; a secluded and tranquil haven yet close to all the great attractions of the Ezulwini Valley.

Mgenule Motel

P.O.BOX 711
Mbabane
Tel: (+268) 41-1041/2
30 rooms with private bathroom, telephone and self-contained kitchenettes. TV rooms and bar. Just nine kilometers, from the Mbabane on the main Manzini road, the Diamond Valley caters for businessmen and tourists alike. It is close to the famous Casino complex, sporting facilities, night clubs, handicraft market and Mlilwane Wildlife Sanctuary.

Happy Valley Motel

P.O.BOX 5
Ezulwini
Tel: (+268) 416-1061
Fax: (+268) 416-1050
57 air-conditioned rooms with private bathroom en suite, with telephone, fridge, coffee machines and satellite TV. The complex includes a swimming pool, 3 restaurants, Roadhouse, Nightclub, Disco and GO-Go Bar as well as a conference and functions room. Situated in the Ezulwini Valley it is at the center of all the principle attractions and offering economic accommodation the motel is popular with both businessmen and tourists. The busy "Bella Vista" Pizzeria and Sir Loin Steakhouse are open till very late. The famous "Why Not" Disco and Nightclub offers a lively cabaret nightly and often features international music groups.The Go GO bar is open Monday to Saturday.

TSHANENI

Impala Arms Hotel
P.O.BOX 34
Tshaneni

18 rooms, A small hotel in the north-east where all rooms have bathroom, air-conditioning and radio. The "Gringo's" a la carte restaurant is famous in the area for its excellent cuisine and well stocked wine cellar and there is a disco.

MANZINI

New George Hotel

P.O.BOX 51
Manzini
Tel: (+268) 505-2061
Fax: (+268) 505-2061
55 rooms
With its central location, Manzini is rightly called the "Hub of Swaziland". Here, at the "Hub" is the George Hotel standing about one kilometer from the town center and offering air conditioned comfort, swimming pool, fine cuisine and special care and attention for guests. The main restaurant, where buffet lunches and a la carte dinners are served has tall, arched windows overlooking the hotel garden. There is always time for morning coffee or a cold beer on the terrace, shaded from the sun by flowering shrubs and trees. The terrace bar is informal and City Pub, which is still in its original decor, is a favorite meeting place. Withiin easy reach are the town

center with shops, handicraft markets and sport facilities as well as Matsapha Airport (10km away) and the Industrial Estate.

Royal Park Lodge

9, Manchisana St, Manzini
Tel: (+268) 505-7423/4-7
Fax: (+268) 505-7428
38 ensuite bedrooms, TV
air-contioning, undercover, safe parking, conference facilities

PIGGS PEAK

Protea Piggs Peak Hotel and Casino

Private Bag, Piggs Peak
Tel: (+268) 437-1104/5
Fax: (+268) 437-1382
Toll free: 0800 1190000 (RSA)
106 luxury rooms with private facilities, telephone and television. This is the finest hotel in the northern Swaziland, 74 kilometers from Mbabane and 10 kilometers north of the village of Piggs Peak on tarred roads all the way. The hotel enjoys a superb view down the Phophonyane Valley and every room faces this vista of mountains and forests.
The Protea Piggs Peak Hotel features an elegant casino and restaurant, renowned for modern and traditional cuisine. The coffer shop is open throughout the day and serving meals from light snacks to full a la carte menu and there are no less than five conference rooms. Other facilities include four bars, a gymnasium and sauna, curio shop, boutique and book shop. There are two squash courts, two floodlit tennis courts, a disco, live entertainment and a swimming pool overlooking the view. Activities include horse-riding, walking and lawn bowls in the clear, crisp mountain air.

Highlands Inn

P.O.BOX 12
Piggs Peak
Tel: (+268) 437-1144
18 rooms with private bath and shower. The tarred road to Piggs Peak in the North has provided the Kingdom with fine scenic drive of majestic mountains, deep river valleys and magnificent views. Originally an old farmhouse, the Highlands stands on two hectares of gardens, with a swimming pool, and provides homely comfort and good food. Here is the perfect base from which to explore much of geological and archaeological interest. Swaziland's most famous rock paintings are at the Nsangwini Shelter only 16 kilometers distant. You may also climb the highest mountain, Emlembe at 1862 meters, search for semi-precious stones or visit a disused gold mine.

Phonphonyane Lodge

PO.BOX 199
Piggs Peak
Tel: (+268) 437-1319, 437-1429, 437-1579
Fax: (+268) 437-1319

Thatched cottages, a guest suite and an exclusive tented camp accommodates 18 persons. Set in delightful, natural garden just 14 kilometers north of Piggs Peak.

All accommodation at Phophonyane Lodge adn Nature reserve is full equipped for self catering . Guests who prefer their meals prepared may be served in thier accommodation or visit the Dining Hut, a fullly licenced, intimate, 16 seat a la carte restaurant. Overlooking the Phonphonyane River,the Dining Hut offers a menu and wine list to match many larger restaurants.

The true attraction of Phonphonyane is the setting. Guests are encouraged to walk through the extensive indigenous Middleveld forests, alive with the sound of bird calls and cascading water. The Reserve is situated on the Escarpment and there are magnificent views over rivers and mountains, forests and valleys.

NHLANGANO

Nhlangano Sun and Casino Hotel

Private Bag, Nhlangano
Tel: (+268) 207-8211
Fax: (+268) 207-8402
Telex: 2089WD
47 air-conditioned, chalet type rooms with en suite bathroom, TV radio, telephone and private terrace. Located in Southern Swaziland near the town of Nhlangano. This small, charming hotel is set in 45 acres overlooking the spectacular Makhosini Valley. The 47 chalet style rooms all have en suite bathroom, TV radio, telephone and a private terrace.
The rooms are linked by covered walkways to the central building which houses the Makhosini Restaurant, Two kings bar and lounge, Casino, Casino Bar, slot area, small curio shop and large patio for outdoor dining. The swimming pool area is set in landscaped gardens with spectacular views of the surrounding countryside.
The Nhlangano Sun offers volley ball, target golf, and two tennis courts with squash, lawn bowls, and golf at the nearby Country Club. Conference facilities for seminars, workshops and groups of up to 80 are available with good conference equipment and back-up Secretarial Services.

BIG BEND

The New Bend Inn

P.O.BOX 37
Big Bend
Tel: (+268) 363-6111/2
Fax: (+268) 363-6384
24 rooms
Situated in the Eastern Lowveld where the Great Usutu River takes a farewell swing and plunges through the "poort" in the Lubombo Mountains and into neighbouring Mocambique. The Bend Inn is popular stopping point for its comfortable rooms, friendly atmosphere and good cuisine. There is a wide range of sporting facilities nearby. Alternatively, relax by the pool with a sundowner as the setting sun turns the spray of irrigation sprinklers on the sugar fields into a hundred rainbows.

Riverside Hotel

P.O.BOX 114
Matata, Big Bend

Tel: (+268) 363-6012
Fax: (+268) 363-6032
18 ensuite bedrooms, secure carports, restaurant, bar, satellite T.V Dish, terrace. Situated in the Lavumisa/Big Bend road north just before Big Bend. The Riverside Hotel is an ideal stop-over with a charming restaurant overlooking the Great Usutu River, offering excellent Portuguese style cuisine. A separate room is used for pool and darts events, a great favorite with locals and visitors. Stay awhile in this pleasant motel, enjoy the stillness of the Lowveld where the pace of life is easy and the proximity to Mkhaya Game Reserve is very convenient.

RESTAURANTS

Visitors to Swaziland may wish to take a break from the restaurant at their hotel and dine out. If, so there are many possibilities offering every type of cuisine. This listing represents only some of the many restaurants in the Kingdom and also features some hotel restaurants where they are of particular note. They are arranged according to location - Mbabane, Mhlambanyatsi, Malkerns, Ezulwini, Manzini and Piggs Peak.

MBABANE

Friar Tucks' Restaurant
Continental cuisine at the Mountain Inn
Tel: (+268) 404-2781

Hwa Li
Chinese food for the family
Tel: (+268) 404-5986

Diners Restaurant
Delicious Steaks for the family
Tel: (+268) 404-4302

Pablo's at the City Inn
Wholesome food all day long
Tel: (+268) 404-2406, 404-2034

La Casserole
Omnicenter, Allistar Miller Street
Continental cuisine
Tel: (+268) 404-6426

Lourenco Marques (L.M)
Portuguese and continental cuisine
Tel: (+268) 404-3097

Mediterranean
Seafood's, curries and vegetarian dishes
Tel: (+268) 404-3212

Phoenix Spur House
New Mall, Mbabane

Quality family fare
Tel: (+268) 404-9103

MHLAMBANYATSI

Forester's Arm
Country Cuisine a la carte
Tel: (+268) 467-4177, 467-4377

MALKERNS

Malandela's
Country cooking
Tel: (+268) 528-3115

EZULWINI

Calabash Continental Restaurant
German, Austrian, International cuisine and Seafood
Tel: (+268) 416-1187
Fax: (+268) 416-2098

First Horse Restaurant
International and curry dishes
Tel: (+268) 416-1137

Gigi's
French, at the Royal Swazi Sun
Tel: (+268) 416-1001

Gourmet Grub
A la carte, at the Smokey Mountain Village
Tel: (+268) 416-1291

Valley Blues
International cuisine at the Ezulwini sun
Tel: (+268) 416-1201

Sir-Loin Steak-house
at the Happy Valley Motel
Delicious steaks and continental dishes
Tel: (+268) 416-1061

Hippo Haunt
Traditional Swazi food at Mlilwane Wildlife Sanctuary
Tel: (+268) 416-1591

Likhaya
Buffet island at the Lugogo Sun
Tel: (+268) 416-1101

Tandoori
Indian Cuisine, at the Mgenule Motel
Tel:(+268) 416-1146

The Great Taipei Chinese Restaurant
next to Mantenga Craft Center
Chinese dishes, eat in or take away
Tel: (+268) 416-2300

Mantenga Lodge
Ezulwini Valley
Island style a la carte and Sunday lunches
Tel/Fax: (+268) 416-1049

The iNkhundla
An open-air facility of Swazi-sibaya style, seating 300, for theme evenings and functions
Tel: (+268) 404-4541

MANZINI

Fontana di trevi
Trattoria and Coffee Bar
Tel: (+268) 505-3608

Gil Vincente
Portuguese cuisine
Tel: (+268) 505-3874

Mocambique Restaurant
Fish and Seafood
Tel: (+268) 505-2489

Sailor Sam
Fish and Halal Dishes
Tel: (+268) 505-3950

PIGGS PEAK

Highlands Inn
A la carte, hotel restaurant Tel: (+268) 437-1144

Forest
Informal, at the Protea Piggs Peak Hotel
Tel: (+268) 467-1104 Fax: (+268) 437-1382

BASIC PUBLICATION ON SWAZILAND

IMPORTANT!
All publications are updated annually!
Please contact IBP, Inc. at ibpusa3@gmail.com for the latest ISBNs and additional information

TITLE
Swaziland Business in Swaziland for Everyone: Practical Information and Contacts for Success
Swaziland A "Spy" Guide - Strategic Informtion and Developments
Swaziland A Spy" Guide"
Swaziland Business and Investment Opportunities Yearbook
Swaziland Business and Investment Opportunities Yearbook
Swaziland Business and Investment Opportunities Yearbook Volume 1 Strategic Information and Opportunities
Swaziland Business Intelligence Report - Practical Information, Opportunities, Contacts
Swaziland Business Intelligence Report - Practical Information, Opportunities, Contacts
Swaziland Business Law Handbook - Strategic Informtion and Basic Laws
Swaziland Business Law Handbook - Strategic Informtion and Basic Laws
Swaziland Business Law Handbook - Strategic Informtion and Basic Laws
Swaziland Business Law Handbook - Strategic Informtion and Basic Laws
Swaziland Business Law Handbook Volume 1 Srategic Information and Basic Laws
Swaziland Business Success Guide - Basic Practical Information and Contacts
Swaziland Constitution and Citizenship Laws Handbook - Strategic Information and Basic Laws
Swaziland Country Study Guide - Strategic Informtion and Developments
Swaziland Country Study Guide - Strategic Informtion and Developments
Swaziland Country Study Guide - Strategic Informtion and Developments Volume 1 Strategic Information and Developments
Swaziland Criminal Laws, Regulations and Procedures Handbook - Strategic Information, Regulations, Procedures
Swaziland Customs, Export-Import Regulations, Incentives and Procedures Handbook - Strategic, Practical Information, Regulations
Swaziland Diplomatic Handbook - Strategic Information and Developments
Swaziland Diplomatic Handbook - Strategic Information and Developments
Swaziland Ecology & Nature Protection Handbook
Swaziland Ecology & Nature Protection Handbook
Swaziland Ecology & Nature Protection Laws and Regulation Handbook
Swaziland Economic & Development Strategy Handbook
Swaziland Economic & Development Strategy Handbook
Swaziland Electoral, Political Parties Laws and Regulations Handbook - Strategic Information, Regulations, Procedures
Swaziland Energy Policy, Laws and Regulation Handbook
Swaziland Fishing and Aquaculture Industry Handbook - Strategic Information, Regulations, Opportunities
Swaziland Foreign Policy and Government Guide
Swaziland Foreign Policy and Government Guide
Swaziland Immigration Laws and Regulations Handbook - Strategic Information and Basic Laws
Swaziland Investment and Business Guide - Strategic and Practical Information
Swaziland Investment and Business Guide - Strategic and Practical Information
Swaziland Investment and Business Guide - Strategic and Practical Information
Swaziland Investment and Business Guide - Strategic and Practical Information
Swaziland Investment and Business Profile - Basic Information and Contacts for Succesful investment and Business Activity

TITLE
Swaziland Investment, Trade Strategy and Agreements Handbook - Strategic Information and Basic Agreements
Swaziland Labor Laws and Regulations Handbook - Strategic Information and Basic Laws
Swaziland Land Ownership and Agriculture Laws Handbook
Swaziland Mineral & Mining Sector Investment and Business Guide - Strategic and Practical Information
Swaziland Mineral & Mining Sector Investment and Business Guide - Strategic and Practical Information
Swaziland Mineral, Mining Sector Investment and Business Guide - Strategic Information and Regulations
Swaziland Mining Laws and Regulations Handbook
Swaziland Recent Economic and Political Developments Yearbook
Swaziland Recent Economic and Political Developments Yearbook
Swaziland Recent Economic and Political Developments Yearbook
Swaziland Tax Guide Volume 1 Strategic Information and Basic Regulations
Swaziland Taxation Laws and Regulations Handbook
Swaziland: Doing Business and Investing in ... Guide Volume 1 Strategic, Practical Information, Regulations, Contacts
Swaziland: Doing Business and Investing in Swaziland Guide
Swaziland: How to Invest, Start and Run Profitable Business in Swaziland Guide - Practical Information, Opportunities, Contacts

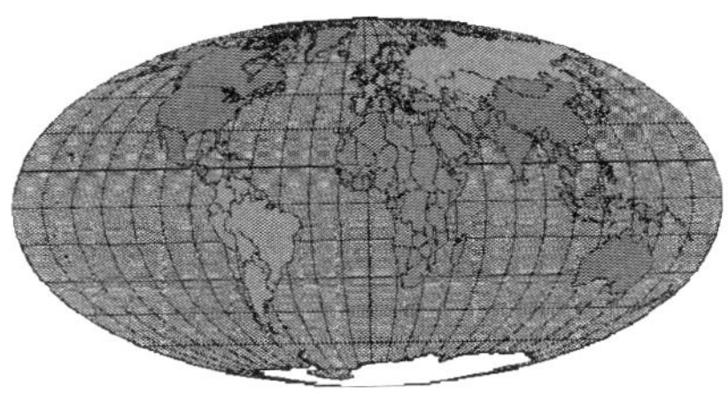

WORLD MINERAL AND MINING SECTOR INVESTMENT AND BUSINESS GUIDES LIBRARY

Price: $149.95 Each

1. Afghanistan Mineral and Mining Sector Investment and Business Guide - Strategic Information and Regulations
2. Albania Mineral and Mining Sector Investment and Business Guide - Strategic Information and Regulations
3. Algeria Mineral and Mining Sector Investment and Business Guide - Strategic Information and Regulations
4. Angola Mineral and Mining Sector Investment and Business Guide - Strategic Information and Regulations
5. Argentina Mineral and Mining Sector Investment and Business Guide - Strategic Information and Regulations
6. Armenia Mineral and Mining Sector Investment and Business Guide - Strategic Information and Regulations
7. Australia Mineral and Mining Sector Investment and Business Guide - Strategic Information and Regulations
8. Austria Mineral and Mining Sector Investment and Business Guide - Strategic Information and Regulations
9. Azerbaijan Mineral and Mining Sector Investment and Business Guide - Strategic Information and Regulations
10. Bahrain Mineral and Mining Sector Investment and Business Guide - Strategic Information and Regulations
11. Bangladesh Mineral and Mining Sector Investment and Business Guide - Strategic Information and Regulations
12. Belarus Mineral and Mining Sector Investment and Business Guide - Strategic Information and Regulations
13. Belgium Mineral and Mining Sector Investment and Business Guide - Strategic Information and Regulations
14. Benin Mineral and Mining Sector Investment and Business Guide - Strategic Information and Regulations
15. Bolivia Mineral and Mining Sector Investment and Business Guide - Strategic Information and Regulations
16. Bosnia and Herzegovina Mineral and Mining Sector Investment and Business Guide - Strategic Information and Regulations
17. Botswana Mineral and Mining Sector Investment and Business Guide - Strategic Information and Regulations
18. Brazil Mineral and Mining Sector Investment and Business Guide - Strategic Information and Regulations
19. Brunei Mineral and Mining Sector Investment and Business Guide - Strategic Information and Regulations
20. Bulgaria Mineral and Mining Sector Investment and Business Guide - Strategic Information and Regulations
21. Burkina Faso Mineral and Mining Sector Investment and Business Guide - Strategic Information and Regulations
22. Burundi Mineral and Mining Sector Investment and Business Guide - Strategic Information and Regulations
23. Cambodia Mineral and Mining Sector Investment and Business Guide - Strategic Information and Regulations
24. Cameroon Mineral and Mining Sector Investment and Business Guide - Strategic Information and Regulations
25. Canada Mineral and Mining Sector Investment and Business Guide - Strategic Information and Regulations
26. Cape Verde Mineral and Mining Sector Investment and Business Guide - Strategic Information and

For additional analytical, business and investment opportunities information, please contact Global Investment & Business Center, USA at (202) 546-2103. Fax: (202) 546-3275. E-mail: ibpusa@comcast.net

Regulations
27. Cayman Islands Mineral and Mining Sector Investment and Business Guide - Strategic Information and Regulations
28. Central African Republic Mineral and Mining Sector Investment and Business Guide - Strategic Information and Regulations
29. Chad Mineral and Mining Sector Investment and Business Guide - Strategic Information and Regulations
30. Chile Mineral and Mining Sector Investment and Business Guide - Strategic Information and Regulations
31. China Mineral and Mining Sector Investment and Business Guide - Strategic Information and Regulations
32. Colombia Mineral and Mining Sector Investment and Business Guide - Strategic Information and Regulations
33. Comoros Mineral and Mining Sector Investment and Business Guide - Strategic Information and Regulations
34. Congo Mineral and Mining Sector Investment and Business Guide - Strategic Information and Regulations
35. Congo, Dem. Republic Mineral and Mining Sector Investment and Business Guide - Strategic Information and Regulations
36. Cook Islands Mineral and Mining Sector Investment and Business Guide - Strategic Information and Regulations
37. Costa Rica Mineral and Mining Sector Investment and Business Guide - Strategic Information and Regulations
38. Cote d'Ivoire Mineral and Mining Sector Investment and Business Guide - Strategic Information and Regulations
39. Croatia Mineral and Mining Sector Investment and Business Guide - Strategic Information and Regulations
40. Cuba Mineral and Mining Sector Investment and Business Guide - Strategic Information and Regulations
41. Czech Republic Mineral and Mining Sector Investment and Business Guide - Strategic Information and Regulations
42. Denmark Mineral and Mining Sector Investment and Business Guide - Strategic Information and Regulations
43. Djibouti Mineral and Mining Sector Investment and Business Guide - Strategic Information and Regulations
44. Dominican Republic Mineral and Mining Sector Investment and Business Guide - Strategic Information and Regulations
45. Dubai Mineral and Mining Sector Investment and Business Guide - Strategic Information and Regulations
46. Ecuador Mineral and Mining Sector Investment and Business Guide - Strategic Information and Regulations
47. Egypt Mineral and Mining Sector Investment and Business Guide - Strategic Information and Regulations
48. El Salvador Mineral and Mining Sector Investment and Business Guide - Strategic Information and Regulations
49. Equatorial Guinea Mineral and Mining Sector Investment and Business Guide - Strategic Information and Regulations
50. Eritrea Mineral and Mining Sector Investment and Business Guide - Strategic Information and Regulations
51. Estonia Mineral and Mining Sector Investment and Business Guide - Strategic Information and Regulations
52. Ethiopia Mineral and Mining Sector Investment and Business Guide - Strategic Information and Regulations
53. Fiji Mineral and Mining Sector Investment and Business Guide - Strategic Information and Regulations
54. Finland Mineral and Mining Sector Investment and Business Guide - Strategic Information and Regulations
55. France Mineral and Mining Sector Investment and Business Guide - Strategic Information and Regulations
56. Gabon Mineral and Mining Sector Investment and Business Guide - Strategic Information and Regulations
57. Gambia Mineral and Mining Sector Investment and Business Guide - Strategic Information and Regulations
58. Georgia Mineral and Mining Sector Investment and Business Guide - Strategic Information and Regulations
59. Germany Mineral and Mining Sector Investment and Business Guide - Strategic Information and Regulations
60. Ghana Mineral and Mining Sector Investment and Business Guide - Strategic Information and Regulations
61. Greece Mineral and Mining Sector Investment and Business Guide - Strategic Information and Regulations
62. Greenland Mineral and Mining Sector Investment and Business Guide - Strategic Information and Regulations

63. Guatemala Mineral and Mining Sector Investment and Business Guide - Strategic Information and Regulations
64. Guinea Mineral and Mining Sector Investment and Business Guide - Strategic Information and Regulations
65. Guinea-Bissau Mineral and Mining Sector Investment and Business Guide - Strategic Information and Regulations
66. Guyana Mineral and Mining Sector Investment and Business Guide - Strategic Information and Regulations
67. Haiti Mineral and Mining Sector Investment and Business Guide - Strategic Information and Regulations
68. Honduras Mineral and Mining Sector Investment and Business Guide - Strategic Information and Regulations
69. Hungary Mineral and Mining Sector Investment and Business Guide - Strategic Information and Regulations
70. Iceland Mineral and Mining Sector Investment and Business Guide - Strategic Information and Regulations
71. India Mineral and Mining Sector Investment and Business Guide - Strategic Information and Regulations
72. Indonesia Mineral and Mining Sector Investment and Business Guide - Strategic Information and Regulations
73. Iran Mineral and Mining Sector Investment and Business Guide - Strategic Information and Regulations
74. Iraq Mineral and Mining Sector Investment and Business Guide - Strategic Information and Regulations
75. Ireland Mineral and Mining Sector Investment and Business Guide - Strategic Information and Regulations
76. Israel Mineral and Mining Sector Investment and Business Guide - Strategic Information and Regulations
77. Italy Mineral and Mining Sector Investment and Business Guide - Strategic Information and Regulations
78. Jamaica Mineral and Mining Sector Investment and Business Guide - Strategic Information and Regulations
79. Japan Mineral and Mining Sector Investment and Business Guide - Strategic Information and Regulations
80. Jordan Mineral and Mining Sector Investment and Business Guide - Strategic Information and Regulations
81. Kazakhstan Mineral and Mining Sector Investment and Business Guide - Strategic Information and Regulations
82. Kenya Mineral and Mining Sector Investment and Business Guide - Strategic Information and Regulations
83. Korea, South Mineral and Mining Sector Investment and Business Guide - Strategic Information and Regulations
84. Kuwait Mineral and Mining Sector Investment and Business Guide - Strategic Information and Regulations
85. Kyrgyzstan Mineral and Mining Sector Investment and Business Guide - Strategic Information and Regulations
86. Laos Mineral and Mining Sector Investment and Business Guide - Strategic Information and Regulations
87. Latvia Mineral and Mining Sector Investment and Business Guide - Strategic Information and Regulations
88. Lesotho Mineral and Mining Sector Investment and Business Guide - Strategic Information and Regulations
89. Liberia Mineral and Mining Sector Investment and Business Guide - Strategic Information and Regulations
90. Libya Mineral and Mining Sector Investment and Business Guide - Strategic Information and Regulations
91. Lithuania Mineral and Mining Sector Investment and Business Guide - Strategic Information and Regulations
92. Macedonia Republic Mineral and Mining Sector Investment and Business Guide - Strategic Information and Regulations
93. Madagascar Mineral and Mining Sector Investment and Business Guide - Strategic Information and Regulations
94. Malawi Mineral and Mining Sector Investment and Business Guide - Strategic Information and Regulations
95. Malaysia Mineral and Mining Sector Investment and Business Guide - Strategic Information and Regulations
96. Mali Mineral and Mining Sector Investment and Business Guide - Strategic Information and Regulations
97. Mauritania Mineral and Mining Sector Investment and Business Guide - Strategic Information and Regulations
98. Mauritius Mineral and Mining Sector Investment and Business Guide - Strategic Information and Regulations
99. Mexico Mineral and Mining Sector Investment and Business Guide - Strategic Information and Regulations

100. Moldova Mineral and Mining Sector Investment and Business Guide - Strategic Information and Regulations
101. Mongolia Mineral and Mining Sector Investment and Business Guide - Strategic Information and Regulations
102. Morocco Mineral and Mining Sector Investment and Business Guide - Strategic Information and Regulations
103. Mozambique Mineral and Mining Sector Investment and Business Guide - Strategic Information and Regulations
104. Myanmar Mineral and Mining Sector Investment and Business Guide - Strategic Information and Regulations
105. Namibia Mineral and Mining Sector Investment and Business Guide - Strategic Information and Regulations
106. Nepal Mineral and Mining Sector Investment and Business Guide - Strategic Information and Regulations
107. Netherlands Mineral and Mining Sector Investment and Business Guide - Strategic Information and Regulations
108. New Zealand Mineral and Mining Sector Investment and Business Guide - Strategic Information and Regulations
109. Nicaragua Mineral and Mining Sector Investment and Business Guide - Strategic Information and Regulations
110. Niger Mineral and Mining Sector Investment and Business Guide - Strategic Information and Regulations
111. Nigeria Mineral and Mining Sector Investment and Business Guide - Strategic Information and Regulations
112. Norway Mineral and Mining Sector Investment and Business Guide - Strategic Information and Regulations
113. Oman Mineral and Mining Sector Investment and Business Guide - Strategic Information and Regulations
114. Pakistan Mineral and Mining Sector Investment and Business Guide - Strategic Information and Regulations
115. Papua New Guinea Mineral and Mining Sector Investment and Business Guide - Strategic Information and Regulations
116. Paraguay Mineral and Mining Sector Investment and Business Guide - Strategic Information and Regulations
117. Peru Mineral and Mining Sector Investment and Business Guide - Strategic Information and Regulations
118. Philippines Mineral and Mining Sector Investment and Business Guide - Strategic Information and Regulations
119. Poland Mineral and Mining Sector Investment and Business Guide - Strategic Information and Regulations
120. Portugal Mineral and Mining Sector Investment and Business Guide - Strategic Information and Regulations
121. Qatar Mineral and Mining Sector Investment and Business Guide - Strategic Information and Regulations
122. Romania Mineral and Mining Sector Investment and Business Guide - Strategic Information and Regulations
123. Russia Mineral and Mining Sector Investment and Business Guide - Strategic Information and Regulations
124. Rwanda Mineral and Mining Sector Investment and Business Guide - Strategic Information and Regulations
125. Sao Tome and Principe Mineral and Mining Sector Investment and Business Guide - Strategic Information and Regulations
126. Saudi Arabia Mineral and Mining Sector Investment and Business Guide - Strategic Information and Regulations
127. Senegal Mineral and Mining Sector Investment and Business Guide - Strategic Information and Regulations
128. Serbia Mineral and Mining Sector Investment and Business Guide - Strategic Information and Regulations
129. Sierra Leone Mineral and Mining Sector Investment and Business Guide - Strategic Information and Regulations
130. Slovakia Mineral and Mining Sector Investment and Business Guide - Strategic Information and Regulations
131. Slovenia Mineral and Mining Sector Investment and Business Guide - Strategic Information and Regulations
132. Somalia Mineral and Mining Sector Investment and Business Guide - Strategic Information and Regulations
133. South Africa Mineral and Mining Sector Investment and Business Guide - Strategic Information and Regulations
134. Spain Mineral and Mining Sector Investment and Business Guide - Strategic Information and Regulations
135. Sri Lanka Mineral and Mining Sector Investment and Business Guide - Strategic Information and Regulations
136. Sudan Mineral and Mining Sector Investment and Business Guide - Strategic Information and Regulations

137. Suriname Mineral and Mining Sector Investment and Business Guide - Strategic Information and Regulations
138. Swaziland Mineral and Mining Sector Investment and Business Guide - Strategic Information and Regulations
139. Sweden Mineral and Mining Sector Investment and Business Guide - Strategic Information and Regulations
140. Syria Mineral and Mining Sector Investment and Business Guide - Strategic Information and Regulations
141. Taiwan Mineral and Mining Sector Investment and Business Guide - Strategic Information and Regulations
142. Tajikistan Mineral and Mining Sector Investment and Business Guide - Strategic Information and Regulations
143. Tanzania Mineral and Mining Sector Investment and Business Guide - Strategic Information and Regulations
144. Thailand Mineral and Mining Sector Investment and Business Guide - Strategic Information and Regulations
145. Togo Mineral and Mining Sector Investment and Business Guide - Strategic Information and Regulations
146. Trinidad and Tobago Mineral and Mining Sector Investment and Business Guide - Strategic Information and Regulations
147. Tunisia Mineral and Mining Sector Investment and Business Guide - Strategic Information and Regulations
148. Turkey Mineral and Mining Sector Investment and Business Guide - Strategic Information and Regulations
149. Turkmenistan Mineral and Mining Sector Investment and Business Guide - Strategic Information and Regulations
150. Uganda Mineral and Mining Sector Investment and Business Guide - Strategic Information and Regulations
151. Ukraine Mineral and Mining Sector Investment and Business Guide - Strategic Information and Regulations
152. United Arab Emirates Mineral and Mining Sector Investment and Business Guide - Strategic Information and Regulations
153. United Kingdom Mineral and Mining Sector Investment and Business Guide - Strategic Information and Regulations
154. United States Mineral and Mining Sector Investment and Business Guide - Strategic Information and Regulations
155. Uruguay Mineral and Mining Sector Investment and Business Guide - Strategic Information and Regulations
156. Uzbekistan Mineral and Mining Sector Investment and Business Guide - Strategic Information and Regulations
157. Venezuela Mineral and Mining Sector Investment and Business Guide - Strategic Information and Regulations
158. Vietnam Mineral and Mining Sector Investment and Business Guide - Strategic Information and Regulations
159. Yemen Mineral and Mining Sector Investment and Business Guide - Strategic Information and Regulations
160. Zambia Mineral and Mining Sector Investment and Business Guide - Strategic Information and Regulations
161. Zimbabwe Mineral and Mining Sector Investment and Business Guide - Strategic Information and Regulations

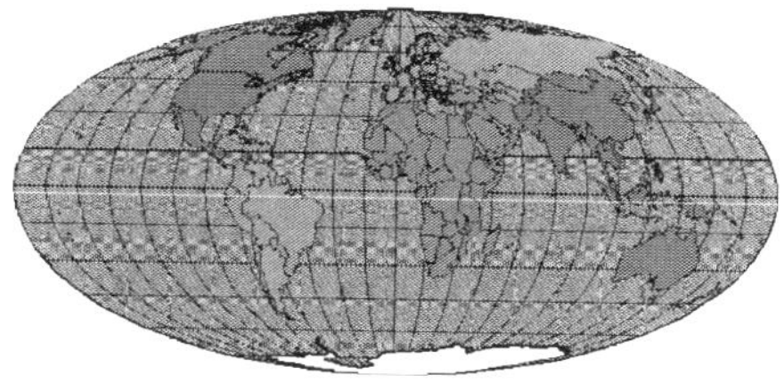

TITLE
Cape Verde Investment and Business Guide Volume 1 Strategic and Practical Information
Cayman Islands Investment and Business Guide Volume 1 Strategic and Practical Information
Central African Republic Investment and Business Guide Volume 1 Strategic and Practical Information
Chad Investment and Business Guide Volume 1 Strategic and Practical Information
Chile Investment and Business Guide Volume 1 Strategic and Practical Information
China Investment and Business Guide Volume 1 Strategic and Practical Information
Colombia Investment and Business Guide Volume 1 Strategic and Practical Information
Comoros Investment and Business Guide Volume 1 Strategic and Practical Information
Congo Investment and Business Guide Volume 1 Strategic and Practical Information
Congo, Democratic Republic Investment and Business Guide Volume 1 Strategic and Practical Information
Cook Islands Investment and Business Guide Volume 1 Strategic and Practical Information
Costa Rica Investment and Business Guide Volume 1 Strategic and Practical Information
Cote d'Ivoire Investment and Business Guide Volume 1 Strategic and Practical Information
Croatia Investment and Business Guide Volume 1 Strategic and Practical Information
Cuba Investment and Business Guide Volume 1 Strategic and Practical Information
Cyprus Investment and Business Guide Volume 1 Strategic and Practical Information
Czech Republic Investment and Business Guide Volume 1 Strategic and Practical Information
Denmark Investment and Business Guide Volume 1 Strategic and Practical Information
Djibouti Investment and Business Guide Volume 1 Strategic and Practical Information
Dominica Investment and Business Guide Volume 1 Strategic and Practical Information
Dominican Republic Investment and Business Guide Volume 1 Strategic and Practical Information
Ecuador Investment and Business Guide Volume 1 Strategic and Practical Information
Egypt Investment and Business Guide Volume 1 Strategic and Practical Information
El Salvador Investment and Business Guide Volume 1 Strategic and Practical Information
Equatorial Guinea Investment and Business Guide Volume 1 Strategic and Practical Information
Eritrea Investment and Business Guide Volume 1 Strategic and Practical Information
Estonia Investment and Business Guide Volume 1 Strategic and Practical Information
Ethiopia Investment and Business Guide Volume 1 Strategic and Practical Information
Falkland Islands Investment and Business Guide Volume 1 Strategic and Practical Information
Faroes Islands Investment and Business Guide Volume 1 Strategic and Practical Information
Fiji Investment and Business Guide Volume 1 Strategic and Practical Information
Finland Investment and Business Guide Volume 1 Strategic and Practical Information
France Investment and Business Guide Volume 1 Strategic and Practical Information
Gabon Investment and Business Guide Volume 1 Strategic and Practical Information
Gambia Investment and Business Guide Volume 1 Strategic and Practical Information
Georgia Investment and Business Guide Volume 1 Strategic and Practical Information
Germany Investment and Business Guide Volume 1 Strategic and Practical Information
Ghana Investment and Business Guide Volume 1 Strategic and Practical Information
Gibraltar Investment and Business Guide Volume 1 Strategic and Practical Information
Greece Investment and Business Guide Volume 1 Strategic and Practical Information
Greenland Investment and Business Guide Volume 1 Strategic and Practical Information
Grenada Investment and Business Guide Volume 1 Strategic and Practical Information
Guam Investment and Business Guide Volume 1 Strategic and Practical Information
Guatemala Investment and Business Guide Volume 1 Strategic and Practical Information
Guernsey Investment and Business Guide Volume 1 Strategic and Practical Information
Guinea Investment and Business Guide Volume 1 Strategic and Practical Information

TITLE
Guinea-Bissau Investment and Business Guide Volume 1 Strategic and Practical Information
Guyana Investment and Business Guide Volume 1 Strategic and Practical Information
Haiti Investment and Business Guide Volume 1 Strategic and Practical Information
Honduras Investment and Business Guide Volume 1 Strategic and Practical Information
Hungary Investment and Business Guide Volume 1 Strategic and Practical Information
Iceland Investment and Business Guide Volume 1 Strategic and Practical Information
India Investment and Business Guide Volume 1 Strategic and Practical Information
Indonesia Investment and Business Guide Volume 1 Strategic and Practical Information
Iran Investment and Business Guide Volume 1 Strategic and Practical Information
Iraq Investment and Business Guide Volume 1 Strategic and Practical Information
Ireland Investment and Business Guide Volume 1 Strategic and Practical Information
Israel Investment and Business Guide Volume 1 Strategic and Practical Information
Italy Investment and Business Guide Volume 1 Strategic and Practical Information
Jamaica Investment and Business Guide Volume 1 Strategic and Practical Information
Japan Investment and Business Guide Volume 1 Strategic and Practical Information
Jersey Investment and Business Guide Volume 1 Strategic and Practical Information
Jordan Investment and Business Guide Volume 1 Strategic and Practical Information
Kazakhstan Investment and Business Guide Volume 1 Strategic and Practical Information
Kenya Investment and Business Guide Volume 1 Strategic and Practical Information
Kiribati Investment and Business Guide Volume 1 Strategic and Practical Information
Korea, North Investment and Business Guide Volume 1 Strategic and Practical Information
Korea, South Investment and Business Guide Volume 1 Strategic and Practical Information
Kosovo Investment and Business Guide Volume 1 Strategic and Practical Information
Kurdistan Investment and Business Guide Volume 1 Strategic and Practical Information
Kuwait Investment and Business Guide Volume 1 Strategic and Practical Information
Kyrgyzstan Investment and Business Guide Volume 1 Strategic and Practical Information
Laos Investment and Business Guide Volume 1 Strategic and Practical Information
Latvia Investment and Business Guide Volume 1 Strategic and Practical Information
Lebanon Investment and Business Guide Volume 1 Strategic and Practical Information
Lesotho Investment and Business Guide Volume 1 Strategic and Practical Information
Liberia Investment and Business Guide Volume 1 Strategic and Practical Information
Libya Investment and Business Guide Volume 1 Strategic and Practical Information
Liechtenstein Investment and Business Guide Volume 1 Strategic and Practical Information
Lithuania Investment and Business Guide Volume 1 Strategic and Practical Information
Luxembourg Investment and Business Guide Volume 1 Strategic and Practical Information
Macao Investment and Business Guide Volume 1 Strategic and Practical Information
Macedonia Investment and Business Guide Volume 1 Strategic and Practical Information
Madagascar Investment and Business Guide Volume 1 Strategic and Practical Information
Madeira Investment and Business Guide Volume 1 Strategic and Practical Information
Malawi Investment and Business Guide Volume 1 Strategic and Practical Information
Malaysia Investment and Business Guide Volume 1 Strategic and Practical Information
Maldives Investment and Business Guide Volume 1 Strategic and Practical Information
Mali Investment and Business Guide Volume 1 Strategic and Practical Information
Malta Investment and Business Guide Volume 1 Strategic and Practical Information
Man Investment and Business Guide Volume 1 Strategic and Practical Information
Marshall Islands Investment and Business Guide Volume 1 Strategic and Practical Information

TITLE
Mauritania Investment and Business Guide Volume 1 Strategic and Practical Information
Mauritius Investment and Business Guide Volume 1 Strategic and Practical Information
Mayotte Investment and Business Guide Volume 1 Strategic and Practical Information
Mexico Investment and Business Guide Volume 1 Strategic and Practical Information
Micronesia Investment and Business Guide Volume 1 Strategic and Practical Information
Moldova Investment and Business Guide Volume 1 Strategic and Practical Information
Monaco Investment and Business Guide Volume 1 Strategic and Practical Information
Mongolia Investment and Business Guide Volume 1 Strategic and Practical Information
Montserrat Investment and Business Guide Volume 1 Strategic and Practical Information
Montenegro Investment and Business Guide Volume 1 Strategic and Practical Information
Morocco Investment and Business Guide Volume 1 Strategic and Practical Information
Mozambique Investment and Business Guide Volume 1 Strategic and Practical Information
Myanmar Investment and Business Guide Volume 1 Strategic and Practical Information
Nagorno-Karabakh Republic Investment and Business Guide Volume 1 Strategic and Practical Information
Namibia Investment and Business Guide Volume 1 Strategic and Practical Information
Nauru Investment and Business Guide Volume 1 Strategic and Practical Information
Nepal Investment and Business Guide Volume 1 Strategic and Practical Information
Netherlands Investment and Business Guide Volume 1 Strategic and Practical Information
New Caledonia Investment and Business Guide Volume 1 Strategic and Practical Information
New Zealand Investment and Business Guide Volume 1 Strategic and Practical Information
Nicaragua Investment and Business Guide Volume 1 Strategic and Practical Information
Niger Investment and Business Guide Volume 1 Strategic and Practical Information
Nigeria Investment and Business Guide Volume 1 Strategic and Practical Information
Niue Investment and Business Guide Volume 1 Strategic and Practical Information
Northern Cyprus (Turkish Republic of Northern Cyprus) Volume 1 Strategic Information and Developments
Northern Mariana Islands Investment and Business Guide Volume 1 Strategic and Practical Information
Norway Investment and Business Guide Volume 1 Strategic and Practical Information
Oman Investment and Business Guide Volume 1 Strategic and Practical Information
Pakistan Investment and Business Guide Volume 1 Strategic and Practical Information
Palau Investment and Business Guide Volume 1 Strategic and Practical Information
Palestine (West Bank & Gaza) Investment and Business Guide Volume 1 Strategic and Practical Information
Panama Investment and Business Guide Volume 1 Strategic and Practical Information
Papua New Guinea Investment and Business Guide Volume 1 Strategic and Practical Information
Paraguay Investment and Business Guide Volume 1 Strategic and Practical Information
Peru Investment and Business Guide Volume 1 Strategic and Practical Information
Philippines Investment and Business Guide Volume 1 Strategic and Practical Information
Pitcairn Islands Investment and Business Guide Volume 1 Strategic and Practical Information
Poland Investment and Business Guide Volume 1 Strategic and Practical Information
Polynesia French Investment and Business Guide Volume 1 Strategic and Practical Information
Portugal Investment and Business Guide Volume 1 Strategic and Practical Information
Qatar Investment and Business Guide Volume 1 Strategic and Practical Information
Romania Investment and Business Guide Volume 1 Strategic and Practical Information
Russia Investment and Business Guide Volume 1 Strategic and Practical Information
Rwanda Investment and Business Guide Volume 1 Strategic and Practical Information
Sahrawi Arab Democratic Republic Volume 1 Strategic Information and Developments
Saint Kitts and Nevis Investment and Business Guide Volume 1 Strategic and Practical Information

TITLE
Saint Lucia Investment and Business Guide Volume 1 Strategic and Practical Information
Saint Vincent and The Grenadines Investment and Business Guide Volume 1 Strategic and Practical Information
Samoa (American) A Investment and Business Guide Volume 1 Strategic and Practical Information
Samoa (Western) Investment and Business Guide Volume 1 Strategic and Practical Information
San Marino Investment and Business Guide Volume 1 Strategic and Practical Information
Sao Tome and Principe Investment and Business Guide Volume 1 Strategic and Practical Information
Saudi Arabia Investment and Business Guide Volume 1 Strategic and Practical Information
Scotland Investment and Business Guide Volume 1 Strategic and Practical Information
Senegal Investment and Business Guide Volume 1 Strategic and Practical Information
Serbia Investment and Business Guide Volume 1 Strategic and Practical Information
Seychelles Investment and Business Guide Volume 1 Strategic and Practical Information
Sierra Leone Investment and Business Guide Volume 1 Strategic and Practical Information
Singapore Investment and Business Guide Volume 1 Strategic and Practical Information
Slovakia Investment and Business Guide Volume 1 Strategic and Practical Information
Slovenia Investment and Business Guide Volume 1 Strategic and Practical Information
Solomon Islands Investment and Business Guide Volume 1 Strategic and Practical Information
Somalia Investment and Business Guide Volume 1 Strategic and Practical Information
South Africa Investment and Business Guide Volume 1 Strategic and Practical Information
Spain Investment and Business Guide Volume 1 Strategic and Practical Information
Sri Lanka Investment and Business Guide Volume 1 Strategic and Practical Information
St. Helena Investment and Business Guide Volume 1 Strategic and Practical Information
St. Pierre & Miquelon Investment and Business Guide Volume 1 Strategic and Practical Information
Sudan (Republic of the Sudan) Investment and Business Guide Volume 1 Strategic and Practical Information
Sudan South Investment and Business Guide Volume 1 Strategic and Practical Information
Suriname Investment and Business Guide Volume 1 Strategic and Practical Information
Swaziland Investment and Business Guide Volume 1 Strategic and Practical Information
Sweden Investment and Business Guide Volume 1 Strategic and Practical Information
Switzerland Investment and Business Guide Volume 1 Strategic and Practical Information
Syria Investment and Business Guide Volume 1 Strategic and Practical Information
Taiwan Investment and Business Guide Volume 1 Strategic and Practical Information
Tajikistan Investment and Business Guide Volume 1 Strategic and Practical Information
Tanzania Investment and Business Guide Volume 1 Strategic and Practical Information
Thailand Investment and Business Guide Volume 1 Strategic and Practical Information
Timor Leste (Democratic Republic of Timor-Leste) Investment and Business Guide Volume 1 Strategic and Practical Information
Togo Investment and Business Guide Volume 1 Strategic and Practical Information
Tonga Investment and Business Guide Volume 1 Strategic and Practical Information
Trinidad and Tobago Investment and Business Guide Volume 1 Strategic and Practical Information
Tunisia Investment and Business Guide Volume 1 Strategic and Practical Information
Turkey Investment and Business Guide Volume 1 Strategic and Practical Information
Turkmenistan Investment and Business Guide Volume 1 Strategic and Practical Information
Turks & Caicos Investment and Business Guide Volume 1 Strategic and Practical Information
Tuvalu Investment and Business Guide Volume 1 Strategic and Practical Information
Uganda Investment and Business Guide Volume 1 Strategic and Practical Information
Ukraine Investment and Business Guide Volume 1 Strategic and Practical Information
United Arab Emirates Investment and Business Guide Volume 1 Strategic and Practical Information

TITLE
United Kingdom Investment and Business Guide Volume 1 Strategic and Practical Information
United States Investment and Business Guide Volume 1 Strategic and Practical Information
Uruguay Investment and Business Guide Volume 1 Strategic and Practical Information
Uzbekistan Investment and Business Guide Volume 1 Strategic and Practical Information
Vanuatu Investment and Business Guide Volume 1 Strategic and Practical Information
Vatican City (Holy See) Investment and Business Guide Volume 1 Strategic and Practical Information
Venezuela Investment and Business Guide Volume 1 Strategic and Practical Information
Vietnam Investment and Business Guide Volume 1 Strategic and Practical Information
Virgin Islands, British Investment and Business Guide Volume 1 Strategic and Practical Information
Wake Atoll Investment and Business Guide Volume 1 Strategic and Practical Information
Wallis & Futuna Investment and Business Guide Volume 1 Strategic and Practical Information
Western Sahara Investment and Business Guide Volume 1 Strategic and Practical Information
Yemen Investment and Business Guide Volume 1 Strategic and Practical Information
Zambia Investment and Business Guide Volume 1 Strategic and Practical Information
Zimbabwe Investment and Business Guide Volume 1 Strategic and Practical Information

For additional analytical, business and investment opportunities information,
Please contact Global Investment & Business Center, USA
at (202) 546-2103. Fax: (202) 546-3275. E-mail: rusric@erols.com